Blank Forms 10
ALIEN R[O

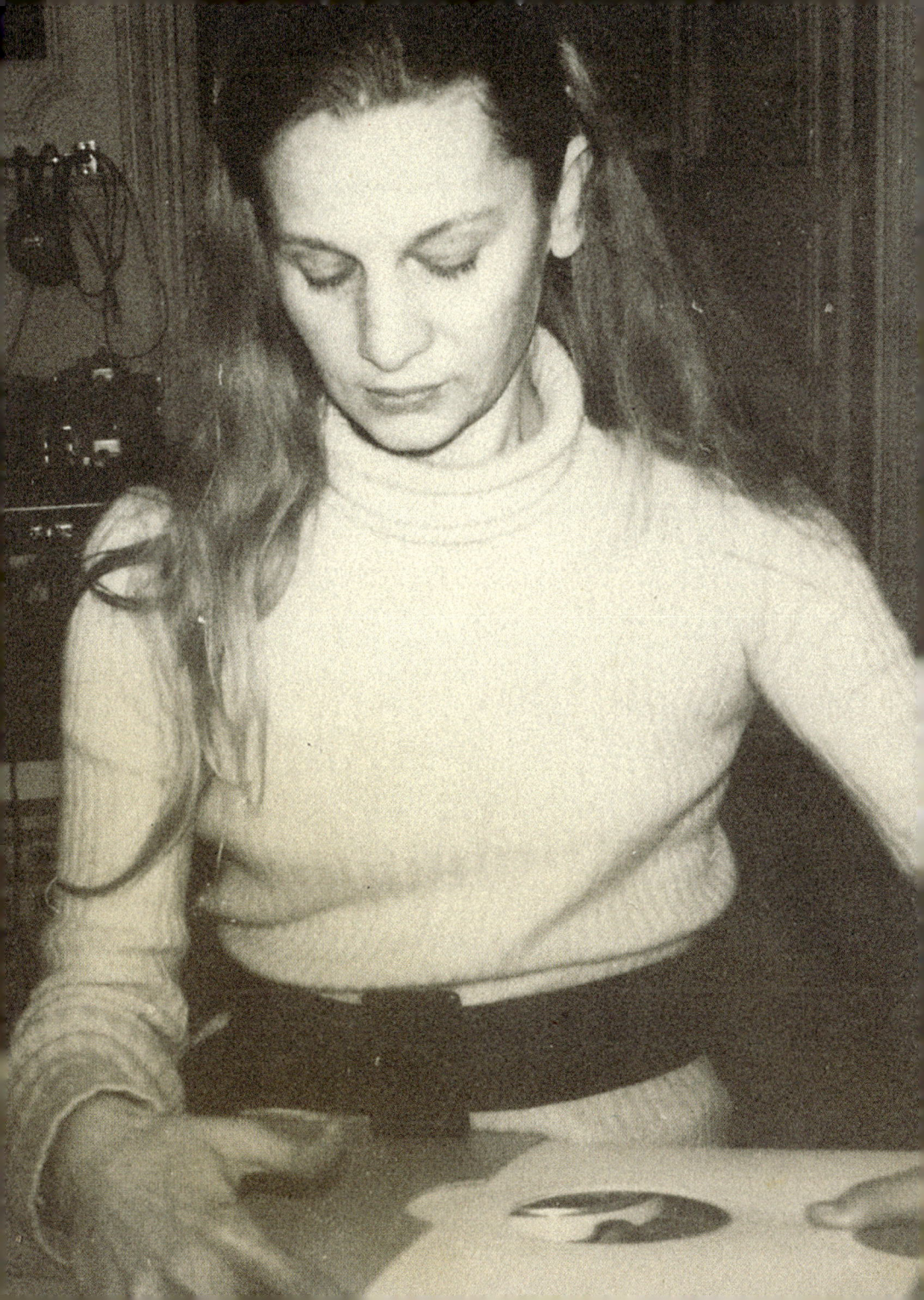

Previous page   Éliane Radigue, Paris, 1969. Photo: Yves Arman. Courtesy Éliane Radigue.

At first, to a distracted listener, nothing could be heard. Then, little by little, from the silence itself came an almost imperceptible resonance. It was as if a hum of life, a vibration from the depths, an indefinable reverberation were radiating from the overall complex of the machine, from the global vastness of the apocalyptic valley. Slowly, to their astonished ears, a melodious sonority arose, its substance so tenuous as to make you doubt whether it was real or hypnotic suggestion. Perhaps a colossal breath rising and falling calmly, a sovereign ocean wave that occasionally receded with joyous eddies in the clefts of the smooth cliffs.

—Dino Buzzati, *The Singularity* (1960)

Cover   Éliane Radigue's studio at 22 rue Liancourt, Paris, ca. 1980s. Courtesy Fonds Éliane Radigue.

9	INTRODUCTION		133	SHREDDING THE CLIMAX CARROT (*Village Voice*) Tom Johnson
17	ÉLIANE RADIGUE AND AN "UNREAL, IMPALPABLE MUSIC" Charles Curtis			
			143	INTERVIEW WITH ÉLIANE RADIGUE Patrick de Haas
	50	DREAMING MACHINES (*Journal de Genève*) Helene Cingria		
			171	ON THE FRINGE OF PARIS (*Village Voice*) Tom Johnson
53	COMBINATORY MUSICS Éliane Radigue			
			188	SONGS OF MILAREPA Éliane Radigue
55	LES MUSIQUES SANS FIN Éliane Radigue			
59	Σ = A = B = A + B Éliane Radigue		201	15TH YEAR OF AVANT-GARDE (*New York Times*) John Rockwell
83	RADIGUE THRESHOLD Paul Jenkins		208	SAMSARA ON THE SYNTHESIZER (*EAR Magazine*) Neil Strauss
	91	MUSIC TO EXHIBIT BY ÉLIANE RADIGUE (*Le Point*) Jack Gousseland	223	INTERVIEW WITH ÉLIANE RADIGUE Ian Nagoski
101	... IN REALITY: FROM AN INTERVIEW WITH ÉLIANE RADIGUE Georges Haessig		243	CONVERSATIONS WITH ÉLIANE RADIGUE Bernard Girard
	123	MISS RADIGUE GIVES A CONCERT ON TAPE (*New York Times*) John Rockwell	285	MODE DIFFUSION ÉLECTRONIQUE Éliane Radigue
	127	MINIMAL MATERIAL: ÉLIANE RADIGUE (*Village Voice*) Tom Johnson	287	BEING AND NONBEING: AN ANALYSIS OF *KYEMA* Daniel Silliman

331 SOUND, OFFERING, AND LIBERATION: LOCATING ÉLIANE RADIGUE'S *TRILOGIE DE LA MORT* (1988–93) IN TIBETAN BUDDHIST THOUGHT AND HISTORY
Dagmar Schwerk

365 CONTOURS OF THE SENSES
Madison Greenstone

389 AN ANTI-IDEAL: RADIGUE AND THE PARADOXES OF RECORDING
Anthony Vine, Charles Curtis, and Madison Greenstone

409 Editors and Contributors

411 Colophon

INTRODUCTION

I first met Éliane Radigue fifteen years ago, in the fall of 2010, when I presented *Naldjorlak* (2005–2009)—an acoustic work written for and performed by Charles Curtis, Carol Robinson, and Bruno Martinez—and two sections of *Songs of Milarepa* (1983) in concert as part of the series "The Propensity of Sound," showcasing Radigue's compositions alongside those of her American colleagues Pauline Oliveros and Laurie Spiegel. At the time there was very little English-language information available on Radigue's work. I was first exposed to her music through the 2002 CD release of *Adnos I–III* on Table of the Elements, and later those of *Kyema, Intermediate States* (1990) and *Trilogie de la Mort* (1998) on Phill Niblock's Experimental Intermedia XI. The Lovely Music releases, *Songs of Milarepa* (1983 and 1998), *Mila's Journey Inspired by a Dream* (1987), and *Jetsun Mila* (1987), were out of print and proved a bit harder to track down, but I managed to find copies while planning the concert series, which led me to discover Radigue's connection to Robert Ashley.

Without much context for this music, I had initially associated Radigue's sounds with those of Niblock and other downtown musicians like Tony Conrad or Rhys Chatham, artists that labels like Table of the Elements were championing at the time. As a result, I listened to Radigue's music at high volume, savoring the resonances and difference tones that such conditions engendered. The elusive and contingent nature of sound is no secret, nor is the fact that conventions of music consumption create conditions for playback that are out of the control of the composer. While Radigue herself has stated that she is not necessarily interested in controlling how one listens to her work on CD (or now, digitally), once I heard her presentation of *Songs of Milarepa* and, later in the week, *Naldjorlak*, my conception of how one should listen to this music was completely transformed, prompting the realization that I had not even really heard what I had spent so much time listening to.

Alien Roots, edited by Charles Curtis and myself, collects writings that reflect on the early electronic work of Éliane Radigue. This publication comes at a time when interest in Radigue's practice as a musician and composer has increased dramatically. Today there are entire books, journals, papers, and conferences dedicated to her music; her work is presented frequently and around the world, especially selections from her ongoing series *Occam* (2011–); her acoustic and electronic compositions are readily available for home listening on CD, LP, digital download, and streaming platforms. Much of this discourse, however, has proliferated in the echo chamber of the internet, and because Radigue no longer gives interviews, each new article or review seems only a reformulation of its predecessors. Conversations around her work tend to focus on the subjective and pseudospiritual experiences of listening to the music; since Radigue herself is a practicing Buddhist, writers often get hung up on the slowness of the compositions, reading the work through a Western pop-cultural understanding of Buddhism (i.e., as "meditative"). Despite the fact that her compositions contain multiple sections and continuous change in sonority and mood, at times seemingly in reference to the movements and structures intrinsic to classical European music, they are often incorrectly referred to as drone music. Likewise, home media has a way of flattening our perception of Radigue's work; when heard through headphones or fixed speaker placement, one loses the sense that the sound is, as Tom Johnson notably put it in an early review of *Ψ 847* (1973), "ooz[ing] out of the side wall."[1]

In 2018 Charles Curtis and I embarked on a project with Radigue to produce analog reel-to-reel editions of all of her electronic compositions, using playback systems that mirrored her original setups. We also attempted to write standard instructions for playback following Radigue's own notes. The first phase required the help of musician and sound engineer Lary 7, who created a duplication system to make clean backup submasters for the first group of compositions we set out to work on: *Chry-ptus* (1971), *Vice–Versa, etc...* (1970), *Trilogie de la Mort* (1988–93), and *Adnos I–III* (1972–82). The results were ultimately presented in a series of concerts in New York (Blank Forms), Houston (Nameless Sound), and San Francisco (The Lab) in 2019, with Curtis and me overseeing the diffusions. Historically, Radigue herself would oversee the diffusion of her concert pieces, carefully arranging the speakers and adjusting the EQ to create the effects that would become emblematic of her sound. We modeled the sound system for the New York concerts after Phill Niblock's setup at Experimental Intermedia Foundation, using four Klipsch La Scalas with a four-band EQ on each of the four channels. While Radigue used Altec Voice of the Theatre speakers in her studio, Niblock's setup seemed appropriate since she premiered the majority of her work at his venue.

In the first of her presentations to move away from the installation-based work she called *propositions sonores*, usually presented in galleries, Radigue premiered *Chry-ptus* in 1971 at the New York Cultural Center, a seated theater near Columbus Circle. She composed the work while in residence at New York University, using two tape reels of music produced on a Buchla synthesizer that could be played "with or without synchronization," resulting in changing subharmonics and overtones. At the Cultural Center, Radigue presented three variations of the composition back-to-back, shifting the synchronization each time to produce markedly distinct effects.

While the presentation in a theater was new, *Chry-ptus* continued Radigue's engagement with themes of repetition and variation, using and elaborating on the combinatorial techniques that she had begun to investigate in her earlier body of work. It was around this time, in the early seventies, that Radigue made a comment (in reference to *Chry-ptus*) suggesting that her compositions were intended to be presented only once, emphasizing the importance of the singularity of the listening experience against the assumed repeatability of magnetic tape, and revealing a prejudice that she would interrogate over the next three decades.

---

1   Tom Johnson, "Minimal Material: Éliane Radigue," *Village Voice*, March 29, 1973.

If we accept magnetic tape, along with other forms of recorded media, simply as a means to capture, store, and play back sounds, we miss two subtle, yet essential concerns of Radigue's: the experience of almost imperceivable changes and variations unfolding over the duration (and through each successive presentation) of her compositions and the fundamental unrepeatability of perceptual experience. Both *Vice-Versa, etc...*, originally published as an edition of ten three-inch reel-to-reel tapes, and $\Sigma = a = b = a + b$ (1969), a double seven-inch that Radigue self-released in an edition of 250, came with instructions for the listener to create their own versions of the compositions by playing the recordings in a variety of different combinations and synchronizations.[2] Equipping the listener with her raw materials and instructions, Radigue invites them to create a unique collaborative work. Despite the open-ended nature of its original release, the first CD reissue of *Vice-Versa, etc...* (Important Records, 2009), along with subsequent releases, simply presents four versions of the orginal tape played at various speeds on the reel-to-reel, first forward and then backward, resulting in a total of eight tracks.[3] When Blank Forms presented a live concert of *Vice-Versa, etc...* in 2019—performed by Charles Curtis and Judith Hamann—we had a more expansive and intuitive interpretation of Radigue's instructions. We made multiple tape duplications of the two tracks at different speeds, sometimes isolated and sometimes in combination with one another, that could then be presented live in different combinations. Ultimately the concert produced a version of *Vice-Versa, etc...* that resembled Radigue's later work on the ARP 2500, in which sections composed with a minimal vocabulary slowly and subtly blend into one another. While *Vice-Versa, etc...* and $\Sigma = a = b = a + b$ both actively engage the listener in the creation of "the composition," this emphasis on participation also predicates a kind of listening that is foundational to Radigue's practice. The composer considered her early tape-based installation work, such as *USRAL* (1969) and *OMNHT* (1970), as "combinatory musics," in that they comprised short loops of various lengths to be played simultaneously, causing them to desynchronize over time and "respond to one another, combine, meet, and

---

2 The instructions for *Vice-Versa, etc...* read, "*Toute combinaison des deux voix, dans un sens ou dans l'autre, sur plusieurs magnétophones, ad libitum...*": "The piece can be played, track 1, separately, track 2, separately, tracks 1 and 2, simultaneously, any combination of two tracks, in one direction or another, on several tape recorders, ad libitum." For those unfamiliar with the mechanics of magnetic tape, the piece was made on quarter-inch tape with two discrete tracks that play out of the left and right speakers during playback, most commonly used for a stereo effect. These tracks can be isolated and copied with another machine, which the instructions suggest. One could take the left channel and make a copy of that at one speed and then copy the right channel at a different speed and play them back simultaneously, creating a unique effect. The instructions for $\Sigma = a = b = a + b$ read, "*Les faces A et B peuvent être écoutées séparément ou simultanément synchrones ou asynchrones. Les faces A et B de ce disque peuvent se combiner entre elles à l'infini à n'importe quelle vitesse 78, 45, 33 ou 16 tours*": "Sides A and B can be listened to separately or simultaneously, synchronously or asynchronously. Sides A and B of this disc can be combined indefinitely at any speed 78, 45, 33 or 16 rpm."

3 The Important Records release uses the European metric CPS (centimeters per second): 9.5, 19, 38, 75.

then lose each other, only to find themselves in their initial form once the cycle is complete."[4] While Radigue's iterative approach is not exhaustive, it opens up a set of choices for the listener/performer that reconfigure their relationship with the composer, "the composition," and time itself in ways that are essential to understanding and appreciating the approach to co-composing with acoustic musicians she would adopt in her latest body of work.

Radigue's early experiments in the manipulation of standard playback techniques would eventually subside as she settled into producing her longform compositions, though she would continue to champion the medium of tape for its singularity and imperfection. Reflecting on the then-recent CD releases of her work in conversation with Ian Nagoski in the late nineties (reprinted in this volume on page 223), Radigue muses:

> I think that analog sounds have a special life-quality—it is just like the skin. No skin is absolutely perfect, but when you touch the skin it has a quality of life-ness. When you touch a balloon or glass, this is another feeling. To me, digital sounds have this perfect—*too* perfect—quality. There are not enough defects, not enough life, because life is made of little defects. We know that even with acoustic instruments, if you listen close-up to any acoustic instrument—a piano, a violin—you can hear some cracking, very slight cracking of the wood. From far away, you don't hear it, but I am very sure that this very small cracking makes the very special quality of acoustic sounds.[5]

Such remarks on the digital betray an ambivalence in Radigue's own thinking about the work she made for tape: on one hand, she notes a qualitative difference between media and states her preference for the analog form explicitly; on the other, she has subsequently authorized almost all of her compositions to be released on CD, including stereo mockups of her combinatory music installations, and has enthusiastically praised diffusions of her work from digital sources in large concert settings.

Radigue presented her final electronic composition, *L'île re-sonante* (2000), on a short US tour in 2002, after which she temporarily ceased composing before embarking on her late body of acoustic compositions. While Radigue rarely gave concerts of her older electronic compositions, interest in this body of work continued to grow, creating an incentive for her to establish guidelines for others to present these pieces on her behalf. During Radigue's hiatus in the aughts, Lionel Marchetti began regularly giving concerts of her electronic compositions using the original masters. The relationship between Radigue and Marchetti began earlier, in 1996, when Marchetti oversaw a diffusion of *Biogenesis* (1973), with Radigue in attendance, for the concert series "Cinema for the Ear," organized by the record label Metamkine. Since 2017,

---

4   Éliane Radigue, "Combinatory Musics," in *Alien Roots: Éliane Radigue* (New York: Blank Forms Editions, 2025), 53.

5   Ian Nagoski, "Interview with Éliane Radigue," *Blank Forms Journal* 1 (2017): 223.

François Bonnet has presented diffusions using high-quality digital transfers made at INA-GRM (Groupe de Recherches Musicales), where Radigue's archives are currently housed.[6] While unsanctioned presentations of Radigue's electronic works persist—usually with someone playing back a CD—Radigue considers Marchetti, Bonnet, and Curtis the only individuals authorized to present such concerts.

Looking back at correspondence I had with Robert Ashley, who was meant to introduce *Songs of Milarepa* when I presented the piece in 2010, he tellingly expressed surprise that the pieces would be presented from a digital source and not the original magnetic tape, noting that he would want to understand "how the piece has changed from analogue tapes to the new form."[7]

* * *

Alien Roots collects a number of key texts, historical documents, and a handful of newly commissioned essays that provide invaluable insights into Radigue's early electronic compositions and beyond. While some of these texts served as guideposts for Charles and me to understand how to approach presenting her work in concert, others are extensions of broader conversations and deeper investigations into less-examined aspects of Radigue's practice. A number of primary documents appear here in English for the first time, including one of Radigue's earliest interviews with Georges Haessig, published in *Musique en jeu* in 1972; another short interview with Patrick de Haas in 1975 for *Art Press*; and the substantial interview conducted by Bernard Girard in 2013, published as *"Entretiens avec Éliane Radigue."* Ian Nagoski's interview with Radigue from 1999 was published for the first time in the inaugural Blank Forms anthology, now out of print, and we felt it was worth reprinting in this volume as important documentation of a transitional point in Radigue's career and as one of the few interviews she gave while composing with the ARP 2500. These interviews are complemented by translations of Radigue's early reflections on her practice: "$\Sigma = a = b = a + b$" and "Combinatory Musics," as well as guidelines for diffusion sent to the Darmstädter Ferienkurse, here titled "Mode diffusion électronique." English-language reviews, along with ones newly translated from French, offer glimpses of the reception of Radigue's work at the time of its debut, and are presented here alongside a number of archival documents, sketches for unrealized projects, fliers, and correspondence from Radigue's collection. Charles Curtis's "Éliane Radigue and an 'Unreal, Impalpable Music'" is an edited and expanded version of an essay that originally appeared in the 2021 *Oxford Handbook of Spectral Music* and gives one of the best overviews of Radigue's work to date, with specific attention to her early compositions. The conversation between Curtis, Anthony

---

6 At INA-GRM, Bonnet has overseen the process of digitizing and cataloguing Radigue's tape collection, as well as creating and maintaining a physical archive of her work. The Fonds Éliane Radigue will be accessible for research at Inathèque, located at Bibliothèque Nationale de France in Paris.

7 Robert Ashley, email correspondence with the author, June 7, 2010.

Vine, and Madison Greenstone that concludes this volume was part of "Éliane Radigue at 90," an event organized by the journal *Contemporary Music Review* in May 2023, in Paris, France (an edited version of the text will appear in a forthcoming special issue of the journal dedicated to Radigue's work.) Also included are two radically different readings of one of Radigue's most well-known compositions, *Kyema* (1988), which she would later designate as the first part of her *Trilogie de la Mort*. Daniel Silliman's is, to our knowledge, one of the only attempts to elucidate the highly technical aspects of Radigue's compositional method and her use of the ARP; a new essay by scholar of Tibetan Buddhism Dagmar Schwerk offers a similarly close listening of the *Trilogie de la Mort*, providing historical context for the Western reception of Buddhism in the sixties and an interpretation of Radigue's late compositions as Buddhist offerings. And, finally, Madison Greenstone's "Contours of the Senses" was specially commissioned for this volume to consider Radigue's earliest body of work, exclusively composed with feedback captured on magnetic tape—a practice that would inform the entirety of Radigue's electronic work, as well as her collaborations with Curtis on *Naldjorlak*.

* * *

Alien Roots concludes the series of anthologies that Blank Forms launched in 2017. As our organization has grown, we've shifted the focus of Blank Forms Editions toward monographic publications, publishing shorter commissioned essays in our online journal. A number of essays from our out-of-print publications will gradually be made available online as we continue to build out our website.

This publication would not have been possible without the support of François Bonnet, Director of INA-GRM, whose invaluable work preserving Radigue's archives has resulted in the publication of *Œuvres Électroniques* (INA-GRM, 2018), the definitive collection of Radigue's compositions for the ARP 2500. In addition to overseeing the diffusion of Radigue's compositions, Bonnet has also written extensively about her work. Special thanks are due to Jean-Baptiste Garcia for producing high-quality scans of our requests from The Fonds Éliane Radigue, and to Marc Moreau for licensing these materials for use. We are indebted to a number of publications that have preceded this one. The major English-language work on Radigue, *Éliane Radigue: Intermediary Spaces/Espaces intermédiaires* (2019), is centered on a long interview with Radigue conducted by the book's editor (and Radigue's collaborator), Julia Eckhardt, and is an invaluable resource for anyone interested in her work. *Intermediary Spaces* also offers the first complete catalogue of Radigue's compositions, including a detailed list of unrealized works and all her installations and tape compositions, along with a comprehensive list of the *Occam* works and their various combinations. For those interested in this particular, latter body of work, "The OCCAM Issue," a special issue of *Sound American* edited by Nate Wooley, is an excellent reference.

We hope that *Alien Roots* will add to the rich discourse around Radigue's music. And, as a continuation of the effort that Charles and I began in 2018, we hope to open up new ways of thinking about and listening to Radigue's work. These endeavors raise serious questions regarding what it means, what it might look or sound like, *to preserve* a body of work like Radigue's—to hold the "very slight cracking" that, while perhaps unheard, animates her music.

Lawrence Kumpf
New York, Summer 2024

GALERIE 22 · J.P. WILHELM · DÜSSELDORF
KAISERSTR. 22   TELEFON 447739   TÄGL GEÖFFNET 0 13, 15 19

Eliane Radigue - Fernandez

vom Studio für Konkrete Musik des Pariser Rundfunks

spricht am Donnerstag, 14. 11 1957, 20 Uhr

in der Galerie 22 über

10 Jahre Konkrete Musik

Zahlreiche Tonband- und Schal plattenaufnahmen.

Eintritt DM 2,-

Flyer for "10 Jahre Konkrete Musik" ("10 Years of Concrete Music") with Éliane Radigue-Fernandez, November 11, 1957. Courtesy Fonds Éliane Radigue.

ÉLIANE RADIGUE AND AN "UNREAL, IMPALPABLE MUSIC"
Charles Curtis

Charles Curtis offers a comprehensive introduction to the major biographical, technical, and art-historical aspects of Éliane Radigue's body of work, and many of his poignant insights are further elaborated upon elsewhere in this book. Curtis acquaints readers with Radigue's use of analog synthesis and various feedback techniques; closely examines two of her works for acoustic instruments and live performance, *Naldjorlak* (2005–2009) and *Occam Ocean* (2011–present); identifies and analyzes several characteristics of her oeuvre; and broaches the question of authorship in the composition of self-generative music, which he returns to in the discussion that closes this anthology. This essay was originally published (in slightly different form) in *The Oxford Handbook of Spectral Music*, Oxford University Press (in progress; online publication 2021).

Aber weder unser Wissen noch unser Handeln gelangt in irgend einer Periode des Daseins dahin, wo aller Widerstreit aufhört, wo Alles Eins ist; die bestimmte Linie vereiniget sich mit der unbestimmten nur in unendlicher Annäherung.

But neither our knowing nor our doing ever reaches, in any cycle of being, that point where all conflict ends, where all is one; the intended line unites with the unintended only in an unending coming-nearer.

—Friedrich Hölderlin, Foreword to the penultimate version of *Hyperion*[1]

I.

The long arc of Éliane Radigue's creative output begins in the late sixties with a series of electronic pieces made directly to magnetic tape; these are relatively short sound essays, modest in scope and in the production techniques employed. The first of these carries the unassuming title *Jouet Électronique* ("Electronic Toy," 1967). By contrast, her *Trilogie de la Mort* of some twenty-five years later (completed in 1993), made on tape with the ARP 2500 synthesizer, stands as a dense and monumental requiem nearly three hours in length. Radigue's final electronic work, *L'île re-sonante*, was completed in 2000, and as of 2004 her practice has shifted to the crafting of pieces for live performers and acoustic instruments. In light of the fact that Radigue had never before this point composed with acoustic instruments, nor worked in the uncertain space of collaboration and live performance, one would have to account this a radical and courageous change, especially in the late stages of a composer's career.[2] But Radigue's pace of production has actually increased since this shift, and as of this writing, the number of instrumental works, ranging from solos and small ensemble pieces all the way up to small orchestra, has reached well past seventy; performances, recordings, scholarship, and general appreciation of her imposing oeuvre are also increasing exponentially.

To this last point one must add that recognition has come late to Radigue; until the late nineties her work was known only to a limited circle of enthusiasts in Europe and the United States.[3] That a figure now so widely celebrated might spend the first three decades of an extremely productive career on the peripheries of the new music scene, particularly in her home country, is now indelibly stamped on her public identity and that of her music. As a woman, working largely in what might now be described as a "DIY" mode, continuing to produce work after work despite her underground status, she has come to be revered as a pioneer on multiple levels: aesthetic, cultural, and technological. Various biographical and societal factors undoubtedly contributed to this state of affairs, and in turn her semiobscurity arguably entered her music as a kind of freedom: freedom from self-assertion, from the pressure of commissions, from the tyranny of deadlines. Her music is inwardly directed, projecting an indifference to outward effect or attention-grabbing spectacle. One could go so far as to call her music insular; understood in the full particularity of its formal and methodological detail, the work is unassimilable to genre or movement. One of its great strengths is that it does not conform; this is true of its manner of production and presentation, and to some extent, its use: it balances between the worlds of sound art, concert music, and recorded media, but its location within or across these worlds seems fluid. Consequently, her work has been realized largely outside official and institutional channels; recognition has come through the admiration of her peers and, more recently, through the spread of her recordings, especially to younger generations of musicians and listeners.

Biographical Sketch

Born in Paris on January 24, 1932, Radigue absorbed a musical education that included piano and music theory lessons and membership in an all-Paris high school youth choir. Radio broadcasts were a substantial part of her introduction to formal music, as they were for so many experimental musicians of her generation, the first to encounter music largely through this medium.[4] It seems to follow that a relationship to music mediated by loudspeakers and the distinctive presence of amplification would set the stage for a creative practice centered in electronic sound. Throughout her life she has maintained an active interest in the Western art music canon, citing one element of tonal harmony in particular: modulation between keys.[5] The span of music stretching from the arrival of the dissonant tone to just before the resolution in a new harmonic center, and the feeling of uncertainty and suspension of identity that the modulation bridges, represent for Radigue a desired state that she has endeavored to prolong, using entirely different means, in her own music. Though she never took formal instruction in composition, she pursued various compositional projects on her own based on her reading of Schoenberg and Leibowitz and her study of Webern, but the few actual attempts at composition using serial techniques she later discarded.[6]

In the very early fifties, having moved to Nice, Radigue began a relationship with Armand Fernandez, later known internationally as the sculptor Arman. Radigue's life for the next decade would revolve around their marriage, the raising of their three children, music theory and harp classes at the Nice Conservatory, and tentative, private compositional ventures. Arman and Radigue's circle of friends included several of the artists who in 1960 would sign the manifesto declaring *Nouveau réalisme*: Yves Klein, Daniel Spoerri, Jean Tinguely, François Dufrêne, Raymond Hains, and others. There is very little formal affinity between the works of these artists and Radigue's music, but one principle must have remained with her from these years of friendship and interaction: the notion that work is made directly by the artist, using material near at hand, and not, as would have been the customary model for a new music composer, as a set of plans or instructions to be realized by another artist—a performer—after the fact.

The possibility of such a hands-on approach to the making of sound pieces was exemplified in another crucial influence from the fifties: Radigue's encounter with the *musique concrète* of Pierre Schaeffer. Appropriately, it was the radio that initiated this encounter, a broadcast of one of Schaeffer's tape pieces in which sounds from the everyday world are manipulated electronically.[7] Radigue probably heard this broadcast in 1955, in Nice; shortly afterward, on a visit to Paris, she chanced to meet Schaeffer at a lecture on Hinduism.[8] An invitation to assist Schaeffer as a musical apprentice in the Studio d'Essai followed, and Radigue's path toward mastering the techniques of the midcentury electronic music studio was set.

In 1961 Radigue and her family spent three months, and in 1963 the better part of a year, in New York City, leading to another set of significant encounters. Partly through Radigue's initiative and partly through Arman's associations, friendships developed with artists and composers loosely related within the network of post–John Cage experimentalism—Rauschenberg, Lichtenstein, Warhol, Fluxus artists, La Monte Young, and, in particular, James Tenney (at that time working at Bell Labs).[9] Radigue must have recognized shared interests and ideas, drawing encouragements and permissions from these artistic and personal engagements. In 1967 Radigue and Arman separated; Radigue moved back to Paris, taking on a two-year stint as assistant to Pierre Henry in the Studio Apsome, where she again had access to electronic equipment. It was in the breaks between her working shifts for Henry that she made the first sound compositions bearing her name, *Jouet Électronique* and *Elemental I* (1968).[10] She has described the making of these pieces as a recreational activity, something she did for personal amusement while working for Henry.

Radigue worked as a guest on various occasions in the United States, at New York University (1970), the University of Iowa and Cal Arts (both in 1973), and Mills College (1974 and 1998), among others. In 1974 she became acquainted with the principles of Tibetan Buddhism and took a three-year break from composition to study its teachings. After resuming her practice in 1978, Radigue worked at a slow but regular pace, laboriously constructing the long-duration works made with the ARP 2500 synthesizer for which she is now famous; her output equates to approximately one piece every two to three years. These pieces were typically presented in tape playback concerts under her direction. After completing *L'île re-sonante* in 2000, the ARP 2500 was put aside, and slowly the work with live performers began. Between 2000 and 2005 two live versions of *Elemental II* appeared (a reworking of the tape feedback and *concrète* piece from 1968, first for electric bassist Kasper T. Toeplitz, and then for the laptop ensemble The Lappetites); and the composition of the three parts of *Naldjorlak* (for solo cello, for two basset horns, and for cello and basset horns, respectively) stretched over the period from 2005 to 2009. Radigue regularly traveled to be present at concerts of the *Naldjorlak* cycle, observing and consulting in the gradual development of a new compositional and performance practice. Since 2011 Radigue has been occupied with the *Occam Ocean* series, and the rate of her work has accelerated precipitously.

In 2006 Radigue received the Golden Nica award from the Ars Electronica in Linz, Austria, for her last electronic work, *L'île re-sonante*; in 2019 the Zentrum für Kunst und Medien (ZKM) in Germany awarded Radigue the Giga-Hertz Award for Lifetime Achievement. IRCAM and the Musée national d'art moderne in Paris honored Radigue with an event at the Centre Pompidou, "Le Monde d'Éliane Radigue," in conjunction with a special prize from the Evens Foundation, in September 2020. Radigue continues to live and work in Paris.

The Work
Feedback Techniques

Radigue's earliest compositions apply sound generated in real time through feedback techniques to magnetic tape. Already in *Jouet Électronique* the concern for precisely controlled sustaining frequency is clearly evidenced, belying the source as microphone-speaker feedback. A limited, timbrally changing sonority sustains across minimally varying rates of rhythmic interference. The unusually short (for Radigue) duration of less than twelve minutes may reflect the difficulty in capturing a source of such volatility with this degree of control. Subsequent pieces such as *USRAL*, using progressively slowed-down ultrasound frequencies, and *In Memoriam-Ostinato*, using tape feedback as opposed to microphone-speaker feedback (both 1969), push toward greater length through the multiplication of sources and looping. The technique of creating ensembles of multiple tapes of slightly varying duration, to be looped simultaneously such that repetitive features are lost in a gradually shifting displacement over time, dates from 1968. A number of Radigue's most important concerns are already apparent in this technique: long, even indefinite, duration; the setting in motion of a form that, despite the repetition of the individual tapes, diverges irreversibly from its point of origin; the consequent relinquishing of direct control over the form of the piece as heard in performance; and a working process through which complex musical results can be achieved by Radigue alone, without the aid of institutional support or additional musicians.

The work with nonsynchronous loops converges with the concept of the *propositions sonores*, pieces issued to the public in a format that encourages the user to create an at-home playback setup with multiple machines. Here Radigue's noncontrol over the final musical form is taken to another degree, inviting the user to make of the piece what they will; the listener is tacitly invited to be more than a listener, indeed, to be a curator, an editor, even a performer. The two principal examples of this approach are $\Sigma = a = b = a + b$ (1969) and *Vice-Versa, etc...* (1970). The former was released by Galerie Yvon Lambert in Paris as a limited edition with two identical seven-inch vinyl discs, the two sides of which are to be freely combined (as the title makes clear) at any available playback speed; the total edition numbered 250 copies. The latter was self-released in an edition of only ten copies, as a two-track stereo tape on a three-inch reel, presumably to be copied by the user and then played back in any combination, at any speed, backward or forward, "ad libitum," as the handwritten instructions on the tape state.[11] A decisive nonlinearity marks these pieces; the conglomeration of altered speeds, backward and forward orientations, displaced sources, and unexpected points of onset suggest a Cubist multiplicity of planes and points of address, but set in motion in the real time of performance.

All the work from this highly productive period (nine substantial pieces appeared in 1969 and 1970) involves the application of feedback techniques with great ingenuity and displays a fecundity borne of admirable technical parsimony. *OMNHT* (1970) specifies that the three asynchronously looping feedback sounds are to be projected through speaker drivers built into the backs of walls that enclose the listening space; thus, the walls themselves function as unpredictable speaker membranes, adding partials, resonances, and unpitched vibrations that correlate to their dimensions and materials. *Opus 17* (1970) is a remarkable suite of five individual pieces using recordings of canonic Western masterpieces (a Chopin prelude, an excerpt from *Parsifal*) subjected to the distortions of all manner of feedback treatments. Remarkably, despite the range of techniques and interventions, the signature sound of patiently sustained sonority, undulating in gradually varying rhythmic interference patterns, emerges again and again—a remainder recurring despite incommensurable and willfully unequal factors.

Analog Synthesis

Opus 17 is the last of the feedback pieces; in 1970, while in residence at New York University, Radigue had access to a Buchla 100-series modular synthesizer, and began the gradual transition to the medium she would use for the next thirty years: analog synthesis and magnetic tape.[12] The first result of this transition is *Chry-ptus* (1971), a single piece made of two stereo recordings to be played back simultaneously. The product of months of experimentation and investigation into the Buchla and its possibilities, *Chry-ptus* manages to elicit from the new instrument sustaining sonorities of subtly changing acoustical beating patterns and partial content that are astonishingly similar to certain earlier feedback pieces.[13] An electronic system customized for maximal variation and the expansion of expressive ranges in all musical parameters, the Buchla is thus chastened by Radigue into the agent of extreme concentration. But again, an element of openness in realization is built into the composition: the two recordings are slightly unequal in length, and in playback a desynchronization of up to one minute is advised, at the discretion of the performer. Radigue does not furnish a definitive mix or a fixed edit of what is in essence a four-voice piece; by requiring two separate tape machines for concert playback, she implies a double-stereo loudspeaker setup, introducing another set of spatial variables in performance, independent of the making of the piece.

At the end of 1971 the Buchla synthesizer gave way to the ARP 2500, which remained Radigue's instrument of choice (along with an array of Revox tape machines) for nearly three decades.[14] The degree of minute control afforded by the ARP, with its extraordinarily sensitive gain controls, modulators, and filters, proved an enduring source of inspiration to Radigue, providing the matrix for the development of her mature longform compositions through the seventies, eighties, and nineties. The elements that entered her work during this period are coextensive with the possibilities afforded by the ARP: long cross-fades and transitions in gain, timbral content, and filtering paced to challenge the listener's awareness of whether change is even occurring, and a consequent increase in overall length commensurate with the pacing of the musical structure. Already *7th Birth* (1972) is a full hour in length, and *Ψ 847* (1973) reaches a duration of eighty minutes. With the *Adnos* cycle (1974–82), the structuring of the work as a monumental triptych of long, independent, but interrelated movements is established, which will hold for both the *Trilogie de la Mort* (1988–93) and *Naldjorlak I–III* (2005–2009); in the case of *Adnos*, the individual movements each approach a length of eighty minutes; in the other pieces, movements are between fifty and sixty minutes.[15]

The magnification of scale and the elongation of the internal articulation of the music correspond to the technical possibilities of the ARP synthesizer, and to Radigue's gradual mastery of them. But the investigation of continuity, sustain, duration, and nearly imperceptible change is clearly anticipated in all her prior work. For the compositions of such long duration, Radigue adopted a system of preparing sections in advance as recordings of approximately ten to twenty minutes, carefully planned and practiced on the ARP. While Radigue has never used scores or musical notation in any conventional sense, she has prepared charts to designate levels and positions of the matrix switches on the module faceplates of the ARP. One could think of these diagrams as a kind of tablature notation, indicating physical registrations on the instrument, rather than notational signs representing sounds and musical states. Having prepared her sounds, noted the levels and positions, and determined that a section was ready for recording, she would commit the section to tape in a single take, without editing or correcting, fully complete as a musical gesture in time, and as a mix. If something went wrong along the way, she would invariably stop and rerecord the section from the beginning. As these individual sections—or "sub-mixes," as Radigue calls them— were completed, a plan would gradually emerge for the linking of the sections into the larger form of the entire movement. Once the final decisions on ordering and approximate durations had been made, the act of connecting the sub-mixes would commence, again, as a single continuous "performance" in which an individual sub-mix would be dubbed from one Revox machine to a master machine. As that sub-mix approached its end, the next would be slowly cross-faded onto the master machine from a third machine, at which point the tape would be removed from the first machine and replaced with the next sub-mix while the previous one was still playing, to be cross-faded onto the master machine as the second sub-mix ended, and so on, until the final section had been dubbed over and faded to silence.[16] In a case like *Kyema* (1988), the first movement of the *Trilogie de la Mort*, the changeovers from section to section are somewhat audible, lending the piece an unusually episodic character. In the third movement of the same three-part work, *Koumé* (1993), by contrast, one is utterly at a loss to identify cross-fades or points of transition.

In this description, one can observe Radigue's commitment to a tactile, handmade, real-time, and fully participatory approach to the making of a piece—not the distantiated, analytical perspective of the all-controlling composer. This approach embraces the striving to wrest from a complex set of simultaneous tasks a result that makes audible the efforts and limitations inherent in the process. The perspective is from within this process, not from outside, beyond, or above it. Here the composition does not represent an ideal, or an idealized object, independent of its realization in time and place, but rather a decidedly subject-dependent transaction, responding to and constituted by the resistances and particularities of a set of actions in a specific material environment.

From the present vantage point, it is difficult to imagine that the works on tape were not intended for commercial release. Almost all of Radigue's work has by now been issued on CD, LP, cassette tape, or digitally. But it is important to remember that, with the exception of $\Sigma = a = b = a + b$ and *Vice-Versa, etc...*, none of Radigue's music saw publication at the time of its making until the mid-eighties. Radigue seems to have intended these pieces for public presentation in concert or, in a handful of cases, in galleries as installations.[17] The works from the seventies would have sprung the bounds of available fixed media without the breaks of side-changes, and thus could be properly heard only from tape with live cross-fades between multiple reels and machines.[18] But even more important to an understanding of Radigue's aesthetic is her approach to multiple speaker setups and the adjustment of sound in a given playback space.

Multiplication of speaker setups has remained a favored playback strategy for Radigue, even for pieces with only a two-channel stereo source, or indeed a monophonic source. In discussing her strategies for speaker placement in concert playback events, Radigue expresses a preference for an evenly diffused sound that discourages any sense of source-locateability, frontality, or stereo field.[19] A stereo pair would be placed at opposite corners of the room, and an additional pair in the remaining corners. Speakers would sometimes be turned toward the wall, tilted slightly, or otherwise angled, all in response to onsite adjustments. Volume levels would be kept low to encourage a floating, disembodied sound presence. Placing two stereo pairs crisscross in a room leads to doublings and phase discontinuities; in addition to disrupting any discernible stereo orientation, the out-of-phase wave fronts will boost and cancel each other in a manner somewhat akin to a gentle and intermittent feedback effect. The multiple angles of address promote an orientation-less surfeit of sources and reflections, in some cases giving rise to acoustical illusions and anamorphosis-like distortions, yet without a single vantage point from which they are to resolve. Indeed, there is no single vantage point for Radigue's music, and multiplication of sources means multiplication of listening experiences. The example of *Chry-ptus* (1970) is paradigmatic. The sounding properties of either one of the two tapes constitute themselves only in convergence with those of the "partner" tape, and only at a time lag (variable, according to the discretion of the performer) and at a spatial remove (also variable, through the distribution and angling of loudspeakers). Thus, one can understand the internal compositional details of each tape to be subsumed in an expanded field of superimposition and virtuality. Here again Radigue's willingness to surrender the exact physiognomy of a listening experience to a set of momentary factors appears programmatic.

Listening Away: Effect as Cause, Resonance as Source

Radigue's art is rigorously fashioned around the play of partials, resonance, and acoustical beating, activated through the medium of continuous sound at a low dynamic. Over and over again Radigue points to the incorporealities of sound, the unpredictable multiplications, specters, and secondary effects that emerge as it propagates and resounds in space. Crucial to her compositional process is a directed listening that is uncompromisingly attuned to "a delicate sound world fashioned from breath, pulsation, beating, murmurs and the richness of the natural harmonics that radiate from it."[20] Far from an impressionistic aesthetic of delicacy, the priorities of this attentional posture define a highly personal relationship to acoustical physics. Paradigmatically, her listening seems to exclude any interest in a sound's fundamental frequency. "[W]hen you play a *la* or a *re* on a string, it's a *la* or a *re*, but what is really interesting is the whole immaterial zone emanating from the bow's friction on the string. For me, the manner of making the string vibrate, and all the richness that exudes from that, is music itself."[21] The fundamental frequencies that inevitably make up her music may in fact be derived from her exploration of the spectral content emerging from those very fundamentals; that is to say, compositional decision making is directed toward resultant features, not their sources. The secondary becomes primary, as if one were handling an object based on one's observation of its shadow or reflection rather than of the object itself. The root is thus inverted, or alienated, from its source position, and made collateral to the desired effects.

This reorientation brings with it the characteristic embrace of uncertainty and unknowability that is a cardinal premise of Radigue's music. A compositional project dedicated so concretely to listening, observing, and reacting, rather than asserting or defining, invites a reciprocal effort of listening on the part of the auditor. As though a kind of transference were being facilitated, the sounding results serve as the medium for one to "hear as Radigue hears," uncertain as such an undertaking may be. This listening situation is mirrored in her manner of working, which is preeminently hands-on, praxis-based, and open to the risk of failure, erasing any distance between the *making* of sound and the resulting composition. She does without scores; the electronic works from 1967 through 2000 were made alone in her studio with only minimal diagrams to guide their realization, and the works for acoustic instruments, from 2004 through the present, rest upon discussion, collaborative exploration with the performers, and memory, without any written prescription whatsoever. Radigue's embrace of uncertainty is likewise reflected in a certain diffidence toward theory, and a disinterest in technology as such. "Technology bores me. It has always been a mandatory means by which I had to pass, but which I hurried to forget."[22] Her interest in science leans toward the unexplainable: "But I am also—even especially—interested in what happens beyond the scientific explanations, in what actually cannot be explained . . . [w]hat interests me above all is what happens when we transgress [*si on déroge un tout petit peu*] these scientific laws a bit. It's their irrational side, their minute features."[23]

Music for Acoustic Instruments and Live Performers

What a strange experience after so much wandering, to return to what was already there, the perfection of acoustic instruments, the rich and subtle interplay of their harmonics, sub-harmonics, partials, just intonation left to itself, elusive like the colors of a rainbow.
—Éliane Radigue, "The Mysterious Power of the Infinitesimal"[24]

Naldjorlak I–III (2005–2009)

Naldjorlak is Radigue's first composition for a live performer on an unamplified instrument. The idea to make this piece was suggested to Radigue by the composer Gérard Pape after my performance of La Monte Young and Marian Zazeela's *Just Charles and Cello in the Romantic Chord in a Setting of Abstract #1 from Phase Angle Traversals in Dream Light* at the Maison de la Poésie in Paris in December 2003. The gestation of *Naldjorlak* took nearly two years; the very idea that a major solo cello composition could be brought into existence by Radigue, with no direct experience of the instrument and no background in composing for orchestral instruments, seemed implausible, especially to her. The making of the piece was thus predicated on an involved collaborative process during which both composer and performer proposed, tried out, discarded, and revisited a very wide range of possible techniques and sound morphologies. One could say that the piece was made ex nihilo; ways of causing the cello to resonate indirectly, as it were, to engage as much as possible of the instrument's resonant capacity at once, were examined empirically. The breakthrough occurred with my suggestion to Radigue that the entire cello, across nearly all its resonating elements—strings, tailpiece, endpin, tailpiece wire—could be tuned to one sonority, that of the so-called wolf tone. The instability of the wolf tone notwithstanding, this tuning transforms the instrument into a bell-like resonator, such that any bowed action on a string or other tuned element prompts sympathetic resonances from every other string or element. This unified resonance of the entire instrument echoes the meaning of the title, *Naldjorlak*, which combines a Tibetan honorific form of address and the concept of yoga, or unity. The structure of the piece traces a physical trajectory over the strings and body of the instrument, paced such that each location is explored exhaustively through slow bowing techniques until no further partials or resonances can be uncovered, at which point the next location is explored, and so on, following the instrument down to the endpin and the tailpiece wire, where the process ends. Usually, the piece runs for nearly one hour.

There is no written score for *Naldjorlak*. In effect a kind of real-time acoustical investigation of an instrument in an unstable tuning, interacting unpredictably with the acoustical space of performance, its compositional framework must be limited to the designation of the techniques to be deployed and their sequence. The actual sounds and dynamics, the rhythms of bow lengths and bow changes, the exact durations of individual sections can only emerge through the act of performing; and the act of performing becomes not the reconstructing of a set of prescribed sounds, but a careful process of listening and reacting, altering the minutiae of technique in response to real-time acoustical cues.

At the time of this collaboration, no one could have predicted that a late florescence in compositions for acoustic instruments would result. But it is not an exaggeration to suggest that *Naldjorlak* laid the groundwork and set forth the methodology for all Radigue's works that have followed. The collaborative process in which a piece is planned and tested out by performer and composer together is certainly not new in the Western musical tradition, but one would be hard-pressed to find other instances in which the composer yields to the performer so much of what is brought to the piece in the first place. This has since become the model for Radigue's practice: to ask the performer to contribute not just expertise and ability but the actual materials of instrumental technique and their specific, personal relationship to those materials. The piece is not so much tailored to that performer as it is a cladding of that performer in the fabric of Radigue's music. In the absence of any written score, the piece is internalized through practice and critical discussion and is expected to continue to change over the space of many performances.

Such an approach to composition sheds light on the making of the earlier tape pieces. In effect, the performers of *Naldjorlak* and of the other instrumental compositions, while bringing their own material to each piece, must present this material in the agreed-upon form as a sort of surrogate for Radigue's own performance of sounds onto tape. From the standpoint of the performer on an acoustic instrument, extracting complex, sustained sonority from an unwieldy instrument made even more unwieldy by the focus on diffuse and complex sounds, the crucial challenge is to enact this exchange as if Radigue herself were performing. One must hear as she hears, react as she reacts, shape as she shapes, but on an acoustic instrument, and in front of an audience. Thus the tape pieces and the instrumental pieces potentially relate to each other as a kind of inside and outside of performance.

Naldjorlak I premiered in New York in 2005 and was followed by *Naldjorlak II* for two basset horns, doubled primarily to make possible the continuous sustaining of sound through overlapping breaths. *Naldjorlak II* was premiered in Aarau, Switzerland, by Carol Robinson and Bruno Martinez in 2007, and was in turn followed by a third piece, *Naldjorlak III*, an approximate palimpsest of its immediate predecessors, in which the first two pieces are overlaid with slight, variable offsets in time and adjustments in material. The three pieces together, performed as a complete cycle, last nearly three hours, with short breaks as between movements in a sonata-form work. The full three-part cycle was premiered in Bordeaux, France, at the CAPC Musée d'Art Contemporain on January 24, 2009, Radigue's seventy-seventh birthday.

Occam Ocean (2011–present)

Since 2011 Radigue has worked on an interlocking series of shorter pieces for individual performers on acoustic instruments under the general title of *Occam Ocean*. The title pays homage to scholastic philosopher William of Ockham and his famous razor, the protominimalist teaching that entities should not be multiplied unnecessarily, and that the simplest solution is the optimal one.

The first in this series, *Occam I*, composed for bowed harp for the Welsh harpist Rhodri Davies, premiered in London in the summer of 2011. As in the process established for the *Naldjorlak* cycle, a performer comes to Radigue to suggest a personal and distinctive approach to their chosen instrument; if Radigue finds the techniques and materials appropriate and compelling, a shared process ensues in which the materials are shaped into a coherent piece, under Radigue's direction. Once again, a written score is eschewed, and the performer relies on memory and the real-time confrontation and negotiation with the dynamic conditions of performance to give the piece its immediate form.

Occam Ocean was initiated as a series of solos; but the interest in combinatoriality and multilayering that persists throughout Radigue's career here reaches a point of utter profusion. More than seventy pieces now comprise a virtual ocean of instrumental forms, spanning solos (*Occam I–XXVII*), duos (*Occam River I–XXII*), trios (*Occam Delta I–XVIII*), and larger groups (*Occam Hexa I–IV, Occam Hepta I*) including small orchestra (*Occam Ocean I*). The instruments employed vary from bassoon, trumpet, tuba, violin, viola, cello, and other standard orchestral instruments to bagpipes, birbyn, saxophone, organ, contrabass recorder, and voice. The choice of these instruments rests not with Radigue, but follows from the personal encounters with instrumentalists who have presented themselves to her in hopes of making a new *Occam*.

The ensemble pieces layer and combine the solos with slight adjustments to optimize the transparency of the individual layers. It seems no accident that this combinatorial procedure (and that of the *Naldjorlak* cycle) revisits the *propositions sonores* of 1968 to '71, in which tapes of differing lengths are looped or repeated ad libitum. These works reveal a commitment to formal results that are unforeseen by the composer and that carry within them a guarantee of unrepeatability and incompletability. Indeed, Radigue views the *Occam* series as one that will remain unfinished. Given the number of individual pieces and the unlikelihood of realizing every possible combination, Radigue states, "the overall construction . . . implies, by nature, the impossibility of completing the oeuvre."[25]

II.

Characteristics and Techniques
Making the Work in Real Time, Performed Composition

Analyzing Radigue's music—or, more properly, investigating its formal and sonorous appearance, identifying its musical contours, assessing its power, tracing its creative sources—is not a straightforward matter. Radigue has almost never worked with scores or notations that might offer themselves to score analysis. The pieces (as of the early seventies) are long; one can hear them as static, absent of identifiable musical activity, or conversely as bearing considerable complexity and variation, but within a perceptually narrowed range. Descriptions range from the entirely metaphorical, in which sound textures are assigned tactile values,[26] to more blunt timeline-based accountings of musical events (interval, relative amplitude, appearance/disappearance of frequency areas)[27] to computer spectrogram analysis of recordings.[28] These approaches raise the question of what is to be gained through description; the pieces exist for themselves, and it is hard to imagine how the immersive listening experience they call forth would benefit from informational pointers of this kind.[29] Such attempts to identify or label or graph its features may distract from a music that is fundamentally conceived as moment-to-moment entrainment in the lived time of its being listened to—a music, for lack of a better term, of personal experience.

Essential to an understanding of Radigue's process is her eschewal of editing. Even the very long pieces from the seventies onward were made in a series of single takes by Radigue alone, without assistance or after-the-fact correction. This is not, however, to suggest that Radigue extemporizes; rather, the sound materials, techniques, and the general shape of the piece were planned in advance and carefully tested out, but its final making was always in a single thrust. Tape, like film, is a medium suited to the capture of discrete elements that can be cut and spliced and reordered in the technique of montage. This would be the characteristic advantage of tape over live performance, and the medium-specific approach to tape is exemplified in works like John Cage's *Williams Mix* (1951–53) or Pierre Schaeffer's *Étude aux chemins de fer* (1948).

Nothing could be more different from these dense concatenations of sound units than Radigue's calmly extended processes. A parallel can be found in contemporaneous film such as Chantal Akerman and Babette Mangolte's *La Chambre* (1972). With a single take of a slow circular pan, the film as much captures Mangolte's calm, controlled camera movement inscribed as gradual gesture as it does the slowly shifting image of the room, its occupant, and its contents. The same can be said of Radigue's technique of recording sound. Tape for her is not a bulletin board or conveyor belt for fragments to be combined; it is a surface upon which Radigue's hand draws, continuously, without pause. The audible tracing of her actions can be considered as much the music as the sound images that result.

In this sense, her electronic music was made in a performance, but one without an immediate audience. To understand her music from the inside, to comprehend the internal dynamics that determine its outer form, it must be understood in precisely this sense, as single-take recordings, not edited or assembled or constructed. Similarly, the public presentations of her works in the form of playback concerts were, invariably, carefully prepared through speaker placement and angling, amplitude balancing, and any other possible adjustments in response to the dimensions and acoustics of the space. Playback itself was performed—not through added theatrical or visual elements but in the fastidious and at times willful preparation of the sound-reproduction apparatus. One can also point to the fact that sustained frequencies tend to produce standing waves, far more so than rhythmic music that focuses primarily on sequences of attacks; the phenomenon of standing waves leads to listening experiences that differ widely from room to room, and especially from location to location within a room. Thus even the playback of Radigue's commercially released recordings will vary according to environment. Finally, the sheer length of many of Radigue's pieces tends to exceed the span of what a listener can remember or refer back to on repeated listenings; the listener is confronted with a music that defies definition and concrete recollection. What is true of any performance is thus to some extent true of these seemingly fixed tape pieces: there is no definitively closed, complete, and authentic version of them.

First and foremost, it is the act of their making that radically embraces an expressive state of uncertainty. A case in point would be the early feedback pieces. Generating frequency through the spatial relationship between a microphone and an amplified speaker sets in motion a volatile sequence of reactions. Given enough gain, once the feedback tone is established, it increases of its own accord. To keep the signal under control one must either move the microphone or ride the gain. In the pieces that involve so-called tape feedback, a single tape is run from one tape deck to another, at some distance from the first. The input signal is run from the playback head of the first deck to some combination of playback and record heads on the second deck, frequently with erase heads disabled; the self-propagating signal saturates the tape, creating all manner of harmonic distortion and overload symptoms, which are then managed through any available controls (pitch, gain, and tone would have been the onboard regulators on Radigue's Tolana Magnetophones).

What both approaches entail is the attempt to control a force that is in the process of escaping, of outstripping its input. In this sequence of actions, a paradigmatic reordering of the assumed priorities of music composition is enacted: emphasis is placed not on the production of the sound, its frequency, location, duration, or timbral qualities, but instead on a physical action in response to a situation of elective volatility. What happens to sound after it is initiated is framed as the site of artistic invention; the composer hovers in a liminal space between noncontrol and the attempt to control.

Sustained Sound

Sustained sound is one nearly irreducible feature of Radigue's work; it may even be its defining feature. But sustained sound is not an end in itself.[30] Sustain must be understood here as more than the prolongation of one, or few, frequencies. It can mean the sustaining of an initiated dynamic, of amplitude, or the upholding of any underlying patterns within a texture (acoustical beating, for example); sustaining equates to duration. It means the concerted act of sustaining: the effort, in many cases palpable or audible (even in a recording), to suspend a continuous signal through the unavoidable changes that interfere with it, often drastically. This effort can again be conceptualized through the example of feedback: When holding a microphone in proximity to a speaker, the input and output will couple, producing a sustained tone. That tone itself may, under certain circumstances, increase precipitously in amplitude, resulting in a sudden peak or an abrupt change, or it may suddenly abate. For the signal to sustain, the location of the microphone must be continuously adjusted to avoid either the sudden cessation or overload of sound. Sustaining then becomes a directed physical effort managed through careful listening and reacting. This concerted, physical act of sustaining becomes even more dramatically present in the works for instruments in live performance (the *Naldjorlak* cycle in particular), in which the audience is directly confronted, visually as well as aurally, with the difficulty of the act.

Sustaining carries other meanings beyond the material facts of sound production. The consistency of Radigue's output, her commitment to a very specific range of musical expression and aesthetic experience, suggest a kind of creative sustaining over a very long time span. In this respect, her output hearkens back to the message of La Monte Young's *Composition 1960 #10* (1960): "Draw a straight line / and follow it." The reference for straightness is never obvious nor given; this is legible in Radigue's labor-intensive works of the nineties, and the extended work periods, over years, required for the production of each new piece. The drawing of the line—the sustaining of the signal—is an ongoing process that points only forward, that is in some sense irreversible. This forward motion touches on the formal aspects of Radigue's music, which tends to not go back. Notions of reprise or recapitulation or return are largely absent from her formal thinking; sustaining proceeds in one direction. Finally, listeners must sustain their attention as a reciprocal effort of concentration, an invitation to participate mentally and affectively in a shared sustaining.

The Experience of Time

As Radigue's works became longer during the seventies, beginning with *7th Birth* and *Ψ 847*, stretching to lengths of one hour and more, sustaining took on an added significance: contributing to a broader aesthetic reconsideration of the experience of time. Though her music was not widely disseminated in the seventies, her ideas must still be understood as participating in a wide-ranging debate in art circles on time and aesthetic experience. Music of long duration is part and product of this discussion, interfacing with other disciplines such as cinema (Chantal Akerman, Michael Snow) and repetitive performance (Viennese actionists, Marina Abramovíc), as well as cultural traditions (ritual and meditation) and personal-social experiments such as psychedelic drugs. All these projects share an interest in testing limits, whether physical, mental, emotional, or purely perceptual.

Radigue's work explores and illuminates very slight change over time. In a sense, the lower limit of perceived change is the subject of the work; sustaining thus emerges as a way of framing barely perceptible change against a sustaining medium. Change is characteristically managed as existing in a near-balance between the changes effected upon the sustaining medium and changes that return, unpredictably and largely uncontrollably, from the overall system or sounding environment. The degree of change is held within very tight bounds, and this fact structurally determines the length of each work. Only within a very slow, gradual unfolding are the minuscule markers of change revealed.

This relationship to time is very different from that of La Monte Young's work. In Young's music, *time stands still*; its aspiration is toward absolute nonchange, approached through a kind of measuring of time in sound (*X for Henry Flynt* [1960]; *Composition 1960 #7* [1960]), which, paradoxically, reveals slight change as an irreducible remainder. In contrast, the late works of Morton Feldman, similar in duration to Radigue's work of the same period, explore near-repetition or microvariation, but on the level of musical utterance. In his very long works, Feldman seems to create figural, thematic, gestural, rhythmic statements (the parallels to language are explicit) that then shift and recast themselves in a listener's memory. Radigue seems less interested in memory, or in the contextual changes in musical materials imposed by long listening phases. As a music that does not repeat, her work seems to exclude the kind of musical material (gesture, figure, ornament) that would lend itself to repetition, pointing to the incompatibility of her entire process with semiotically mediated forms of notation, and the fixed ordering of elements in time.

Sound Figures

It is not the case, however, that figures or gestures do not arise in Radigue's music. They do, but as byproducts of other, nonfigural and nongestural actions. Sometimes they arise as faint acoustical emanations from the sustaining texture (the opening stretch of *Kyema* introduces high partials that have an almost nonacoustical presence), and sometimes as pronounced stretches of roughness (the heavily bowed sections in the 2011 solo for bowed harp, *Occam I*, for example). These are figures specific to the sustaining context, not composed into the music directly. Mostly they take the form of beating, shifting patterns of overtones, or other less clearly defined acoustical distortions. Examples abound: toward the end of *Kyema*, the sustained sonorities seem to produce slowly pealing bell sounds;[31] in *Adnos II*, the "Danse des Dakinis" section reaches a rhythmicization that can almost be heard as percussive; in *Naldjorlak I*, the pulsations of the wolf tone take the form of a nearly uniform thrumming action; many of the early feedback pieces exhibit pronounced rhythmic interference patterns as well.

In fact, such figural patterns are so specific to the unique conditions of the sustained actions that they cannot be predicted with any degree of certainty. Therefore, these "figures" are not controlled directly—neither by Radigue in the electronic music nor by the performer in the instrumental works—but indirectly, and the degree of control is severely limited. They are most certainly not composed; instead they arise, sometimes more and sometimes less readily, in response to the acoustical or instrumental conditions at a particular moment. Their independence from the direct control of the composer is a crucial, even constitutive feature of all Radigue's music. To voluntarily relinquish control over those elements that are most often perceived as foreground figures (with rhythmic, quasi-melodic associations and discrete durations), and yet to seek those elements as a second-order indexing of another sustained and nondiscrete action, itself requiring considerable direct control, frames a paradox that is central to any understanding of musical perspective in Radigue's work.

Surface and Depth

One could begin to see the actual signal production—whether electronic or instrumental—as the laying out of a medium, not as the making of a piece per se. The piece then becomes the sum total of reactions upon the medium. These reactions are not random, and indeed a considerable amount of control is exerted, both in the choice of medium and in its handling, in order to induce reactions upon it—but the reactions themselves, the exact sounding results, organize themselves in a realm of considerable freedom from control. They are not random, but incalculable.

If signal production here is to be viewed as a medium, and the piece proper as the sum total of reactions upon it, one is confronted with a reassessment of the foreground-to-background or figure-to-ground relationship. The sense of immersion in a listening experience that Radigue's music elicits may have something to do with an experience of falling into this gap, and of the continuous process of reorientation as one seeks out signs pointing to continuity, variation, material, resonance, subject, work, listener. Immersion is far from passive, and the figure of the listener easily conflates with the figure of the music. The movement from figure to ground and from ground to figure, from the "in back" of background to the "in front" of foreground, is constantly in process.

Radigue's music is curiously homophonic, at times even monophonic. A notable case in point is *Transamorem–Transmortem* (1974). In this hourlong piece, one monophonic tape is to be played back simultaneously through four speakers, one in each of the four corners of a room. In Radigue's words: "The impression of different localisations of the sound is solely due to the allocation of the different frequency zones, as well as to displacements from simple head movements occurring within the acoustic space of the room."[32] While the model of the single monophonic signal multiplied by four is probably unique in Radigue's output, the sound image thus proposed takes one to the heart of her notion of musical perspective. Abstaining from complex simultaneities, polyrhythms, competing layers, her music projects a sounding front that is largely unified or even singular; and the listener encounters this front initially as a kind of surface. The music does not evoke a sense of depth, a region of profound truth lying concealed below the surface, or a set of symbolic references wrested from notation or inherited tradition. Rather, one is drawn to the surface itself, and to that which arises from it: an interchange between surface and atmosphere, a spatial manifold that extends outward toward the listener, including, paradigmatically, the full dimensions of a listening space. Far from being flat or shallow, another depth extends in this direction, a spatial depth that lies not below or behind the surface, but around the sound source and those in its presence.

Irreversible Process

Notable in many of Radigue's works is the sense that change proceeds slowly, in some cases so slowly that one tends to register the change only after the fact. It is often only when beginnings and endings of pieces are compared that one realizes significant change has occurred, and that the form that the piece has taken is that of a continuous *going-away* from its starting point. In *Naldjorlak I* (2005), the distance traversed turns out to be a visible, physical distance spanning the body of the cello, in the direction of the floor. The gradual change in location on which the cellist bows the instrument visually articulates a stepwise change in the sounds themselves over a nearly one-hour duration. At the end, bowing on the endpin, the cellist can go no further. In the first piece of *Opus 17*, "Étude" (1970), a recording of a Chopin solo piano prelude is looped and sent through a recursive tape-feedback process. The loop is approximately two minutes and forty seconds long, and is repeated eight times, each time receding further behind the feedback frequencies elicited by the process. By the end, the loop is no longer recognizable; one can go no further. A piece that began in A-flat major ends among sustained B-naturals, A-naturals, and

F-sharps—pitches that are, even in a tonal sense, remote from the loop's home key, its point of departure.[33]

Similar instances of gradual displacement from a starting point can be found throughout Radigue's output. While the process of "electro-erosion," as Radigue calls it, in *Opus 17* and the traversal of the cello's geography in *Naldjorlak I* are the most schematic examples, the directionality of away is not always so straight or linear. In more sectionalized pieces like *Kyema*, or audibly looped pieces like *Maquette* (1970), which loops a recorded excerpt from Wagner's *Parsifal*, cyclical, symmetrical, or ritornello ideas are nowhere to be found. Invariably a going-away is present, whether as a drifting apart or as a steady and purposive procession in stages.

A variant of this characteristic may be found in the works from the late sixties that involve the playback of simultaneous loops of different lengths, the *propositions sonores*. The unequal lengths of the loops ensure that no sounding combinations will ever repeat (at least not discernibly, within the expected time span of a listening). In pieces such as *Accroméga* (1968), *USRAL*, *OMNHT*, $\Sigma = a = b = a + b$, *Labyrinthe Sonore* (1970), and *Vice-Versa, etc...*, going-away must be understood as a kind of gradually revolving process in which the repetitiveness of the loops themselves is obscured by constantly new—theoretically nonrepeating—juxtapositions. Especially given that these pieces are largely made up of sustaining sounds, no repetitive quality at all remains in the repeating of the loops.

Propagation and Diffusion

This notion of going-away can stand as a central image in Radigue's way of working with her materials. What can perhaps be said broadly of her work is that the stage of sound production is less interesting to her than the stage of sound propagation. Sounds directly produced are chosen for their capacity or inclination to be transformed in the process of their diffusion; conversely, the acoustical conditions to which those sounds are exposed are chosen to create unpredictable reactions only after the onset of the sounds, necessitating a reactive or responsive rather than predictive attitude. Her creative act, grounded primarily in the medium of sustained sound, is arbitrating between two factors that reciprocally invade, disrupt, and transform each other: the one, a setting in motion of sound energy, and the other, a force field of mechanical, spatial, or electronic stresses that exceed direct control. The act, then, is casting out information into a swirl, attending to the results, and attempting to shape them despite their unruliness. This dynamic presupposes a readiness to relinquish subjective domination, to renounce a posture of prediction in favor of listening for what may be—in effect, to coexist with material in a kind of entente.

This orientation is visible even in the public distribution of Radigue's work. $\Sigma = a = b = a + b$ was released in 1969 as a double seven-inch vinyl edition, containing two copies of the same disc and instructions for the user to play both discs simultaneously—either the same side at once or opposite sides, either synchronized or not, and at any playback speed—in a series of possible combinations "*à l'infini*," as Radigue writes on the sleeve.[34] This is a proposition in the sense conveyed by the French language, an *invitation* to see what will happen, and to make of these discs a sound piece of the user's liking. Here the work has moved far away from the composer's control, and the fact that the sounds on the discs are already the result of an unruly feedback process goes without saying.

An even more illuminating case is Radigue's relationship with the performers of her acoustic pieces. The sound-production stage is that set of playing techniques or instrumental habits brought to the conversation by a particular performer, not conceived or invented—and certainly not composed—by Radigue. The piece itself is the joint construction of a framework in which these techniques and actions may unfold in the uncertain space of live performance. Without score, with only the verbal planning and testing of the actions and the memory of the performer linking performance to performance, a slippage or displacement from the point of origin is inevitable; indeed, it seems to be desired. Radigue is in the habit of releasing responsibility for the piece to the performer; often, when she has determined that the piece is ready for performance, she will declare to the performer that the piece is "yours."

The sound materials and techniques Radigue is drawn to share a quality that might best be called anomaly, deviation, or even flaw. Feedback, for example, is conventionally considered a defect in the system, something to be held at bay. Yet it is intrinsic to amplified systems; it reveals and defines the gain relationships of output and input. In *Transamorem-Transmortem* the mono signal was created on the ARP 2500 and recorded onto tape, then rerecorded with a microphone placed inside Radigue's Altec-Lansing Voice of the Theatre speaker, layering a slight tinge of feedback into the original signal.[35] *Naldjorlak I* for solo cello takes as its central feature the so-called wolf tone, again, a stigmatized acoustical distortion that stands outside the accepted norms of cello sound. Yet it, too, is intrinsic to that instrument; it is a point of resonance that indexes very precisely a particular instrument's dimensions and vibratory mechanics. Acoustical beating is yet another marginal, chimerical effect that stands outside notions of unison or pure intonation or harmonic stability, but is also an inextricable feature of the act of sustaining multiple frequencies and cannot be eliminated in any human scale of perception. All these examples share a dual status as distortions that are nonetheless central attributes of their source systems. In all cases, they also bring about a surplus, an actual increase in energy (sometimes even in amplitude) when fully revealed in the diffusion phase of the sound process. For Radigue, these anomalies act as guarantors of complex, unpredictable, and perceptually rich consequences. The surplus in richness they bring about corresponds to a reduction in the degree of possible control over their behavior; wrestling in sound with this contradiction is key to the particular expressivity of Radigue's music.

Epilogue: The Composer Paradox

The "open door" of the *Occam* series proposes both a radical extension of Cage's notion of "accepting" rather than "making"—accepting the performer who literally knocks at the door to present themself as the material for a new musical work—and a radical equating of the musical work with the performer who volunteers.[36] This latter idea also extends the standard concept of collaboration to its breaking point: there are situations in which one might even question whether the resulting work is indeed a composition by Radigue or a composition by the performer as a sort of homage to Radigue, channeling and emulating her relationship to sounds and their organization—an imitation, in effect. That the musical works brought into being through this process will vary considerably in interest, closeness to the object being imitated, intensity of experience, not to say artistic quality, goes without saying. But it is a remarkable achievement of Radigue's to have thus shuffled the hierarchies of authoriality, interpretation, originality, and even the ignis fatuus of artistic quality in such distinctive and potentially far-reaching ways. The result is, at least in concept, a tacit critique of received notions that have adhered to the economy of "classical music" for at least a century, notions revolving around professionalism, expertise, division of labor, and ownership, in addition to the hierarchies noted above.

In dissolving the fixities of these relationships, Radigue may have conceptualized and elaborated, with infinite patience and resolve over decades, an entirely different set of properties with which to define the musical work. Heightening the perceptual labor of the listener and illuminating the changing phases of attention, Radigue's music suggests an interrelation more inwardly directed than listening would seem to propose. Ultimately, her compositional practice has dismantled the conventions of the internally organized musical work as a stable entity or closed system, engaging musician and listener alike within a field of shifting relations, one in which the subject herself is invited to dissolve the inherited forms of a separate, boundaried consciousness.

1   Friedrich Hölderlin, *Sämtliche Werke und Briefe, Fünfter Band* (Leipzig: Im Insel Verlag, 1926), 341.

2   An apparent exception is the composition *Geelriandre* (1972), which included live performance by the pianist Gérard Frémy on prepared piano and gong; however, Frémy's part seems to have been semi-improvised and created independently of Radigue's tape piece. The shift to live performers and acoustic instruments in the early 2000s involved a definitive end to her work with electronics. It is difficult to find historical parallels to such a radical shift in medium—as if the painter Agnes Martin had suddenly decided, in her early seventies, to henceforth make only films.

3   Apart from two limited gallery publications in 1969 and 1970, the first commercial release of Radigue's music is a 1983 LP released on Lovely Music, *Songs of Milarepa*. The next is a cassette from 1987, likewise by Lovely Music, *Jetsun Mila*. By 1998, only four full-length releases had appeared; since then, more than twenty-five separate works have been released, several in multiple editions. In a 1973 review in the *Village Voice*, Tom Johnson is at a loss to describe the effect that Radigue's Ψ 847, presented at The Kitchen in New York, had on him. He remarks: "Most people would have been unimpressed by the modest sounds and uninterested in the tiny things that happen to them." See Tom Johnson, "Minimal Material: Éliane Radigue," *Village Voice*, March 29, 1973. One indication of the more recent attention her work has received in mainstream consciousness is the use of an excerpt from *Jetsun Mila* (1986) in the 2015 Hollywood movie *The Revenant*, which claimed three Academy Awards and grossed over a half-billion dollars.

4   Julia Eckhardt and Éliane Radigue, *Intermediary Spaces/Espaces Intermédiaires* (Brussels: Q02/Umland Editions, 2019), 59, 64. See also Bernard Girard, *Entretiens avec Éliane Radigue* (Paris, France: Éditions Aedam Musicae, 2013), 27.

5   "'What I always loved in classical music were those moments when a modulation takes place,' says Radigue, 'when the ear is no longer in the preceding tonality but hasn't yet arrived in the new one. That moment of *in-between-ness*.' Radigue's music is about extending and superimposing such moments to create a constantly evolving sound mass that plays with our perception of both musical and clock time. 'The material repeats,' she explains, 'but it also evolves, and that evolution has to be almost imperceptible, so the ear only recognises it once it's happened.' In short, Radigue . . . revels in ambivalence and ambiguity." Dan Warburton, "Into the Labyrinth," *The Wire*, no. 260 (October 2005): 26–32. See also Eckhardt and Radigue, *Intermediary Spaces*, 42.

6   Warburton, "Into the Labyrinth." Webern and Leibowitz are also mentioned in Emmanuel Holterbach et al., *Portraits Polychromes: Éliane Radigue* (Paris, France: INA/Groupe de Recherches Musicales, 2013), 12.

7   Radigue's recollections of this event make it impossible to ascertain exactly which piece of Schaeffer's she heard. In one interview she cites *Étude aux chemins de fer* (see Eckhardt and Radigue, *Intermediary Spaces*, 64); in another she states that she cannot recall which piece it was (see Warburton, "Into the Labyrinth"). It is possible that the broadcast she heard was an extended program of pieces by Schaeffer, and that she heard more than one.

8   Eckhardt and Radigue, *Intermediary Spaces*, 64.

9   Eckhardt and Radigue, *Intermediary Spaces*, 72.

10 Eckhardt and Radigue, *Intermediary Spaces*, 76.

11 Instructions reproduced in the CD booklet for *Vice–Versa, etc…* on Important Records, IMPREC 259 (2010). It is probable that the recording on the first of the two channels is the same as on the other channel but recorded backward, hence the title; Radigue as much as confirmed this in conversation with the author, September 2019.

12 There is some uncertainty as to the sound source for *Vice–Versa, etc.…* Dated 1970 and presented at Galerie Lara Vincy, Paris, in 1971, it fits chronologically with the last of the feedback pieces, and Eckhardt maintains that the sound source is "feedback on

45

magnetic tape." See Eckhardt and Radigue, *Intermediary Spaces*, 178. Likewise, the CD release on IMPREC identifies the piece as "the very last feedback loop composition." But Radigue insists that the sounds were produced on the ARP 2500 synthesizer (conversation with the author, August 2020). The ambiguity in sound source underlines the seamlessness of Radigue's transition; *Vice-Versa, etc...* presents a kind of aesthetic fulcrum between the two work periods.

13 "The synthesiser not only allowed me to combine, but also to develop the two main elements of the vocabulary I had found with feedback: sustained sound and beating, to which could be added the search for natural harmonics . . . I could work on making the sound progress much more slowly and precisely. But maybe I would not have found this way of working with the synthesiser without first going through the period of research into feedback, where I learned not to try to bend the sounds to my liking, but rather to give them a framework." Quoted in Eckhardt and Radigue, *Intermediary Spaces*, 111.

14 *Arthesis* (1973) is the only exception, made with a Moog system at the University of Iowa.

15 In *Naldjorlak* the durations are somewhat variable in concert, since the pieces are untimed, live instrumental performances.

16 This process was described to the author in considerable detail in conversation, September 2019. For a helpful description, see Eckhardt and Radigue, *Intermediary Spaces*, 119. See also Tara Rodgers, *Pink Noises: Women on Electronic Music and Sound* (Durham: Duke University Press, 2010), 57–58; and Girard, *Entretiens*, 70–71. Additionally, in this volume, Daniel Silliman describes in detail the technical procedures that Radigue likely followed in the making of *Kyema*, proposing a slight variant to my understanding of the preparation of the submix tapes. See Silliman, "Being and Nonbeing: An Analysis of *Kyema*," in *Alien Roots: Éliane Radigue* (New York: Blank Forms Editions, 2025), 287–321.

17 In fact, for much of her career Radigue would not allow a piece of hers to be presented publicly more than once: "I thought it was part of my duty to not repeat myself, to move on once one of my works had been presented." Girard, *Entretiens*, 59–60.

18 An early offer to release $Ψ 847$ on the prominent new music imprint Shandar in the early seventies was declined by Radigue, on the grounds that the continuity of the piece would have been destroyed by the interruptions necessary to change sides. Conversation with the author, August 2020.

19 Eckhardt and Radigue, *Intermediary Spaces*, 120–21.

20 Éliane Radigue, "The Mysterious Power of the Infinitesimal," trans. Anne Fernandez and Jacqueline Rose, *Leonardo Music Journal* 19 (2009): 47–49.

21 Eckhardt and Radigue, *Intermediary Spaces*, 54.

22 Eckhardt and Radigue, *Intermediary Spaces*, 116.

23 Eckhardt and Radigue, *Intermediary Spaces*, 49–50.

24 Radigue, "The Mysterious Power of the Infinitesimal," 49.

25 Eckhardt and Radigue, *Intermediary Spaces*, 158–59.

26 Emmanuel Holterbach, in *Portraits Polychromes*, as well as in numerous CD and LP liner notes, excels in this approach, at times rivalling Marcel Proust in his allusiveness. See his description of $Ψ 847$ in Holterbach et al., *Portraits Polychromes*, 41.

27 See Joanna Demers, *Listening Through the Noise: The Aesthetics of Experimental Electronic Music* (Oxford, UK: Oxford University Press, 2010), 94–95, in which Demers descriptively contrasts differing strategies of "drone" music.

28 An interesting investigation of a recording of *Naldjorlak* based on formant theory is found in Jacob Wiens, "Acoustical Resources for Music Analysis and Scale Formation" (PhD diss., McGill University, Montreal, 2016).

29 Salomé Voegelin, in *The Political Possiblity of Sound-Fragments of Listening* (New York and London: Bloomsbury, 2019), 166–75, raises this very issue. Voegelin opts for a writing that interweaves description, theorization, and sensate observation. Her prose traces a listening experience through writing that

captures both the sounding object and the inner logics of the listening subject, arguing compellingly for "the possibility of a sonic materialism as a feminist science fiction" (166).

30 Radigue has said as much on numerous occasions: for example, see Eckhardt and Radigue, *Intermediary Spaces*, 42: "Continuous sound is a means, it's not an end in itself."

31 As a case in point, these bell-like sounds may be the result of one of the ARP 2500 oscillators set to a fractional Hertz value—a sustaining, but one that is intrinsically intermittent.

32 Description on tape box. Text reproduced in CD booklet for Éliane Radigue, *Transamorem–Transmortem* CD, Important Music, IMPREC 337, 2011.

33 This process superficially resembles Alvin Lucier's contemporaneous *I Am Sitting in a Room* (1969), in which recursive rerecordings of a spoken text elicit the prominent resonances of a given space. Radigue was not acquainted with this work of Lucier at the time (conversation with the author, September 2019). Despite clear parallels, it is most helpful to understand the differences in these apparently similar approaches. For Lucier in *I Am Sitting in a Room*, it is the acoustic signature of the resonant void that he seeks to articulate. For Radigue in "Étude," it is larsen, the feedback sonority itself, determined by microphone and speaker placement and gain relationships, recorded in a nonresonant space, a closet full of clothing with the door closed. The resonance of the space was not a primary consideration. In fact, the very first iteration of the Chopin recording already betrays a slight aura of feedback sustain.

34 Galerie Yvon Lambert, limited edition, 1969, 2nd ed., in identical format to the original issue by Povertech Industries, Sacramento, California, 2000.

35 This was disclosed by Radigue in conversation with the author, December 2018.

36 Discussing the early music of Morton Feldman, Cage praises Feldman for having "changed the responsibility of the composer from making to accepting." See John Cage, "Lecture on Something," in *Silence: Lectures and Writings* (Middletown, CT: Wesleyan University Press, 2011), 129.

Marc HALPERN
Designer
4, rue François Girardon
91 - CHILLY-MAZARIN

368.80.56 + 920.15.33

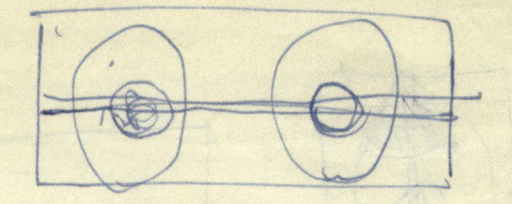

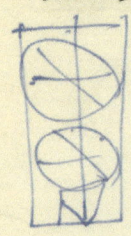

Spécialisé dans les recherches de structures cinétiques, présente, au SALON DES ARTISTES DECORATEURS, dont le thème est cette année

E S P A C E   E T   L U M I E R E

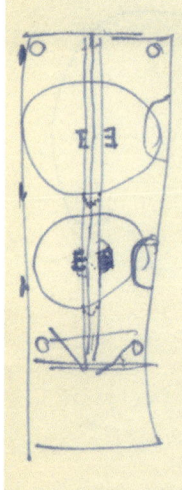

qui se tient au GRAND PALAIS, à partir du 19 Septembre prochain, une structure "CHROELEC-MOUVE" constituée par une sphère de plexiglas de 1,60 m de diamètre, tournant au rythme de 1/4 mn le tour, dans laquelle cinq sphères de 0,40 m de diamètre tournent à des rythmes et dans des sens différents.

Dans ces sphères qui les protègent et les isolent dans l'espace de pesanteur, se meuvent des éléments électroniques chromosomes en aluminium.

Le but est de leur donner un rythme dans l'espace par un jeu de lumière et de propos sonores qui leur donnent un état d'anti-pesanteur.

Ce mouvement, lent et décomposé de chaque élément, est rythmé par des propos sonores d'Eliane RADIGUE.

Le jeu de lumière s'appuyant sur le mouvement, ce sont les ombres et les réflexions venant de rayons projetés sur un complexe de surfaces mouvantes qui créent une sorte de firmament fortuit sur les murs, les pièces et les spectateurs se trouvant dans l'enceinte du cylindre de circulation.

Pris dans ce mouvement de lumière et de propos sonores, les spectateurs sont baignés d'une sérénité exceptionnelle.

Press release for "Espace et Lumière" with Marc Halpern, 1969. Courtesy Fonds Éliane Radigue.

Marc H A L P E R N
Designer

4, rue François Girardon
91 – CHILLY-MAZARIN

368.80.56 + 920.15.33

Specializing in research on kinetic structures, in the SALON DES ARTISTES DÉCORATEURS, on this year's theme

S P A C E   AND   L I G H T

which will take place at the GRAND PALAIS starting September 19, presents a structure called "CHROELEC-MOUVE" comprised of a plexiglass sphere 1.6 meters in diameter, turning at a rhythm of 1/4 minute per turn, in which five spheres of 0.4 meters in diameter rotate at different speeds and in different directions.

Electrical elements (chromosomes) made of aluminum move, isolated and protected within the spheres, in a space of gravity.

The goal is to give them a rhythm in space through the play of light and through *propos sonores*, which imbue them with a state of weightlessness.

The slow and decoupled movement of each element is accompanied by the *propos sonores* of Éliane Radigue.

The play of light relies on the movement, the shadows and the reflections created by the rays of light projected on a number of moving surfaces, creating a type of accidental firmament on the walls, the parts, and the audience located at the heart of the circulating sphere.

Enveloped within the light's movement and the *propos sonores*, the audience is bathed in an exceptional serenity.

DREAMING MACHINES
Helene Cingria

After a few hours at the Grand Palais in Paris, where the 46th Salon des Artistes Décorateurs held its annual conference during the first fortnight of October, one has to ask oneself how it's still possible to put up with the furniture of past generations, when one finds oneself standing before these new creations—prototypes with multiple purposes, the use of light to reveal unimagined decorative possibilities, and astonishing synchronizations of sound, movement, and forms, as well as curiosities of kinetic art that introduce a way of living which one must promptly adapt oneself to, in order to appreciate its advantages even more quickly. This is the opinion of those who, in collaboration with the French Lighting Association, brought the products of their research to this show.

Research of which the best example is without a doubt the work *Chroelec-Mouv* [sic] of Marc Halphern [sic]: the kinetic structures made from a plexiglass sphere 1.6 meters in diameter, turning at a rhythm of a quarter [minute per] turn, in which five other spheres turn at different rhythms and in different directions. Inside the spheres, different electronic elements in aluminum move, rotating in a state of weightlessness: the slow and decoupled movement of each element is punctuated by the *propos sonores* of Éliane Radigue. The play of lights creates a type of accidental firmament on the walls, the parts, and the audience located at the heart of the circulating sphere. In short, it's a dreaming machine, in which all the means of modern technique are used to put human beings into a relaxed state, relieving them of all fatigue and suffering.

Once in the ambiance of this wonderful invention, I could only admire the spirit of research that permeated this space, where light reigned supreme. A capricious light that now exploded in fireworks and scattered in multicolored sparks, now hurled over you, aggressive, in successive attacks, now playing a mysterious game of hide-and-seek, surging across the walls of a brick claustra, disappearing behind a stainless steel panel, refracting on glass inner walls, scintillating in The Ting Tien's fountain, to envelop, in the same iridescent light, the water falling in pearly cascades, and the shining curve of the metal volute encircling the spray. It could surge suddenly from a steel pipe like an enormous glow-worm, pouring out in puddles of brightness on the vegetation of a flowerbed, or, within the fifty-something opalescent eggs, project all the colors of a sun-catching prism over a white screen mounted on a black wall (*Ben Swildens*).

I came to a stop before a group of reclining chairs by Laporte, whose white polyester frames, garnished with orange and green foam cushions, formed the movements of petals around a central couch, the heart of a gigantic flower. The steel piping, terminating in spot lamps, lit up a group of curious magnifying mirrors by Mirolège, enlarging or diminishing the furnishings at the slightest motion, accentuating the unreality of the armchairs.

Journal de Genève, November 1969

"OHMNT"

« .. Qui ne soit jamais ni tout à fait la même ni tout à fait une autre ... »

(Paul Valéry)

Les « musiques combinatoires » se développent selon un processus continu et variable. Enregistrées sur bandes sans fin de durées différentes (de 10 à 30 minutes), les structures sonores sont organisées de façon à subir une désynchronisation progressive.
Les « propos sonores » se répondent, se conjuguent, se rencontrent, puis se perdent, pour ne se retrouver dans leur forme initiale qu'une fois le cycle accompli (120 à 150 heures)

ELIANE RADIGUE

ONE MORE NIGHT

MOURAUD
DESIGN

ELIANE RAD GUE
PROPOS SONORES

VERNISSAGE MARDI 3 FÉVRIER A 18 HEURES

GALERIE R VE DRO TE
3 RUE DE DURAS   PARIS-VIII

Top — Éliane Radigue, notes for *OMNHT*, ca. 1969–70. Courtesy Fonds Éliane Radigue.

(Editor's note: Early appearances of the title of this work use the variant spelling *OHMNT*, rather than the standard *OMNHT*, which may indicate that Radigue had not yet made a definitive decision regarding the title.)

Bottom — Postcard for "One More Night" with Éliane Radigue at Galerie Rive Droite, Paris, February 3, 1970. Courtesy Fonds Éliane Radigue.

COMBINATORY MUSICS
Éliane Radigue

> "... Who is, each time, neither quite the same, nor quite another..."
>
> Paul Valéry [sic]

Combinatory musics develop according to a continuous and variable process.

Recorded on tapes without end, of different lengths (of ten to thirty minutes), the sound structures are organized to undergo a progressive desynchronization.

The *"propos sonores"* respond to one another, combine, meet, and then lose each other, only to find themselves in their initial form once the cycle is complete (120 to 150 hours).

Éliane Radigue

LES MUSIQUES SANS FIN

Concept des années 70

Réalisées sur bandes sans fin de durées différentes, minimum 3 bandes qui évoluent en continuité par désynchronisation progressive.

Ce procédé a donné naissance à plusieurs projets - concepts dont seulement trois ont été présentés.

"... Et qui n'est chaque fois ni tout à fait le même ni tout à fait une autre."
        Paul Verlaine

Éliane Radigue, notes for "Les Musiques Sans Fin," 1970. Courtesy Fonds Éliane Radigue.

LES MUSIQUES SANS FIN
Éliane Radigue

Concept from the '70s

Realized on tape loops of different durations, minimum 3 tapes that continuously evolve by progressive desynchronization.

This process gave birth to several projects–concepts of which only three were presented.

"... Who is, each time, neither quite the same, nor quite another ..."

Paul Verlaine

Cover for Éliane Radigue, $\Sigma = a = b = a + b$, ca. 1969. Courtesy Lawrence Kumpf.

$$\Sigma = a = b = a + b$$

Concept de la fin des années 60 cette réalisation appartient à une série de travaux, nommés à 'époque "propositions sonores" Le produit final de ces oeuvres, est constitué de juxtaposition aléatoire de trames sonores, selon le déroulement de bandes sans fin de différentes durées. Les sons eux-mêmes étaient créés avec deux magnétophones, mis en circuit de ré-injection (feed-back) controlés par d'infimes modifications des dosages de lecture et/ou enregistrement.

La première des oeuvres de ce type, "USRAL" (Ultra-Sons RALentis) fut présentée au Salon des Artistes Décorateurs en 1969 accompagnant une sculpture mobile de Marc Halpern. Réalisée sur cassette Philips CE-10 3 bandes sans fin, de durées respectives 9'28" - 9'33" - 9'35" - en lecture continue, ont évoluées pendant un mois en se désynchronisant progressivement

Selon un procédé identique, "OHMNT" fut présenté à la galerie Rive Droite en Janvier 1970 dans un environnement de Tania Mouraud, utilisant un mode de reproduction sonore par diffusion murale ·"Rollenstar" inclus derrière les panneaux qui doublaient les murs de la galerie. 3 cassettes sans fin, "Fidélipac" de durée respective 19'20" - 27'55"- 31 - Système réalisé par Jean Heuzé.

Parm les projets non réalisés à ce jour " les paroles gelées" sculptures flottantes contenant chacune leur propre sytème sonore évoluant sur un bassin.
"la tour sonore" "les bulles d'écoutes" De cette même époque, mais plus tardivement realisés "E-5th" en 1975 à "The Kitchen"- New-York. Puis le "Labyrinthe Sonore" en Novembre 1998 à Mills College, Californie.

Seule survivante de ces créations éphèmères, cette oeuvre sur disque vinyl deux disques identiques, sous une même pochette, les deux faces pouvant être lues à différentes vitesses. 16 - 33 - 45- 78 tours, puis mixées au gré de 'auditeur- manipulateur Présenté pour la première fois au Festival de Como, le 3 Octobre 1970 sur six tourne disques, dans les trois vitesses standard, reliés à une console de mixage, le tout organisé et présenté par les soins de Giuseppe Englert, premier DJ de l'histoire

Éliane Radigue, notes for $\Sigma = a = b = a + b$, ca. 1969. Courtesy Fonds Éliane Radigue.

$\Sigma = A = B = A + B$
Éliane Radigue

A concept from the end of the sixties, this production belongs to a series of works, at the time named *propositions sonores*. The final product of these works consisted of the aleatoric juxtaposition of audio tracks according to the unwinding of endless tapes of different lengths. The sounds themselves were created with two tape players, placed into a reinjection (feedback) circuit, controlled by minuscule modifications of playback and/or recording settings.

The first work of this kind, *USRAL* (*Ultra-Sons RALentis*),[1] was presented at the Salon des Artistes Décorateurs in 1969, accompanying a mobile sculpture by Marc Halpern. Presented on Philips CE-10 cassettes, three endless tapes—of the following lengths: 9'28", 9'33", 9'35"—in continuous playback, evolved during a month, progressively desynchronizing.

Using an identical process, *OHMNT* was presented at Galerie Rive Droite in January 1970, in an installation by Tania Mouraud, using a method of sound reproduction by mural diffusion: Rolen Stars enclosed behind the panels which doubled the gallery walls and three endless Fidélipac cassettes of the following lengths: 19'20", 27'55", 31'00". The system was realized by Jean Heuzé.

Among the unrealized projects of the time: "the frozen words," floating sculptures each containing their own sound system evolving over a pool, "the sound tower," "the listening bubbles". . . Of this same period but produced later: *E-5th* in 1975 at The Kitchen in New York. And then the *Labyrinthe Sonore* in November 1998 at Mills College in California.

The only survivor of these ephemeral creations was this work on vinyl record, two identical discs, in the same jacket, the two sides playable at different speeds: 16, 33, 45, and 78 rpm, and then mixed at the discretion of the listener-manipulator. Presented for the first time at the Festival de Como, October 3, 1970, on six turntables, at the three standard speeds, connected to a mixing console, the whole thing was organized with care by Giuseppe Englert, the first DJ in history.

---

1   Slowed-down Ultra-Sounds

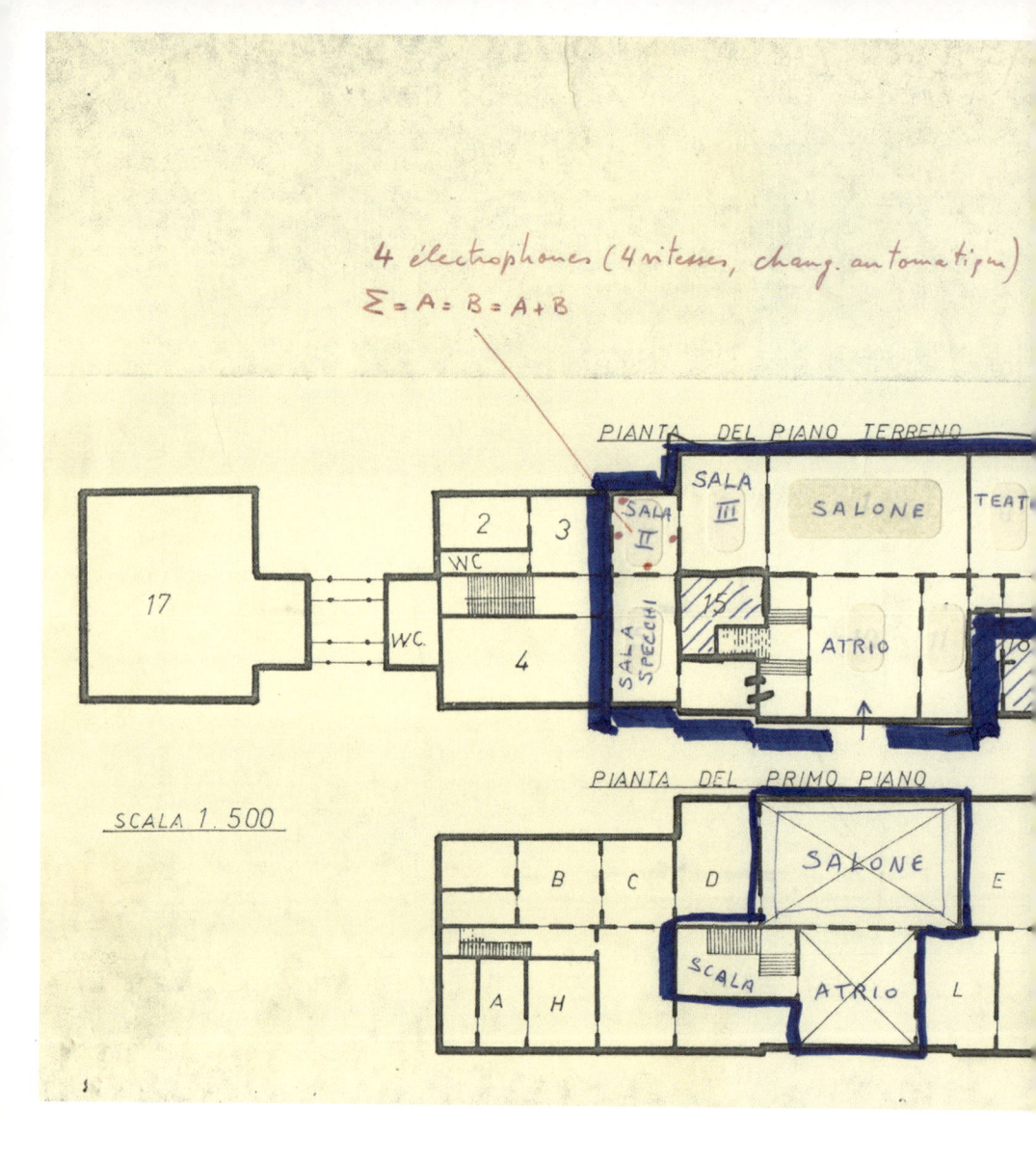

Gallery map for $\Sigma = a = b = a + b$ installation, ca. 1969. Courtesy Fonds Éliane Radigue.

WC 14 16

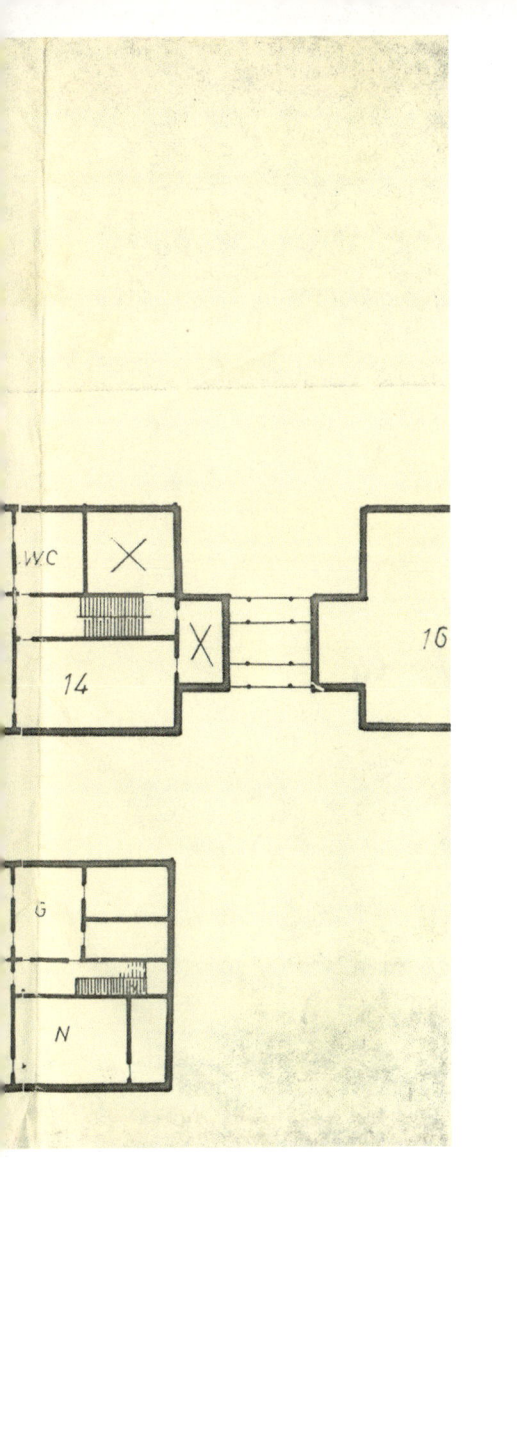

G
N

Above and right   Éliane Radigue, sketches for *Vice–Versa, etc…*, ca. 1969.
Courtesy Fonds Éliane Radigue.

Bande stéréo 2 pistes
La lecture peut se faire
    piste I – séparément
    piste II – séparément
    pistes I et II – simultanément
Toute combinaison ~~possible~~ ~~dans un sens ou dans~~ l'autre
des deux ~~pistes~~ sur plusieurs
magnétophones – ad libitum

Bande stéréo . 2 pistes .
La lecture peut se faire
    Piste I . séparément .
    Piste II . séparément .
    Pistes I et II . simultanément
Toute combinaison de ces
deux voix dans un sens ou
dans l'autre sur plusieurs
magnétophones – ad libitum

Éliane Radigue

9, Décembre 1969

Cher Ami,

Suite à notre entretien hier soir :
En ce qui concerne la section " Technologie ", je pourrais réaliser une animation musicale d'une dizaine de minutes pour la somme forfaitaire de 5.000 FF.

Pour la section "Arman", il serait souhaitable de définir un progamme musical lié , tel une introduction - parcours à celui de "Technologie", dont il serait le "Prélude ". Je serais bien entendu, disposée à effectuer moi-même , sur place, le réglage des masses, volumes et dosages de cet itinéraire sonore.

Enfin, il semblerait interessant de réaliser dans la section "Scientifique" dont nous avons parlé, une atmosphère musicale faite d'une sonorisation "bruissante" ou "murmurante", par micros de contacts reliés à des circuits d'amplification et des filtres, dont les éléments combinatiores constitueraient la "trame musicale" en une composition instantanée qu'il me serait possible d'effectuer sur place.

Dans tous les cas, je reste à votre disposition, et vous prie de croire cher Ami, à mes sentiments les meilleurs.

Letter from Éliane Radigue to unknown addressee, December 9, 1969. Courtesy Fonds Éliane Radigue.

Éliane Radigue

December 9, 1969

Dear Friend,

Following our conversation yesterday evening:

Concerning the "Technology" section, I could create for it a ten-minute piece of music for a flat rate of 5,000 FF.

For the "Arman" section, it would be desirable to design a related musical program as an introduction—leading up to the one on "Technology" for which this would be a "Prélude." I would of course be willing to carry out the adjustments of the masses, volumes and dosages of this sonic program myself on site.

Finally, in the "Scientific" section we talked about, it would be interesting to create a musical atmosphere with a "noisy" or "murmuring" sound system, using contact mics connected to amplifying circuits and filters, whose combinatorial elements would constitute the "soundtrack" in an instantaneous composition that I would create on site.

In any case, I remain at your disposal, and please accept, dear Friend, my best regards.

```
Éliane Radigue
24, rue de Bourgogne                    14 Janvier 1970
   Paris 7
```

Monsieur,

    Suite à notre entretien téléphonique, je vous confirme mon accord pour la réalisation d'une animation musicale d'une dizaine de minute, sur bande enregistrée, pour la section "Technologie", réalisée par Monsieur Tallon.

    Je vous serais obligée, de m'adresser en même temps que la confirmation de votre propre accord, 50% de la somme forfaitaire dont nous sommes convenus de 5.000 FF. soit 2.500 FF. le solde me sera versé à réception de la bande.

    Dans l'attente de vous lire, je vous prie d'agréer Monsieur, mes salutations distinguées.

                                           Éliane Radigue

Letter from Éliane Radigue to unknown addressee, January 14, 1970. Courtesy Fonds Éliane Radigue.

Éliane Radigue
24 rue de Bourgogne
Paris 7

January 14, 1970

Sir,

Following our phone conversation, I'm confirming with you my ability to create a ten-minute piece of music, on recorded tape, for the section titled "Technology," produced by Monsieur Tallon.

I would be much obliged if you would also give confirmation of your own agreement, as well as 50% of the flat-rate sum which we agreed would be 5,000 FF, so 2,500 FF, the rest being paid to me upon receipt of the tape.

I look forward to hearing from you, and please accept my best wishes.

Éliane Radigue

Labyrinthe Sonore

L'idée générale est de jalonner un parcours.
Deux éléments principaux :
   I Principe de deconnection, dépaysement sonore.
   2 le "Fil d'Ariane"

I les éléments de "deconnection" sont réalisés avec des évènements sonores réalistes, pour la plupart captés par micro dans l'environnement immédiat et reproduits dans un contexte différent du lieu originel Ex ; Bruit d'ascenseur ou d'escalier mécanique dans un espace uniforme voué à la marche, bruit de pas ou de foule dans un lieu immobile et solitaire etc . Bruits enregistrés : Vagues de l'ocean dans les pierres de la ville, de torrent déferlant sur une place isolée etc. .

2 le Fil d'Ariane
Une progression de plusieurs trames sonores s'enchevêtrant en certains points du parcours. Réalisées sur bandes sans fin de différentes durées 7 à 9 éléments sont nécessaires Ex; Au départ du parcours, diffusion de la source sonore 'A' un peu plus loin, diffusion de la source 'B' , un "Noeud" sonore se produit par la perception simultanée de 2 ou plusieurs sources. La rencontre dans l'oreille de l'auditeur de ces différentes sources sonores , au rythme de son parcours, constitue son propre "Fil d'Ariane", sa propre musique dont la durée est celle de son parcours, et la forme celle des rencontres occasionelles de ce discours musical, aléatoire par essence, selon le principe de base des musiques sans fin, principe étendu pour la circonstance à l'espace et aux rencontres des différents moments, hasard du cheminement

Proposé en 1970 pour le pavillon Français à la Foire Internationale d'Osaka, aucune suite n'y étant donné, le "Labyrinthe sonore" fut ensuite proposé à la ville de Strasbourg, pour les ruelles pietonnes de la vieille ville. Sans suite également. Réduit à son "Fil d'Ariane" constitué de sept trames musicales de différentes durées, une réalisation "fermée" dans une vaste salle du musée d'Art Moderne de cette ville fut ultérieurement envisagée.
Le tout se solda par une simple "lecture" successive des "7 petites pièces" réalisées pour ce projet.

Éliane Radigue

Éliane Radigue, notes for *Labyrinthe Sonore*, 1970. Courtesy Fonds Éliane Radigue.

Handwritten insertion above the text: a disposition and integration of the sonic environment will be realized [*illegible*] after transformation (filtering, coloration, etc.) to these events

To Alain Bizos [*illegible*]

Labyrinthe Sonore

The general idea is to mark out a route.
Two principal elements:

    1) The principle of disconnection, sonic disorientation
    2) "Ariadne's Thread"

1) The elements of "disconnection" are created with realistic sonic events, for the most part captured by microphones in the immediate environment and reproduced in a context different from the original location. E.g.: sound of an elevator or escalator in a space totally dedicated to walking, noise of footsteps or of a crowd in a still and solitary place etc... Recorded sounds: waves of the ocean in the rocks of a city, torrents breaking in an isolated place etc...

2) Ariadne's Thread[1]
A progression of several sonic tracks entangling at certain points along the route. Realized on tape loops of different durations. 7 to 9 elements are necessary. E.g.: at the start of the route, diffusion of sound source "A," and a bit further away, diffusion of source "B," a sonic "knot" arises from the simultaneous perception of 2 or more sources. The meeting of these different sound sources in the ear of the listener, at the rhythm of their route, constitutes its own "Ariadne's Thread," its own music whose duration is that of the journey, and whose form is that of the occasional encounters in the musical discourse, aleatoric in essence, according to the basis of *musiques sans fin*, a principle extended to the space for the occasion and to the meeting of different ~~knots~~[2] according to the path's chance

---

1 Hand-drawn bracket around this section of the text, with the annotation "*mise en œuvre*" (implementation).

2 Crossed out by hand with "*points du rencontres*" (points of encounter) inserted in its place.

Proposed in 1970 for the French pavilion at the International Fair in Osaka, but was never realized there, the "Labyrinthe Sonore" was then proposed to the city of Strasbourg, for the small pedestrian streets of the old city. No further action was taken. Reduced to "Ariadne's Thread," comprising seven musical tracks of different durations, a "closed" realization in a vast hall of [Strasbourg's] Museum of Modern Art was subsequently envisioned.

The result was[3] a simple successive "playback" of the "7 little pieces" created for this project.[4]

---

3 Illegible handwritten insertion here.

4 Hand-drawn bracket around this section of the text with three annotations: "7 movements 1998," "ad libitum–," and a third, illegible annotation.

Caroline Corre et
Antoni Miralda, Joan Rabascall, Eliane Radigue, Dorothée Selz, Jaume Xifra,
vous invitent à la

FÊTE EN BLANC

LE SAMEDI 23 MAI 1970

prise de la cape à 16 heures
- l offrande des fleurs
- accouplement et ibération des colombes
- a procession des draps
- bération des cygnes sur e ac
- apparition des mariées
- e repas blanc
- passage dans le cie
- temps blanc
- fumées
- m se à blanc de a nuit

capes de Paco Rabanne
dôme blanc de HW Mu ler

parking sur la place du village
entrée par la grille du château
fleurs blanches de rigueur

participation aux frais repas compris 20 F

IMPRA - PARIS

Flyer for "Fête en Blanc," May 23, 1970. Courtesy Fonds Éliane Radigue.

TOUR SONORE

4 Trompettes J B LANZ G
d ffusant haute fréquence
ULTRA SONS + 18 000 Hz

P afond † ssus b anc sous
trompettes

P ancher sur Wooffers

4 Wooffers d ffusant basse
fréquence NTRA SONS - 50 Hz

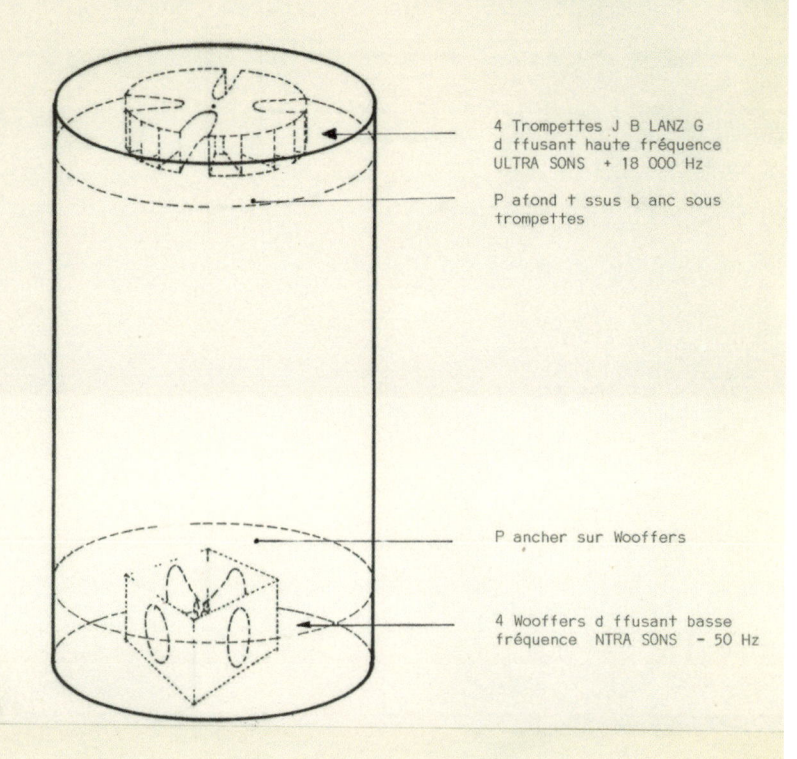

Tour Sonore.

L'auditeur entre dans la tour-cylindre-espace de diffusion.
L'énergie dégagée par les hout parleurs est perçue par le corps autant que par
l'oreille D'où le concept de "Tour" associé à l'idée d une densité palpable
A la base et au sommet de la tour sont émises des fréquences -limites du seuil de
perception auditive.

Seul le "sommet" de cette tour a été réalisé en Février 1975 à "The Kitchen"- New-York
Le titre "E 5th" avait été donné à cette expérience, en référence au rapport de quinte
juste sur lequel étaient accordés les oscillateurs, controlés par oscilloscopes

E ane RAD GUE - 970 -

Éliane Radigue, notes for "Tour Sonore," 1970. Courtesy Fonds Éliane Radigue.

TOUR SONORE [SONIC TOWER]

⟵──────── 4 J B LANZIG [sic] 'trumpet' speakers diffusing ULTRASONIC high frequencies + 18,000 Hz

●──────── White fabric ceiling under trumpets

●──────── Floor above Wooffers [sic]

⟵──────── 4 Wooffers [sic] diffusing INTRASONIC[1] [sic] bass frequencies — 50 Hz

Sonic Tower.

The listener enters into the tower-cylinder-space of diffusion.
The energy released by the speakers is perceived by the body as well as by the ear.
Hence the concept "Tower" associated with the idea of a palpable density
At the base and summit of the tower frequencies are emitted— limits of the threshold of auditory perception.

Only the "summit" of the tower was produced in February 1975 at "The Kitchen" — New York.
The title "E 5th" was given to this experience, in reference to the relationship of the perfect fifth that the oscillators were tuned to, controlled by oscilloscopes.

Éliane RADIGUE – 1970

---

1 Translator's note: Here, Radigue means infrasonic, which refers to frequencies below the human threshold for hearing.

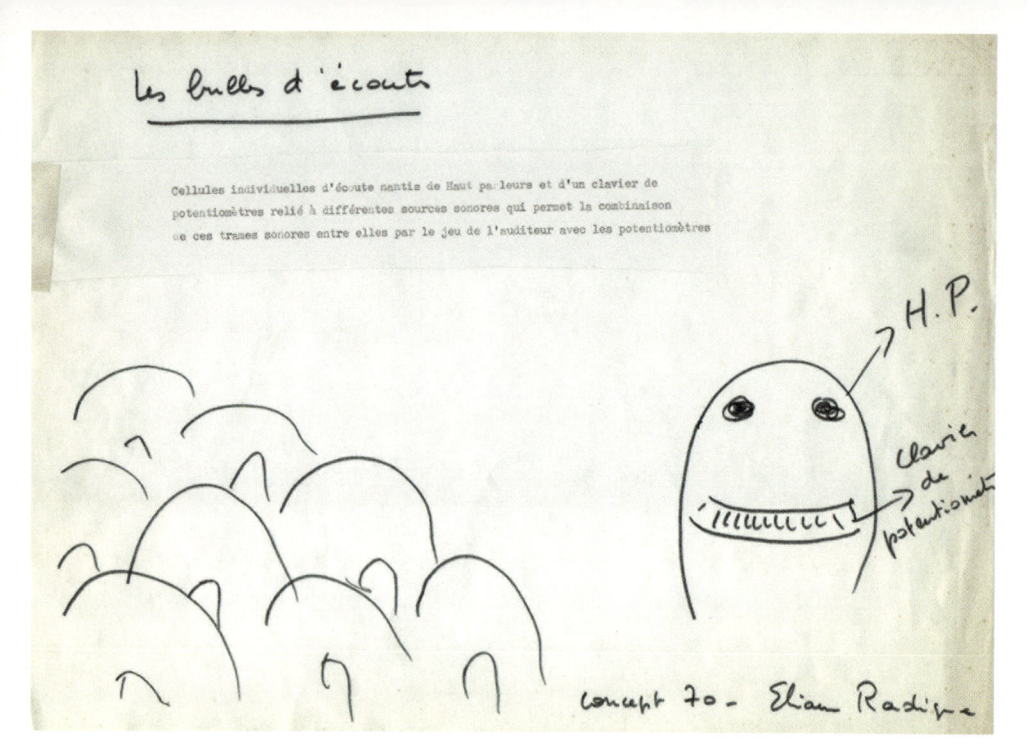

Listening Bubbles

Individual listening cells equipped with loudspeakers and a keyboard of potentiometers connected to different sound sources, allowing for the combination of these different audio tracks through the listener's playing of the potentiometers.

H.P. [Haut-parleur, loudspeaker]
Keyboard of potentiometers

Concept 70 — Éliane Radigue

Éliane Radigue, notes for "Les bulles d'écoute," 1970. Courtesy Fonds Éliane Radigue.

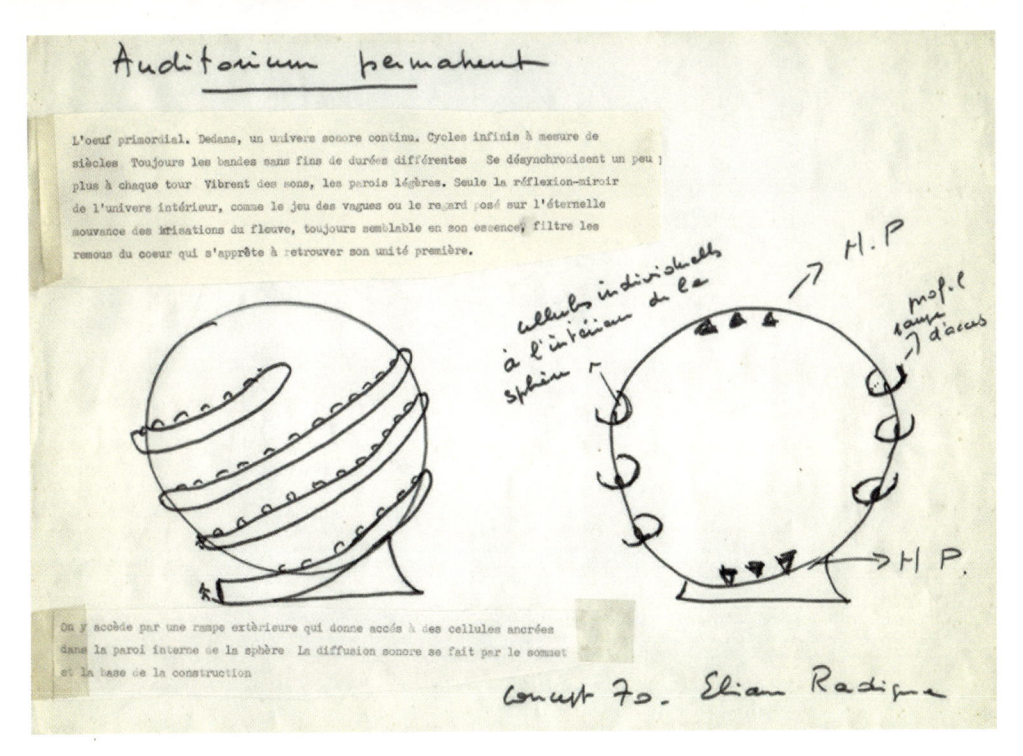

Permanent Auditorium

The primordial egg. Inside, a universe of continuous sound. Infinite cycles on the scale of centuries. Always tape loops of different durations. They desynchronize a bit more with each turn. The light-weight walls vibrate with sounds. Only the mirror reflection of the interior universe, like the play of waves or the gaze fixed on the eternal movement of the iridescence of the river, always similar in its essence, filters the eddies of the heart preparing to find its first unity.

Individual cells on the inside of the sphere
H.P. [loudspeaker]
Profile of the access ramp
H.P. [loudspeaker]

One enters by an exterior ramp which gives access to cells fixed on the interior wall of the sphere. Sound is diffused through the top and the base of the construction.

Concept 70 — Eliane Radigue

Éliane Radigue, notes for "Auditorium permanent," 1970. Courtesy Fonds Éliane Radigue.

"ART CONCEPTS FROM EUROPE"

Cher Ami,

J'organise chez Alfredo Bonino, dans sa galerie de New-York (7 West 57 th. N.Y.C.), une manifestation documentaire intitulée : "Art Concepts from Europe", des conceptions artistiques en provenance d'Europe. 50 artistes européens de l'est comme de l'ouest sont contactés en même temps que vous et je leur pose le même problème.

La technologie actuelle des moyens de communication permet une grande flexibilité dans la diffusion des idées. Je vous propose d'en faire la démonstration et de faire parvenir à New-York l'une de vos idées, par n'importe quel moyen et sous n'importe quelle forme. Le document correspondant pourra être visuel (plan, texte manuscrit ou imprimé, télégramme, insertion ou article de revue, photographies et photocopies), audio-visuel (film, TV, magnétoscope), codé (formule technique ou mathématique), sonore (enregistrement sur bande magnétique, communication téléphonique, disque) etc...

L'essentiel est que le message à son arrivée soit parfaitement clair, tangible et immédiatement réalisable. La galerie Bonino mettra ainsi à la disposition du public un stock d'idées pleinement disponibles.

L'ensemble des projets et documents circulera par la suite dans les diverses galeries de la chaîne Bonino en Amérique du Sud, à Rio de Janeiro et à Buenos Ayres : aucune oeuvre proprement dite ou présentant un état de réalisation avancée ne sera admise.

Tous les documents doivent parvenir à la galerie Bonino avant le Ier mars 1970. Le délai est impératif : il est conditionné par les nécessités de l'aménagement technique de la galerie en fonction du matériel rassemblé. La présentation publique débutera le 9 mars 1970.

J'espère que vous accepterez cette invitation et je vous prie de croire, cher Ami, à mes sentiments les plus cordiaux.

Pierre RESTANY

P.S. - Votre envoi devra être accompagné d'une notice biographique complète en vue de l'établissement du catalogue-témoin de la manifestation.

Letter from Pierre Restany to Éliane Radigue, ca. 1970. Courtesy Fonds Éliane Radigue.

"ART CONCEPTS FROM EUROPE"

Dear Friend,

I'm organizing at Alfred Bonino's gallery in New York (7 West 57th St., NYC) a documentary exhibition titled "Art Concepts from Europe," with artistic conceptions coming from Europe. 50 artists from Eastern and Western Europe are being contacted alongside you with the same proposal.

Current communications technology allows a great flexibility in the dissemination of ideas. I propose that you make a contribution demonstrating this and send one of your ideas to New York, by any means and in any form. The corresponding document can be visual (plan, a handwritten or printed text, telegram, introduction or review, photographs, and photocopies), audio-visual (film, TV, video recorder), in code (technical or mathematical formula), sonic (recording on magnetic tape, telephone communication, disc) etc. . .

What is essential is that the message be perfectly clear, tangible, and immediately realizable upon its arrival. <u>Gallery Bonino will thus provide the public with a fully available stock of ideas.</u>

The entirety of the projects and documents will then continue to circulate in different Bonino galleries in South America, to Rio de Janeiro and Buenos Aires: nothing that is, strictly speaking, a finished work or in an advanced state of completion will be admitted.

All the documents must arrive at the Gallery Bonino before March 1, 1970. The deadline is imperative: it is based on the technical requirements for the installation of the materials collected. The public presentation will open March 9, 1970.

I hope that you will accept this invitation, and please accept, dear Friend, my warmest regards.

Pierre RESTANY

P.S. – Your submission should be accompanied by a complete biography to be included in the exhibition catalogue.

423 Broadway
New York, N.Y. 10013
September 28, 1970

Dear Eliane,

How do. Are you still in Paris? I think perhaps I will finish typing this and you will call me saying you are in New York. I hope you are still planning to come here.

How was your summer? I managed to go to Ghana where I took daily private lessons from an Ewe (tribe) master drummer until I got sick with malaria and had to return here rather quickly. I'm all recovered now and I think I managed to learn quite a bit musically in the short period (5 weeks) I was there.

It turns out that Philip Glass has arranged several concerts for himself and his ensemble (including me) for late February through early March in different parts of Europe. Since I and all the musicians who play with me will be over there, I was hoping to set up concerts for my own group some time after the 10th of March when Philip is through with his tour. I suppose I could stay there through ####### April, if there was enough work.

As to money, the minimum fee would be $600. for a small concert of live and electronic music. For $900. we could do a really full evening —or 2— of music including both those new pieces for 4 electric organs which you seemed to enjoy and which many of the people who heard them at the Guggenheim Museum (including myself) thought were the best pieces I've ever done. I suppose we could always negotiate something about prices providing someone is seriously interested.

I have also written or am about to write other people in Paris that you may be in contact with. Namely Dominique Larre who I guess you know, and Jacqueline and Daniel ##### Caux who some musician friends have told me are extremely helpful in setting up concerts. I am also writing to Jean Larcade of the Galerie Rive Droite and Tania Mouraud who knows Jon Gibson, one of my closest friends and best musicians who was recently touring with LaMonte Young. I saw a brochure of Tania's and you were included in it, so I imagine you must be friendly. Perhaps with all these people it will be possible to set up a few concerts during the March 10th through April period. Perhaps there could be something arranged for elsewhere in France besides Paris?

I hope all is well with you and look forward to hearing from you soon.

All the best—

Steve

Steve Reich

Letter from Steve Reich to Éliane Radigue, September 28, 1970. Courtesy Fonds Éliane Radigue.

Dear Éliane   13 Dec '71

    Hello from New York. I'm sorry not to write to you but life is complicated for me now and I have little time to do everything I would like to. I am afraid I have not been studying my french lately but hope to start up again soon. I wish I could be more consistent.

    Musically, I have been very busy. I did a series of outdoor performances in different NY park spaces with a dancer, which were quite satisfying to me and also well received. I was thinking it would be nice to do some outdoor performances in France (and Europe) this summer, traveling from village to village performing in city squares or at local wine festivals (?). Perhaps we could be financed by some French government agency like the Maison de Culture. Do you think there is any possibility of something like this happening?

    Phil Glass and I wonder when you will come to NY again. I will be in Europe with Steve Reich in Jan–Feb 72 and in Paris from about Jan 12 to 18. On Jan 18 we will perform at the Teatre de la Musique. If you are in Paris at this time I will certainly see you.

    I hope you and your children are all well & I look forward to seeing you soon.

                    Your friend
                      Jon

Jon Gibson
339 E. 6th St #10
New York, NY 10003
USA   (22 673-135)

Letter from Jon Gibson to Éliane Radigue, December 13, 1971. Courtesy Fonds Éliane Radigue.

Éliane Radigue and Giuseppe Englert at Palais de Tokyo, Paris, ca. 1971. Courtesy Éliane Radigue.

Éliane Radigue at the New York Cultural Center, New York, 1971. Photo: Yves Arman. Courtesy Éliane Radigue.

Éliane Radigue at the New York Cultural Center, New York, 1971. Photo: Yves Arman. Courtesy Éliane Radigue.

RADIGUE THRESHOLD
Paul Jenkins

Sounds which enter
you like pulsating beads.......
They spin in your head cavities
Fluttering moths with panic, just
before dying.
The absurdity of imagined mortality
make evident—
and the
Ultimate thereness
exposed and
made manifest.
Pierced by a million multitudes
Memory not yet remembered.
Carving out dormant crevices
in the brain
Where only certain sounds   may enter.
Walls of shadows in the brain come tumbling down
Tapping on the brain pan of your tomorrow
You are awake
Not awakened.
Not sky but the inner sight on your
own universe.
The bowl of your celestial brain pan
Held in its
Original form   released from the finite
It listens—you
After it decides
You give to it the chance and it will decide
Something haunting for you.
You are the cavity of it to enter
And having done so—you
Cannot be the same.
You become the instrument on which it plays
You are the point fixe
Between two sources which differ and relate
You are awake
Not awakened.

NEW YORK UNIVERSITY
Schoo of the Arts
Intermedia Program
144 BLEECKER STREET NEW YORK N.Y 10012

Dear Éliane —

Thank you for being a part of the COMPOSERS' WORKSHOP this past season. I want you to know that all the members of our group were honored by your presence and wish to extend an open invitation for your return whenever our studio facilities can be of use in your creative work. We look forward to seeing you this fall.

Sincerely Yours,

MICHAEL CZAJKOWSKI
DIRECTOR - COMPOSERS' WORKSHOP
NYU - SCHOOL OF THE ARTS
40 E 7
NYC NY 10003

Letter from Michael Czajkowski to Éliane Radigue, ca. 1971. Courtesy Fonds Éliane Radigue.

NEW YORK UNIVERSITY
School of the Arts
Intermedia Program
144 BLEECKER STREET NEW YORK, N Y 10012

6/1/71

To Whom it May Concern —

Eliane Radigue spent November to June working as a participating artist of the Composers' Workshop at New York University – School of the Arts. As Director I was delighted to make our facilities available to Eliane to aid her in her work as a composer preparing for concert performances. Her presence was appreciated by all the members of the workshop and we fervently hope she will be able to make use of our studio and participate in our program again in the near future!

Sincerely
Michael Czajkowski

Letter from Michael Czajkowski to New York University, School of the Arts, Intermedia Program, 1971. Courtesy Fonds Éliane Radigue.

Éliane Radigue, Paris, 1971. Photo: Yves Arman. Courtesy Éliane Radigue.

Éliane Radigue, Paris, 1971. Photo: Yves Arman. Courtesy Éliane Radigue.

Éliane Radigue at the New York Cultural Center, New York, 1971. Photo: Yves Arman. Courtesy Éliane Radigue.

Catalogue des oeuvres d'Eliane Radigue

Titre de l'oeuvre : CHRYP-TUS

Mise en oeuvre : Deux bandes qui sont jouées simultanément synchrones ou a-synchrones (jusqu'à 1 minute de désynchronisation pour chaque bande), ce qui n'affecte pas la stucture de l'oeuvre, mais créé d'infinies variations, principalement dans le jeu des harmoniques. Trois versions avaient été présentées lors de la création de cette oeuvre, incluant des variations d'amplitudes et/ou désynchronisation.

Réalisé sur Buchla synthesizer, New-York University
Date de l'achèvement : 1971

Durée : Environ 23 min.

Création et lieu de diffusion : 6 avril 1971 au New-York Cultural Center

Where 3 different version of this piece has been given - the same night

Two tapes are played simultaneously, synchronously or asynchronously (up to 1 minute of desynchronization for each tape), which doesn't affect the structure of the work, but creates infinite variations, principally in the play of harmonics. Three versions were presented during the creation of this work, including variations in volume and/or desynchronization.

Éliane Radigue, notes for *Catalogue des œuvres d'Eliane Radigue*, ca. 1971.
Courtesy Fonds Éliane Radigue.

MUSIC TO EXHIBIT BY ÉLIANE RADIGUE
Jack Gousseland

White walls, bare, softly lit, a gray close-cropped fitted carpet, no furniture: a place that doesn't fix the gaze, but marks absence. A place that effaces itself to show what occupies it: Galerie Yvon Lambert—the location of this exhibition. But what was "exhibited" escaped the eye: deep opaque hums, glissandi—as if, piling over one another, the purring of machines—took over the space from the back wall: Yvon Lambert received the "sound exhibition" of Éliane Radigue.

Recorded and synthesized sounds—one doesn't know which—on tapes of different lengths, collated in "loops," played continuously at the same time, at variable speeds on hidden tape recorders: discrepancies and slow overlaps; the sounds sometimes grow deeper, sometimes prolong themselves, comment on themselves, repeat in echo. From one shape toward another, in an instant, the sonorities organize and undo themselves—instantaneous Construction / Destruction—like a kaleidoscope of sound brought to perpetual movement.

That this music would be presented in such spaces isn't an accident: it was conceived for them. Éliane Radigue wants to escape the concert setting: from its ceremony, its theatricality, from its strict time—the work inscribed between two slices of applause—two sagging trenches—marking it as a closed object. Escaping as well from Notation, cast onto a musical utterance only to reify it and render it easily imitated and reproducible. At its most extreme: Éliane Radigue researches "pure music." Her "works," which she herself calls "music to exhibit," attack time; the listener has few footholds for what they perceive: no articulations, frequent incomprehensible shifts in timbre, unexpected registers; identifiable sonic events are too rare, too spaced out, to discern such an ordinary structure by listening, for a form to emerge. Even at the moment when this music is restored to the time of memory: music being an "art of time," it attempts to subvert this pleasant idealism.

Unpredictable, left to the hazards of playback devices, variations in the intensity of electrical current, etc., it doesn't correspond to any notation that would be able to preserve or capitalize on it: the sonic configuration depends on the combination of tapes in the moment. "Chance" is the principal parameter here, which intervenes each time a piece of music is "produced" (even, above all, from a score). Without doubt, after all, it would be possible to write down what one heard—yet it would only be a transmission of a listening session—a snapshot of a continuous creation, in which one would have eliminated the only active element that grounds it as a work: the listener.

Tape recorders can surely run for weeks, for months, their noise will not have "meaning," it will only become music once LIVED. It's only during the moments when whoever is put in a position to perceive the resulting sounds—to register them in their own time—will they become "works." With their past, their culture, the listener is always implicated in what they hear. No matter what time they enter the gallery, they will have heard a complete work, their own, responding only to their need.

In this space where nothing catches the eye, this music of the here-and-now doesn't propose a succession of sonic events but a state of listening; nothing that would articulate a discourse, nor recount a story. It refers to nothing other than itself, to its material, to its "grain": sinusoidal sounds now lumpy, sticky, harsh, now flaky and acidic—but never "pure."

Once through the door, the music provokes the visitor: the moment is ritualized, their attention to listening heightened. Because the sound sources are invisible, their defenses can't establish themselves: the visitor is in part powerless to choose "good" sounds; the quotidian world—goings-on in the street, the typewriter in the office next door—invades the universe of music. Rather, music participates in the quotidian.

Also utilizing analog combinatory processes, Éliane Radigue's two works presented in the second room of the gallery were less interesting: they lacked spatial and visual dimension; to hear them, one had to put on headphones; the equipment operated in plain sight, and, for one of the pieces using vinyl instead of tape loops, the listener had to intervene by means of potentiometers to select such or such a source. Guided by ear, it necessarily recreated sonic "events," a spontaneous structure: music regained its anecdote.

Putting aside all mythology of "expression," the meaning of music—according to tonality at the very least—is generally its structure. Now, during the time I heard them at Yvon Lambert, no structure was perceptible in the two works for magnetic tapes; they almost totally escaped from rhetoric, from an organizing Logos. This is their only sense: they MEAN NOTHING other than themselves: sonic matter lived by the listener. As with literature (and sometimes theater), music today fundamentally reveals itself as a hesitation of (sound) images and meaning.

Le Point, 1997

Éliane Radigue, untitled sketch, 1971. Courtesy Fonds Éliane Radigue.

Éliane Radigue

Exposition Sonore

chez Yvon Lambert du 24 au 31 Mai 1972

Musiques à exposer - nommées aussi "musique combinatoire" - faute d'un autre terme Se "combinent" en des cycles de plusieurs centaines d'heures Réalisées sur bandes sans fin de durées différentes - évoluent en continuité par désynchronisation progressive
Musique qui n'est jamais "ni tout à fait la même, ni tout à fait une autre"

USRAL - 1969

présenté au Salon des Artistes Décorateurs en 1969, pour une sculpture mobile de Marc Halpernn, pendant une durée d'un mois. Réalisée sur cassette Philips CE-10
3 bandes de 9'28" - 9'33" - 9'35" -

$\Sigma = a = b = a + b$ - "Pour Farhi" - 1969

Processus analogue adapté au disque Faisant également intervenir des possibilités de variations par changement des vitesses de lecture A été présenté au Festival de Como, par les soins de Giuseppe Englert

OHMNT - 1970

Présenté à la galerie Rive Droite en Janvier 1970, pendant un mois, dans un environnement de Tania Mouraud. Utilise un mode de reproduction sonore par diffusion murale Système conçu et réalisé par Jean Heuzé
3 bandes de 19'20" - 27'55" - 31' -

Cette exposition a été réalisée avec la collaboration technique de Jean Heuzé

Éliane Radigue
Exposition Sonore
Chez Yvon Lambert from May 24 to 31, 1972

Music to exhibit—also called "combinatory music," for lack of a better term. They "combine" in cycles of more than several hundred hours. Realized on tape loops of different durations, continuously evolving by progressive desynchronization.

Music which is "never quite the same, nor quite another."

USRAL - 1969

presented at the Salon des Artistes Décorateurs in 1969, for a kinetic sculpture by Marc Halpernn [sic], for the duration of one month.
Produced on Philips CE-10 cassettes.
3 tapes of 9'28" - 9'33" - 9'35" -

$\Sigma = a = b = a + b$ - "For Farhi" - 1969

Analog process adapted to disc.
Involving possible variations by changing playback speeds.
Presented at Como Festival, through the curation of Giuseppe Englert.

OHMNT - 1970

Presented at the Gallery Rive Droite in January 1970, for the duration of one month, in an environment by Tania Mouraud. Using a sound reproduction system mounted inside the walls. System designed and realized by Jean Heuzé.
3 tapes of 19'20" - 27'55" - 31' -

This exhibition was produced with the technical assistance of Jean Heuzé.

ELIANE RADIGUE

EXPOSITION SONORE

CHEZ YVON LAMBERT, 15 RUE DE L'ÉCHAUDÉ PARIS 6e DU 24 AU 31 MAI 1972

Postcard for "Exposition Sonore" with Éliane Radigue at Yvon Lambert, Paris, 1972.
Courtesy Fonds Éliane Radigue.

G. Haessig
81 bd Saint Marcel
PARIS 13e

Voilà le résultat de mon travail de coupage - montage sur vos expressions phoniquement emprisonnées dans la boîte noire...

Dans l'espoir que ma compréhension analytico-synthétisante n'aura pas trahi votre pensée..

Comme bien entendu je n'y suis pris au dernier instant (dira-t-on assez le déchirement dramatique de l'acte de coupure-césure, avec son aspect de censure, qui retarde toujours ce travail réducteur) et j'ai fini hier seulement...

Dans l'espoir que vous retrouverez dans ce texte la sympathie que j'ai pour le compositeur, "pauvre travailleur solitaire face à l'incompréhension générale" (exemple de ce qui se trouve précieusement engrangé dans ma "mémoire" mais n'a pas passé la rampe)

Dans l'espoir aussi que vous ne crierez pas à l'interprétation tendancieuse, parce que mon tardif texte part demain chez l'imprimeur et que cela m'obligerait à des acrobaties lors de la correction des épreuves...

Letter from Georges Haessig to Éliane Radigue, ca. 1972. Published in *Musique en jeu* no. 8, 1972. Courtesy Fonds Éliane Radigue.

G. Haessig
81 Bis Saint Marcel
PARIS 13e

Here are the results of my cutting and editing of your expressions, the sounds of which are imprisoned in the black box . . .

In the hopes that my analytical-synthesizing understanding didn't betray your thinking . . .

As always, I didn't get to it until the very last moment (enough has been said on the dramatic heartbreak of cutting and tearing, with its aspect of censorship, which always slows down this reductive work), and I only finished yesterday . . .

In the hopes that you find in this text the sympathy I have for the composer, "poor laborer, alone in the face of general incomprehension" (an example of something that preciously ingrained itself in my "memory," but didn't make the cut)

In the hopes that you won't be too upset by a tendentious interpretation, because my now-late text is going to the printers tomorrow, and this would require acrobatics outside of correcting proofs . . .

In the hope of, and looking forward to, our next telephone conversation . . .
and more . . .

Musical salutations,
Georges Haessig

...IN REALITY:
FROM AN INTERVIEW WITH ÉLIANE RADIGUE
Georges Haessig

"In Reality: From an Interview with Éliane Radigue" was originally published in 1972 under the title *"Dans la réalité cinglante"* (In the harsh reality). It appeared in *Musique en jeu* (Music at play), a French quarterly magazine specializing in intellectual and philosophical interrogations of contemporary music. Georges Haessig was a cofounder of the magazine, which ran from 1970 to '78; and, in accordance with its mission, Haessig and Radigue's conversation takes a particular interest in theory and notation. Translated by Adrian Rew, this interview is now available in English for the first time.

GEORGES HAESSIG

... the particularity of an independent composer's work?

ÉLIANE RADIGUE

First, there's the handicap of weak equipment, the small studio, which makes it necessary to rely on the resources of the imagination, but solutions made on a shoestring sometimes bring about astonishing and very satisfying results. In fact, one can succeed, even with terrible material, to inflect the sonic material in sought-out directions with other, different solutions; for the rest, one always submits technique to what one wants to do. In terms of production, the problem is the same for anyone who wants to do something with sound, whether it's on paper or not; one personally manages their problems, one submits them to their own doubts, their own critiques, their own certainties ... The other problem, in fact, is material, first of possession, of improvement of equipment; it's a problem of investment, and then of upkeep, of the maintenance and fine-tuning of the instrument. The great misery of solitary people is the lack of technicians to take care of the upkeep and repairs.

GH Why choose the electroacoustic path rather than instrumental composition?

ÉR Lightning first struck me for this kind of music long ago. One morning, I was working on my Leibowitz while doing my housecleaning when I heard something extraordinary on the radio; it was Pierre Schaeffer, who did a series of programs presenting *musique concrète*. It was my road to Damascus: *this* was it ... With the twelve tones, there is a dead end; the limits of a marvelous music, the traditional Western music, could be pushed no further, at least by me, and [at that moment] I discovered a fantastic field to explore, in which the mode of autonomous formulation remains to be discovered.

I believe that these new sound materials must also have their internal logic; like with traditional music, and the natural resonance of a sounding body, the relations between fourths, fifths ... Why, in electroacoustic music, this tendency to always return to the frequency of a *larsen*,[1] or to certain

1 The larsen effect, also known as acoustic feedback, is a phenomenon that occurs when a sound system, such as a microphone and a speaker, creates a loop where the output sound from the speaker is picked up by the microphone and then reamplified. It is named after the Danish engineer Søren Absalon Larsen, who discovered and studied the phenomenon in the early twentieth century.

frequencies that come spontaneously, naturally? There's a whole observation to be made, which begins simply with humble listening to what is happening; I try to understand while knowing that it's my own subjectivity that perceives the sound material. Perhaps there exist phenomena, natural structures of this material, like a kind of natural resolution of frequencies; but it's a difficult terrain in which to venture because . . . to do so is to hang on to the paintbrush, there is no ladder yet . . . And then you must pass from *homo sapiens* to *homo ludens*, which isn't easy to own up to.

GH   And for composition?

ÉR   There's a part of research in alternation with a phase in which I rush headlong and let myself go completely, and pick myself up at the end, and I listen again, and I submit to the critical goal.

GH   Of an aesthetic?

ÉR   I prefer the terms *option* or *choice*. I don't know if the notion of aesthetic comes into play. Actually, in my research there is a concern for continuous form, the linear fluidity of the sound process, that's an option; I also took a strong interest myself in electronic microsounds, in sounds that go a little outside, above the frequencies of encounter, in the summits of phases if you'd like, all while trying to eliminate fundamentals, keeping only subharmonics and revealing them to themselves. Can this be translated in aesthetic terms? I don't know . . .

I've noticed that, since I've been working in this direction, I've developed a greater auditive acuity to unusual frequencies, to ultrasounds inaudible to the average ear; this, I know I've acquired by dint of hearing and listening, it's all an education of perception and sensations.

In fact, these are experiments, research. For a long time, I called what I did *propositions sonores*; it allowed me to avoid a lot of questions—being asked and asking myself: "Is it music?"

GH   And is it an oeuvre?

ÉR   Of course, there is the problem of longevity. Creating something is an attempt to outlive oneself, beyond biological survival; I believe that the best way to ensure this in what one does, is if someone finds in what you propose a sufficient motive to develop it, to go further, to surpass it, which is perfectly compatible with the terms *experience*, *research*, or *proposition*.

I'd like to compose on paper to go faster, to go directly from the idea to its translation into a sign and entrust the performance to an interpreter. The ideal would be the ability to conceive of the work in one's head.

GH   Hence the need for a written form.

ÉR   The first need, at the level of a mode of writing, would be to find myself thanks to it, or to indicate certain figures of sounds, without having to go through the manipulations of all the parameters. Writing is the economy of loss, of forgetfulness, the suppression of a negative side of chance, a system that allows you to find your way back. To transition from the idea to its realization, it would be easier to be able to throw the idea onto paper. I am not trying to hinder experimentation, which is extremely important, nor the role of discovery during manipulation, which one accepts, rejects, integrates, and which changes the direction of the thing; but first there's the sketch of the idea, then the idea, then the realization of the idea is put into question by the discovery in progress, then the final result... The role of notation is to make possible the remaking of the piece, it's the basis of a work that I made last year: a notebook of synthesizer études, progressive études, of more and more complex modulations, figures, for the user, to enable the assimilation of the instrument.

GH   Returning to your *propositions*: you have a series of records.

ÉR   It was crude sound material. What interested me was to capture its versatility and the different possibilities of adjustment: the sounds on these records can be played at all speeds on two, three, four, [or] five record players; when it comes down to it, the outcome is less important than the process itself.

I also made pieces for continuous tape, on endless tapes of different lengths, that create indefinite cycles through successive synchronization.

What's important is the *acoustic space* that represents the sound box of the instrument. Tapes are traveling electrons that produce sounds, but it is space that is in play. In a way, space produces its own vibrations: when we listen, we find ourselves inside the instrument, inside the sound box itself.

Chers Christian et Françoise,

Vous me demandez beaucoup, je n'arrive pas à penser un article sur "la musique électro-acoustique aux Etats Unis, les studios, leurs activités et leur rayonnement" autrement qu'en terme de pensum. Je ne peux donc vous livrer que ces quelques notes maladroites, de caractère anecdotique.

D'abord le terme "électro-acoustique" n'est pas usité là-bas. On distingue même en les mélant, les techniques de l'"Electronic Music" et celles de la "Concrete Music" qui fait figure d'ancêtre respectée. Faite avec des sons électroniques issus d'instruments de synthèse des sons, (le terme synthétiseur est aussi indigeste dans les deux langues, mais malheureusement on n'y coupe pas) associée à des procédés appelés ici électro-acoustiques, sons enregistrés, amplifiés en direct, l'"Electronic Music" suit encore la vague très forte amorcée il y a quelques dix années par le phénomène "happening". La forme "live performance" reste privilégiée, musique produite en direct sur synthétiseur (impossible d'échapper à ce mot barbare malgré son air faussement civilisé) "home-made" ou signé Moog, Arp ou Buchla, le plus souvent associée à des techniques d'expression visuelle, circuits télé-video, danse et lumières. Annotée selon signes et symboles inventés par le compositeur, grande place est laissée à l'improvisation contrôlée ou utilisée comme fin en soi, lors de ces représentations.
Les studios : De tous poids, formes et mesures, chaque Université en est nantie. La section "School of Music" en contiendra au moins deux : Mini Arp ou miniMoog, ou vieux Buchla, 2ou 3 magnétophones type Revox (très prisé là-bas comme ici) un "petit " 4 pistes type Sony, et un monitoring system constitura le petit studio. Super Moog ou super Buchla ou super Arp, 2ou 3 sérieux ampex , autant de sérieux 4 pistes, console de mixage associée à Dolby syste ou/et filtres, equalizer, constitueront le grand. En annexe à ces nécessaire ment double, voire souvent triples studios; salles et auditoriums dans lesquelles des concerts sont régulièrement proposés. Ouverts aux étudiants qui bénéficient chaque semaine d'un certain nombre d'heures individuelles d'utilisation, pour lesquelles il leur suffit à jour fixe de signer le calendrier mis à l'affichage, pour le nombre d'heures qui leur est accordé, La plupart de ces studios fonctionnent 24 heures sur 24, week-end inclus. Le problème commence pour ces étudiants, lorsque formation acquise, ils n'on le choix pour conserver leurs prérogatives d'accès, qu'entre redoubler, tripler, rester étudiants à vie, ou guetter un poste d'assistant qui maintie ne ce droit. Une solution se fait jour : la fabrication de son propre instru ment de travail. Il est maintenant possible d'acheter plans et circuits imprimés, permettant avec un minimum requir de connaissances techniques, de construire son propre synthétiseur de sons "le seul risque est que ça ne marche pas du premier coup, ou de griller un haut parleur" (citation entendue d'un graduate student). Le coût de cette opération peut varier de 500 à 1.000 $ U.S. soit le prix d'un bon instrument pour n'importe quel instrumentiste.

Éliane Radigue to Christian Clozier and Françoise Barrière, ca. 1972. Courtesy Fonds Éliane Radigue.

Dear Christian and Françoise,

You've asked me many times, but I still haven't come up with an article on "electroacoustic music in the United States, the studios, their activities and their influence" other than in intellectual terms. I can only send these few clumsy and anecdotal notes.

First, the term "electroacoustic" isn't used there. They distinguish between the two, even while mixing together techniques of "Electronic Music" and "Concrete Music," which takes on the airs of a respected ancestor. Made with electronic sounds from sound synthesis instruments (the term synthesizer doesn't sit well in either language, but unfortunately we can't get rid of it), associated with processes that are called here electroacoustic, recorded sounds, amplified live, "Electronic Music" in this way follows from the very strong wave begun about ten years ago by the "happening" phenomenon. "Live performance" is still privileged, music produced directly on the synthesizer (it's impossible to escape from this barbarous word despite its false air of civility) which are "homemade," or produced by Moog, ARP, or Buchla, which is most often associated with techniques of visual expression, video circuits, dance and lights. Annotated according to signs and symbols invented by the composer, great importance is left to controlled improvisation as an end in itself, as well as its representations. Each university is equipped with studios of all shapes and sizes. The "School of Music" will have at least two of these: a mini ARP or mini Moog or an old Buchla, 2 or 3 Revox tape recorders (very expensive over there as they are here), a "small" 4-track Sony, and a monitoring system all make up a small studio. Super Moog, super Buchla, or super ARP, 2 or 3 serious Ampex's, as well as a serious 4-track, a mixing console part of a Dolby system and/or filters, and equalizer, all constitute a large studio. One often sees triple studios: halls and auditoriums attached to a double studio in which concerts are regularly presented. Open to students who are individually able to use them each week for a certain number of hours; on a given day, it suffices to sign up for their allotted hours on a calendar, and the majority of studios are open 24 hours a day including weekends. The problem starts for these students when they've finished school, they don't have the ability to keep their access privileges, so they double, triple their studies, stay students their entire lives, or research in an assistantship post which allows them this right of access. One solution is emerging: building one's own working instrument. It's now possible to buy schematics and printed circuit boards, and permitting a certain minimum technical

Outre ces activités intérieures à vocation d'enseignement, chaque "Electronic Music Studio" s'efforce d'entretenir un courant d'échanges avec ses voisins, et se tient rigoureusement informé des activités des plus lointains. Et si le rayonnement de ces studios est d'abord circonscrit à sa situation géographique à peine étendue de quelques miles, jusqu'à la réputation internationale de ceux dont nous connaissons les noms, cet intérêt porté à l'ensemble, crée un très interessant climat d'émulation professionelle.

Actuellement, des sommes énormes sont investies dans le contrôle par computer électronique des nouveaux instruments. Depuis la fabrication de banques de mémoires intégrées, en passant par la computerisation analogique digitale, jusqu'aux tentatives de programmation intégrale, toutes les recherches sont orientées vers l'asservissement de la machine par des "intelligences artificielles". Un musicien complet devra donc être également habile dans l'utilisation du "Fortram" ou quelque autre langage de ses esclaves cérébaux.

Bon artisan aussi, s'il veut construire lui-même son instrument, mais dans ce cas il lui faudra besogner à modeler ses propres sons de ses dix doigts, tout potentiomètre attentivement gardé sous son unique contrôle. Car si le home-made synthetiseur est une réalité d'aujourd'hui en voie de développement, la computerisation à domicile est encore pour demain. Aux anxieux d'y voir la bouteille à moitié vide d'un fossé se creusant, aux incorrigibles optimistes de boire ce qui reste de la bouteille à moitié pleine, en attendant que soit mûrie la nouvelle cuvée.

Éliane Radigue to Christian Clozier and Françoise Barrière, ca. 1972. Courtesy Fonds Éliane Radigue.

knowledge, to build one's own sound synthesizer where "the only risk is that it won't work the first time, or it'll blow out a speaker" (overheard from a graduate student). The cost of this endeavor can vary between 500 and 1,000 USD, which is the price of a good instrument for any instrumentalist.

Outside of these activities particular to the vocation of teaching, each "Electronic Music Studio" strives to keep up a current exchange of dialogue with its neighbors, and keeps itself rigorously informed of the activities of those further afield. And if the influence of these studios is at first constricted by its geographical situation, extending at most to several miles, up to the international reputations of those who are household names, this focus on the whole creates a very interesting climate of professional emulation.

Currently, enormous sums are invested in new computer-controlled instruments. Since the fabrication of integrated memory banks, passing through analog digital computerization, and up until forays in integral programming, all research is oriented toward the subjugation of the machine to "artificial intelligence." A complete musician must therefore be equally at home using "Fortram," or some other language of its cognitive puppets, because if the homemade synthesizer is today already a path of development, at-home computerization follows tomorrow.

One must be an artisan too, if one wants to build their instrument themselves. But in this case one will have to toil hard to model their own sounds with their ten fingers, all potentiometers attentively watched over under their own control. To those who anxiously see in the half-empty bottle a deepening chasm; and to those incorrigible optimists who drink what remains from the bottle half-full, while waiting for the new vintage to mature.

7th Birth.

- Multitude de l'infinitésimal.
  7th like anything like 7th.
- 7th gate
- 7th seal
- 7th sin
- 7th chord - - - -

Birth like any birth. The frightening anguish of any change from one state to an other one. The long and deep scream of any being - born -

Éliane Radigue, handwritten notes for *7th Birth*, ca. 1972. Courtesy Fonds Éliane Radigue.

> 7th Birth –
> Electronic Composition
> by Éliane Radigue
> at
> Sonnabend Gallery,
> 420 West Broadway
> on Saturday, March 18 at 4 p.m.
>
> V E. A U S – 254 12 24 –
> 74 – 42

Éliane Radigue, handwritten invitation for "7th Birth" at Sonnabend Gallery, New York, March 18, 1972. Courtesy Fonds Éliane Radigue.

GEELRIANDRE.

Has been performed recently at the Sonnabend Gallery. Made on the Arp Synthesizer. Represents research on the play of the upper ranges of cycles, cut from the fondamental which generate them.
World of intentions rather than form, made of sound molecules captured by enlargment.
"Out of Chaos vibrations seeking to be born"

Dedicated to GERARD FREMY.

Éliane Radigue, handwritten notes for *Geelriandre*, ca. 1972. Courtesy Fonds Éliane Radigue.

THEATRE DE LA MUSIQUE
Ancien GAITÉ-LYRIQUE   Tél 277 88-40   Square Emile Chautemps
Métro Réaumur-Sébastopol

LUNDI 29 MAI à 20 h 30
CONCERT
DE L'ENSEMBLE INSTRUMENTAL
DE MUSIQUE CONTEMPORAINE DE PARIS

SOLISTES : Arlette Bonnard, Amelia Salvetti, Mario Haniotis, Michel Jarry

DIRECTION
KONSTANTIN SIMONOVITCH

Places de 10 à 25 F   Adhérents Alpha 12 F   Etudiants, J.M.F., A.M.J., COPAR 8 F
Location au Théâtre de la Musique, et dans toutes les Agences théâtrales Bureau des Concerts
Marcel de Valmalète, 11 avenue Delcassé, Paris 8e.

CARTE BLANCHE

A

Georges et **Gérard**
APERGHIS   **FREMY**
COMPOSITEUR   PIANISTE

ŒUVRES DE

G APERGHIS
J S BACH
E RADIGUE

Flyer for a concert with Georges Aperghis and Gérard Frémy at Theatre De La Musique, Paris, May 29, 1972. Courtesy Fonds Éliane Radigue.

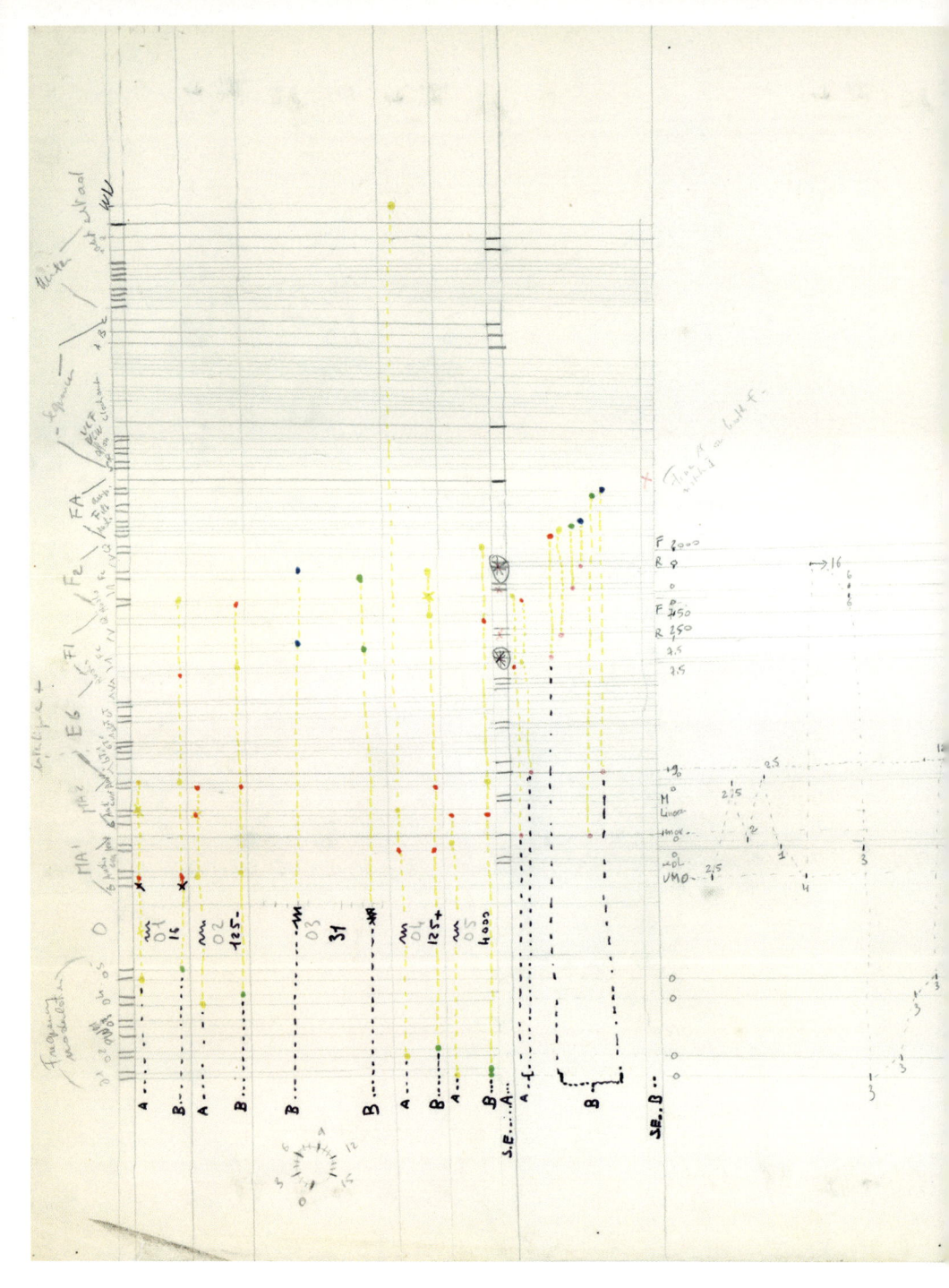

Éliane Radigue, score for *Geelriandre*, ca. 1972. Courtesy Michele Cone.

THEATRE DE LA MUSIQUE

☆

LUNDI 29 MAI 1972

☆

carte blanche à :

Georges APERGHIS   et   **Gérard FREMY**

compositeur   pianiste

œuvres de APERGHIS   J.-S. BACH   Eliane RADIGUE

ENSEMBLE INSTRUMENTAL DE MUSIQUE CONTEMPORAINE DE PARIS

direction

KONSTANTIN SIMONOVITCH

BUREAU DE CONCERTS MARCEL DE VALMALETTE   45, RUE LA BOËTIE, PARIS-8ᵉ   359-28-38

Program for a concert with Georges Aperghis and Gérard Frémy at Theatre De La Musique, Paris, May 29, 1972. Courtesy Fonds Éliane Radigue.

ELECTRONIC MUSIC STUDIO

HARPER HALL, UNIVERSITY OF IOWA

4:00 P.M.

MONDAY, 19 FEBRUARY 1973

Ψ - 847 . . . . Eliane Radigue

    for tape

    duration: c. 80 min.

        (Final mixdown courtesy of the Studios of the
        "Groupe de musique experimentale de Bourges")

"Dedicated to Francoise ORLY, my daughter. For what she is committed to: a better insertion into consciousness of the Ψ factor."

The following notes have been provided by the composer:

    Quivering, murmur of sound material.

    Slow stretching. Time suspended within the time unit.

    Feline softness masking capriciouss savagery.

    Impossible taming.

    Distances between proximity and familiarity.

        . . . .

    1) Primary material

    2) First elaboration

    3) Conflict

    4) Resolution

Mme. Radigue is visiting the University of Iowa for two weeks, during which time she has been working at the Electronic Music Studio. Her experience in electronic music includes study at the Club d'Essai with Pierre Schaeffer, a period as assistant to Pierre Henry, and work at the studio of New York University. She presently resides in Paris where she has her own private studio.

Flyer for "Ψ 847" with Éliane Radigue at the University of Iowa, Iowa City, February 19, 1973. Courtesy Fonds Éliane Radigue.

MUSIQUE ELECTRONIQUE

BENEFIT FOR FEMINIST MUSIC/MULTIMEDIA WORKSHOP   DONATION OPTIONAL

SUNDAY, MARCH 4, 1973   8:00 P.M.   MUSIC HALL, B 312

♀-847 . . . . ELIANE RADIGUE

    For Tape
    Duration: c. 80 minutes

    "Dedicated to Francoise Olry, my daughter, for what she is
    committed to: A better insertion into consciousness of
    the ♀ factor."

    Final mixdown courtesy of the studios of the "Groupe de Musique
    Experimental de Bourges."

. . . .

        The following notes have been provided
                by the composer:

Quivering, murmur of sound material.
    Slow stretching. Time suspended within the time unit.

        Feline softness masking capricious savagery.

           Impossible taming.

                Distances between proximity and familiarity.

                    1) Primary material
                    2) First elaboration
                    3 Conflict
                    4 Resolution

Mme. Radigue has been visiting Cal Arts for the past two weeks, during which time she has been working with the Buchla 200 equipment. Her experience in electronic music includes study at the Club d"Essai with Pierre Schaeffer, a period as assistant to Pierre Henry, and work at the studio at New York University. She presently resides in Paris where she has her own private studio.

Flyer for "Benefit for Feminist Music/Multimedia Workshop," March 4, 1973.
Courtesy Fonds Éliane Radigue.

Poster for "Ψ 847" with Éliane Radigue at The Kitchen, New York, March 19 and 20, 1973. Courtesy Fonds Éliane Radigue.

MISS RADIGUE GIVES A CONCERT ON TAPE
John Rockwell

Éliane Radigue is a Parisian electronic composer of impeccable credentials. She studied with Pierre Schaeffer and served as Pierre Henry's assistant. Monday night she presented an eighty-minute, four-channel tape at The Kitchen, 240 Mercer Street, that proved something of an exercise in the need for meditative concentration, but had its subtle rewards, too.

Miss Radigue's piece, which, was dedicated to her daughter, had some rather enigmatic relationship to the psychoanalytic experience and was coupled in the program with some poetically metaphorical phrases ("feline softness masking capricious savagery," etc.). The program also indicated that the work divided itself into sections dimly suggestive of sonata form.

On a first hearing, however, the parts blended into one another in what seemed like seamless flow. Realized on an ARP synthesizer, the work consisted almost entirely of thin, soft, sustained sounds. There were no sharp attacks or rhythms (a periodic, regular, muted, plucking effect aside), nothing loud, nothing dramatically contrasted. One kept waiting for something to happen. Then one became aware that on a far smaller level, the sounds were constantly permutating in texture, that a steady stream of sonic activity was in fact taking place right at the edge of one's perceptions. The program was repeated last night.

New York Times, March 23, 1973

Éliane Radigue, score for Ψ 847, ca. 1973. Courtesy Fonds Éliane Radigue.

Poster for "Arthesis" with Éliane Radigue at Theatre Vanguard, Los Angeles, May 1, 1973. Courtesy Fonds Éliane Radigue.

MINIMAL MATERIAL: ÉLIANE RADIGUE
Tom Johnson

There is something very special about the music of Éliane Radigue, but after thinking about it for almost a week, I still can't put my finger on what it is. Is it the intimacy? The way one feels that the music is speaking only to him regardless of how many other listeners may be sitting in the room? Is it the sheer efficiency with which it accomplishes so much with so little? Is it the enormous care and devotion which must have been required to make something so sensitive out of electronic sounds which most composers would consider drab and unpromising? Is it that Radigue sustains her minimal material for 80 minutes without ever repeating herself or becoming boring, and yet without ever leaving the restricted area within which she works?

Psi 847, the piece presented at the Kitchen on March 19 and 20, was created on an ARP synthesizer. It is built out of a number of themes or motifs, but they are not motifs in the usual sense. One is simply a low fuzzy tone which goes on for a long time, hardly changing at all. One is a very high tone, so high that it is difficult to tell exactly what pitch it is, so it sounds different, depending on what else is going on. One changes color from time to time. One is a clear middle-range tone which fades in and out quite a bit, sometimes dominating the other motifs and sometimes hovering in the background. Later there are some more elaborate motifs. There is a tone that wobbles quite a bit. There is a five-note descending melody. There is a tone that pulses every five seconds or so, something like a muffled department store bell.

The texture is never very thick. Often only three or four motifs are working at once. But there is always much to listen to, since the motifs fade in and out in many combinations and interact in many ways. The focal point often shifts from one motif to another, sometimes giving the impression that the music is changing key. As a motif changes color, it may begin to blend with some other motif which sounded alien to it. As a new motif fades in, everything else may begin to sound quite different.

Perhaps the most interesting thing about *Psi 847* is the way its motifs seem to come from different places. They were all produced by the same loudspeakers, and many of them seemed to come directly out of the loudspeakers. But some of the sounds seem to ooze out of the side wall, and others seem to emanate from specific points near the ceiling. I am told that this is actually true with any kind of music, and that the acoustical properties of a room will always affect different pitches in different ways.

But one only becomes sensitive to this phenomenon in pieces like this, where tones are sustained for a long time.

For me this piece represents the height of musical sensitivity, but perhaps I should temper that statement by admitting that it is a minority opinion. Most people would have been unimpressed by the modest sounds and uninterested in the tiny things that happen to them. I am told that supermarket products which have no red on their packages are usually passed by, and the music of Éliane Radigue will probably be overlooked for similar reasons.

Strength and brilliance are certainly to be valued, but I am often more moved by simplicity and subtlety. Perhaps I was influenced by Morton Feldman a few years ago when he wryly mentioned that, since this is the Jet Age, everyone thinks that we ought to have Jet Age music to go with it. Things have simmered down a little since the multimedia craze of the late sixties, but quite a bit of the music written today is still oriented toward speed, loudness, virtuosity, and maximum input, Éliane Radigue's music is the antithesis of all that.

Village Voice, March 29, 1973

Iowa State Studio, ca. 1973. Courtesy Fonds Éliane Radigue.

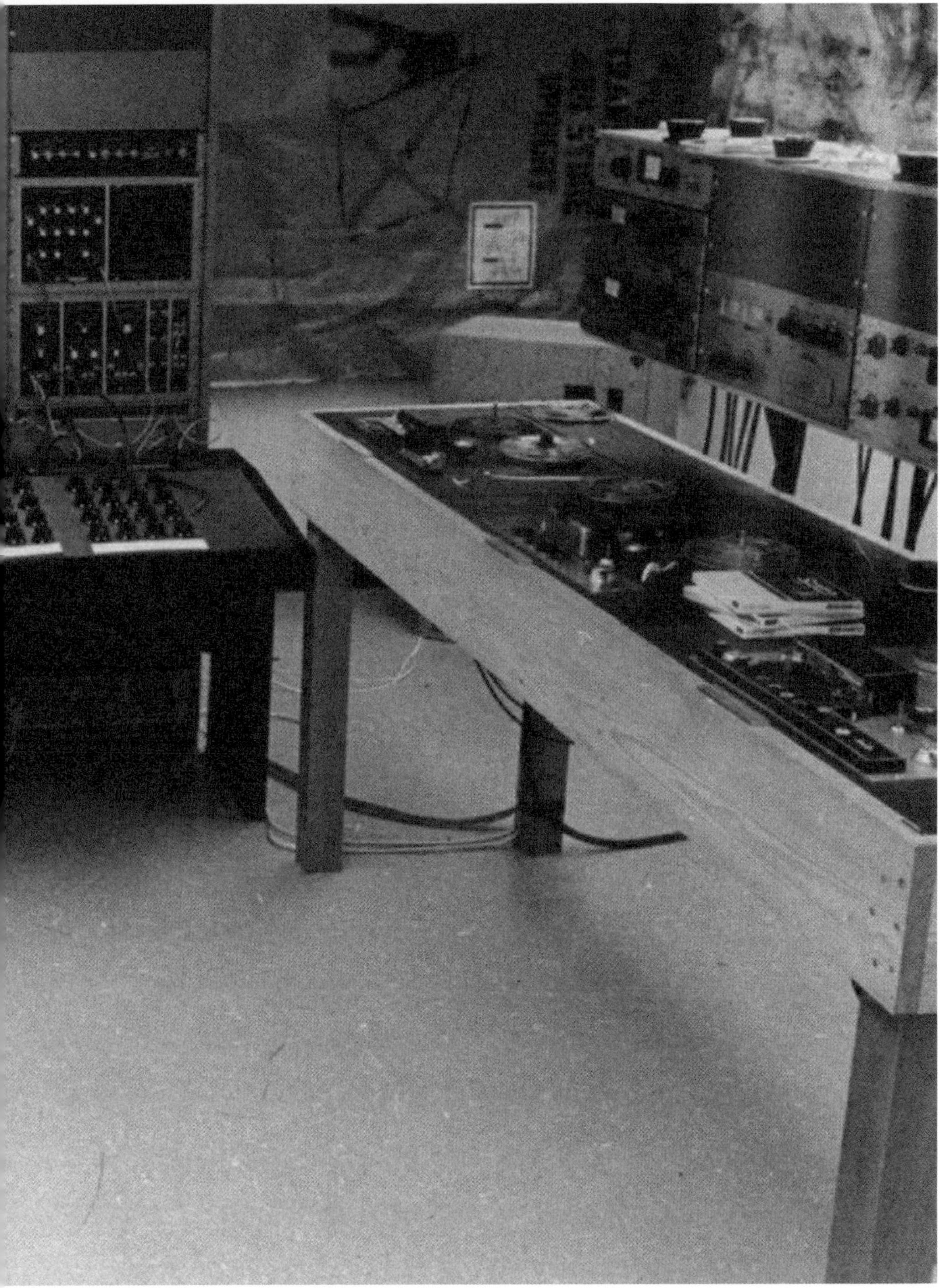

SHREDDING THE CLIMAX CARROT
Tom Johnson

When I was a composition student, the one thing which was always held up to us as an unassailable criterion for good music was whether or not it would "hold the attention." This seems obvious enough until one begins to consider what it involves.

In order to hold our attention for an entire evening, a work must jolt us once in a while with a well-timed surprise, hold a climax carrot in front of our noses so that we will have something to look forward to, lift us up and let us down in an appealing sequence, and titillate us with interesting details all along the way. Otherwise our minds might wander.

There is something manipulative about pieces which force themselves on us, conning us into following every move they make, and I think this process begs a few questions. What right does an artist have to tell his audience what to feel and when to feel it? Shouldn't it be possible to have an enjoyable evening in a theater or concert hall without constantly being manipulated? When we go to something like *Rigoletto* aren't we really just sitting there like so many Pavlovian dogs, salivating when the bell rings, laughing when we are supposed to, and weeping on cue?

I am not saying anything is wrong with Verdi, not to mention Beethoven, Shakespeare, Bartók, or any of the other masters whose works hold our attention so well. We give ourselves willingly to these things, just following them along, allowing them to manipulate us, feeling whatever we are supposed to feel, and loving every minute of it. But I am not sure this kind of art, which actually tyrannizes its audience, is what people really want and need today. And I am not sure that we should continue to insist that a performance must hold us in rapt attention from beginning to end in order to be beautiful.

Some of the performances I enjoyed most this past season are ones in which my mind wandered a great deal. They did not try to manipulate me or ring any Pavlovian bells, and they did not struggle to hold my attention. They simply said what they had to say, leaving me free to listen or not listen, and respond in my own way.

I think the first time I began to think along these lines was the night Victor Grauer read his *Book of the Year 3000* at the Kitchen (see Dec. 14, 1972). This was a truly non-manipulative performance, and it is a good example of what I am talking about, because Grauer made his intentions quite clear at the outset. His introductory remarks, as well as I can remember them, went something like this.

"I'm going to be reading for about three hours against this electronic sound. There won't be any intermission, but I don't want anyone to feel tied down. If you would like to hum along with the electronic tone, or echo back some of the words or phrases I read, that's fine too. And if you get sleepy, don't force yourself to stay awake. We can take in a lot of things even when we're asleep. The important thing is just to make yourself comfortable." I listened attentively much of the time, sometimes humming along with the electronic background. But I also took a couple of intermissions, and I spent quite a bit of time just lying on the floor, allowing the mellifluous words of the repetitious text to wash over my wandering mind. The piece was not holding my attention much of the time, but I would not have walked out for anything. Whenever I was able to tune in on the specific images and rhythms, I liked what I heard. And when I came to the end of a concentration span, the atmosphere itself was quite enough to keep me content.

In a very broad sense, all art is manipulative, and Grauer was pulling a few strings himself. After all, he did prime us with those introductory remarks. The lighting he used, the electronic tone, and the text itself all had a calculated effect. But this is not manipulation in the specific sense I was talking about before. No climax carrot. No surprises. No titillation. No insistence on holding the attention. He left us pretty much alone, allowing us to decide for ourselves how we wanted to respond, and leaving plenty of room for each individual to respond differently.

I encountered this non-manipulative attitude again when I heard Éliane Radigue's *Psi 847*, a wonderfully sensitive, though extremely subtle hour-long electronic piece, a few months later (see March 29, 1973). I had a chance to meet Radigue after the concert, so I decided to sound her out. "I like your music very much," I explained, "but I must admit that I wasn't able to concentrate on it all the time." "Of course not," she was quick to reply. "No one can concentrate on such tiny differences for such a long time. But it's not necessary. The piece can go along without you for a while. You come back to it when you're ready. And maybe the things you were thinking about while you weren't focused just on the music were also meaningful. That's all part of the experience. How you get into the music, leave it, come back again, and so on. And it's different for everyone." It is different. In my case I listened attentively for the first fifteen or twenty minutes before my mind finally took its first intermission. But I remember the critic John Rockwell saying that night that he hadn't paid much attention at first, thinking it must be kind of an introduction, but that he got into it later, after he realized it was going to continue on this same minimal plane. We were not being manipulated. We were simply exposed to something beautiful and allowed to deal with it in our own ways.

Grauer and Radigue are convenient examples, since they have expressed their attitudes verbally. But they are really only a small part of a large picture which has been evolving for some time. I think the seeds of this non-manipulative attitude could be traced back at least as far as Gertrude Stein and Charles Ives. Certainly the bulk of John Cage's work has been relatively non-manipulative, though this was never his main concern. In 1956, for example, Cage introduced an evening of collaborations with Merce Cunningham with this remark, "The activity of movement, sound, and light, we believe, is expressive, but what it expresses is determined by each one of you—who is right, as Pirandello's title has it, if he thinks he is." The works of dozens of current artists could be considered non-manipulative. Many of the things I heard this past season reflected this attitude. Like the three-day event presented by the Sonic Arts Union at WBAI, where people were free to come and go all day (see June 7, 1973). Or Max Neuhaus's permanent sound installation in front of the Transit Authority building (see June 28, 1973). Or Alvin Lucier's *The Queen of the South* (see March 15, 1973), or Rhys Chatham's "Two Gongs" (see June 7, 1973), or David Behrman's concert (see February 1, 1973), or Phill Niblock's "Ten 100-Inch Radii" (see March 8, 1973).

In some of these works a great deal of information is presented, and the audience pays close attention most of the time. But none of them require us to feel or think particular things at particular times. We are not treated as Pavlovian creatures, but as free agents who have our own ideas, our own fantasies, and our own curiosities. Pieces of this sort do not manipulate the audience, actively demanding anyone's attention. They are passive in nature, and the audience is allowed to approach them in different ways.

I am less familiar with current playwrights, choreographers, and filmmakers, but I have the feeling that this new wave of non-manipulative art is coming at us from all directions. It is a cool wave, reminiscent of the kind of coolness McLuhan was talking about when he discussed hot and cool communications media. And it threatens to drown our last sure-fire dictum for evaluating performance pieces: that they must hold the attention in order to be valid.

Village Voice, July 3, 1973

Bonjour Eliane!

      I hope this letter finds you and your family happy and well. I am fine except for the awful heat which haunts NYC during August and early September. I am sorry I have not written sooner ----- sometimes I am bad at such things ----- and then a spirt of enthusiasm inspires me again to communicate with my friends ----- often a letter seems so slow --- ones thoughts fermenting constantly. Much music lately for me ----- a sonority made with three consecutive whole tone fifths --------- and then a two fifth version with the middle fifth excluded. Also my first piece of written music in six years ---- symbolizing the fundamentals of my approach to overtones in a simple sonority and a new addition of rhythmic overtone relationships as well -------- very new for me and very frightening -------
How is your music progressing? I played your piece for my class in Nova Scotia ----- it came off very beautifully --- I spent much time trying to set the mood just right for it ----- and as I remembered watching you meditating, concentrating very hard before your performance at the Kitchen in NYC I tried to imitate the sense of that kind of concentration and centering myself to create a invisible feeling of warmth and focus in the room before I played the work ----- the room felt very magical during it ----- and the aural aroma of the work seemed to remain many days after in that room and in my mind ----- your work is most, most beautiful ------ it even brings tears to my eyes -----

      Simone and I arrive in Paris about the first of October ----- our performances the 13th, 14th and 15th. I think we are being put up in a hotel so I won't need a place to stay ------ thanks for offering your place though ---- recently I've been thinking how strange we met in California not knowing eachothers work at all --- having dinner hearing Jim Tenny's concert together never dreaming how much our music's had in common with eachothers until later through other peoples observations. Very strange indeed ------

      Well , off to the fan ----- this heat induces even a touch of madness ----- it will be good to see you and talk to you at length ----- I wish I were better at foreign languages ----- maybe soon I will be ---- but now my French is still nowhere ----- I apologize for not writing to you in your native tongue and promise soon in the future to learn.

                    Take care   be well   good luck in Montreux

Letter from Charlemagne Palestine to Éliane Radigue, ca. 1973. Courtesy Fonds Éliane Radigue.

Dear Eliane,

Back in Fun City again after a wonderful stay in Paris. I can't thank you enough for your kindness. I hope I can repay you someday. I assume that you have seen Charlemagne and that he may even be staying with you. I am now very busy getting ready to go to Houston and also to Louisiana for a concert at the old college of Dickie Landry. Should be fun. Will be gone about a week and then back again to New York and I'm not sure what.

I hope everything is working out OK with your family. I can see why you hate to leave them but I'm sure its all for the best. I also hope you continue with your music. I like it in my simple way although I'm not sure if I understand all of the ramifications of it, other than its meditative, cleansing quality — that's enough! Let me know when you will be coming to the States again.

Thank you again

Love,
Jon

Letter from Jon Gibson to Éliane Radigue, ca. 1973. Courtesy Fonds Éliane Radigue.

C

PALAIS JACQUES COEUR

Mardi 5 juin   18 h 15

CONCERT   oeuvres en CREATION de E   Radigue
et L   Ferrari (réalisées dans les studios du Gmeb)

PALAIS JACQUES COEUR

Mardi 5 juin : 21 h

CONCERT G. M. E. B   CREATIONS d'oeuvres de
P. Kolman, L   Ferrero, P. Boeswillwald, E. Sikora,
A   Savouret

avec le GMEBAPHONE

Flyer for a concert with Éliane Radigue and Luc Ferrari at Palais Jacques Coeure, Bourges, March 5, 1973. Courtesy Fonds Éliane Radigue.

Patrick de Haas
216 Bd Raspail
75014 Paris

Le 19 juillet 1974

Madame,

Puis-je me permettre de vous demander de bien vouloir répondre à ces quelques questions; cet interview sera publiée dans le prochain numéro de la revue "Artpress". Je regrette de n'avoir pas pu vous rencontrer; Catherine Millet m'a dit que vous avez accepté de répondre par retour de courrier; je vous en remercie vivement.

Si vous préférez développer plus longuement certaines questions, vous pouvez bien sûr en abandonner d'autres.

En espérant pouvoir faire votre connaissance, veuillez croire, madame, à l'expression de mes sentiments les meilleurs,

Letter from Patrick de Haas to Éliane Radigue, July 19, 1974. Courtesy Fonds Éliane Radigue.

Patrick de Haas
216 Bd Raspail
75014 Paris

July 19, 1974

Madame,

Please let me ask you to kindly answer these few questions; the interview will be published in the next issue of the magazine "Artpress." I regret not having been able to meet you in person, Catherine Millet told me that you agreed to respond by return mail; I thank you kindly.

If you prefer to work longer on certain questions, you can of course turn in the others sooner.

Hoping to get to know you, and please accept, madame, my best wishes,

Patrick de Haas

INTERVIEW WITH ÉLIANE RADIGUE
Patrick de Haas

In 1975, *Art Press* published this brief dialogue between Radigue and art historian Patrick De Haas, which the pair had conducted via mail over the previous year. Translated by Madison Greenstone, their exchange appears here in English for the first time.

PATRICK DE HAAS

One could characterize your music (or your musics) as "elemental" or "minimal"; in working with well-defined sonic material (but which develops indefinitely through time), your preoccupations seem to align with those of "minimal art." However, you have participated in exhibitions of artists whose thinking couldn't be further from this movement: Marc Halpern, Tania Mouraud, Fahri, and the Selz-Miralda-Rabascall-Xifra group. What exactly is the importance that you attach to the collaboration between two artistic practices: painting and music?

ÉLIANE RADIGUE

Elemental, "minimal," without a doubt. In deliberately reducing the field of possibilities of sound synthesis to just a very thin slice, to which I apply a "microphonic" quality of listening (analogous with microscopic): this is to discern the tiniest variations/modulations of the sound material, which is the source material of my constructions. My different collaborations can each be explained on a level that comes close to my fundamental preoccupations: with Marc Halpern, an affinity with nonrepetitive kinetic elements of his sculpture; with Tania Mouraud, the meditative character of her white environments, which suited the mode of sound reproduction through wall panels without using classic loudspeakers—associated with a slow unfolding of the musical discourse reproduced at low amplitude—were my primary concerns. The ritual aspect of the gatherings "Memorial" and "*Fête en Blanc*" by the Selz-Miralda-Rabascall-Xifra group was another meeting point. Concerning Fahri, it had less to do with a collaboration than with a type of exchange: a piece of time (the piece that is dedicated to him) for one of his sculptures (a piece of space).

PDH   Is there a particular reason that you have your creations heard outside of cultural institutions specially conceived of for listening to music?

ÉR   I like to make my "sound productions" heard in open places, which offer the possibility of permanent listening, where the duration of a piece is subjectively linked to the personal attention that the listener brings to it during the time of their listening. I would love to one day realize a "*labyrinthe sonore*" ["sound labyrinth"] in which the listener would be able to reconstruct to their liking a piece with their own pauses, landmarks, continuity, and duration, which would be that of their own meandering, with their own stops, with the crossing/intersecting of different sound sources and instantaneous mixing in and by their ear; this could be realized as an aleatoric pathway through a city, a town, or any closed space.

PDH Your music realized with tape loops that combine together in cycles of several hundreds of hours by progressive desynchronization, seems to be without a story, without a beginning or an end, without events, without privileged moments: this absence of a center, of points of redress, calls into question the notion of a work as well as that of a closed process.

ÉR What interests me is to submit the listener to a predesigned process that privileges the active participation of listening in the determination of the expressive field according to their attention or appetite . . . I sometimes complete the cycle myself, according to my own arbitrary choice, by taking sonic material in one state and leading it into a different state that could be the start of a new cycle: this is almost always the case, as I will often start a new piece where I decided to leave off with the previous one.

PDH There are perhaps two ways to apprehend this music: Should it be considered as a kind of conceptual proposition where, in the result (that which is heard), one must see above all what is demonstrated? Or rather does it necessitate, as in non-Western music, a certain state, a certain participation of the listener?

ÉR This is a difficult question, delicate in nature—by which I mean it involves concepts that cannot be explored in informal conversation, since the conversation itself is a transposition into words of a value whose sound-music vocabulary is already a transcription. I'll only say that any sound phenomenon that is perceived as a musical event requires the listener's participation, a state of perfect openness to the musical experience, in order to be experienced fully; on the other hand all musical structure is conceptual in essence and necessarily calls on often unconscious analytical functions during its perception. In the end, these two approaches aren't mutually exclusive but directly complementary.

PDH How do you situate yourself in relationship to the work of other composers of electroacoustic music, like Charlemagne Palestine and La Monte Young?

ÉR What we have in common is a commitment to the linear unfolding of musical discourse, related to the need for inner modifications inherent to the substance of sonic material . . . But here I'm taking risks, because I don't know if Charlemagne Palestine or La Monte Young would agree with what I've proposed. Our differences lie in the choice of "dramatic events" that punctuate this discourse: the use of the voice and light art in La Monte Young's work, and gestural action in Charlemagne Palestine's, whereas in my work there's a total absence of participation associated with presence or the visual, leaving only a "reflection" to be established be between the listener and the sonic phenomena that I propose.

PDH Could you speak more specifically about what sound manipulation techniques you work with, and the history of your work with sound?

ÉR I don't think that a little excursion into the land of potentiometers, frequency generators, filters or modulators of any kind, voltage control, or alternating current could shed any light, whether it be green or red, on your question.

It's always tempting to lose oneself in the fog of technical vocabulary that obscures the most elementary concepts, and to shroud in hermeticism tinged with intellectualism questions that are ultimately only of interest to the person responding.

ÉLIANE RADIGUE
FOUR NIGHTS OF THREE YEARS' WORK

224 CENTRE ST.-
WEDNESDAY, MARCH 6, 1974 9:00 PM

ARTHESIS (1972-73)

    Whirlpools come from the depth of the ages, with a secret and fierce ascendancy. Indiscernible light which seeks to dawn, trails its frail coming when sleep overtakes everything.

    Realised on the Moog Synthesizer at the Univ. of Iowa.

BIOGENESIS (1973)

    To my daughter Anne Person, for the child she bears within herself and will bear up for a long time.

    Paris - Arp Synthesizer and natural sound sources.

CHRY-PTUS (1971)

    Originally two tapes which are to be played simultaneously. (with or without synchronisation, which does not affect the structure of the work, but creates changes in the game of sub-harmonics and overtones. Three variations of this piece were performed at the New York Cultural Center in 1971, with variations of amplitude and location modulation as well as synchronisation. This concert is the third variation on the tape performance.

    Realised on the Buchla Synthesizer at New York University.

THURSDAY, MARCH 7, 1974 9:00 PM

ARTHESIS (1972-73)

    See above date for notes.

7th BIRTH (1971)

    7th like anything 7th,
    7th gate
    7th seal
    7th sin
    7th chord - - -
    Birth like any birth - -
    The frightening anguish of any change from one state to another one. The long and deep scream of any being-born.

Program for "Four Nights of Three Years' Work" with Éliane Radigue at Experimental Intermedia Foundation, New York, March 6 and 7, 1974. Courtesy Fonds Éliane Radigue.

FRIDAY, MARCH 8, 1974 9:00 PM

Ψ-847 (1972)   (Duration: c. 80 minutes)

Dedicated to Francoise Olry, my daughter, for what she is committed to: A better insertion into consciousness of the Ψ factor.

Quivering, murmur of sound material.
Slow stretching. Time suspended within the time unit.
Feline softness masking capricious savagery.
Impossible taming.
Distances between proximity and familiarity.

. . . .

1) Primary material
2) First elaboration
3) Conflict
4) Resolution

THE KITCHEN -
SATURDAY, MARCH 9, 1974 8:30 PM

BIOGENESIS (1973)

See March 6 for notes.

TRANSAMOREM-TRANSMORTEM (1973)

"Preceding the greatest achievement
 Preceding the greatest detachment."*

Outer edge of the frontier space of the unconscious. Waves in tune, "the consonant things are vibrating together."* Where is the changing point? Within the inner field of perception, or the external reality of something on the way to becoming.

"Then, time is no longer an obstacle, but the means which permit the realisation of the possible."*

* from an anonymous author.

Paris - Arp Synthesizer

This series of works represents a cycle of researches with electronic sounds through Moog, Buchla, and Arp synthesizers.

Program for "Four Nights of Three Years' Work" with Éliane Radigue at Experimental Intermedia Foundation and The Kitchen, New York, March 8 and 9, 1974. Courtesy Fonds Éliane Radigue.

ÉLIANE RADIGUE

BIOGENESIS (1973)

A ma fille Anne Person, pour l'enfant qu'elle porte et portera longtemps.

To my daughter Anne Person, for the child she bears within herself and will bear up for a long time.

Paris - Arp Synthesizer and natural sources.

TRANSAMOREM-TRANSMORTEM (1973)

"Avant le plus grand accomplissement
Avant le plus grand detachement." (1)

Outer edge of the frontier space of the unconscious. Waves in tune "les choses qui sont consonantes vibrent ensemble" (2). Where is the changing point? Within the inner field of perception, or the external reality of something on the way of becoming.

"Et le temps n'est plus un obstacle, mais le moyen qui permet la realisation du possible" (3)

(1) "Preceding the greatest achievment
    Preceding the greatest detachment"

(2) "The consonant things are vibrating together"

(3) "Then, time is no longer an obstacle, but the means which permits the realization of the possible".

                            -Anonymous

Paris - Arp Synthesizer

the kitchen   **saturday march 9**

The Kitchen is supported by the NY State Council on the Arts.

Program for "Four Nights of Three Years' Work (*Biogenesis* and *Transamorem–Transmortem*)" with Éliane Radigue at The Kitchen, New York, March 9, 1974. Courtesy Fonds Éliane Radigue.

Poster for "Four Evenings of Three Years' Work" with Éliane Radigue at Experimental Intermedia Foundation and The Kitchen, New York, March 6–9, 1974. Courtesy Fonds Éliane Radigue.

FESTIVAL D'AUTOMNE à PARIS

OCTOBRE.NOVEMBRE 1974

MUSIQUE

MUSEE GALLIERA
2-5 octobre
MILFORD GRAVES (U.S.A)

9-14 octobre
SONIC ARTS UNION (U.S.A.)

6-10 novembre
œuvres électro-acoustiques
JEAN-CLAUDE ELOY : SHANTI (6, 7, 8)
en coproduction avec la Westdeutscher Rundfunk, Cologne
GROUPE DE RECHERCHES MUSICALES (9)
ELIANE RADIGUE (10)

JOURNEES DE MUSIQUE CONTEMPORAINE (SMIP)
14-23 octobre
en collaboration avec le Théâtre de la Ville
et la Compagnie Renaud-Barrault

THEATRE DE LA VILLE
14-18 octobre
Angleterre (14) - Italie (15) - France (16) - Pologne (17) - Espagne (18)

THEATRE D'ORSAY
19-23 octobre
sessions IRCAM
Musique et débats avec le public
BERIO (19) - **GLOBOKAR** (20) - **RISSET** (21) - **BOULEZ** (23)

PALAIS DES CONGRES
25 octobre
INORI «adorations» pour soliste et orchestre
de KARLHEINZ STOCKHAUSEN
Orchestre du Südwestfunk, Baden-Baden
direction **KARLHEINZ STOCKHAUSEN**

SALLE WAGRAM
31 octobre
MUSIQUE PLUS
SCHOENBERG - LIGETI - CASTIGLIONI - GRISEY

ARTS PLASTIQUES

MUSEE GALLIERA
2 octobre-10 novembre
Galerie Daniel Templon
L'ART AU PRESENT

ESPACE PIERRE CARDIN
10 octobre-30 novembre
TAKIS
SCULPTURES MUSICALES

CENTRE NATIONAL D'ART CONTEMPORAIN (C.N.A.C.)
15 octobre-2 décembre
BOLTANSKI-MONORY
ASPECTS RECENTS

VIDEO

ARC-MUSEE D'ART MODERNE DE LA VILLE DE PARIS
8 novembre-8 décembre
ART VIDEO ET CONFRONTATIONS VIDEO 1974
en collaboration avec le Centre National pour l'Animation
Audio-Visuelle (C.N.A.A.V.)

Program for Festival d'Automne à Paris at Musée Galliera, Paris, 1974.
Courtesy Fonds Éliane Radigue.

Éliane Radigue, handwritten notes for *Adnos*, ca. 1974. Courtesy Fonds Éliane Radigue.

ADNOS.

80′

Éliane Radigue

"From adage in adynamia, for all the adolescents and the adnos, this addendum."

Éliane Radigue

"ADNOS": Moving stones at the bottom of a stream doesn't affect the course of the water, but modifies its liquid shape.
Thus, a highly powerful sonic energy transforms the course of the fluid zones of resonance and generates an emergent sonic activity.
Like the needle of time, the wheel mechanism of an open watch punctuates, integrated into its movement.
In the conch formed by the course of sound, the ear filters, selects, privileges, like a gaze would, resting on the shimmering of water.
Only listening is called on, like an absent and double gaze, turned both toward an image proposed from outside, of which the reflection lives in thought in the interior universe.

Produced on the ARP synthesizer. Final mixing carried out in the GRM studios. Paris.

Premiere at Festival d'Automne ~~1974~~ Musée Galliéra November 10th 1974

Sept 74. Éliane Radigue.

Eliane,

Since I am now in charge of music at the Kitchen, I had a meeting with Ann McMillan yesterday. We decided the following things.

    Ripert Center series of six concerts
        January 28 - Feb. 2
        half of proceeds go to Ripert Center for publicity etc.
        Equiptment available; Teac 3340 4-track tape ($\frac{1}{4}$ inch) recorder with 4 channel amplification system

    Eliane Radigue concert
        weekend of 7th + 8th of February
        (you may play as many concerts as you wish around then)

If you have any reservations about these plans, could you please notify us soon?

Looking forward to all of these concerts.

                      Arthur Russell

Letter from Arthur Russell to Éliane Radigue, ca. 1975. Courtesy Fonds Éliane Radigue.

MILLS COLLEGE OAKLAND, CALIFORNIA 94613

CENTER FOR CONTEMPORARY MUSIC

Dec 8, 1974

Dear Eliane, I hope this letter reaches you, or that you have assumed that the concert at Mills is as we talked in Paris. We have scheduled a concert by you for February 15 (Saturday evening.) The fee is embarrassingly low --- $250 --- but as I explained, it's all we have. If you will be in California, we will be expecting you with delight.

I dont know what you intend to perform, but we have all variety of tape equipment and good loudspeakers, so I dont see any difficulty for any sort of tape. We have:

1/2 " four channel
1/4 " four channel
1/2 " two channel

and mixers, etc.

If something more complicated is involved, please just spell out your technical requirements in a letter.

I cant say how much we appreciated you dinner for us in Paris. It was wonderful being in France for the first time, but your party was the only chance we had to meet people socially, and you made us feel "at home."

I hope Ripert plans go well. I have tried and tried to get time to contribute something, but I pay for the chance to be away from this job whenever I need to be (Sonic Arts, Paris, etc.) byt the kind of work I have to put in when I am here. I cant complain, it's a fair trade, but pretty much cuts out any sort of personal work during the academic year. I hope to take some time off during next year, and maybe that will change things in my relationship with the outside world.

Very best regards and love to you.

Bob

Bob Ashley

Letter from Robert Ashley to Éliane Radigue, December 8, 1974. Courtesy Fonds Éliane Radigue.

Poster for "Adnos" and "E-5th" with Éliane Radigue at The Kitchen, New York, February 8, 1975. Courtesy Fonds Éliane Radigue.

The Center for Contemporary Music

Saturday, February 15, 1975

Mills College Concert Hall

ELIANE RADIGUE

ADNOS:

D'adage en adynamie, pour tous les ados et les adnés, cet addenda.

Adage: Slow exercises to improve the equilibrium of dancers and the form of their movement. First part of a pas de deux.

Adné: This is said of any part tied or welded to another and which appears to be part of it.

Ados: A bank of earth used to protect plantings from the north wind and expose them more directly to the rays of the sun.

Addenda: That which is added to something to complete it.

Adynamie: Total lack of physical strength which accompanies some serious illnesses.

Realized in the artist's studio, Paris, 1974
Final mixing courtesy the Groupe de Musique Experimentale de Bourges.

This concert made possible by a grant from the Rockefeller Foundation.

Program for "Adnos" with Éliane Radigue at The Center for Contemporary Music, Oakland, February 15, 1975. Courtesy Fonds Éliane Radigue.

Eliane RADIGUE

à partir du 26 Février 1976, à 18 heures

audition continue de

Chry-ptus	♉ 847
Adnos	Biogénésis
7th Birth	Arthesis
Transamorem-Transmortem	Geelriandre

Galerie Shandar   40, rue Mazarine   75006 Paris   326.84.35

Postcard for a concert with Éliane Radigue at Galerie Shandar, Paris, February 26, 1976.
Courtesy Fonds Éliane Radigue.

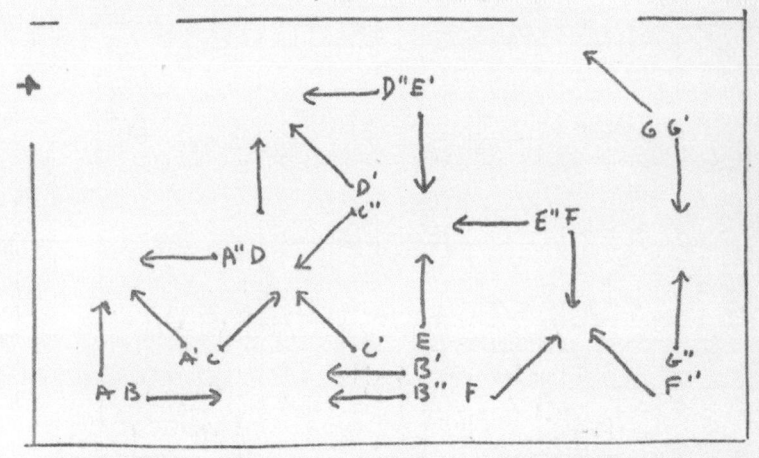

Poster for a concert with Éliane Radigue at GERM, Paris, October 11, 1977.
Courtesy Fonds Éliane Radigue.

Éliane Radigue, sketch for *Les Paroles Gelées*, ca. 1977. Courtesy Fonds Éliane Radigue.

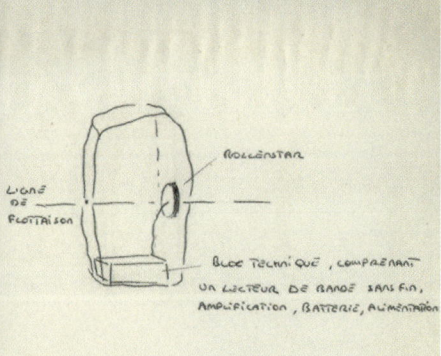

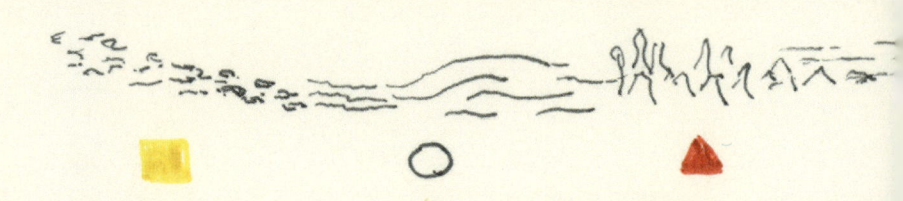

Éliane Radigue, score for *Triptyque*, ca. 1978–79. Courtesy Fonds Éliane Radigue.

17' 29"

24' 15"

Triptyque.
14.11.79.   3-2-80.

Valencia
California 9 355
805 255-1050

California Institute of the Arts

School of Music

September 30, 1980

Ms. Laetitia de Compiegne
Mills College
Seminary at McArthur
Oakland, CA 94613

Dear Laetitia

    I would like very much to have Eliane do something at CalArts. We have a very limited budget and the time table around the 22nd of November is quite full. However, would the 17th and 18th be possible with an evening performance on the 17th and a lecture to the students on the 18th? If so, we could offer $250, and that would have to be inclusive of travel

    I will try to reach you by phone before I leave, but in case I don't, I will be returning to the United States on November 3rd. If you need to contact someone before then you could speak with Mel Powell. I hope that something can be worked out

My best wishes,

Morton Subotnick
Head, Composition Department

MS kh

home # 805.259.5739

Letter from Morton Subotnick to Éliane Radigue, September 30, 1980. Courtesy Fonds Éliane Radigue.

10 / 1 / 80

Dear Mr Radigue,

I hope while you are in California that we can meet

I have asked J.C. François to try and arrange a visit for you at UC San Diego Music Dept.

If you are nearby please telephone me at 714-753 7400.

My address is 1602 Burgundy Rd., Leucadia, California.

I will leave for Bonn, West Germany ~~Oct~~ November 18.

With best wishes
Pauline Oliveros

Letter from Pauline Oliveros to Éliane Radigue, October 11, 1980. Courtesy Fonds Éliane Radigue.

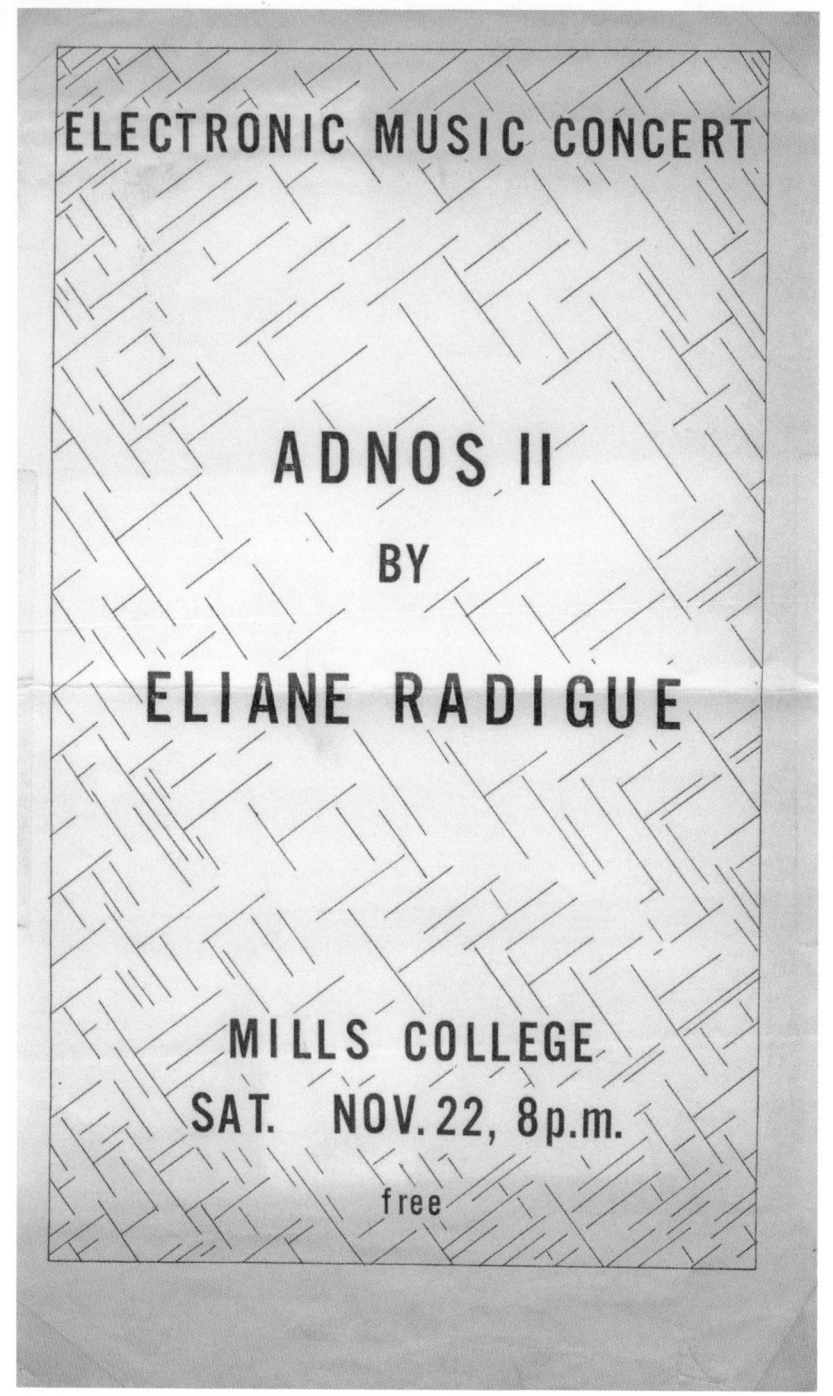

Poster for "Adnos II" with Éliane Radigue at Mills College, Oakland, November 22, 1980.
Courtesy Fonds Éliane Radigue.

ELIANE RADIGUE - ADNOS II -
1980
75'30"

To move stones around in the bed of a river does not affect its course, but can only change the play of the waves on the surface

And so, the sound energy alters the course of the flowing fields of resonnance

Pulsation, like the hand of a watch, marks out the mecanism of the gear of time, integrated in its motion.

In the conch formed by sound waves, the ear filters, selects and emphasizes some areas of hearing, the same way as one's eyes would look at the shimmering of water, at the same time absent and multiple, oriented towards an outside whose image lives reflected in the inner universe

Éliane Radigue, notes for *Adnos II*, 1980. Courtesy Fonds Éliane Radigue.

The Kitchen Center for Video and Music

press release

ELIANE RADIGUE

December 23, 1980 - 8:30pm
$4.00/$2.50 members/TDF music
The Kitchen, 484 Broome Street
Res: 925-3615

On December 23, the Kitchen's Contemporary Music Series will present the world premiere of ADNOS II (1980, a composition by French composer ELIANE RADIGUE. A resident of Paris, Ms. Radigue has been composing for tape and electronic media since the late 1950's, using facilities which she built independently. ADNOS II presents a delicately continuous transformation, a fragile sonic texture resembling, in the composer's words, "the shimmering of water in sunlight". Ms. Radigue, inspired by the idea of moving water as metaphor for sound in motion, writes:

"In the conch formed by sound waves, the ear filters, selects and emphasizes some areas of hearing, just as one's eyes would look at the shimmering of water: at the same time absent and multiple, oriented toward an outside whose image lives reflected in the inner universe.

ELIANE RADIGUE studied electro-acoustic techniques under Pierre Schaeffer at the Studio d'Essai and under Pierre Henri at the Studio Apsonne In 1970 she came to the United States and for the following three years worked in New York at School of the Arts, at Iowa Institute and at California Institute of the Arts. Her principal compositions include Chry-ptus 1971, 7th Birth 1972, Geelriandre 1972), 847 (1973, Triptych 1980 and Adnos II (1980. Internationally known, Ms Radigue has presented her work at the Pavillon Français of Expo '70 in Osaka, at Festival of Como (Italy, 1970, at Exposition Sonore in Paris 1972, Fondation Maeght in 1973 and the Kitchen in 1973

484 Broome Street between West Broadway and Wooster, New York City

Press release for "Adnos II" with Éliane Radigue at The Kitchen, New York, December 23, 1980. Courtesy Fonds Éliane Radigue.

ON THE FRINGE OF PARIS
Tom Johnson

After six months in Paris, it was time to return to New York, and I thought I should try to put together a general column summarizing the new music I'd been hearing in Europe. I soon realized, however, that what was really necessary was an article devoted to a few of the extraordinary independent composers I found there, but have not yet written about. Like most critics, I often find myself reporting on the more prominent public events, and forgetting about what I hear in more modest circumstances. So I want to conclude this series of European reports by telling you about Pierre Mariétan, Éliane Radigue, and Horacio Vaggione.

They have much in common. All are mature and highly experienced musicians. All work more or less on the fringes of Parisian musical life and are more or less ignored by the French press. All are strong individuals with highly personal styles. I've become friendly with all three, and I've gained much by hearing their music, listening to their ideas, and observing the richness of their musical lives. Perhaps you will find their stories rewarding as well.

Pierre Mariétan is one of the few composers who has studied with both Boulez and Stockhausen. Of Swiss origin, he spent two years as a young horn player with the Orchestre de la Suisse Romande, but he then settled in Paris, which offered a more stimulating new music environment. His current life sometimes leads me to describe him as the Phill Niblock of Paris, because he spends so much time presenting the work of other composers and working for the cause of experimental music in general. He is particularly concerned with making people more sensitive to environmental sounds and often organizes programs that encourage school children to listen to the rain, the insects, the sounds of their neighborhoods. Once a week he teaches a course in sound addressed to city planning students. Once a month for the past seven years his organization GERM has presented informal concerts of experimental music which consistently seem to offer some of the most original and professional work around.

Mariétan continues to write some music for conventional instrumental ensembles. I heard a recording of a piece for twenty-four instruments, for example, which consists of forty-two sections, written on fourteen consecutive days. It's a sort of diary, pleasant and whimsical. The composer's heart, however, is outdoors. One of my most pleasant days in Paris was the time Mariétan drove me out to the suburb of Évry, where he has been collaborating with an architect, contributing sound elements to an attractive new public housing project. One area had been acoustically shielded so as to permit quiet conversation right in the middle of the busy garden. At several points, curious looking pipes rise up to the surface allowing children, or other people, to send sounds to one another through underground interconnections. As you walk along the sidewalk, your footsteps produce intermittent clapping rhythms because Mariétan had the fine idea of interrupting the concrete sidewalks with sections of resonant planks. I like the way Mariétan has dealt with acoustics, and his work seems somehow more integrated with the space than the installations of artists like Max Neuhaus or Liz Phillips, who make their effects solely with electronic equipment. But Mariétan has not eliminated electronics. For example, he also played for me a gorgeous tape of sustained overtones, which he made by playing the natural harmonics of the Alpine horn. He wants to realize a computer version of this music, to be triggered off automatically at sunrise and sunset as part of one of his outdoor installations.

Éliane Radigue's music has been familiar to me, and to other New Yorkers, since the early seventies. She worked for a year at the electronic music center at NYU, where she came to know Morton Subotnick, Rhys Chatham, Laurie Spiegel, and others, and she has returned to the States periodically to present programs of her own electronic works at the Kitchen and other places. In 1975, however, she became a Tibetan Buddhist, went into retreat, and dropped her composing career completely. Curiously, when she returned to music four years later, her work went on very much as before. The aesthetic was still minimalist, one might even say ascetic. The sounds were still long and sustained. The source was still her 1970 ARP synthesizer. The medium was still recording tape. The result was still a technically impeccable sequence of carefully tuned tones, which emerge from unexpected places, coalesce into unique modes, and change very slowly. The music still challenged the listener to slow down, be patient, and observe subtle changes. Listening in this way can be considered a form of meditation, and I would say that Radigue's music is clearly religious in nature, though perhaps no more religious than before her own conversion.

Recently Radigue embarked on a long-term project based on the 100,000 songs of the Tibetan master Milarepa. Privileged one night in early March to hear a private playing of the first segment of the new work, which lasts about seventy-five minutes, I was particularly impressed by the distinct personality of every tone in the new piece. This one has a breathy quality. This one has an odd oboe-like edge. Another vibrates in a quirky way. Another is somehow very distant and rather loud at the same time. Another is so soft that you sometimes can't be sure whether it is there or not. There is a rhythmic motif in the second of the four sections of the piece, and for a while Radigue's music seems to be moving, dancing, making gestures in a way that it normally never does. Her style develops over the years with the same kind of subtle progress that can be heard in one of her individual pieces. Only the time-scale is different.

Horacio Vaggione grew up in Argentina and received his early training in South America. As a young composer, however, he came to Europe, where he has been based ever since. He lived for several years in Spain, where he sometimes worked with the members of the innovative Spanish group Zaj, and often toured with Luis de Pablo in the group Alea. In the early seventies, he gravitated to Paris, began working more and more by himself, and gradually developed the unique electronic music that he now presents live in solo concerts, generally out of town.

You could say that Vaggione is basically a synthesizer player, and you could say that his music is a little like the solo presentations of Richard Teitelbaum or Alvin Curran, but this is perhaps misleading. For one thing, Vaggione's repertoire is segmented into specific one-movement pieces, generally about twenty minutes long. Each involves a specific mode, a specific kind of texture, and a specific category of electronic sound. Generally the material is prerecorded on several different tapes, which the composer mixes together with one hand while overlaying improvised lines on an electric keyboard with his other hand. Vaggione has exceptional keyboard technique, and it is impressive to watch the speed and control with which he puts everything together in a performance, standing all the time, and sometimes almost dancing with the music. What really impressed me in the solo concert I heard, however, was the cleanness, both of the ideas and of the sound. Each piece is carefully defined, and neither the prerecorded material nor the improvised lines go ever beyond the vocabulary of the specific piece. And the sounds are about as high in fidelity and low in noise as in any electronic music I have ever heard. This is remarkable for a composer who works mostly in a modest home studio, and I asked Vaggione what his secret was.

"Oh, it's not so hard," he said. "Just get a couple of Revoxes and some good-quality tape. Don't bother to work at fifteen inches per second. Seven and a half is good enough." He neglected to add that you must also have a lot of experience, a sensitive ear, and enough patience to do things over and over until each element attains the same superb sound quality.

As I left Paris, Mariétan was completing a program for the French radio that involved recording and mixing the bells of some thirty Parisian churches. Radigue was preparing to present her new work in some concerts in the United States. Vaggione had just mixed a new composition made with computer-generated sound and was collecting tapes of other composers in preparation for presentations of electronic music he will be making in Argentina. All were doing their customary high-quality work, and none of them seemed particularly bothered by the idea that it would not be taking center stage in Parisian musical life. In fact, I think they feel rather comfortable working on the fringes. It's quieter there, there are fewer hassles, and one can make wonderful music strictly for its own sake, as they do.

Village Voice, May 4, 1982

Albany Composers' Consortium

presents

ELECTRONIC MUSIC

by

ELIANE RADIGUE

in the Art Gallery
State University of New York at Albany

between 2 PM and 5 PM

Thursday, May 6, 1982

PROGRAM MADE POSSIBLE IN PART THROUGH A GRANT FROM MEET THE COMPOSER with support from the New York State Council on the Arts, the National Endowment for the Arts, the American Society of Composers, Authors and Publishers, American Telephone and Telegraph Company, Broadcast Music, Inc., Consolidated Edison of New York, Coopers and Lybrand, Equitable Life Assurance Society of the United States, Exxon Corporation, the Martha Baird Rockefeller Fund for Music, Mobil Foundation, Morgan Guaranty Trust, the New York Community Trust, NL Industries Foundation, Inc., the Edward J. Noble Foundation, Helena Rubinstein Foundation, Xerox Corporation, Warner Communications, American Savings Bank.

Poster for "Electronic Music" with Éliane Radigue at Albany Composer's Consortium, State University of New York at Albany, May 6, 1982. Courtesy Fonds Éliane Radigue.

samaya foundation
PRESENTS

ELIANE RADIGUE

ADNOS III (Prélude to Milarepa)

VOICE MAY 4, 1982

Eliane Radigue's music has been familiar to me, and to other New Yorkers, since the early '70s. She worked for a year at the electronic music center at NYU, where she came to know Morton Subotnick, Rhys Chatham, Laurie Spiegel, and others, and she has returned to the States periodically to present programs of her own electronic works at the Kitchen and other places. In 1975, however, she became a Tibetan Buddhist, went into retreat, and dropped her composing career completely. Curiously, when she returned to music four years later, her work went on very much as before. The aesthetic was still minimalist, one might even say ascetic. The sounds were still long and sustained. The source was still her 1970 Arp synthesizer. The medium was still recording tape. The result was still a technically impeccable sequence of carefully tuned tones, which emerge from unexpected places, coalesce into unique modes, and change very slowly. The music still challenged the listener to slow down, be patient, and observe subtle changes. Listening in this way can be considered a form of meditation, and I would say that Radigue's music is clearly religious in nature, though perhaps no more religious now than before her own conversion.

Recently Radigue embarked on a long-term project based on the 100,000 songs of the Tibetan master Milarepa. Privileged one night in early March to hear a private playing of the first segment of the new work which lasts about 75 minutes, I was particularly impressed by the distinct personality of every tone in the new piece. This one has a breathy quality. This one has an odd oboe-like edge. Another vibrates in a quirky way. Another is somehow very distant and rather loud at the same time. Another is so soft that you sometimes can't be sure whether it is there or not. There is a rhythmic motif in the second of the four sections of the piece, and for a while Radigue's music seems to be moving, dancing, making gestures in a way that it normally never does. Her style develops over the years with the same kind of subtle progress that can be heard in one of her individual pieces. Only the time scale is different.

By Tom Johnson

BENEFIT CONCERT FOR

PAWO RINPOCHE

WED. JUNE 2, 8 PM

SUGGESTED DONATION $3.

75 Leonard Street   925-9763   New York, N.Y. 10013

Flyer for "Adnos III (Prélude to Milarepa)" with Éliane Radigue at Samaya Foundation, New York, June 2, 1982. Courtesy Fonds Éliane Radigue.

Flyer for "Adnos III (Prélude to Milarepa)" with Éliane Radigue at GERM, Paris, October 19, 1982. Courtesy Fonds Éliane Radigue.

EXPERIMENTAL INTERMEDIA FOUNDATION   224 CENTRE STREET   NEW YORK CITY 10013

December 4th, 1983

Eliane Radique
22 rue Liancourt
75014 Paris France

Dear Eliane Radique,

I invite you to do a concert of your music "Five Milarepa Songs" in our Concerts by Composers series. We will schedule the date for March 15th, 1984. We're very happy to support your music here in New York. As you know, our sound system is one of the best in the country for your music.

We have some support from the National Endowment for the Arts and from the New York State Council on the Arts. There will be approximately thirty concerts this year in our series. Look forward to seeing you in March.

Sincerely,

Phill Niblock

Above and right   Letters from Phill Niblock to Éliane Radigue, December 4, 1983.
                  Courtesy Fonds Éliane Radigue.

PHILL NIBLOCK   224 CENTRE STREET   NEW YORK CITY 10013

December 4th, 1983

Eliane Radique
22 rue Liancourt
Paris 75014

Dear Eliane,

We haven't set the exact dates for concerts in March but
I expect to start right about the 15th. So we could
say the 15th or 16th. But we could change it to match
your schedule if you'd like. The fee is $200 this year.
Am enclosing a more formal letter for you to use.
I'll leave New York about the 6th of April and come back
the 24th. I'm doing a concert in Paris on the 18th at
GERM, so I'll miss you. See you in March.

And merry christmas.

Philll

Eliane Radigue
22, rue Liancourt
750 4 PARIS
FRANCE

September 28 , 1984

Far West Translations
c o Jacob Needleman
2855 Jackson St, NO 302
San Francisco, California, USA

To whom it may concern :

As a composer, I am planning to make a work on the "Life of Milarepa", including texts, music, visual effects. For that purpose, I am requesting the authorization to use some quotes from the book published in 1979, The Life of Milarepa , in the new translation by Lobsang P. Lhalungpa.

Included here, you'll find a brief introduction to my career and to the project, but of course, I can provide you any further information about my work if you want it.

Lookink forward to hearing from you and knowing your conditions in using this text ,

Sincerely Yours,

[signature]

Eliane Radigue

Letter from Éliane Radigue to Far West Translations, September 28, 1984.
Courtesy Fonds Éliane Radigue.

Kensington, Février '83

Lama Kunga Rinpoche
254, Cambridge Ave.
Kensington, CA. 94708
Etats-Unis

Eliane Radigue
22, rue Liancourt
75014 - Paris
France

Je, soussigné Lama Kunga Rinpoche, autorise Eliane Radigue à utiliser dans le but d'une création artistique, les chants de Milarépa que j'ai traduits du Tibétain à l'Anglais et publiés en collaboration avec Brian Cutillo, sous le titre "Drinking the Mountain Stream", chez les Editions Lotsawa.
Ces chants sont "Mila's song in the rain", "Symbols for yogic experience", "Elimination of desire", "Song of the path guide" et " Journey inspired by a dream".

Il est entendu que je réserve tous droits de reproduction mécanique qui, si envisagée, fera l'objet d'un autre accord.

Lama Kunga Rinpoche

Letter from Lama Kunga Rinpoche to Éliane Radigue, February 1983. Courtesy Fonds Éliane Radigue.

Kensington, February '83

Lama Kunga Rinpoche
254 Cambridge Ave.
Kensington, CA. 94708
United States

Éliane Radigue

22, rue Liancourt
75014 - Paris
France

I, the undersigned Lama Kunga Rinpoche, authorize Éliane Radigue to use for the purposes of artistic creation, the songs of Milarépa that I translated from Tibetan to English and published in collaboration with Brian Cutillo, under the title "<u>Drinking the Mountain Stream</u>," through Editions Lotsawa.

These songs are "<u>Mila's song in the rain</u>," "<u>Symbols for yogic experience</u>," "<u>Elimination of desire</u>," "<u>Song of the path guide</u>" and "<u>Journey inspired by a dream</u>."

It is understood that I reserve all the rights of mechanical reproduction, which, if envisaged, will be the subject of another agreement.

Lama Kunga Rinpoche

Front covers for Éliane Radigue's *Songs of Milarepa* (Lovely Music, Ltd., 1983), *Jetsun Mila* (Lovely Music, Ltd., 2007), *Songs of Milarepa* (Lovely Music, Ltd., 1998), and *Mila's Journey Inspired by a Dream* (Lovely Music, Ltd., 1987).

LOVELY COMMUNICATIONS, LTD.
325 Spring Street New York, NY 10013
212.243.6153   Telex: 668420 ARTSVC

June 8, 1983

Ms Eliane Radigue
22, rue Liancourt
75014 Paris
France

Dear El ane

Excuse me for not answering sooner

Basical y, what I understand from your letter is that the money from the French government will go to performers to Lama Kunga, Bob, Laetitia, and Maggi That's fine. I can make an agreement with you that Lovely Music pays for the pressing The only problem, of course, is that I have got to wait until I can come up with money, and it will make the record go rather slowly

Would you please let me know if the record you got is all right? It is very important that I know that

Also, p ease send me whatever credits or notes you have as soon as possible That way, I will just be able to proceed little by ittle as the money comes in

Laetitia told me she had an idea for the cover which she could send me I am beginning to think of other ideas, so, again, please let me know if the pressing is OK, and send me your information

Love,

Mimi

Mimi

Letter from Mimi Johnson to Éliane Radigue, June 8, 1983. Courtesy Fonds Éliane Radigue.

FIVE SONGS OF MILAREPA

Tibetan singing : Lama Kunga Rinpoche English translator of the songs.
Recording : Laetitia Sonami and Maggi Payne.
English narrator : Robert Ashley
Electronic composition : Eliane Radigue

1. Mila s song in the rain. 20 min.
2. Song of the Path guides 20 min
3. Elimination of Desires 18 min.
4. Mila s journey inspired by a dream 60 min
5. Symbol for Yogic Experiences 30 min

EXPERIMENTAL INTERMEDIA FOUNDATION

Program for "Five Songs of Milarepa" with Éliane Radigue at Experimental Intermedia Foundation, New York, 1984. Courtesy Fonds Éliane Radigue.

LA MAISON FRANÇAISE
OF COLUMBIA UNIVERSITY

presents an

ELECTRONIC MUSIC

concert by composer

ELAINE RADIGUE

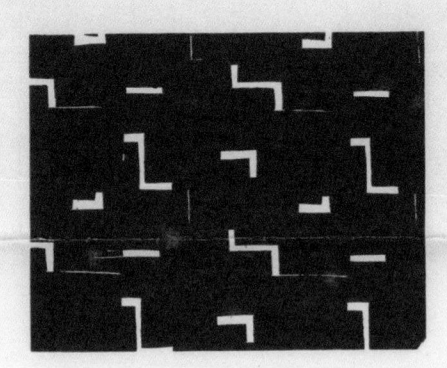

FIVE MILAREPA'S SONGS
Tibetan Singing: LAMA KUNGA RIMPOCHE
Recording: Laetitia de Compiègne & Maggie Payne
English Narrator: Robert Ashley

MONDAY, APRIL 2, 1984   8:00 p.m.
BUELL HALL LOUNGE, Tel.: 280-4482
Broadway at 116th Street, New York

Contribution: $3   Students and members: $1

HOW TO GET THERE   IRT Local #1 to Broadway and 116th Street
BUS #4 on Madison Ave to Broadway and 116th Street
BUS #104 on Broadway

Program for "Five Milarepa's Songs" [*sic*] with Éliane Radigue at La Maison Française of Columbia University, New York, April 2, 1984. Courtesy Fonds Éliane Radigue.

SONGS OF MILAREPA
Éliane Radigue

Milarepa is a great saint and poet of Tibet who lived in the eleventh century. His autobiography, the *Mila Kabum*, or *Namthar*, as told to his closest disciple, Rechungpa, has been translated into several Western languages. In this story of Milarepa's life, we can see how, through years dedicated to meditation and related practices in the solitude of the mountains, subjecting himself to the severest form of asceticism, Milarepa achieved the highest attainable illumination and the mental power that enabled him to guide innumerable disciples. His ability to present complex teachings in a simple, lucid style is astonishing. He had a fine voice and loved to sing. When his patrons and disciples made a request or asked him a question, he answered in spontaneously composed, free-flowing poems or lyric songs. It is said that he composed 100,000 songs to communicate his ideas in his teachings and conversations.

The large collection of stories and songs, *The Jetsun Gurbum*, was translated first into English by Garma C.C. Chang. There is also a rare, little-known collection, *Miraculous Journey: Further Stories and Songs of Milarepa, Yogin, Poet, and Teacher of Tibet* (1986), which existed in an oral state longer than the other works. *Drinking the Mountain Stream: Songs of Tibet's Beloved Saint, Milarepa* (1978, Lotsawa Publications), from which the songs on this album were taken, is the first English translation by Lama Kunga Rinpoche and Brian Cutillo.

Lama Kunga Rinpoche has kindly agreed to record his singing in Tibetan, and Robert Ashley has given his voice to the English translation of these songs.

Poster for "Chants de Milarepa" with Éliane Radigue at GERM, Paris, May 15, 1984.
Courtesy Fonds Éliane Radigue.

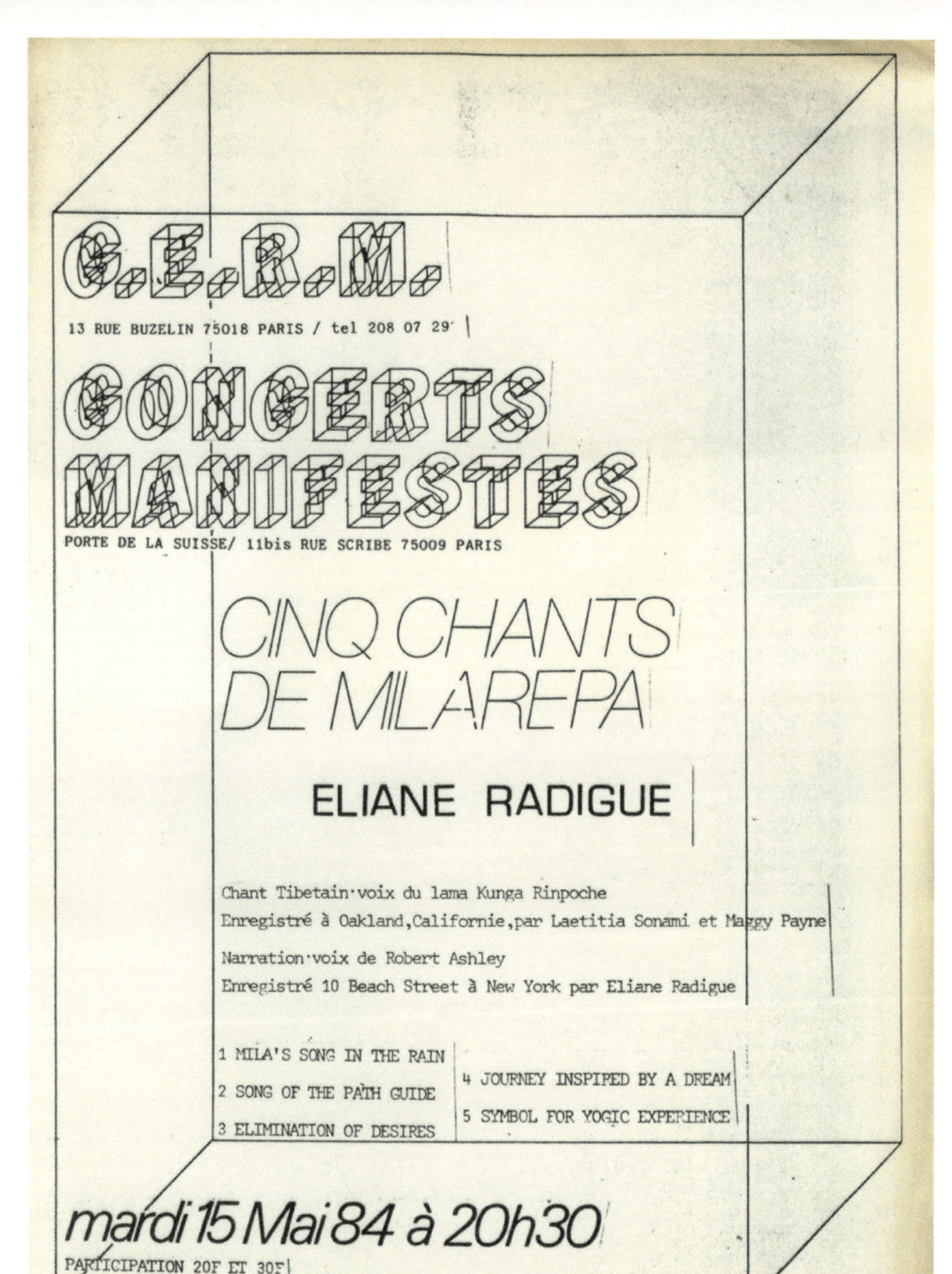

Poster for "Cinq Chants de Milarepa" with Éliane Radigue at GERM, Paris, May 15, 1984.
Courtesy Fonds Éliane Radigue.

THE LIFE OF MILAREPA

Milarepa was a great yogi and poet of Tibet who ived
in the 11th century. The story of his life as told to
his closest disciple, Rechungpa, represents one of the
most famous works w thin T betan culture

The "Mila Kabum", or "Namthar", has been translated into severa Western anguages, including Engl sh and
French. In this story of Mi arepa's ife, we can see
how in one lifetime one can accomplish amazing deeds
through ascetic pract ses and spiritua endeavors.

It seems interesting to bring to Western audiences the
knowledge of this story which belongs to our human patri-
mony. For this purpose, a work including texts, music,
and visua effects within an adaptation of the basic
texts will be simu taneously worked out in English and
in French. The Lobsang Lha ungpa translation wil be
used for the Engl sh vers on and the Jaques Bacot translation will be used for the French version. This adaptation should be narrated either in French or in English.
The music will be made of e ectronic means. Tibetan
songs will be inc uded in the or ginal and traditional
way of Tibetan singing by record ng the voice of a Tibetan
lama. The visual effects, including s ides from T bet,
should recreate the orig nal ambience n which Milarepa
has l ved About two to three years will be necessary
to achieve this project The piece wil be approximately
one and a half to two hours in length.

Éliane Radigue, typewritten notes for *Songs of Milarepa*, ca. 1980s. Courtesy Fonds Éliane Radigue.

Milarepa's Life

Here included is a cassette containing a sample of the work
It cannot be considered as final and may be subject to some
modifications It gives only the "musical color" up to the third
part of the work , which will incude nine parts, namely :

1   Birth and youth
2   Misdeeds
3   Meeting with the gourou
4   Ordeals
5   Practice
6   Visit to homeland
7   Retreats
8   Meditation
9   Nirvana-Death

Above and right   Éliane Radigue, typewritten notes for *Songs of Milarepa*, ca. 1980s.
Courtesy Fonds Éliane Radigue.

Adaptation of the texts English and French	Gérard Fournaison
English narrator	Robert Ashley
French narrator	Danielle Van Bercheycke
Tibetan Songs	Lama Kunga Rinpoche
Visual effects	Laeticia de Compiègne
Music composer	Eliane Radigue
Technical assistance	Marc moreau

Éliane Radigue
22, rue Liancourt
75014 Paris

octobre 22 -

Dear Mimi,

I was so happy to receive the record you sent to Yves. Thank you very much Mimi. Yves will be coming back France next week, around October 29th so, if there would be some message... or new developpement you could call him before he'll leave New York.

I am actually trying to figure out the schedule of my tour over States to present these new works next spring. Actually the only precise date I have is April 12 in Los Angeles. So I try to organise everything around this date. I wrote to Laetitia to ask her if she could arrange something in San Francisco or other place in Area Bay in this period, if by chance you talk with her, or if you have any suggestion could you please check it ? Could you also please check what could be done over New York, I'll like to present this work first in new york, namely anywhere at the end of March or early April; it is so difficult to do this from so far. I told you I think that Phill Niblock was willing to present it, and we thought also may be "The Kitchen". What do you think ? Excuse me to bother you with all that, but the time seems now rather short ahead and I'll be very gratefull to you if you could help.
May be I'll call you sometime this week it will be easier. Many thanks Mimi dear Mimi, with my very best thoughts for you and Bob.

with love

Eliane

Letter from Éliane Radigue to Mimi Johnson, November 10, 1984. Courtesy Fonds Éliane Radigue.

Eliane Radigue
22, rue Liancourt
75014 Paris

Dear Mimi,

I was so happy to receive the record you sent to Yves. Thank you very much Mimi. Yves will be coming back France next week, around October 29th so, if there would be some message . . . or new developpement [sic] you could call him before he'll leave New York.

I am actually trying to figure out the schedule of my tour over [in the] States to present these new works next Spring. Actually the only precise date I have is April 12 in Los Angeles. So I try to organise everything around this date. I wrote to Laetitia to ask her if she could arrange something in San Francisco or other place in Area Bay in this period, if by chance you talk with her, or if you have any suggestion could you please check it? Could you also please check what could be done over New York, I'll like to present this work first in New York, namely anytime at the end of March or early Aril [sic]; it is so difficult to do this from so far. I told you I think that Phill Nibblock [sic] was willing to present it, and we thought also maybe "The Kitchen". What do you think? Excuse me to bother you with all that, but the time seems now rather short ahead and I'll be very gratefull [sic] to you if you could help. Maybe I'll call you sometime this week it will be easier. Many thanks again dear Mimi, with my very best thoughts for you and Bob.

with Love
Éliane

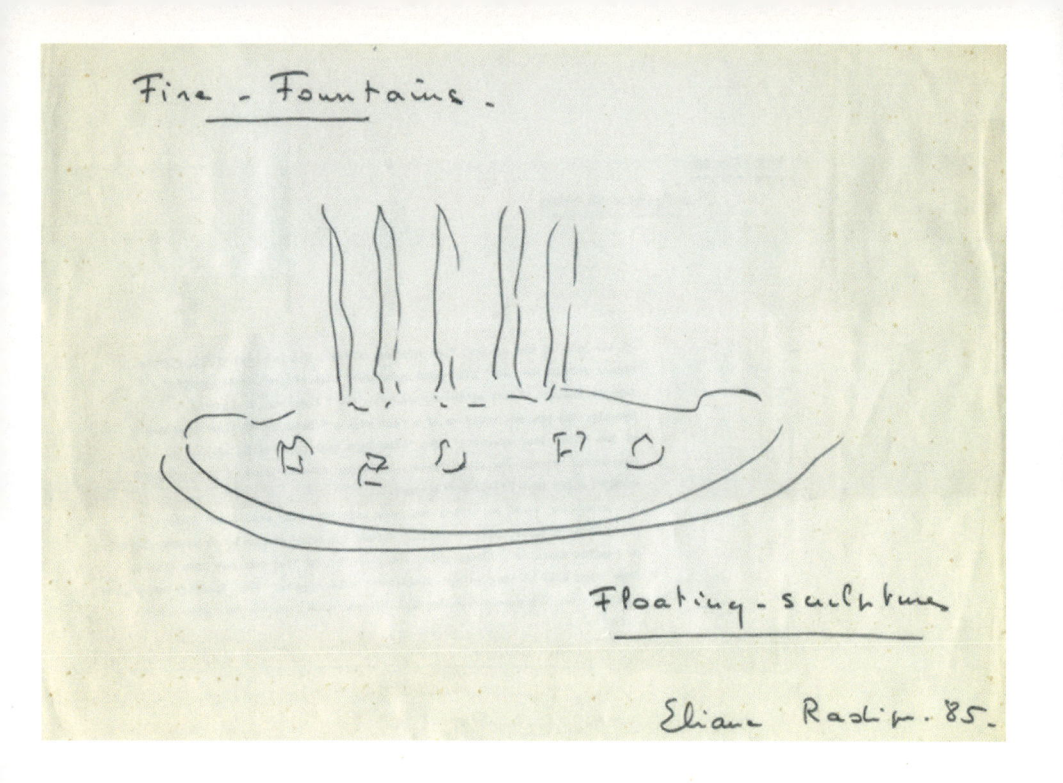

Éliane Radigue, notes for "Fire Fountains," 1985. Courtesy Fonds Éliane Radigue.

FIRE FOUNTAINS

and FLOATINGS SCULPTURES

In the line of the project "Les paroles gelées", and inspired by Maggy Payne's actual researches on " fire-loud speakers", this project would involved a team including visual artist to conceive the " floatings sculptures "
Roughly, the project would be of a pond with a " fountain of fire" produced by the "fire- loud speakers" The "Floatings sculptures would contain an autonomous reproducing sound system, including several types of loud speakers amongst which some "In-water" systems
The monotoring would be from a magnetic induction ring around the pound, transmiting several trcks of musical stream (produced either by an analog-digital or numeric computer Always u ing the principle of "les musiques sans fins".
Each track will be read by the independant units, namely "the floatings sculptures" equiped a necessary de-coder, to read its own track from the "magnetic ring" induction

Program *(front)* for "Jetsun Mila" with Éliane Radigue at GERM, Paris, June 10, 1986. Courtesy Fonds Éliane Radigue.

```
                    JETSUN MILA
                    ============


   Oeuvre  nsp rée de  a v e de M  arepa

   M  arepa est un grand yogu  et poète qui vécut au T bet au IIème
   s èc e

   L histo re de sa vie, te  e qu'el e fut racontée à son p us proche di-
   sc p e, Rechungpa, représente un des ouvrages les p us popu aire de la
   cu ture T bétaine

   Le "M  a Kabum" ou "Namthar" fut un des premiers ouvrages traduit en
    angue occ denta e. Dans cette histoire de  a vie de Mi arepa, faits
    égenda res et réels sont étroitement mêlés

   D'une durée de 80 minutes environ, cette évocat on comprend 9 "temps",
   précédés d'un pré ude, correspondant aux grandes périodes de  a vie du
   cé èbre yogui

   Ces 9 pér odes s'enchaînent musicalement sans discontinuité, l'une
   donnant nature lement naissance à  'autre


                            Pré ude

                         1  Les origines
                         2   es méfaits
                         3  Rencontre avec Marpa
                         4  Les épreuves
                         5  La prat que
                         6  Visite au pays nata
                         7  Les retra tes
                         8  La réa isation
                         9  La mort




       mixage final : atelier GERM
       assistance technique : MARC MOREAU
```

Program *(back)* for "Jetsun Mila" with Éliane Radigue at GERM, Paris, June 10, 1986. Courtesy Fonds Éliane Radigue.

EXPERIMENTAL INTERMEDIA

We're beg nn ng our fifteenth anniversary season The first series of formal (?) concerts at the Centre Street studios of EIF was n December of 1973. This month, we will present the composers from that first series with the addition of two other kindred spirits Since that time we have presented more than six hundred performances, curated by Phill Niblock.

DECEMBER 1988

JON GIBSON   **TUE 13**
SOME OLD, SOME NEW, SOME SOLO, SOME .

JOEL CHADABE   **WED 14**
LIVE ELECTRON C PERFORMANCE WITH COMPUTERS AND MUSICIANS

GARRETT LIST   **THU 15**
SOLO TROMBONE AND SOLO VOICE WITH SEQUENCER, PLAYING THE HUMAN AFFA R

RHYS CHATHAM   **FRI 16**
TWO GONGS, 1971, A RECREATION OF THE CONCERT OF F FTEEN YEARS AGO WITH THE OR G NAL PERFORMERS, YOSHI WADA

DAVID GIBSON   **SUN 18**
SOLO ON A FOR F VE (NO MORE HANG NG PIANOS, WE'RE TO OLD AND THEY'RE TO HEAVY)

DAVID BEHRMAN   **MON 19**
OUT OF TOWN N BERLIN, BUT MAY BE BACK

ELIANE RADIGUE   **TUE 20**
KYEMA, NTERMEDIATE STATES

PHILL NIBLOCK   **WED 21**
OWED TO THE FIFTEENTH ANNIVERSARY, EIGHT HOURS OF MUSIC AND F LM, BEGINNING AT 6PM

with support from the New York State Counci on the Arts and the National Endowment for the Arts and the Mary Flagler Cary Charitable Trust

224 CENTRE STREET AT GRAND   NEW YORK   212 431 5127   9PM $3

Flyer for concert series at Experimental Intermedia Foundation, New York, December 13–21, 1988. Courtesy Fonds Éliane Radigue.

15TH YEAR OF AVANT-GARDE
John Rockwell

In December 1973, the composer and filmmaker Phill Niblock offered a series of concerts at his loft at 224 Centre Street. The Niblock loft concerts have continued as a branch of the Experimental Intermedia Foundation and have become a small but telling part of New York's musical avant-garde.

This month, to mark the 15th anniversary of those first concerts, Mr. Niblock reassembled all but one of the original composer-performers (the missing link was Charlemagne Palestine) and added two more longtime associates of that group (Éliane Radigue and David Gibson) to present an eight-concert retrospective.

This critic, who reviewed Mr. Niblock's own concert in the 1973 series, attended the final three events in the series, which began with Jon Gibson on Dec. 13 and continued with Joel Chadabe, Garrett List, Rhys Chatham, and David Gibson before reaching the final trilogy—David Behrman on Monday, Ms. Radigue on Tuesday and Mr. Niblock on Wednesday.

Mr. Niblock's concerts have always prided themselves on their scruffy casualness: the chairs are ratty (though comfortable), the loft could be cleaner, the concerts begin late and one never quite knows from either the erratic programs or the vague announcements just what is being played or who is playing it. But all this informality encourages conversation and inquiry, and the relaxed circumstances foster true experimentation.

For this series, Mr. Niblock asked all the composers to present work from 1973 or thereabouts as well as newer pieces. There are significant differences among these musicians, especially as they have evolved in the intervening years. But what united them, and especially the final three, was more significant.

All three composers use electronic means; their music issues forth from loudspeakers, with which Mr. Niblock's loft is admirably outfitted. They all deal in slowly unfurling planes of sound; shifting textures without the narrative drama of conventional Western music. This is true Minimalism, not the minimalist subcategory of kinetically propulsive music espoused by composers like Steve Reich and Philip Glass.

Mr. Behrman presented two pieces he has recorded, "Figure in a Clearing" (1977) and "Leapday Night" (1985). Both involve the interaction of a live performer with a microcomputer program that accompanies (in 1977) or actually responds (in 1985). The performers were Ben Neill for "Leapday Night," playing his specially designed "mutantrumpet," with its three bells and two sets of valves, and David Gibson, playing the cello, in "Figure."

Both soloists are sensitive performers, deeply attuned to the quiescence that lies at the root of Mr. Behrman's art. And art it is: over the years, no electronic composer has made more poetic uses of the now-common interaction of live musicians and electronic circuitry.

Ms. Radigue, who is from Paris, and Mr. Niblock are like soft and loud siblings. Both make taped music (although a live flutist piped along during one portion of the bits I sampled from Mr. Niblock's eight-hour performance Wednesday). This is dense, layered sound, lacking harmonies in the conventional sense but dealing instead in shifting sonorous clouds, sometimes consonant and sometimes wildly dissonant.

But there are big differences. Ms. Radigue, who offered one brand-new, hourlong piece called *Kyema* and one shorter effort from 1973, plays at the lower levels of audibility. Hers is a music of whispering subtlety, toying with our limits of perception. Yet within her delicately restricted dynamic range, big dramas take place.

However she actually assembles her tapes, they sound like a particularly refined extension of the *musique concrète* that Pierre Schaeffer made in the 1950s. There are intimations of throbbing machines and whispering winds and cosmic heartbeats and animal groans, yet all within the most abstract of contexts.

Mr. Niblock plays his tapes to accompany his films, or vice versa. The films, which now include both large-screen projections and various television monitors, offer competing images shot around the world, mostly of people laboring at humble tasks.

The music, dating from various points along the 15-year continuum, consists of recordings of sustaining instruments (trombone, cello, flute, etc.) with many of their attacks and decays clipped off to form steady streams of sound. But at the volume Mr. Niblock plays his tapes, and with the density of the intervals, the music sets up all manner of shimmering, pulsing acoustical beats and overtones. By now, he seems to have tuned his room more exactly than he once had; in any event, his music, which had seemed sometimes uneventful on previous occasions, glowed with powerful life on Wednesday.

New York Times, December 23, 1988

ELIANE RADIGUE
electronica

zondag 2 april 1989
15.30 uur ƒ 7,50 of ƒ 12,50
voor een passepartout

Elektra is een serie van 3 concerten met electronische muziek van Eliane Radigue Caroline Wilkins en Sonja Mutsaerts en georganiseerd in samenwerking met Ooyevaer Desk en Theater Zeebelt Den Haag

Eliane Radigue (Parijs) studeerde electroacoustische muziektechnieken aan de Studio d Essai van de RTB onder leiding van Pierre Schaeffer. Eliane Radigue werkt met electronische muziek op tape Zij combineert de geluiden van verschillende oneindige tapes tot muziek die klinkt als een continue stroom van geluid Werk van Eliane Radigue was eerder te horen in het Apollohuis in 1985

Jetsun Mila is geïnspireerd op de Tibetaanse dichte en yoga-beoefenaar M larepa, die leefde in de 11e eeuw De geschiedenis en de legenden over Milarepa, verteld door zijn volgel ng Rechungpa, vormen een van de popula rste werken van de Tibetaanse cultuu

Jetsun M la' is uitgebracht op cassette bij Lovely Music LMC2003

HET APOLLOHUIS
TONGELRESESTRAAT 81 EINDHOVEN
5613 DB. H O L L A N D
TELEFOON 040-440393

Dit concert is tot stand gekomen met financiële steun van de provincie Noord-Brabant.

Postcard *(front and back)* for "Elektra" with Éliane Radigue at Het Apollohuis, Eindhoven, April 2, 1989. Courtesy Fonds Éliane Radigue.

CONCERT PRIVE

Madame Colette de Charnières

et

le G E R M.

vous invitent à la première audition en France

de

K Y E M A

Etats Intermédiaires

d' E L I A N E   R A D I G U E

Le mardi 9 Mai à 20h 30

(durée 60 mns)

2, avenue Frédéric Le Play
75007 Paris

Métro   Ecole Militaire

Program for "Kyema" with Éliane Radigue at GERM, Paris, May 9, 1989.
Courtesy Fonds Éliane Radigue.

K Y E M A

Etats ntermédia res

. à mon fils, YVES ARMAN

Inspirée du texte-racine du BARDO - THODOL (le Livre des Morts Tibètains), cette pièce évoque les six états intermédiaires qui constituent la "continuité existentielle" de 'être

Achevée en octobre 1988, "KYEMA" a été présentée en décembre 1988 à San Francisco (CA), puis New York (NY)

Six états intermédiaires

1- KYENE   La Naissance

2- MILAM   Le Rêve

3- SAMTEN   La Contemplation - Méditation

4- CHIKAI   La Mort

5- CHÖNYE   . La Claire Lumière

6- SIPPAÏ   Traversée et Retour

Christian Marclay
304 East 5th St 4B
New York, NY 10003

Chère Élianne Radigue,
merci infiniment de nous avoir prêté votre disque pour l'exposition "Extended Play". Vous trouverez ci-joint une critique de presse. Un catalogue a été publié, malheureusement il est en réimpression, il vous sera envoyé en septembre. Je regrette d'avoir mis si longtemps pour vous rendre ce disque, j'attendais ma venue en Europe pour vous l'envoyer avec plus de sécurité.
L'exposition a eu beaucoup de succès, l'article Tichu vous donnera une idée du context en attendant le catalogue.

Très cordialement,
Christian Marclay

Letter from Christian Marclay to Éliane Radigue, ca. 1990s. Courtesy Fonds Éliane Radigue.

Christian Marclay
304 East 5th St. 4B
New York, NY 10003

          Dear Elianne [sic] Radigue,
Infinite thanks for lending us your disc for the exhibition "Extended Play." You'll find enclosed a press review. A catalogue was published, unfortunately it is being reprinted, it will be sent to you in September. I regret taking such a long time to return the disc to you, I waited until coming to Europe to send it more securely.
         The exhibition was very successful, the enclosed article will give you an idea of the context while you wait for the catalogue.

         Very cordially,

         Christian Marclay

SAMSARA ON THE SYNTHESIZER
Neil Strauss

Imagine a rope stretched snugly against the Earth along the equator. Now imagine a piece one yard long added to that rope. If the rope was kept tight and in a circular shape, how far above the surface of the Earth would it be? One might think the distance would be imperceptible, but actually the rope would rest nearly six inches above the Earth's surface.

Similarly, six words are enough to rend all the earthly thoughts, ambitions, and material cohesiveness from a person's life. After a concert at Mills College in 1974, a group of people came up to composer Éliane Radigue and told her, "You're not doing your music yourself." This blow left an indelible impression on her. She felt that she was getting inspiration then, but she didn't know from where it came. The people, it turns out, were studying Tibetan Buddhism and they gave Radigue the address of a center in Paris which she instantly visited upon returning home. Soon afterward, she left her musical and material world to pursue a spiritual life dedicated to Tibetan Buddhism.

But there's a catch to the rope riddle: knowing the right answer is not enough. We have a mental picture of the way things are supposed to be, but the truth doesn't always dissolve our illusions. The difficulty is not in finding the answer, but in confronting the habits and assumptions embedded in our psyches. When Radigue found the same old sounds running through her head during the ensuing years of musical abstinence and spiritual practice, she tried to let them go, but was unable to. Even her lama recognized the dilemma; after four years he decided that Radigue should go back to music even though her new life had no need for it.

So, she returned, reluctantly, to her analog ARP synthesizer and gave freedom to the trains of sounds that were uncontrollably running through her mind. The only changes in the music were the text and source material for the works—such as the life of the eleventh-century Tibetan master Milarepa, photographs of sacred places in Tibet, and the six intermediate states in the Buddhist continuum of existence. The rest was the same electronic flow of sounds and subtleties, technically difficult because they were mere physical manifestations of imagined and inspired sounds.

In Tibetan Buddhism, music is used for ritual activity and spiritual growth. Radigue admits that her music is profane, but she cannot escape the internal impulse that draws her to her synthesizer, no matter how much it troubles her.

What takes place is a compromise between the ancient and the new, the spiritual and the material. These separate forces in her life make allowances for one another, perhaps even engage in a dialectic. So, even though different spiritual lifestyles can be chosen like food off a menu in today's society, the modern myths of science and individuality are not simply superseded by a more spiritual way of thinking. Instead, a bargain is struck, whereby both disparate forces grow concurrently, and redirect each other. Radigue's is not an isolated case, either; the Gyuto Tibetan Monks are experiencing the same dilemma, except in reverse, as they tour the States entertaining in commercial venues and performing with Philip Glass, Kitaro, and Grateful Dead drummer Mickey Hart. As the world's cultures bleed like colored shirts in a hot wash, one wonders what fashion statement will emerge.

EAR Magazine, June 1990

Dear Phill –

Thank you for your sending and Thanks to Neil Strauss if he agrees to use his text. But then is a confusion to the meaning of Kyema, due to me. and the direct subtitle, may be we should put " or 6 Intermediate States " to avoid this confusion

I hope that Neil will agree to correct this part of his text (from the quote "Kyema" at the bottom of the first page to the first line of second page – Of course he can rewrite it to correct my English, but the real meaning is important also ---

Letter from Éliane Radigue to Phill Niblock, ca. 1990. Courtesy Fonds Éliane Radigue.

Front cover for Éliane Radigue's *Kyema, Intermediate States* (XI Records, 1990).

Poster for "Kailasha" with Éliane Radigue at Mills College, Oakland, March 19, 1991.
Courtesy Fonds Éliane Radigue.

The Center for New Music & Audio Technologies CNMAT
University of California Berkeley • Department of Music

Eliane Radigue
"Koume"

The French composer wi present her atest electron c
composition — the th rd part of her triology on death

March 8, 1994   **8:30 pm**

CNMAT
1750 Arch Street   5 0-643-9990
Berkeley CA 94709   Limited Seating

Postcard for "Koumé" with Éliane Radigue at the Center for New Music & Audio Technologies, Berkeley, March 8, 1994. Courtesy Fonds Éliane Radigue.

CONCERT PRIVE

Patrice et Elisabeth de Laage

Vous nvitent à 'audition

de

"KOUME"

"Ô Mort, où est ta victoire ?"

corynthiens xv

d' Eliane RADIGUE

Le jeudi 9 juin 1994 à 20h30

(durée 51 minutes)

2, avenue Frédéric Le Play
75007 Paris

Réponse souhaitée au 47 05 66 00

KOUME

"Ô Mort, où est ta victoire ?"

Corynthiens XV)

.. à Colette de Charnières

3ème partie de la "Trilogie de la Mort"

Oeuvre de cendres - Des cendres de l'illusion devenue lumière - Des-cendre au plus profond des sources de la vie. Là où naît la Mort, où Mort devient naissance. Activement re-commencement - Eternité d'un perpétuel de-venir

I   "Certainement l'homme se promène parmi ce qui n'est que apparence"

(Psaumes XXXIV 7)

II - "Qua resurget ex favilla judicantus homo reus"

(Messe de Requiem)

III   "Have lightning ans thunders their fury forgotten"

(Passion selon Saint Mathieu)

IV   "Ô Mort, où est ta victoire ?"

Commande réalisée au studio CIRM à Nice

Program for private concert of "Koumé," Paris, June 9, 1994. Courtesy Fonds Éliane Radigue.

KOUME 3ème partie de la trilogie de la Mort

TRILOGIE DE LA MORT

" aller au delà de la mort dans cette vie même, dépasser la dichotomie de la vie et de la mort, afin de devenir témoin de la vie . " Thomas Merton

Les trois parties de la Trilogie de la Mort se composent de

Kyema - La première partie est inspirée du Bardo Thodol, livre des Morts Tibétain et représente l'aspect théorique et littéraire de cette Trilogie. Achevée en 1988.

Kailasha - La seconde partie, structurée selon un pèlerinage imaginaire autour du Mont Kailash, l'une des montagnes les plus sacrées des Himalayas est empreinte d'un réel vécu et retrace l'ambivalence d'une traversée émotionnelle Achevée en 1991.

Koumé - La troisième partie se voudrait l'expression du pouvoir transcendant de la Mort dans la vie même, de la Vie sur la mort même Achevée en 1993.

L ntégrale de cette trilogie a été présentée au Monastère de Cimiez et au Musée d'Art Contemporain à Nice dans le cadre du Festival MANCA en Novembre 1993.

Merci au GERM, et à Pierre Mariétan, d'avoir bien voulu réaliser 'installation sonore de ce concert

.. ***Eliane Radigue*** propose des musiques à la fois sombres, méditatives et infiniment subtiles. D'une grande exigence, elle entraîne ses auditeurs dans un voyage intérieur, au coeur de sons incroyablement étirés, qui changent la perception du temps et permettent de s'immerger dans un univers sonore épuré, profondément humain

La musique contemporaine.

M chel Thion

Program for private concert of "Koumé," Paris, June 9, 1994. Courtesy Fonds Éliane Radigue.

Top   Éliane Radigue with Luc Martinez at Festival Manca, Nice. Courtesy Fonds Éliane Radigue.
Bottom Éliane Radigue at Festival Manca, Nice. Courtesy Fonds Éliane Radigue.

Top   Éliane Radigue with Michel Redolfi and Luc Martinez, October 15, 1992. Courtesy Fonds Éliane Radigue.

Bottom   Éliane Radigue with Morton Subotnick and Joan La Barbara, October 15, 1992. Courtesy Fonds Éliane Radigue.

Top   Éliane Radigue with Daniel Charles at Festival Manca, Nice.

Bottom Éliane Radigue with unknown man, Michel Redolfi (partially blocked), Beatrice Heiligers, and unknown woman, October 15, 1992. Courtesy Fonds Éliane Radigue.

Front cover for Éliane Radigue's *Trilogie de la Mort* (XI Records, 1998).

Eliane Radigue

Wednesday January 25th
1:00pm
ROD

L'île re-sonante
(analog electronic music)

"Radigue's works nduce in the listener an altered state of ecstatic spirituality " - *Kyle Gann*
Radigue creates "A steady stream of sonic activity taking place right at the edge of one's perception " *New York Times*

Flyer for "L'île re-sonante (analog electronic music)" with Éliane Radigue at ROD, January 25, 2006. Courtesy Fonds Éliane Radigue.

Éliane Radigue, ca. 1989. Photo: Marc Moreau. Courtesy Fonds Éliane Radigue.

INTERVIEW WITH ÉLIANE RADIGUE
Ian Nagoski

Ian Nagoski's interview with Éliane Radigue was conducted in 1998 for *Halana* magazine, published in 2009 by *Yeti* magazine, and reprinted in 2017 in the inaugural anthology of Blank Forms Editions. All three aforementioned publications are now out of print—the first two folded, and the last sold out. Nearly thirty years after its initial conception, however, the interview stands as much as a testament to the gradual, deliberate growth of Radigue's artistry as to the tenacity of young writers like Nagoski, who sought this conversation with Radigue across continents in his early twenties.

> Once upon a time, there were some kids who found a shell. Some of them collected the shell. Some disfigured it. Others just threw it. The object became enormous, awful, voracious, insignificant, discouraging, venomous . . . There was a naive with blond hair, alone, for herself. The shell intact at her ear, pursuing, inexorably, backwards and against any fate, the reassuring, respectable sound of the blood. For Éliane, always lost and found. Faithfully, Pierre Schaeffer.
>
> —Pierre Schaeffer's dedication in Éliane Radigue's copy of *Traité des objets musicaux*

At the age of twenty-one, my education had turned out to be a total failure. I had just given up after six months of studying with La Monte Young and Marian Zazeela, after having dropped out of high school at sixteen and then dropping out of a state university at twenty. I was living in my parents' attic when I spoke to my friend Jason Glover on the phone—he told me about Éliane Radigue's recording *Kyema* (1988). He was insistent that it was something I should hear. He could not have been more right.

Almost two years later, in 1998, my parents took my younger twin sisters to Paris as a gift for their twenty-first birthdays. They told me I could come, too, because the difference in cost to bring one more person was somehow negligible. I didn't see any particular reason to go until I remembered that Éliane Radigue lived in Paris. So, I sent her an earnest letter asking her for an interview, telling her how much I loved *Kyema* and *Biogenesis* (1973), the two of her works available at the time, as well as *Jetsun Mila* (1987), which I had managed to track down despite being out of print. She wrote back and very sweetly said, "No, thank you. No one is interested in my work."

I wrote back, "I am interested. And if I am interested, others will be. Please." I let her know that I would arrive on a particular weekend in April, and she wrote back consenting to the interview. Shortly thereafter, I met Phill Niblock, who had published *Kyema* on his label XI Records in 1990. I asked him what I should know about Éliane in advance. There was nothing published about her except for Tom Johnson's reviews of her concerts in the seventies collected in his 1989 book *The Voice of New Music*. Phill said, first of all, that her name was not "Elayne Radigyoo," as I had pronounced it; then he added, "She hates speaking to anyone, particularly in English." He didn't say anything else.

Immediately upon arriving in Paris for the weekend in question, I phoned Éliane from my hotel room: no answer. Later that night, I tried again: no answer. The next morning, I phoned again with the same result. I also phoned the Erik Satie museum: it was not open. So, I phoned Éliane again. Nothing. I got a map and started walking to the address that I had for her.

It was a long walk, an hour or so. When I arrived, I rang the buzzer, and there was no answer. I found her mailbox and saw that it was stuffed. Backing away from the apartment building, I looked up and saw Buddhist stickers in the window. This was definitely her place, I thought, but she wasn't home. I scrawled a note saying I had arrived and hoped to speak with her and jammed it in the box with the other mail. I left and, later, listened to Jean Guillou play organ at Saint-Eustache, attended Easter Mass at Notre Dame, and looked at the instruments in the Cité de la Musique—including the old GRM (Groupe de Recherches de Musicales) mixing desk. That was my trip to Paris. Not bad, but not why I came.

About a week after I got home, a postcard arrived from Éliane apologizing. She had forgotten that I'd be in Paris on Easter weekend and had gone to visit her daughter. I wrote back asking if we could do the interview by phone. She consented. Nearly a year after I first wrote to her, we spoke on the phone for the first and only time.

The magazine for which I conducted the phone interview, *Halana*, folded shortly after the interview took place, before it could be published. A recording of Éliane's *Ψ 847* (1973) was supposed to have been issued in an edited, one-hour edition with the magazine. Both the interview and *Ψ 847* remained unpublished for years and years. It pained me. When I finally met Éliane at her apartment in 2009, I was deeply embarrassed to admit—eye to eye—the total failure of the project.

Now, nearly twenty years have gone by since I first spoke to her on the phone. I am middle-aged; nearly all her music has now been released to the world. I admire every bit of it, and a much larger audience has finally given her the love and recognition she deserves. During this time, her work evolved away from the synthesizer that had been central to it for decades and into collaborations with instrumentalists, and her considerable oeuvre has been catalogued and largely released to the public, creating a thorough discography of new and old work. This conversation was, at the time, a window into one of the most extraordinary and forceful minds in European music.

ÉLIANE RADIGUE
As far as I can remember, one of my first memories with music was when I was a very little girl. I was going through the garden under the long beans growing there with my teddy bear, and I was chanting some sort of song that I was just inventing, to my teddy bear. I was somewhere between three and five. I remember this and watching the clouds in the sky. That was the beginning. But that was long, long, long, *long* ago!

IAN NAGOSKI
Did your parents get you music lessons?

ÉR No. I am from a middle-class family. My parents were business people, and I was not helped much on that level. My coming to music has been mainly from my will. I am rather stubborn. I had some piano lessons, of course. I remember that my teacher was very fond of me, and I now understand why. I know now what a tremendous pleasure it is to give lessons to someone who really wants to learn.

IN You were a good student?

ÉR I don't know if I was a *good* student, but I was passionate. If you see someone who is passionate, you like it, no?

IN How did you begin to study with Pierre Schaeffer?

ÉR I was in my twenties. My husband [Armand Fernandez] and I were living in Nice at the time—a big provincial town, but touristy. I was a young mother: I already had three children who were very near in age to one another, with just about a year between them. I was taking care of them at home and listening to radio broadcasts, and one morning, I heard something tremendous. It was Pierre Schaeffer, talking and presenting his work. It was 1954, '55, something like that. At that time, I was more or less writing with the twelve tones on paper, and I found what I was doing a little bit frustrating. But what Pierre Schaeffer was doing was something absolutely fantastic. In life, when things are ripe or ready, they happen.

During those same years—around '55—my parents were still living in Paris, and I came to Paris regularly to visit them with my children. One night I was invited by a friend to a lecture with Lanza del Vasto, a personality involved in

Hinduism in France in that period. I went to this roundtable lecture that included Luc Dietrich, a French writer who was also into spiritual philosophy, and the most fantastic thing happened. Who did I see at this table but Pierre Schaeffer himself! At the end of the lecture, I asked my friend, "Do you, by chance, know Pierre Schaeffer?" And she said, "Yes, I was just with him for dinner tonight." I said [*laughs*], "Okay! Introduce me to him!"

IN   Hearing him on the radio was the first time you had heard *musique concrète*?

ÉR   That was the first I heard about *musique concrète*, and the very same year, a few months later, I happened to meet him. I was so fond of the sounds I had heard. I guess it was something like his *Étude aux chemins de fer* [1948] or "Étude pathétique" [1948], something like that—early pieces, from the late forties. And I was just as involved with what he was saying as I was with the music. Pierre Schaeffer was a wonderful, very bright person.

IN   How did he react to you approaching him?

ÉR   He was pleased. At that time, he appeared quite old, even though he was just around forty or fifty. When you're in your twenties, everyone above twenty-five is old. So, for me, he was already an old man—and I was a young woman! Anyone who has been working in a marginal sort of way all their life is pleased to see young people take an interest in their work; immediately, he took me on as a student. I went to the Studio d'Essai de la rue de l'Université in Paris—at that time, it was not the GRM, it was the Studio d'Essai. I had my first informal lesson. At that time, there were not very formal teachings about this discipline. There were only a few people who had interest, who came to watch and listen and try to get involved. There was no frame of teaching around it. The lessons were simply about being in the place, listening, and following what was going on. And participating. I cut my first magnetic tape there. I made my first edits and started to learn all of the technical processes necessary for this way of making something out of sounds.

    Around this time something very funny happened. After I had this introduction to the techniques, Pierre Schaeffer wrote a letter on my behalf to a radio station in Nice. Studio d'Essai was the only place where I could use these instruments at the time because they were very, very expensive. A tape recorder cost a fortune; *everything* cost a fortune. But I had a nice letter for the director of the station from Pierre Schaeffer himself. When I visited and gave the director the letter, he was not at all convinced. He was polite, but he made me understand that they were making very *serious* things, and they didn't have time to waste with such baloney! [*Laughs.*] So, I went back to writing my work on paper, waiting, and dreaming for the time I would be able to get the equipment that would allow me to do what I really wanted to do. I just had to wait and see. From time to time, when I came to Paris to visit my parents, I visited the Studio d'Essai. I would visit Pierre Schaeffer and Pierre Henry, cut a little tape, do little things.

IN How do you remember your pieces from that time?

ÉR I don't have any real memories, I must say. The only thing I know, which is strange, is that one of the edits I was doing at the time was used by Pierre Henry, like a quote. He used quite a few of my sounds in his own things. But that was it. Nothing remains of that period.

IN What happened to the pieces?

ÉR I have no idea. I guess they were lost, completely lost somewhere. They stayed at the Studio d'Essai. After the Studio d'Essai moved, what was born from it became the big institution that you know: the Groupe de Recherches Musicales. I guess they didn't keep anything of mine . . . At the time I was very young—a young, little nothing—and no one paid attention to this *fantasy* [*laughs*]. This world of music was rather macho, it was for men. Any woman who was coming into that was "just having fun." It couldn't be serious.

IN Did they accept you?

ÉR Yes, they accepted me because of my enthusiasm. I guess it was refreshing to have me around. But still, it was often just, "Okay, she's nice." They thought I was kidding around, that I wanted to have fun. They didn't know about me—that I was more serious, not just kidding around.

IN — Tell me about Pierre Henry. You were also a student of his as well?

ÉR — Much later, I was an assistant to Pierre Henry. But in the fifties, I was a student of Pierre Schaeffer. I was the main follower—the first follower—of Pierre Schaeffer. Later, around 1967, when I separated from my husband and came back to live in Paris, I was an assistant for Pierre Henry. Of course, you know about him?

IN — Bits and pieces. I have heard a little music and a few stories. I know a little about his role in creating a place for *musique concrète* in Paris and as a figurehead in the history of tape music. And that he and Schaeffer collaborated for a while and parted ways at a certain point. My general impression is that Henry was dreamier. Does this make sense?

ÉR — That makes sense, but since I am a slow person, I will have to think about my answer . . . Yes, Pierre Henry is a dreamer, but a dreamer in the sense of *phantasm*. Pierre Schaeffer was a genius discoverer. Schaeffer was really a genius, definitely. The main thing he did in life was his music. He was not as good a technician as Henry, who took much more care about things. But Schaeffer had tremendous intuition.

IN — Am I right in thinking that Schaeffer was interested in orientalism?

ÉR — He was interested mainly in the philosophy of Gurdjieff; he would often quote Gurdjieff. There was something very special about Pierre Schaeffer. He was, by his formation, rather mathematic and scientific. He was from the École Polytechnique—this big school in France that makes great engineers and such. This was very deep in him, but he was also a deeply creative artist. There was an ambivalence between these two aspects of his personality. The *polytechnicien* in him aspect did not take his artistic creativity seriously, and he, himself, did not take the music he was making that seriously. It is very subtle what I am saying and not sharp the way I am saying it. Of course, I guess he was happy with what he was making—with the sounds and music—but he always had to reassure himself about what he was doing.

IN   It was an inspired move to start creating in the way that he did.

ÉR   Absolutely. When he started, in the late forties, even John Cage had not been that far. And we all know that John Cage is one of the geniuses of the second half of the twentieth century in music. But at that time, Pierre Schaeffer was the real discoverer of everything.

IN   You have so much respect for them. Do you see yourself as their *disciple*?

ÉR   No, I am sort of a black duck. I have not gone in that direction. I have not followed either Pierre Schaeffer or Pierre Henry. I must say, I am quite sure neither of them likes the music I am making. I remember I once invited Pierre Schaeffer to one of my concerts in Paris. Since everything at my concerts has always been on tape, I put all the equipment in a cupboard or in any other room, because I didn't want the equipment in the room where the audience was listening. I like to have just the audience with the loudspeakers around them. I would carefully adjust the sound in the rehearsal space beforehand so that the audience would be able to listen as well as possible from anywhere in the space. I don't like the idea of: you sit here in the middle; this is the best place. For me, that is not right. Everywhere, everyone should have something. This works very well with the sounds that I work with; when they are correctly projected into the space, the sounds go everywhere and come from everywhere. Coming back to this particular concert, which was fifteen, maybe twenty, years ago, I could see the people in the room, but no one could see me. About fifteen minutes into the concert, Pierre Schaeffer left. So, I said to myself, "Okay, he doesn't like it."

IN   Were you upset?

ÉR   No, but since I consider him like a kind of father—it was like being rejected by one's own father. A little bit painful, but not that serious, because I also have other fathers, like John Cage. We are all the sons and daughters of John Cage, all the musicians of my generation and your generation and several generations to come. I have never worked with John Cage, but I have always had more recognition from him than from my . . . if I could say so, from my natural father! [*Laughs.*]

When my time with Pierre Henry ended, it was also mainly for these reasons. We are friends now, but at one point we had a very difficult relationship. He didn't agree at all with what I was doing or what I wanted to do. I made the music I made because I wanted to make it. After that, I did everything I could to give myself the means of doing it, like going to the United States to use a synthesizer that didn't exist in France. In the late sixties and early seventies, there were no synthesizers in France. To the GRM, the synthesizer appeared to be a kind of devil-object. So, to have access to this instrument, which I had heard make the sort of sounds I wanted to make, I had to go to the United States.

IN   What sounds were you after?

ÉR   What I wanted to do was to work with sounds that were continuously moving from their inside. To do that, there is nothing but the synthesizer, from which you take the basic components of any sound, namely some frequencies, and you treat them, or cook them, through all the operations of modulation—of filtering and such—to control them permanently, very slowly, from the inside.

There were two main things that I wanted to do. First of all, like I said, I wanted to have a space for a concert such that anyone could hear the whole piece from anywhere; just by turning their heads right or left, they can have different feelings about the sounds. Ideally, the sounds should give the impression of coming from everywhere but the loudspeakers. The loudspeakers should be forgotten. The space should be filled up with the sounds, like a shell, as though you were inside the body of a piano or any instrument. I mean, the room being like the body of the instrument, and the people being inside the body. All the air should be moving, and we should bathe in it! One of the important things that I have been trying to do in making sounds is to drive them slowly, to change them unnoticeably, so that by the time the ear realizes that something has changed, the process of change has started long, long before. I was fascinated by the quality of some—*some*—electronic sounds. Not all! I immediately rejected all the big effects. That was not my thing, big effects [*laughs*].

IN	The music of yours that I've heard is very subtle, very understated, which is not a quality I hear in the music of American artists, especially of the late sixties and early seventies. La Monte Young is one example, but many other American artists also make meditative music which, like yours, uses the physicality of sound, but is bombastic and overwhelming. Did you find your music to be strikingly different from what was going on in the US when you got here?

ÉR	No, I actually found that people understood my music best in America. My musical family is from the United States, and all my musician friends are American—La Monte Young, for example, to whom I feel very close. When I went to New York in the early seventies to work at NYU for a year on the Buchla—which had been left there by Morton Subotnick just a year before or something like that—I also came to meet people like Philip Glass, Steve Reich, and Jon Gibson, and we became rather close. There was this branch of people with whom I felt much more familiar than I did with anyone in Paris at that time. At NYU, I met Rhys Chatham and Laurie Spiegel. We shared the same studio. Charlemagne Palestine said we met once then, but I remember meeting three years later at CalArts. I felt much more complicity with Americans in terms of using sounds.

IN	Was there more a sense of complicity because of personalities or aesthetic reasons?

ÉR	I would say both—personality often aligns with aesthetics.

*   *   *

IN	I recently heard Pierre Henry's piece *Le Voyage* from 1962, which is based on *The Tibetan Book of the Dead*.

ÉR	I know this piece very well and like it very much. There is one part that is by far one of my favorite pieces in the whole oeuvre of Pierre Henry: the "Après le mort (fluide et mobilité d'un larsen)." He made it before I was working with him, but like I told you, I was keeping track of what all these men were doing; every time I came to Paris, I saw them. If I may anticipate your next question, because you probably know I made a piece involved with the *Bardo Thödröl* (*The Tibetan Book of the Dead*) called *Kyema*—

IN Yes.

ÉR I think that the concept was not the same as Pierre Henry's piece, because, as we said about him, all his work is the work of a dreamer, which is into some *phantasm*. It can go from *The Tibetan Book of the Dead* to *Les Chants de Maldoror* to *L'Apocalypse de Jean* and all that. As far as I know Pierre Henry, and I think I know him quite well, he has a spiritual direction—but his spirituality is not really driven. It is a free, natural spirituality that can go here and there, in any direction.

When I made *Kyema* in 1988, I had been involved with Tibetan Buddhism since 1975; I have been studying it all these years and am still studying. I am a real practitioner, every day. This is my discipline. And within my practice, if I could just realize just a portion of a fingernail of what my master, Pawo Rinpoche, has taught me, that would be good enough; I wouldn't have any more problems in my life. *Kyema* is inspired by the deep teachings I was receiving from my master. I make music out of this experience and conviction, which is not the same approach as Pierre Henry's. He has a more or less literary approach to the *Bardo Thödröl*, whereas my own approach is really driven by my spiritual involvement. I cannot say it was based on experience [of dying and being reborn], but in a way, we could all say so.

IN Buddhism has had an effect on the thematic dimension of your work, as in the *Songs of Milarepa* [1983] and the *Trilogie de la Mort* [1998]. Do you think it has had an effect on how you approach the work, or your aesthetic in sound?

ÉR This is another story because I came to Tibetan Buddhism through music. In the early seventies, I was going to the United States every year, and in 1973 at CalArts, I presented *Ψ 847*, which is the first very long piece I did—an eighty-minute piece. A few days after, I was in San Francisco, where I had come to meet my friend Terry Riley, and I met a girl who had just received a card that said, and I quote, "I have just heard a concert at CalArts of a meditative music of a French girl named Éliane." So, the music I made was called meditative before I was actually involved with Buddhism.

Through music, too. In 1975 in California—but this time at Mills College, where I had been presenting *Adnos*, another one of these very long pieces—three French men came up to me after the concert and said, "You know that you are not *yourself* doing your music." And that struck me. It was really quite shocking, but it made sense somehow. It happened that the three men were involved with Buddhism. After we talked, they gave me an address here in Paris, and the day after I returned to Paris, I jumped into this center. I dug into it, and I never came back! Buddhism came to me through music. I don't try to understand anything about that, I just quote the facts as they are!

IN   I only know a little about Tibetan sound culture, but I think it does have some parallels to your music—this meditative quality, which we have been talking about, but also the use of harmonic aspects as a kind of tool for coming to a personal awakening.

ÉR   When I made pieces like *Ψ 847* and *Adnos*—I use the past tense, because I don't do this so much anymore—I was working with all the passion I could, following the trajectory of sounds I was pulling from my ARP synthesizer, following them with absolute fascination. I always knew what I wanted to do. I could give some description of the piece, like *Ψ 847*. Long after I did it, a friend told me that I had explained to her that I wanted to create a sort of sound-mass, like a mountain—the shape of a mountain—and, thread by thread, to bring these sounds to the same state but in reverse, a sort of cup. I don't know if it sounds like that, but I was following sounds that could give me this feeling. At that time, I didn't apply myself to making meditative music. Like I said, I didn't know about meditation—although maybe you're familiar with the philosophy of karma and all that . . . Maybe I was involved already with Buddhism in some way, and I didn't know it. Unconscious, but already there. I don't know. There are a lot of questions for which I have no answers!

IN   I'm interested in your conversion experience—when you became a serious student of Buddhism and didn't make any music for three years.

ÉR It was after the first *Adnos* [1974], when I came back to France and started studying at the center the men in California had recommended. I was at the center almost every day. It seemed so important to me, like, "Here is what I have been looking for all my life." Nothing was more important—and that is why I put my music aside in this period. I was just studying, practicing. At that time we were very lucky because in France, we had wonderful visitors, great Tibetan masters who've now disappeared. It was like fireworks. I won't say that this was the best period of my life, because now is the best period of my life. Day after day, it's now, talking with you. But it was a great period. And then I came to meet Pawo Rinpoche, who was a great Tibetan lama. He had a more personal approach. He had a very small monastery on an old farm in the south of France in the Dordogne, and at that time, I decided that this was the place I wanted to live, and that I would stay there for the rest of my life!

IN Why did you leave?

ÉR It's an interesting story. After a certain period of practicing, I said to my master: "Now I will not make any more music, so I think I should sell my equipment." And he said to me: "Wait a minute. This music is what you have to do." At that time, I didn't understand why he said this, but now I can understand. He brought me to a certain point. He was a very wise, fantastic person and thought that maybe I had something else to do in life. Occasionally, I would sense that maybe he was upset by hearing the train of sounds that were still in my mind all day long. And it was true—I still had a lot of music in my mind. After that experience I made *Adnos II* [1980], *Adnos III* [1982], all the five *Songs of Milarepa*, the *Trilogie*—all of which I never would have made if he had not sent me back to music. He knew better than I did. But at that moment, I thought maybe I was not good enough at being a spiritual student, that maybe I just didn't have the ability to make myself a perfect student, even if I trained for the rest of my life. So I started to spend more time here in Paris where I had my studio.

IN How did you feel reapproaching your ARP?

ÉR Very happy. I have a very bad analogy—it's like when someone stops smoking, and when they can't resist to smoke again, the wonderful feeling of lighting a cigarette! [*Laughs.*]

IN It sounds like you were a little disappointed with yourself, that you couldn't be a better student somehow and stop making music forever.

ÉR Now I don't even ask myself the question. I think that I follow, to the best of my ability, the spiritual path with the training that my master has given me. He stayed in France until 1988, and after that I went to Nepal to visit him. The last time I was in Nepal was for his cremation six years ago. But I have always followed all his precious advice, and I'm still very respectful of it. I think that the music I have been making all along these years, after all, maybe it's not bad to have made it. My master told me: "You should always think of your music as an offering." I always remember this, and I hope that I have been faithful to him. This is why I undergo this process of showing my deep conviction to Buddhism, by making my pieces.

IN Somewhere in your music there is the feeling that what goes on in the mind of the listener, one's own vividness of perception, is a crucial part of the music. The quietness of the sounds and their warmth, their particular quality has a bright, perceptual vividness . . . I don't think I'm explaining this feeling very well.

ÉR I see what you're saying. I agree. I know that when listening to these sounds, if you don't give them the full capacity of your attention, they're just unbearable. I've been living with these sounds for quite a long time; some days, for some reason, when a bad mood descends, which happens to all of us, I'll think, "I can't stand these sounds!" [*Laughs.*] I've learned that on those days, I'm much better off going for a walk in the woods or in the street. Quite often these sounds are like a mirror that reflects whatever is in our minds—they have this very strange effect. Speaking for myself, if I am in a terrible mood, these sounds sound awful. If I am in a good mood, they just—*poof!*—come into me, and I feel happy with them.

I am very happy when people are happy with my sounds. It is like sharing something very precious with someone else. But I can also understand the people who cannot stand these types of sounds. Someone will come up to me and say: "What you are doing is just awful. Are you crazy? It's absolutely silly. I get mad with your sounds!" And I will say: "Yes, I understand very well, because that also happens to me from time to time." Sometimes I wonder to myself [*whispering*]: "But *am* I not crazy doing such a thing?" Really, almost paranoiac! But the goal is to bring peace, a feeling of comfort and happiness. This comes only through this quiet aspect; I am very sure of that. If I would say I have a goal, it would be to bring a feeling of happiness, of being well. This is what I wish for, but I can understand if it doesn't happen.

IN   Do you have hopes that your music will be spiritually or socially beneficial?

ÉR   I like the idea of it being somehow spiritually beneficial, and I have had quite a few reports of this, which really makes me happy. Socially—I must say that I am not antisocial, but I am not the kind of person who is running everywhere with people always around. I'd rather live in a secluded way with a few people with whom I have great affinity. I don't like large social meetings that much [*laughs*]. That's not exactly my cup of tea.

IN   Are you a disciplined music maker? Do you do it consistently?

ÉR   I used to, but that is what I was starting to tell you—now, I work much less. There are several reasons for that. One of these reasons is the technical deficiency of my equipment, with which I have too many troubles. I tried recently, in the past two or three years, to change my technique of working, because working with an analog synthesizer is quite obsolete. I tried working with a digital synthesizer. But I am stubborn, and I fought a lot with it. I have to say that I didn't find my way into that. I couldn't make the music that I wanted to make. I no longer even had to make beautiful sounds—beautiful sounds were there already. You push a button, and you have beautiful sounds; my goal has never been just to make beautiful sounds.

And, I'm sorry to say it, but the fact is that aging creates problems, too. I think the mind is not as supple, not able to get everything as quickly as it does when we are young. This is why I had to fight so much more than I would have had to if I had been forty years younger. When it came time to really work physically with it—with my physical ear, with my physical hand, with my physical body—I couldn't get accustomed to it. It was just impossible, really. I reached the point where I got very high blood pressure. So, I gave it up. I said, "Okay, my health!" And since I gave it up, my blood pressure has gone back to normal. This is for you young people. I have heard beautiful music made with a digital synthesizer, but I already made the music I wanted to make—and I have been very happy with the music I have been doing the past twenty-five, almost thirty years.

I think that analog sounds have a special life-quality—it is just like the skin. No skin is absolutely perfect, but when you touch the skin it has a quality of life-ness. When you touch a balloon or glass, this is another feeling. To me, digital sounds have this perfect—*too* perfect—quality. There are not enough defects, not enough life, because life is made of little defects. We know that even with acoustical instruments, if you listen closely to any acoustical instrument—a piano, a violin—you can hear some cracking, very slight cracking of the wood. From far away, you don't hear it, but I am very sure that this very small cracking makes the very special quality of acoustic sounds. Analogic sounds have a special quality, and I hope that the synthesizer will remain in the musical lutherie like any other instrument, the violin or something, for its special quality.

IN   Do you still use the ARP sometimes?

ÉR   No, my ARP has a real problem. Its main problem, which would be unbearable for anyone, is that sometimes the sound just goes on and off . . . [*Laughs.*] You are just working on a sound and—*oops!*—the whole thing is gone.

IN   I like what you said about the feeling of life in the sound of the synthesizer. I can hear a vitality in the sound of your music, the breath-like quality in "Mila's Journey" and the heartbeat in *Biogenesis*, these bodily rhythms.

ÉR   I will tell you the story of *Biogenesis*. It's a piece I made in 1973, and I made it like an homage for the birth of my first granddaughter, the daughter of my daughter who is a genetic biologist. To make this piece I used a microphone—quite a good microphone, a Sennheiser—as well as a Telefunken tape recorder and a stethoscope. I had a problem finding an adapter to connect the microphone to the stethoscope. I went to a toy shop, where I found a very small plastic bottle containing some sort of small candy. One end of the bottle attached perfectly to the stethoscope, and to the other end, the larger one, I affixed to my microphone. This is how I made recordings of the heartbeat of my daughter and the heartbeat of my son. The father of my granddaughter was too serious to play around with this, but my son consented to give me the beating of his heart, of a man's heart. Last but not least, you hear very rapid beating at the end, which is the heartbeat of the baby in the womb of the mother. This was the first track of the piece. I had to do a lot of editing, because that was very, very raw material; I cooked that through my ARP and then added some of the sounds of my synthesizer.

IN   What did your daughter think?

ÉR   My children were a little bit like my musician-father, Pierre Schaeffer. They were accepting of what their mother was doing [*laughs*]. Now, maybe they are starting to consider it a little bit more seriously. But my daughter allowed me to make *Biogenesis*. For me, that was so important, because I was so happy to be a grandmother—and now this very first granddaughter is pregnant and will have a baby, and I will be a great-grandmother! And I am as happy as I was twenty-five years ago! This is why I can't resist to tell you the story of *Biogenesis*, even if it's very personal.

IN   Is your music still presented often at festivals or concerts?

ÉR   No—and, I would say, luckily. I prefer the idea of people listening to this music quietly, when they want, for the time they want, at their own pace, comfortably. If they're people I know, I always wonder if they're getting bored and staying because they don't want to hurt me. I don't like to make concerts; I had to do it because it's a matter of being correct with the work itself. The work would have been nothing if I had just made it and then put it on a shelf and moved on to something else. It seems to me to be my duty after I have finished a piece to present it. Every piece has been presented one, two, three, four times—no more than that. Then I can put it on the shelf and go on to another piece.

IN   What would you like to do next?

ÉR   [*Giggling.*] Maybe you'll be disappointed, but it's always the same. I am a faithful woman, faithful to the same types of sounds. Listening to the first piece I made almost thirty years ago and the most recent one—a small piece which I am still trying to finish, because I hate to leave things unfinished—there is not much change. Just a little. None of these pieces are exactly the same, but none of them are very different.

IN   Kind of like a person. From one day to the next, you feel different, but you're still the same person.

ÉR   Absolutely. I think it's organic music. It grows like an organism. Slowly. Gets more wrinkled, but that's it. The whole personality doesn't change that much. And maybe the music also gets some wrinkles, but it somehow stays the same as well.

Éliane Radigue, ca. 1980s. Courtesy Fonds Éliane Radigue.

CONVERSATIONS WITH ÉLIANE RADIGUE
Bernard Girard

In this extensive interview with philosopher Bernard Girard (1946–2014), Radigue traces her approach to serial music—an "intellectual game" that entwines her interests in theory, technique, and analysis with play and provocation—back to her mentors Pierre Henry and Pierre Schaeffer, whose creative practices were similarly concerned with a careful negotiation between rationality and artistic intuition. Originally published in French as a standalone volume, *Entretiens avec Éliane Radigue* (Éditions Aedam Musicae, 2013), the interview appears here in English for the first time, translated by Adrian Rew.

> I often have this strange and penetrating dream
> Of an unknown woman, whom I love, and who loves me
> And who, each time, is neither completely the same
> Nor completely another, and who loves and understands me
>
> —Paul Verlaine, "Mon rêve familier"

BERNARD GIRARD

You belong to a generation that witnessed and participated in the great major revival in the world of music in the fifties and sixties, in the discovery of new sounds, concrete and electronic, of new forms, serialism, minimalism, but before speaking of these, perhaps a word on your beginnings. How did you become a musician?

ÉLIANE RADIGUE

My parents were shopkeepers. I discovered music through the radio, on a Radiola model, and I found it fascinating. One of my friends at school—I was still in primary school—was learning the piano. Our mothers knew each other, and the little girl's had suggested to mine that I also take piano lessons with a teacher who lived in her building. This teacher, Madame Roger, was, dare I say, the first truly important person in my life. Without her, my life could really have taken a wrong turn. She had two pianos: an upright piano and a grand piano. I was very curious about everything, about music theory . . . Very quickly, she put me on the grand piano. It was a sign. She gave me everything, against my mother's wishes, who very quickly wanted me to stop.

BG   And why?

ÉR   Out of jealousy, I think. She was possessive, very authoritarian, very jealous. She kept her whole world, my father, me—I was an only child—on a tight leash. One day she brought me to this teacher and, holding me firmly by the hand, explained: "Éliane no longer wants to take piano lessons. Right, Éliane?" Now, when my mom said, "Right, Éliane?" there was really only one response: "Yes, mother." But Madame Roger and my friend's mother understood very well. Every time that my friend invited me to play at her place, her mother told me, "Madame Roger is waiting for you," and I went up to take my piano lessons. And this lady gave me lessons, for I don't know how long, without being paid. I was also sometimes invited to practice alone. And this, seeing how to work alone as a student, I know from having done some teaching myself, is extremely instructive.

This woman was really a teacher. I owe her a great deal. Her daughter was an opera singer. For me this was the discovery of a whole world.

BG   You come from a world hardly interested in music, especially in classical music.

ÉR   It's true, but I was lucky to have a great uncle who, for the new year, gave all his nephews and nieces money. It was enough to buy a season ticket for ten concerts at Chatelet. We lived close by at the time. They were on Saturday afternoons. I remember being fascinated . . . I would be at the edge of the balconies, and there would be nobody, or almost nobody, in front of me.

BG   This was during the war?

ÉR   Yes . . . I was seven years old when it was declared. You see, I came from nothing. Composers have often been raised in environments of music lovers, musicians, this was by no means my situation. I didn't fall into the magic potion as a child, but music, classical music, quickly became my great passion.[1] The simple fact that by putting your hands on a keyboard—the ivories and ebonies—you can produce these sounds really fascinated me.

BG   You then went on to study music?

ÉR   Yes, but my journey was rather anarchic. At nineteen—at the time, the legal age was twenty-one—I rebelled against my family. I had had enough, especially of my mother. So, they sent me to stay with some of their friends in Nice to, as my mother said, "build character." I was only supposed to stay a few weeks, but these friends turned out to be open, very nice, and, at the end of those three weeks, I had no desire to leave, so they suggested that I stay with them. And I stayed. . .

BG   So, it was in Nice that you first studied music?

---

[1] Translator's note: This is a reference to French comic book *Asterix*, in which sidekick Obélix has superhuman strength because he fell into a pot of Gaulish invincibility potion as a child.

ÉR In high school, in Paris, I was part of the choir. Each school had a selection of about ten singers and we did an annual concert at the Sorbonne. One of the first things I did in Nice was continue to sing with Émile Delpierre's choir. I was a nice little soprano, but lacked the lungs, I could never have become a singer. Then I signed up for harmony and harp classes at the conservatory.

BG The discovery of music is thus, for you, associated with rebellion and freedom, while for so many other children it is synonymous with discipline.

ÉR Yes, it was really what I wanted, what I sought out.

BG But back to your conservatory classes . . .

ÉR In Nice, I had a very good piano teacher, Madame Delberre, but I have never been a good pianist or harpist. Because I didn't work hard enough on my technique but also because I have a horrible handicap: as soon as I am touched by emotion, my hands get clammy, which is incompatible with both a keyboard and the strings of a harp. I had no grip, I didn't have what it took to become a good interpreter, which I regret. On the other hand, I immediately became interested in music theory, in the ways in which things are made. I was eight or nine years old when Madame Roger showed me the circle of fifths. She had me analyze a piece before playing it, she asked me to identify the first accidentals, sharps, flats, naturals, which bring about the change of key. I've always been fascinated by transitions, by the few measures, sometimes more, where we leave a tone before falling back into another. We travel, we are between two waters, we never know exactly where we are going.

BG In addition to the piano, you also took harp lessons. Why this instrument?

ÉR It was simply because piano lessons were at capacity when I entered the conservatory at Nice, and because I have a very short pinky finger. It's a handicap on the piano, whereas the harp is played with only four fingers. It's a beautiful instrument. Playing it is very physical, you take it in the arms.

BG The harp is an instrument that's difficult to afford when you're twenty.

ÉR But it can be rented. My teacher had one that I rented for several years and which I kept since my son was interested in the instrument. So I returned it much later when I started composing.

BG How long did you stay in Nice?

ÉR Seventeen years. It was there that I met and married Arman.

BG It was the period during which he created, with Yves Klein and Martial Raysse, what became the Nice school.

ÉR Yes, it was a very exciting, very animated adventure. It must be said that at the time, in Nice, there was nothing, absolutely nothing.

 I quickly discovered that I missed Paris and, since my parents still lived there, I returned regularly with my three children. It was during one of these trips that I met Pierre Schaeffer in 1955.

BG You had three young children to raise, so what was your musical practice like during this time?

ÉR I gave composing a shot, I did exercises during my children's naps, I played with the twelve tones. I have never really been touched musically, deeply, by serial music like I have been by classical music, but it was an intellectual game for me. I tried to cheat, to create series with tetrachords. Apparently, La Monte Young was able to achieve this. I'd like to know how he managed to respect all the rules of verticality and horizontality and of the series, of retrograde, of its inversion, without becoming, at some point or another, stuck in dissonance, in an atonality that I always wanted to avoid. I used to do it like I do sudoku or crossword puzzles, to keep the mind nimble, but it wasn't very satisfying. I also continued to play the piano a little.

BG And that's when you met Pierre Schaeffer? How did you meet him?

ÉR   I took advantage of my visits to Paris and went out a little. I went to meet a friend at a lecture on [Paul-Yves] Nizan by Lanza del Vasto. It was actually a roundtable discussion, and next to Lanza del Vasto was Pierre Schaffer, whose name I knew from listening to the radio. I asked my friend, who had good social skills, if she knew him. She had dined with him, and she offered to introduce us. My interest, my enthusiasm, must have appealed to him because he very quickly accepted me as an intern at the Studio d'Essai, an intermittent intern since I still lived in Nice.

BG   So you didn't see him often at that time?

ÉR   No, especially since he still ran SORAFOM [Société de Radiodiffusion de la France d'Outre-Mer], the overseas radio, and only came to the studio at night. I worked primarily with Pierre Henry, who assigned me editing. He entrusted me with tapes that I would cut and cut for hours; he taught me how to locate a sound. It was there that I learned to make loops, do editing, mixing, slowdowns . . . all the techniques of *musique concrète*.

In 1956, Pierre Schaeffer gave me a letter for the director of radio in Nice, asking him to give me a few hours of studio time per week. This did not come to fruition. I found the copy of the response, which he had addressed to Pierre Schaeffer, dated April 6, 1956: he is sorry, he excuses himself, but he cannot grant me these few hours in the studio. *Musique concrète* really did not have a place at that time. I remember that Pierre Boulez said, when he came to visit the Studio d'Essai, that there was no future in this music. [Iannis] Xenakis, on the other hand, was very interested.

BG   I imagine that during this time you met many people in the Parisian musical world.

ÉR   Yes, but I was an intern, and you know, interns, they don't count. . .

Since I couldn't work at the radio station in Nice, I started to promote this music, I gave lectures, I gave some in Nice, in the surrounding region, abroad in Düsseldorf, Amsterdam, Darmstadt . . . I had tapes, 78-rpm records, which I have since given to the library at Mills College after realizing that they were getting damaged in my home. And when Pierre Schaeffer organized his first internships, he asked me to participate. It was there that I met for the first time François-Bernard Mâche, Luc Ferrari, Beatriz Ferreyra—the people of the very first team. But I came more as a visitor.

BG How was Pierre Schaeffer?

ÉR Dazzling. I remember that during one of my visits to Paris he invited me to attend one of his lectures. He was a superb spirit. We wondered where he was taking us in his lectures, and then, like in *"Les Cinq dernières minutes,"* everything became clear at the end.[2]

At the time he was very preoccupied with the desire to develop a universal music theory. He worked a lot with Abraham Moles, which ultimately led to the [1966] publication of his *Traité des objets musicaux*. When I began to use analog electronic instruments, I tried to follow his example of establishing a system of notation. But now we have everything on computers.

BG Pierre Schaeffer is a bit of a mystery. He is the undisputed inventor of *musique concrète*, but he left behind very little work, as if he hadn't wanted to compose.

ÉR I have always considered him a great artist and creator. I remember seeing Maurice Béjart's dance performance of *Symphonie pour un homme seul* at the Fontaine des Quatre-Saisons. It was splendid, but Schaeffer was, in a way, held back by his training as a *polytechnicien*.[3] For him, there was always a conflict between this artistic, creative instinct, which demands that for a moment one cease to think and reason, but the first works, the railroad studies, were essentially him. Pierre Henry worked during the day; at night, Pierre Schaeffer gave his approval and made corrections.

BG And then there was the quarrel between them.

---

2   Translator's note: *"Les Cinq Dernières Minutes"* ("The Last Five Minutes") is a French crime television series that was broadcast from 1958 to 1996.

3   Translator's note: Pierre Schaeffer's alma mater, the École Polytechnique, is a prestigious French public institution of higher education and research, especially known for its *polytechnicien* engineering program, which, not unlike MIT in the US, has produced leading engineers and politicians alike.

ÉR   I no longer recall the reason. I was a closer friend to Pierre Schaeffer than Pierre Henry, but I found that he had gone too far and I made the mistake of openly and resolutely taking Pierre Henry's side. I was sent off at the same time as him. It was rather harsh. I remember a letter from Arman telling me: "I ran into Pierre Schaeffer, he said that if you wanted to return to the studio, it would be to stick stamps onto envelopes."

The general reconciliation occurred much later, in 1968. I had organized a small dinner for Pierre Henry's birthday, to which I had dared invite Pierre Schaeffer. He came with the *Traité*, which had just been published, and he wrote me a very beautiful dedication, which perfectly reflects his way of being. Going forward, we saw each other only periodically.

BG   So, in Paris you were connected with musicians who made *musique concrète* and in Nice with visual artists of the Nice school. When one thinks of the work, of their respective approaches, one would think that they naturally would have encountered one another and worked together. Yet, this does not seem to have been the case. When, a few years later in 1960, Pierre Restany founded the *nouveaux réalistes* group, he could have included musicians in the movement, but he didn't.

ÉR   I was the only musician. I was a woman, a "wife of," and all these men were extremely "macho."

However, I tried to establish links between the two groups. In fact, I began to. I consulted a number of galleries with which we could have carried out joint operations. Pierre Schaeffer had agreed to the production of a film joining images from avant-garde artists, notably Arman and [Antoni] Tàpies, with *musique concrète*, which was meant to be produced by Jean Grémillon. It consisted of pairing images from these painters with *musique concrète* without the slightest commentary.

Pierre Schaeffer had introduced me to Pierre Braunberger, who was one of the great film producers of the time, and to Anatole Dauman, who was very interested in the project and whom I was supposed to meet when I learned that my son was very sick. Because an indefinite strike was supposed to begin the next day, I returned immediately to Nice. For me, this was a shock. I thought, things can't go on this way. Overnight, I decided to stop . . . But there were other contacts between visual artists and musicians. Pierre Henry worked with François Dufrêne and our poet friend Claude Pascal. His *Variations pour une porte et un soupir* [1963] are dedicated to Arman. He also worked on Yves Klein's *Symphonie monoton-silence* [1960].

BG This symphony is the sole example of a musical creation by a painter of the Nice school. I say creation, but it consists rather of a collaboration between a painter, Yves Klein, who proposed a concept, an idea, to a musician.

ÉR This symphony has a rather peculiar backstory. A group of us would go to the beach at night. Yves Klein's mother, Marie Raymon, hosted salons, and at one of these Yves had met François Dufrêne, Raymond Hains, and Jacques de la Villeglé, who at the time made phonetic poetry they called *glossolalia*, in reference to the universal language that the apostles received at the Pentecost. So we were all on the beach practicing glossolalia when one of us, I don't remember who, said, "But what if we only made one sound?" Being the only musician of the group, I harmonized the voices, the baritones, the tenors. Since they weren't musicians, I gave them very simple relations of fifths, thirds, fourths, which were easier to maintain.

When Yves Klein decided to revisit this in a more systematic manner, he asked me to give him a hand with its writing. Knowing his character and not wanting to jeopardize our friendship, I suggested that he go see a friend, Louis Saguer, a fine musician, who told me later that each time he proposed to Yves elaborate harmonies, he found them too sophisticated. Irritated, he wound up tossing out a harmony in C major and Yves said, "That's it." Perhaps in memory of that improvised beach concert.

BG This took place in Nice at the beginning of the fifties.

ÉR I was pregnant with my son, so it was in August of 1954. There were many exchanges in the Nice school. It was very cheerful, very stimulating, very creative. Many creations were made through play, verbal play, which the surrealists did very spontaneously. It was kind of like playing with a ball: everyone kicks around ideas, and when one of us found one of interest, they would put it in their pocket, and if they made something from it they were credited, even if it came from someone else.

That's why I don't remember who said, "What if we made the same sound?"

BG   Although no link was established between these composers and painters, your husband, Arman, broke, sawed, and burned many musical instruments, violins . . .

ÉR Pierre Restany once joked that he did this when things started to go wrong with his musician wife. He was probably not mistaken. The height of this was when he burned the pianos and broke a harp.

BG   You said to yourself: "He's angry at me."

ÉR It was a provocation. It also happened to be not long before our separation.

BG   Let's go back to your musical career. It is 1956/1957, your children are growing up, what are you up to?

ÉR I abandon everything, my lectures, the seeds of a professional career, to raise my children. And this lasted ten years. When I return to Paris, in the summer of 1967, I learn that Pierre Henry's collaborator, Marie-Luce Staib, is leaving him. I go to see him in his studio on the boulevard Saint-Germain, and he proposes that I join him, which I did.

    He had just met Isabelle Warnier, who later became his wife. Great love is not necessarily compatible with work. He had asked me to get things in order at the studio, and I was often alone there, which left me with some moments of freedom. But since it was a year in which he had planned a twenty-four-hour concert of *L'Apocalypse de Jean* [1968], the last months were madness. He set up two of his first instruments at my home, two Tolanas, which I still have, and I worked without pay. I went to the studio, I brought back piles of tape that he asked me to prepare on separate reels. I had to add start and end leaders and detect whether there were any technical problems. He did the mixing. It was a huge job. We would sometimes work fourteen or sixteen hours a day. It was exhausting. Sometimes, when I was too tired, I would tell him to go get a coffee and would lie down on the floor with my legs up . . . He wound up asking Isabelle Chandon, who lived—who probably still lives—in South America, to come. It was impossible for one person to handle the most complex mixes, the simultaneous starts of three or four tape recorders. Isabelle Chandon had a lot of experience with all the techniques of editing and tape preparation, and had worked with Pierre Henry, who was, of course, at the mixing console.

BG And this went well?

ÉR In general, yes. I prepared several tapes for mixing, which allowed him to choose what he liked best. I recall only one big disagreement. He had instructed me to prepare tapes in a "very different contrapuntal style." We had manifestly different conceptions of this. He became angry; I took it very badly.

I stayed with him until the concert at the Gaîté Lyrique, but with the firm intention of reclaiming my freedom, which I did the next day. I left with my little suitcase without saying anything. When he called me a few days later to ask me to return to the studio to do the musical dictation and create the score for *La noire à soixante* [1961], I refused and never returned to the studio.

BG At the time, you didn't return to composition.

ÉR No, except for when I had a few free moments. I used the studio's instruments, his Studer. I had some sounds, my personal little sound library, which I had assembled with a portable Stellavox that my husband had given to me. But it wasn't much, no more than ten minutes on tape.

BG What has stayed with you from that period?

ÉR The learning or, rather, the relearning of the techniques of *musique concrète* and of listening that I discovered with Pierre Schaeffer. When I returned to working with him in 1967/1968, Pierre Henry had me make many loops, and to do so you really have to listen to connect the tape at the right point for it to be seamless. This requires a *discriminating* listening, through which the different attacks must be carefully located. It was during one of these editing sessions that I rediscovered the power of continuous sounds, which had been revealed to me in the fifties at the Studio d'Essai, and of which I spoke in the lectures I gave at the time.

Pierre Henry had asked me to work on different sounds, to cut the attacks that had to be placed end to end to make a three-minute edit. But I listened to what was left of the sound: it was a splendid drapery, solely harmonics that were infinitely more interesting than the attacks.

When I left I was able to get to work on what I wanted to do: feedback, larsens between a microphone and a speaker. You really have to be quite precise and maintain the right distance, if you move the mic slightly, you can change the sound. It requires a real practice of patience.

BG Feedback, larsens, and the reinjection of sounds are concepts that aren't necessarily familiar to everyone. Can you explain them to us?

ÉR Feedback corresponds to two phenomena. Larsens occur when the microphone is too close to the speaker, the sound of which is picked up by the microphone, which then passes it back into the speaker, and again into the microphone. They come into resonance, which results in a very loud and piercing sound. Reinjections require two tape players: a two-track recorder where one track is picked up by the second tape player before being "reinjected" onto the second track of the first. The combination of the two recordings produces the effects of phase shifting and delay.

BG It is at this time that you begin composing again. You give the impression of having always had this ambition.

ÉR I had no other ambition at the time than to make the music that I wanted to hear. I didn't worry about how it might be labeled. I had been raised in a world where I knew all too well that, at best, my position could be that of an assistant. On this point, the GRM remained very traditional. Only in the United Stated did I find, with people like Tom Johnson or James Tenney, relationships that seemed entirely equitable to me.

BG You belong to the first generation that saw women make their mark in the world of music as creators, composers . . .

ÉR   I had decided once and for all that I didn't have enough energy to fight every battle. I didn't participate in the feminist movements, but I remember a militant feminist telling me, when I explained to her why I had chosen music, that it was also a way to carry out combat.

   I didn't even want to fight to promote my music, I had only one ambition, one objective: to make this music.

BG   You had no other desire than to make the music that you wanted to hear without concerning yourself with its promotion, but you had no obligation to make a living otherwise.

ÉR   Yes, this was very important. When I took my distance in 1957/1958, Arman had much more freedom. His career had begun to take off. He was already well known when we separated in 1967, and he had a comfortable income. He always had the class to support me and our children financially. This was very lucky. I had complete freedom, complete latitude. I had lost ten years, but now I could get back to things full time, that is, when I wasn't taking care of my children.

BG   You were working on music that in no way resembles what others, even Pierre Henry, were making, without the hope of diffusing it—but where did you begin?

ÉR   These sounds that I discovered, the barbarous, wild sounds that I got using larsens or reinjections between two tape players, with the Tolanas, were quite simply marvelous. They ranged from low pulsation to rapid beating. If you controlled their larsen, you could get long, sustained sounds that evolved very slowly. I listened to them first, observed their behavior, and that's what determined my sound color.

BG   You like this slowness?

ÉR   I think I've always liked it. In classical music, I've always had a great passion for slow movements, my whole interior discography is made from them. It is toward them that I gravitate. I'm thinking for example of [the slow movement of] Maurice Ravel's *Piano Concerto* [1929–31]. I can't stand the scherzo that comes immediately after this sublime flight. Far from fearing slowness, I desire it. To get these sounds, to maintain control of them, required a lot of patience, this suited me very well.

BG So at the beginning you listened to these sounds a lot.

ÉR Yes, and I understood very quickly that they could work together, that they could be assembled. That's when I created my first pieces, which I improperly called combinatory music, and which today we would call sound installations. The basis was tape loops of different lengths. I made the first ones, with Philips E-10 cassettes, for Marc Halpern, an artist who had requested them for the Salon des artistes décorateurs.[4] He had made a sculpture in a block of plexiglass with movable elements inside. In the plinth were loudspeakers through which three tapes, each a little over nine minutes, were diffused endlessly, gradually becoming desynchronized. The music thus evolved on its own. This piece is called *USRAL* [1969] because it was made with slowed-down ultrasounds: during one of my hunts for sound, I had captured sounds so high that they were practically inaudible, but when I slowed them down, they became extremely interesting. I made several pieces like this, including the *Labyrinthe Sonore* [1970], which is still played from time to time.

BG These first pieces of music for installation were very quickly diffused in galleries.

ÉR It is indeed in galleries that my works were first diffused—at Jean Larcarde, Galerie Rive Droite, Yvon Lambert—in what today we call sound installations.

In 1968,[5] at Galerie Rive Droite, I created a piece for an installation by Tania Mouraud, *One More Night [OMNHT]*. Three tapes of different lengths, from ten to thirty minutes each, overlapped, yielding a music that imperceptibly transformed itself over very long durations.

---

4 Translator's note: The Societé des artistes décorateurs was a French society of furniture designers, interior designers, and other practitioners of the decorative arts that was active from 1901 until the 2000s. It sponsored an annual Salon des artistes décorateurs in which its members could display their new work.

5 This installation at Galerie Rive Droite actually took place in 1970.

Since Tania's installation was all white, Jean Larcade had agreed to completely cover his gallery in panels. I couldn't figure out where to place the speakers without their being intrusive. My technician had spoken to me about Rolen Stars, speakers that could be screwed into wooden walls, so it was the wall that vibrated. And, since we stop much more easily to listen to music that unfolds slowly, this aligned well with what Tania wanted.

I again presented this piece, which I had renamed *OMNHT*, following a disagreement with Tania, in 2006, in Dijon at the Cumulus festival.[6] Emmanuel Holterbach had the excellent idea of putting carpets throughout the room, on which the audience could seat themselves and receive the sound through their backs. This is what gave Kaffe Matthews the idea of asking me to present it for [an iteration of] her *Sonic Bed* [2005], a very large bed filled with several speakers. The listener is asked to remove their shoes, take cushions, and bathe in a sound universe that feels like waves in their body; we receive the vibration of sound in this way.

I also collaborated with some quite fascinating artists from Barcelona: Antoni Miralda, Dorothée Selz, Jaume Xifra, Joan Rabascall. They organized processions, cortèges. First there was a purple party for All Saint's Day, and then a few months later a party in white given in Verderonne, in Oise, for which I composed a piece that I believe to have been the last of this period made with electronic accidents, feedback, and maybe the first to be made up of five parts: *Opus 17* [1971].

I had chosen a process that David Tudor, Pierre Henry, and Alvin Lucier also used: rerecording a sound loop with the microphone fairly close to the speaker with a slight modification in each cycle. It was fairly constraining because it required taking the loop back up and passing it back through. But after five, six, or seven cycles, all that was left was a light oscillation of synthetic sounds. I had taken a phrase of Chopin that looped very easily, so you could hear the modifications throughout. The second part was made by keeping only the elements from the end, each piece was a mode of exploration of this process. The piece was presented as part of this white party at Verderonne in the castle park. The procession ended with a buffet in all white. Couples began to dance to these

---

6 Editor's note: The festival in Dijon that Radigue refers to here was called Continuum and was organized by a group called Cumulus.

very slow movements. It was very pretty, and it deeply touched me. Maybe that's why I still have soft spot for the piece.

In any case, this was the last work that I made with wild sounds, since immediately afterward I left for the United States.

BG   It's 1970, the beginning of your second period. You leave to establish yourself in the United States. Why?

ÉR   I had always visited the United States. In the sixties, we spent a year there [in New York City] with the kids, who went to the Lycée Français. It was there that I met James Tenney, who was, at the time, married to Carolee Schneemann; we got along very quickly. He introduced me to Philip Corner, Malcolm Goldstein . . . Those were wonderful days. Every evening there were events, concerts, happenings by Jim Dine, Claes Oldenburg. Yvonne Rainer danced at Andy Warhol's Factory, which was just starting up. We all visited one another—Roy Lichtenstein, Jasper Johns, Robert Rauschenberg . . . I went to visual arts events with Arman and nights of avant-garde music with James Tenney. It was a period of abundance, of all kinds of experience. I continued to go to New York every year to visit my son, who had settled there in '74/'75 to open a gallery, Yves Arman, which produced a very beautiful Marcel Duchamp show.

BG   Who you met at this time?

ÉR   We knew him from much earlier. We had met him at the end of the fifties thanks to Bill and Noma Copley, collectors who were very close to him and his wife Teeny. We saw each other regularly during the year we spent in New York. They dined at our place, we dined at theirs, we played chess together. I remember one night when Teeny and Arman played one game, while I played another with Marcel. I was the worst, but Marcel let me catch up anyway. During that time, we played a lot of chess.

Thanks to James Tenney, I met Philip Glass and Steve Reich in the sixties, when they still played together. A little later, in the early seventies, Rhys Chatham introduced me to La Monte Young, who already had his admirers. I remember telling him one day that I had heard one of his works in a gallery, and he replied that he had never done anything in such a space.

BG I imagine that you also met John Cage at this time?

ÉR I heard David Tudor play one of his pieces in a loft. I also heard his music in concert at New York University, and in another concert with [Karlheinz] Stockhausen, but I didn't really meet him until later, thanks to my son, who took me to his place during one of my visits. Another time, my son invited him and Merce Cunningham to a surprise party he had organized. I saw him for the last time at the Opéra de la Bastille. He wasn't fond of small talk and asked me if I could take him home when he'd had enough of the reception organized in his honor.

BG What were you doing, then, in New York in 1970/1971?

ÉR I was a composer-in-residence at New York University, where I shared the electronic studio created by Morton Subotnick at the Tisch School of the Arts with Rhys Chatham and Laurie Spiegel. And it was in New York that I had my first real concert, on April 6, 1971.

BG You returned to work in 1967 after a ten-year hiatus and, having hardly stepped foot in New York, you become a composer-in-residence at an American university. How did you do it?

ÉR It was thanks to Steve Reich. At the end of the sixties we were very close to him and Philip Glass. I also helped them get their very first concert in France with Jean-Étienne Marie, who at the time organized concerts of contemporary music in the south. We knew each other very well. I remember that Philip Glass came to visit me when he was writing *Music in Twelve Parts* [1971–74]. He was, as are all artists in these moments, overcome with doubt. He made me listen to what he had written, and I reassured him. I told him: "But it's brilliant, the way that you carry out this modulation with these repetitions. You should go through the entire circle of fifths with it." When, some years later, he presented the piece in Paris, we had dinner together and he told me that I was its godmother. Steve and Phil were my closest friends at the time, along with Jon Gibson.

So when I got to New York, I went to see Steve Reich and told him that I would like to try the synthesizers; he suggested I go see Michael Cjaikowski, who was then the director of the studio at New York University, and he immediately recruited me.

BG And you wound up in this electronic music studio.

ÉR The studio had a synthesizer, the Buchla, which I shared with Laurie Spiegel. I remember that we signed in on a sheet of paper at the entrance. We crossed paths from time to time, but I usually worked alone. There were also tape recorders. And since I left France thinking that I would stay in the United States, I also had my own tape recorders, my little mixing console. So I also had a small workstation at home where I could listen in peace to what I had created with the Buchla. During the first three months, my attempts were often so discouraging that I wondered why I had come to this studio for results that were so far from those I had previously obtained with the most rudimentary techniques. And then one day I found a small zone of sound that interested me, and I explored it.

BG You never used a synthesizer with Pierre Schaeffer and Pierre Henry?

ÉR No, the synthesizer was completely reviled. It was really considered to be the *diabolus in musica*. Anyway, there were no synthesizers in France.

BG The first time one hears these sounds, especially if one is used to those of *musique concrète*, it can be disappointing; it seems poor. What seduced you even before you discovered all the subtleties, the delicacy that later defined your work?

ÉR It was more of a quest than a discovery. I told you that I had very quickly abandoned the recorded sounds of *musique concrète*. And when I used them, like the recording of the Chopin phrase played on the piano that I spoke of earlier, it was to immediately transform them. My goal was to explore a process. I very quickly began to work with feedback, which was only rarely tolerated by *musique concrète* people. There's a larsen in Pierre Henry's *Le Voyage* [1968], but it is quite exceptional.

Working with larsens or with tape reinjections, another process that I used, requires an enormous amount of patience, of finesse; it takes only a slight displacement of a dial for the whole thing to go haywire. However, I immediately rediscovered this pleasure in working with delicacy on the synthesizer.

Moreover, these sounds immediately interested me in themselves, for themselves. Far from considering them poor, I found that they hearkened back to the very foundations of musical reflection, since they were either sustained tones that could be oscillated and balanced or a whole spectrum going from bass pulsations to the little beating I used in *Chry-ptus* [1971], my first-ever piece with the Buchla. In it you hear [acoustical] beating that transforms little by little into sustained tones, and then sustained tones that become beating. The synthesizer interested me because it allowed me to better realize what I had previously been doing in a very rustic manner. When I listen to my first pieces, I realize that everything I did afterward comes from there.

BG But one doesn't work these sounds like those produced by classical instruments.

ÉR I immediately understood in working with my first wild sounds that I had to stop thinking in traditional terms of pitch, of relationships of fourths or thirds, and that I had to accept the sounds as I managed to create them and as they spoke to me, as I heard them.

BG What interested you? Harmonics?

ÉR That was one of the aspects that immediately fascinated me, but with my first archaic instruments, it was a matter of chance, superb chance. The synthesizer allowed me to better manage all this. The Buchla was a very interesting instrument, without a keyboard, which immediately appealed to me; if it had had one I might have taken a different direction. So I learned to work with patches and dials, which didn't come naturally. I had to connect the different modules with cables, which made it difficult to access the dials. Often it was like being before a labyrinth of intertwining wires. If you weren't careful, you risked unplugging a module and losing everything. So you had to be very careful. This was the only drawback to the instrument, which had, moreover, a beautifully rich and full sound. I soon began to draw graphs to remind myself of my patches. I had a notebook full of these drawings that resembled chemical formulas, to which I gave names like *So What*.

So it was with the Buchla that I created *Chry-ptus*, a piece that retained some of the spirit of what had preceded it since it consisted of two tapes of comparable length, twenty-two or twenty-three minutes, that could be played simultaneously or with a slight desynchronization of no more than a minute, backward or forward. It was interesting to hear the variations that established themselves.

BG This was the first piece that you presented in concert in New York?

ÉR On April 6, 1971, at the New York Cultural Center at Columbus Circle, I presented three rather contrasting variations of this first production. I retained the spirit of the sound installations with loops that desynchronized—always the same but still a little different. I always liked that. A music that is never "completely the same nor completely another." I sometimes quote this line from Verlaine to my musicians. So this was my very first piece for synthesizer.

BG Steve Reich put you in touch with New York University, but how did you manage to get a concert just four months later?

ÉR All of this happened, like many other things in my life, a bit by chance. In January, Bernar Venet had invited us to his wedding with his first wife. His witness—his "best man"—happened to be Donald Karshan, the director of the New York Cultural Center. We chatted, got along. I told him that I made music. He asked me if he could come over for a coffee. One night, I heard the doorbell ring, it was him. He asked me where I was at. I had just finished *Chry-ptus*. He asked me if I could play him five or ten minutes. I refused and said: "Either you listen to the whole thing, or nothing." It was difficult for him to refuse, so he carefully listened to the whole thing.

At the end of this compulsory listening session, he asked me what it would take to present it. And that's how it happened.

BG   And a lot of people showed up? At the time there was an attentive public in New York, eager for experimentation, but what you presented was still very original, very different from what the avant-garde was doing at the time.

ÉR   The auditorium was small, it could barely hold forty people, and the invitations had been made by telephone, but it was full. My friends were there, but also many of Donald Karshan's acquaintances. Notably, Paul Jenkins was present. The next day, he came to see me with a gift, a painting that I still have, *For Elaine Radigue's Sounds*, with my first name misspelled. A painting that, he told me, my music had inspired and that he had composed from notes taken during the concert, notes from which he later made a poem that is now part of the record.

Other listeners sent me a page of the Bible because they saw it as spiritual, people whom I didn't know, friends of the director who, driven by this first success, wanted to present the piece a second time. I refused. At the time I was very purist, very radical. I refused, saying, "The pieces I make, I present them once, and then I move on to something else."

BG   An unusual attitude . . .

ÉR   Yes, but one that I kept for a long time. I remember that a few years later, Ileana Sonnabend had asked me to repeat a concert I had presented the year before. I refused. I was kind of a pain in the ass, speaking my mind, but I thought it was part of my duty not to repeat myself, to move on once one of my works had been presented.

BG   Were there other pieces in this April 6 concert?

ÉR   There was nothing else. Three variations of about twenty minutes each; this was an entirely reasonable length for a concert. But it was a space with excellent programming. There had been, the day before, a piano concert of Morton Feldman's and, the next day, Cage's *Sonatas and Interludes* [1946–48] interpreted by its dedicatee, Maro Ajemian, with a piano that John Cage himself had prepared.

BG   After this first work, we come to what has, for years, been your way, your style.

ÉR   Yes, because when I left New York a few months later—this city was really not for me—I bought a synthesizer so I could continue my work in the same direction. At the time there was the Buchla, the Moog, and the Electrocomp. There was also the ARP and, in England, the little Putney by EMS. I tried them all, but the day I came upon the ARP, it was love at first sight. I thought, this is the one that I need.

BG   Love at first sight, but why?

ÉR   Two things appealed to me: first, the sound color, which was very beautiful, much less metallic than that of its competitors, and second, a much more convenient system of connections that provided complete freedom to manipulate the dials. The device had a keyboard, but I didn't take it in fear of submitting to ease. The manufacturer never understood.

BG   So you bought an ARP synthesizer in New York and returned to Europe with it.

ÉR   I installed it in the cabin of *France*, because we were returning to Europe by ship, and kept it until two or three years ago.[7]

In Paris, I spent the summer exploring it, familiarizing myself with it, and then I composed *Geelriandre* [1972], a piece made in collaboration with Gérard Frémy, whom I had met during a seminar by GERM [Groupe d'étude et realisation musicales], Pierre Mariétan's group. Frémy was a great interpreter of Cage's *Sonatas and Interludes*; he prepared his own piano. I remember speaking about it to Cage, who told me, "Gérard, oh yes, he is a fine musician." He once proposed to Cage that he make a notation of his preparations, but Cage refused, saying that the piece must remain free.

BG   And you participated in GERM's activities?

---

7   Translator's note: The *SS France* was a Compagnie Générale Translatlantique ocean liner put into service in 1962, the longest passenger ship ever built until 2004.

ÉR I met Pierre Mariétan in Marseille for a seminar that he was participating in with his group that was not yet called GERM. They played together every week at the Vieille Grille, a cabaret next to the Grande Mosquée. The following summer, he invited me to Sion, in Switzerland, where he gave a summer seminar. I could have participated in their activities, and I would have done so gladly if I hadn't learned that they had decided during one of their meetings that there would "be no chicks in our group." I didn't insist otherwise. It was of the era. But later they were much more willing to include me. In the seventies, I presented most of my Parisian concerts at Porte de la Suisse, in the small room that Pierre Mariétan and Giuseppe Englert directed on rue Scribe, behind l'Opéra.

Around the same time, I had the opportunity to participate in a work of Cage's. It was in Nevers at a concert by Gérard Frémy with an ensemble directed by Michel Decoust. The program included a Cage piece with a frequency generator, but there was nobody there to play it. Gérard asked me to do it. So, without much notice, I found myself under the direction of a conductor for the first and only time in my life. This very much disconcerted me, but I took a pleasure in it that was not unlike what I feel today when I work with performers.

BG This wasn't your only collaboration with Gérard Frémy. In *Geelriandre* we hear his prepared piano with resonant and bell effects and a vast drapery of very slow electronic sounds that impose themselves progressively, like sounds discovered in silence . . . You say that this piece was meant for him and that he must remain its only interpreter.

ÉR I owe him a lot. He was the first person who made me accept what I was doing. When I began, I worked only for my own pleasure. I didn't pretend to be a professional. I called all of my works *propositions sonores*. I especially did not want to get into long discussions about whether it was music or not. But with encouragement from eminent musicians, the question stopped being asked.

It is also thanks to him that I had my first concert in Paris. He programmed the piece alongside others by Aperghis and J.S. Bach in a concert at La Gaîté Lyrique.

BG And was this piece well received in Paris?

ÉR Georges Aperghis and Luc Ferrari told me they really liked it, unlike a critic who wrote that "nothing happened, but it was still too much." I think the critic also said, regarding the audience, "the miserable people watched the exit without daring to take it."

BG It's a piece that Gérard Frémy commissioned?

ÉR No, I never composed by commission, except in rare cases, like in the late seventies for Douglas Dunn, but none of my pieces went unpresented. And for this I had two solutions: GERM in Paris and Phill Niblock's Experimental Intermedia concerts at 224 Centre Street in New York. I really liked going there because it was an occasion for me to emerge from my isolation and to present my work on a good sound system—which is important—to a small but high-quality audience. In 1974, in collaboration with The Kitchen, he organized my first retrospective with the diffusion of everything I had produced since 1970: "Four Evenings of Three Years' Work."

BG Good sound systems are important because in your work sound behaves in disconcerting ways, takes its freedom; it comes from in front but is heard as if coming from behind.

ÉR You're absolutely right; there are the two speakers in front of you and you can hear them from behind. All it takes is a turn of the head to hear something different. I realized this during the first public presentation of the components of *Labyrinthe Sonore*. In 1970, Roger Tallon had asked me to contribute a work for the French Pavilion of the world's fair at Osaka, of which he was the commissioner. I had proposed the construction of a labyrinth: I had made seven small pieces meant to be looped, desynchronized, and distributed in the space through twenty-one loudspeakers that could be divided by three to have the first tape, the second tape, etc. At the time this was very technically complicated—it still is, actually—and in Osaka we only diffused a short ten-minute tape.

But this piece that Pierre Mariétan had asked me to present at Porte de la Suisse meant a lot to me. So he rented me twenty-one speakers. When we did some tests we noticed that they had the annoying tendency of transforming sine waves to square waves. What a horror! Fortunately, there were two

J.B. Lansing speakers in the space, with an elevated booth for volume control. Only one worked but, fortunately, had very good sound. So I presented the concert with this device without having had time to move all the equipment we had brought . . . At the end, all the spectators told us that the sound came from all sides. This is one of the characteristics of these sounds: They react differently depending on the acoustic space. They respond differently, and each time they have to be reconfigured. This is why a rehearsal is necessary for each concert, to correctly adjust sound that can vary with just a slight change in the position of a speaker. This is the most engaging aspect of my work.

BG Work that always remains close to sound . . .

ÉR Yes. It wasn't the analysis of sounds that first interested me; it was much more instinctive and intuitive than that. Listening to them, seeing what they say, letting them be without seeking to organize them. I chose these kinds of sounds because they interested me in and of themselves. It was out of the question to put them in a mold. I had no desire to connect them to pitches, to constructions based on pitch, or even to great sonic effects.

It was only with *Opus 17* in 1970 that I began to really organize them. It's the first piece in which I discovered that they combine very easily. I varied the speeds, the combinations, but it always worked; it was something else, of course, but it was interesting.

BG Your first pieces made with feedback were relatively short, while those created with the synthesizer are much longer. When did you discover the virtues of durations that modify listening, that force the listener to immerse themselves in the music, to be attentive to the slightest nuances, to await the shifting, the bifurcations?

ÉR It's a logical development of my early works. My first pieces are like long, twenty-minute phrases; the longest pieces I created afterward were made up of a succession of phrases. My first impulse was to respectfully listen to these sounds, to follow them—I did not direct them too much—and then to add my own two cents. I wanted to extend, to begin to talk with, to say, "This goes in such a direction, but it could be interesting to involve something else." The longest pieces are in three, four, or five parts, sometimes even more. It's a little bit like paragraphs of the same story.

It was in 1973, while creating *Ψ 847*, that I began to develop much more precise ideas on the composition of these pieces. I had to feel their structure in order to approach them. For *Ψ 847*, the idea was to take a sound mass, like a cone of music, and to unroll it little by little, to put it in counter-relief and then in cross-section.

BG   This is an architect's image.

ÉR   Architecture and music are two very closely related art forms that demand conception in three dimensions. I've always been very interested in architecture, and I know many architects who have a musical sensibility. . . But this is just an image to construct the work, it doesn't matter whether we hear it or not. I do the same with my interpreters—I give them images—but this is no more than an architect's blueprint.

BG   These very long works have a very particular effect on the listener. They require a listening that stimulates a keen focus, which is sometimes compared to meditation.

ÉR   Recently, in Berlin, Thibaut de Ruyter asked me almost the same question and gave me an embryo of a response that I really liked. When you enter a very dark room, you are forced to focus your attention before your eyes can see; my music also works a little in this way. There is no silence in my pieces, but there is an interior silence. The effect on the listener is undoubtedly this, but in fact I've never asked myself the question.

BG   These very long pieces are also very slow.

ÉR   Yes, both out of necessity and by choice. Whether with feedback or using synthesizers, the manipulation of these machines requires an extreme delicateness that leads to very slow developments. I will add, even though I've already told you, that I've always been partial to slow movements. And it's always the same emotion. I recently heard the last movement of Mahler's Eighth, it's to die for. And I've just discovered

Rossini's *Stabat Mater*, which contains passages of gravity, of magnificent beauty. These are sounds that unfold very slowly.

BG   The sound material in your pieces always evolves very slowly, almost imperceptibly, so that we don't always know where the sound is going. It makes one wonder, while listening, how you go about composing.

ÉR   I began with an idea of the piece, of its structure, an image, and, curiously, the type of sound always came immediately with the idea. Even when the image didn't come from me. Michèle Bokanowski, one of my friends who works a lot with her filmmaker husband, sometimes asked me for sounds. One day she came to me saying: "I'm looking for the sound of the silence of the stars." It's a beautiful image and I found it immediately. When I have this sound, I record it first, and then I check the ten or twelve dials with which I will be able to work.

BG   Just the dials, not the oscillators?

ÉR   Definitely not. Once the oscillators are set, tuned, they remain so for the duration of the piece. And if there's an evolution due to the time spent composing the piece, it issues from the natural discord of the oscillators, which doesn't bother me. So I did my prospecting, my harvesting of sounds. I grabbed what interested me and began recording.

Once I obtained all of the sounds, I let them rest. I didn't do this at first, which is why my early pieces are clumsier. I let them rest for three or four months, and then, when I returned to them, I made a selection, putting aside those that I didn't use. This way, I kept many sounds, telling myself that maybe one day I would have a use for them. Then I began to arrange those that I had selected, to organize them—this could be up to twenty sound elements—and to make overlaps. If I had to redo any, I would let them sit again, which is why it took me so much time. Finally, I organized all this in a very systematic way, taking note of the durations, beginnings, ends. It was like a kind of score. Then I put it all on two tapes with blank tape between them as markers. I had my two tape players with the mixing console and, on the right, the tape recorder to take everything in. It was a massive undertaking. Everything had to be done in one take. If I made even the slightest error, I had to start all over again.

BG This is closer to a painter's practice than a musician's—I'm thinking of Georges Braque, who began a painting, abandoned it, and returned to it a few months later, or never. One day, the painting would appear finished to him, and he would have no desire to retouch it.

ÉR That's it. There's a moment when you know it's finished. Even if there are mistakes, you can't go further.

BG Did you change your working methods over time?

ÉR With my first pieces, I did everything in one take, but this was probably a mistake. In *Y 847* and *Adnos I*, the central parts, the most delicate to handle, drag a little in length. Later, when I better constructed my pieces, they became markedly shorter; they went from eighty to seventy or sixty minutes. The last one lasts only fifty-five minutes, which is a good length for this kind of development.

BG There are longer ones, like *Jetsun Mila* from 1986.

ÉR *Jetsun Mila* lasts eighty-five minutes, but it's a piece in ten parts. This slow development allows me to make the interior sounds evolve. It is the same sound that changes very gently, that passes from one state to another.

BG In this sense, your music is very different from the drones produced by Ellen Fullman or Phill Niblock, who are often associated with your work.

ÉR Drone doesn't change and that's the basic difference. I remember one day I was being interviewed, and the journalist really insisted on drone. I tried to explain to him that it wasn't quite the same thing, but he still titled his article "Drone de dame."[8]

BG The title was amusing.

---

8 Translator's note: The title translates to "lady's drone," which is a play on the French title for the television show *Charlie's Angels* (*Drôles de dames*).

ÉR But it isn't fair. I've often had this discussion with Tom Johnson, who classifies my work with drone or minimalist music. It's a question to which I've responded dozens of times.

BG With the drone composers, there is often a spectacular dimension—whether it's Ellen Fullman or Paul Panhuysen's long strings, or Niblock's films—that is absent in your work.

ÉR There's only one piece that could possibly be considered as drone, *Transamorem-Transmortem*, from 1974, which I made just after *Ψ 847*. It lasts one hour, but I couldn't help but surreptitiously introduce interior variations: there's a small *tick* that periodically returns and at the end appears as a very clear sound. While insignificant at first, it is no longer so at the end.

BG Your music makes me think of a painter, Rothko, who superimposed different layers of color even though many of his paintings appear monochrome, that's why his paintings vibrate. There is in your work, like his, a certain inner vibration.

ÉR I am flattered to be compared to him, because that is indeed what I sought to do.

BG You speak of research . . .

ÉR Yes, because each finished piece, for me, was like a compromise between what I had wanted to do and what I could achieve technically. *Ψ 847* was the first piece about which I said to myself, "*Voilà*, here is something that resembles what I had set out to do." I continued, but I always said to myself, "This isn't quite it, but I'll succeed next time." It was always the next piece that was going to be the right one.

BG And you have finally arrived?

ÉR I think so, with *Naldjorlak*, thanks to the marvelous talents of Charles Curtis, Carol Robinson, and Bruno Martinez. We spent a few days together in the South of France to finish it, and I told them that, for the first time, I had heard the music that I had wanted to make.

BG You made electronic music with a synthesizer for forty years, but a few years ago you began to work with performers. Why?

ÉR It was Kasper Toeplitz who, in 2001, asked me to collaborate. He insisted on it for a while. I was really hesitant, but I accepted because the sound world of his instrument, the electric bass, is quite close to that of synthesizers. I enjoyed working with him so much. I, who had worked in solitude my whole life, took great pleasure in this shared experience.

BG No interpreters had ever approached you?

ÉR Some musicians contacted me about thirty years ago, but none were willing to do the work necessary to realize the music I wanted to make. So they left at full speed. It was Kasper who opened everything up so that when Kaffe Matthews and The Lappetites contacted me next, I kept going. I then went on to work with Charles Curtis in 2005, with Carol Robinson and Bruno Martinez in 2007, and today I work with several other interpreters: Antye Greie, Rhodri Davies, Julia Eckhardt, Silvia Tarozzi, and others.

BG How do you choose your interpreters?

ÉR They are the ones who come to me, who send me records, who make first contact. But each time it's different. I was familiar with the work of Charles Curtis, a tremendous cellist. When we worked together, he came over in the mornings to practice. Hearing him was a pleasure. He began with scales and, very slowly, each note would be chiseled like a diamond. Then he accelerated progressively, beginning with C major, passed through all the keys, and then he did the church modes in the same way. Then he played. For instance, I once heard him play a Bach suite, it was splendid.

I also knew Carol Robinson's work. As for Bruno Martinez, it was Carol who chose him because we needed a clarinetist who had a basset horn of the same make and the same series as hers, which limited us to two candidates. Bruno had never played this kind of music, but he fell into it rapidly. Antye Greie sent me some records of what she was doing by herself and with her friends in The Lappetites. Among these was a CD on which everything that I wanted was contained, but in disorder. So we listened together and she took notes.

BG How do you work with all these performers? There is no score.

ÉR No. We start from images. There are very specific themes. The famous plans and scaffoldings are forgotten once the work is completed, even if their image remains in the title. I already worked this way when composing with the synthesizer. I had begun *Ψ 847* with a reflection on psychoanalysis in mind, hence the *Psi*. While I worked, I drew interlocking *8*s, hence the *8*. I flew to the United States on one of the first Boeing 747 flights, and, shortly after takeoff, one of the engines stopped. We saw big flames and an impressive silence settled in the cabin. We were rerouted to London, where we took a new plane. The whole piece came to me during the flight from London to New York.

BG And so it's the same method that you use when you work with performers, like when you conceived of *Naldjorlak*?

ÉR *Naldjor* is a Tibetan word meaning "yoga," or "union." *Lak* is an affix that is a sign of respect. The *naldjolma* are the female yogis, the *naldjorpa* are the male yogis. We still say *amalak*, meaning "the mother whom we salute respectfully." *Naldjorlak* is a piece in three parts, the first is the yoga of the body, the second is that of speech, the third is that of the spirit. And this provided the images that I gave to the interpreters: Charles Curtis with his cello is the yoga of the body, the two basset horns are speech, and they're accompanied by breath

Thus each piece has a generic theme, a structure that serves as a template, and then each instrumentalist has a personal image that guides us. It may be, for example, images associated with water, with the ocean. This image must correspond to the personality of the interpreter and the nature of the instrument. I'm currently preparing a piece with Antye Greie, who lives on a Baltic island, on the edge of a sea that is quite interesting since it is traveled by sled in the winter, boat in the summer, and between the two is the spring, the thaw. Naturally, each season has its sounds, different noises: cracking ice during the thaw, glorious moments in summer.

It happens that these images are very old. The idea for *Occam Ocean* [2011–] came from a 1970 visit to the geology section of a Los Angeles museum. I came upon a gallery on an upper level in which all the known lengths of frequency were represented: from the length of the earth to the sun, which is a single long wave, to the smallest, which are mini angstroms, passing through more accessible zones that allow us to hear or determine color, with many zones used in multiple domains in between. These undulations, these waves of different sizes, inspired me. And I chose the ocean because it is what, on Earth, best permits us to have the physical feeling of this immensity, of these very big waves but also these light ripples.

BG   Why the title *Occam*? One thinks of the medieval philosopher and his razor . . .

ÉR   It comes from a science-fiction book that I read at that time, *Le rasoir d'Occam* [1957], in which there was a magic ocean and, of course, the razor of Guillaume d'Ockham, the great medieval theologian, whose still-relevant thought was used by great architects like Mies Van der Rohe and comes down to: the simplest is always the best. Starting from these global, general ideas, each develops their own images.

BG   This title is found again in several of your recent works.

ÉR   Yes, because they all form a series of solos, each time made with a different performer, then with duos, trios, quartets, etc., when I can convene several performers. This will end with a tutti, but the number of combinations is so substantial that as long as I live, this work will remain unfinished because it is unfinishable.

BG   But, more specifically, how do you work with your performers?

ÉR   The musicians who come to me know my work and know very well that it is impossible to notate my music. Each has their own technique. Some have a device to record our exchanges, my commentary, others take notes in their notebooks. Carol Robinson notes the keys that she uses, which I can't do since I don't know her instruments. The only instrument for which I did this was Rhodri Davies's, since I know the harp. This served us well in the development of his piece, the first in the *Occam* series.

With Antye, things went differently. She had sent me several CDs that we listened to together, and I told her, "Here's what would be good for the first part, this for the second." She herself decided that she wanted to work with the voice even though she usually works with computers, with electronic means.

BG   It takes you how long, how many rehearsals?

ÉR   It is unforeseeable. An initial part of the work consists of building the overall structure, and then there's the honing of each of the elements, which takes the longest. Between the moment that Silvia Tarozzi and I began to work and the premiere of her piece, almost a year went by. We must have met almost ten times. But this can be quicker. We finished the quartet in a few hours.

BG   But for the performers, it's a real leap into the unknown.

ÉR   For some, no doubt. Silvia Tarozzi is a marvelous violinist who has played a lot of baroque music and it took her a while to, if I may say so, break through the wall of sound. I had to help her unlearn a number of things, to explain to her, for example, that I don't fret about tuning: all musical instruments are sensitive to variations of temperature, when traveling—in heat, in the cold, in humidity—and as a result respond differently. I asked her to work according to space, to listen, and to seek the best resonant threshold of her instrument and to tune it from there. It wasn't a matter of forcing her instrument, to constrain it to the C of concert pitch, it could be a little higher, a little lower . . . I spoke to her of first, second, third string. This I owe to my work with listening.

This requires a different working method. When Julia Eckhardt came to work with me, Carol Robinson told her, "Don't worry if it doesn't work when you practice by yourself because it gets better when working with Éliane." For *Naldjorlak*, Carol and Bruno practiced many times together and always told me that it was much more difficult. This is no longer true for Carol, who can now do everything without me, once the structure is defined, but maybe this is because she is a composer.

BG   Which is the case for several of your performers.

ÉR   This is the case for Thomas Lehn, Kasper Toeplitz, Carol Robinson, but not all. It's one thing to work for yourself and another to put yourself in someone else's service. Antye Greie has highlighted this because she uses her name when she performs my works and her pseudonym, AGF, when she composes.

BG   All this is very personal. These are pieces intended for the performers with whom you have developed them.

ÉR   Each time, it's a completely personal, different thing. They are one-of-a-kind pieces made for a single musician, who are free, if they wish, to transmit it to another. I'm going to work with another cellist; the theme will be different from the one that I developed with Charles Curtis. There are new stories each time.

BG   The first time one hears your music, one is usually very surprised and wonders where you come from, what your sources are. It is known that you worked with Pierre Schaeffer and Pierre Henry, but your music is really quite different from theirs. So different that one struggles, at first listen, to see the connection, and is often tempted to turn toward other horizons. It has been said that your music incites meditation, and that you make no secret of your Buddhism, which is referred to explicitly in the titles of several of your works. Is there a connection there?

ÉR   No. I never made a mystery of my Buddhism, but I also don't show it off. Curiously, Buddhism came to me through music, with *Adnos I*, a piece that I presented in 1974 at Mills College, which at the time was under the direction of Robert Ashley. At the end of the concert, a group of young people came to me and said: "You know, your music, you are not the one making it." It was a little surprising, but I continued to chat with them. They were students of Tibetan Buddhism. For me it was a bit like rediscovering a lost country that I already knew. It was an extraordinary sensation. And their words brought back memories. Notably of a conversation I'd had with Terry Riley's first wife, who had heard about my music. It had been described to her as meditative.

These young people gave me an address in Paris to which I rushed upon my return and started to study. I was working on *Adnos II* at the time, and I had decided to finish the piece and then give everything up to consecrate myself to Buddhism after meeting a Tibetan master who lived in the Dordogne and with whom I spent most of my time.

BG   So you stopped composing?

ÉR   I was no longer making music, and after two or three years I thought it was time to stop officially. The roof of [the retreat center in the Dordogne] was in need of repair, and I was considering selling my synthesizer to help finance the work. But I always asked for the master's advice before making an important decision. It was always interesting. Like all the great masters, he didn't necessarily respond to the question directly, he gave, rather, more of a generalized direction. It was very rare for him to say, "No, don't do this," and yet, this is what he told me: "You must continue to make music." I would later joke that he had probably had enough of hearing the bizarre sounds that went through my head. Actually, I think he figured that I didn't have strong enough shoulders to really handle the great retreats. So, I owe both my encounter with and return from Tibetan Buddhism to music. My master had added, however, during this conversation, "But it must be an offering." And Tibetan Buddhism had given me so much that it felt right for me to give something back. My first offering was *Songs of Milarepa* [1983].

BG   A very long work in which we find two voices, one that reads the texts of the songs in English and another that reads them in Tibetan.

ÉR   I had an English translation of some very beautiful songs made by Lama Kunga, I asked him for permission to use it and for him to read the texts in the original version, so it's his voice that is heard in the Tibetan sections. As for the English, I asked Robert Ashley, whose voice had seduced me one night when we dined together. I started with this, and then, based on the recording of the voices, I made my edits. With this done, I added electronic sounds.

These songs inspired a very nice letter from Albuquerque, from a medical salesman who bought the record and had stopped on the side of the road. "With this music," he wrote, "my medicine is no longer needed."

BG   This isn't the only work that you composed as an offering.

ÉR   There was *Jetsun Mila* and *Trilogie de la Mort* [1998], which is in three sections: *Kyema* [1988], dedicated to my son Yves; *Kailasha* [1991]; and *Koumé* [1993].

Kyema is inspired by *The Tibetan Book of the Dead*, the *Bardo Thödröl*, which describes the six states of consciousness that evoke the continuity of being. The second section of *Trilogie* is an imaginary pilgrimage around Mount Kailash, the most sacred mountain in the Himalayas. I had a whole series of photos. I was familiar with the pilgrimage, and I had to make it internally to set it to music. And it just so happened that between the moment of its conception and the moment I really set myself to creating it, my son had his accident. So, more than a pilgrimage, it also traces the path of a very difficult mourning. For years, I couldn't listen to the piece. It was the only time that I asked my friends, notably Tom Johnson, to come listen to it. I told them: "I cannot hear this piece, I'm ready to destroy it, tell me what you think." In this pilgrimage around Mount Kailash, there are periods of walking and stops, with moments that are very hard for me. It gives me the impression of a dinosaur who sinks into mud and tries with difficulty to raise its feet to walk.

BG   Did you make this pilgrimage?

ÉR   No. It's a very difficult pilgrimage that takes several days, the conditions are very tough, the nights frigid. And I was already too old, but I have friends who have done it and who brought me extraordinary images. That's what gave me the idea.

The third piece, *Koumé*, is associated with the departure of my Tibetan master and with cremation ceremonies. I made the mix at CIRM [Centre International de Recherche Musicale], in Nice, on a computer.

BG   You present these pieces as if they were independent.

ÉR   They are, in fact. It was Michel Redolfi who assembled and wanted to present them together at the MANCA Festival. That's how it became the *Trilogie de la Mort*.

Koumé is the first piece for which I was invited, by the CIRM studio in Nice, to do the final mix with an assistant, Luc Martinez.

BG   Where does the title *Koumé* come from?

ÉR   It's pidgin Tibetan: *mé* is "fire" and *kou*, "the sacred body." The word doesn't actually exist in Tibetan.

BG   So it isn't Buddhism, but we can attempt other associations. In particular, with painting, not that of the *nouveaux réalistes*, whom you knew well, but Rothko, his almost monochrome works that vibrate discreetly, standing out against a background of color.

ÉR   The comparison with Rothko is flattering. I'll accept it. I recently received a letter from someone who found an analogy between my music and Soulages's paintings, these big, flat black blocks, which is close to what you're suggesting. But it's true that connections with *nouveau réalisme* are distant, if not nonexistent.

Two or three years ago, I was asked, as part of an exhibition of *nouveaux réalistes*, to give a lecture on *musique concrète* and *nouveau réalisme*. It was difficult for me to refuse, so I talked about Hains and Villeglé's *Hépérile éclaté* [1953], the poetry of Dufrêne, but it isn't my world. At the same time, I am still moved by Pierre Schaeffer and Pierre Henry's oldest works. They were my first loves. They move me, touch me, because I remember how much I was moved, bowled over when I first heard this world of sound, even if today I know it wasn't necessarily mine.

BG   So, it's neither painting nor Buddhism . . . The first time that we met, you told me that it was the sound of the Caravelle, a plane of the seventies with a daily route between Paris and Nice, that made you want to make this music.

ÉR   There were others. There was a courier between Nice and Corsica, which was a real symphony orchestra. All it took was to lend an ear, to take advantage of the capacity of the ear to wander in an undefined world of sound, to hear, more or less. The music I made really reflects this. I've often been told that my electronic pieces are never heard the same way; the first time you grasp one thing, and another time, something else. It's kind of the same with the plane engines. There's a constant, which one would call a white noise, that is quite harmonious, through which one can wander, favoring one frequency and then another, associating them.

BG   It's the ear that makes its menu.

ÉR   Yes, and this is also true of the music I make now with performers. The situation in concert privileges listening to these partials and harmonics more than the record that captures everything and on which much is missing. It isn't a matter of recording or technique, but rather that the ear doesn't behave in the same way. It was clear from my most recent concerts that one very quickly forgets the fundamentals and retains only the very subtle play of the interpreter, all of their nuances. All it takes is an instant's lapse of concentration for the attention to give way. Anyway, I recommend, in these cases, to abbreviate. That's why I refuse all amplification, which limits the size of the performance spaces. But *Naldjorlak* was performed in this way at the Louvre in front of four hundred people and it was magnificent. No two listeners hear the same thing. Perception becomes more refined.

BG   You seem very aware of the noise of plane engines.

ÉR   We lived close to Nice's airport, which at the time was just a small shed with a single runway and no more than ten planes per day. There was one that I didn't like at all because it was very violent; it was a four-engine propeller plane that made noise of an intolerable violence. It was like those concerts where there are too many decibels. And then there was the Caravelle, and another plane, the sound of which was so rich.

BG   Your music is so unique that it might seem isolating, yet if we consider all the performers who approach you, we can see that this isn't the case.

ÉR   I do receive many letters, recordings of musicians who claim to be followers of my work, who tell me about the influence I've had on them. Very often, at the end of a concert, young composers come to see me, give me CDs to listen to, which I do systematically. Afterward, I send them a note. Sometimes, it takes me a while to respond because I really listen to their recordings, out of respect for their work, but also because I can't stand background music. But I always respond.

This takes so much time that I can't listen to this music in a suitable way every day. I've observed that I listen to these recordings like my own music, in different ways that range from a discreet, lenient listen to a technical listen that highlights flaws, weaknesses, errors, to a bad day's listen, when everything seems disposable. At first, when this happened to me, in the sixties, I was overcome with rage, I took my demagnetizer and I made a big cross on the tape. And when, a few weeks later, I returned to the tape to reuse it, I would discover interesting sounds that I would have used had they not been half erased. So I forbade myself from doing this. The days when I could not hear, I didn't push it; I stopped, I moved on to other things. And then there is, of course, the fascinated listen. So I understand the behavior of the audience at my concerts, those who can't take it and leave after ten minutes, just as I do those who remain, fascinated.

BG   But where do these composers come from?

ÉR   From everywhere, from Europe and North America, the United States and Canada. Sometimes it's embarrassing to respond because you sense that there's a little something . . . but there are some very interesting ones, too. What I like the most are those that haven't settled in my slippers and have developed their own musical world.

BG   Most have discovered your music through concerts or recordings, but have you had students?

ÉR   I have given a few lessons, notably at Mills College, but I've had very few students. I am, however, very proud of one of them: Laetitia Sonami, who found, on the basis of what she experienced with me, her own music.

I feel like I've succeeded when I perceive, in the music of those who claim to be influenced by me, that they have surpassed my influence to come into their own, when listening to my electronic sounds has suggested to them their own inner music. This, I believe, is the most beautiful transmission. I've said it many times: it's my greatest pleasure, I have no fear whatsoever that my work, my name, will disappear with me because I have the feeling that a transmission has been made.

MODE DIFFUSION ÉLECTRONIQUE
Éliane Radigue

No stereophonic effects, no frontal diffusion, but rather an all-over, all-around effect avoiding as much as possible direct projection from the loudspeakers onto the audience.

Ideally, we should forget about the speakers, and get the feeling of sounds coming from everywhere, like being immersed in a shell or in the body of an instrument. Never too loud, from ppp to p with some mf; anyway, the tapes are already recorded that way, so just follow it. The only corrections would depend on the acoustical response from the room. As, for example, the number of loudspeakers, and their placement. The only little trick is to cross the two tracks, let's say right in the front diffused on the left in back, and conversely for the left track. When several loudspeakers are necessary, cross them all along.

To ensure the all-over level for the diffusion according to the size and acoustical response from the space, make a complete listening of the piece, from the beginning to the end, avoid jumping around here and there, stopping, forwarding the tape, losing the feeling of the continuity in listening. Instead, walk around the space while making the adjustments, to make sure that everywhere the diffusion is about the same, finding the best level to maintain the presence of the sound anywhere and everywhere. That way, very few light corrections, made slowly during the diffusion, should be necessary.

To avoid the hiss of the tape recorder, there is a small trick that can be done at the beginning and end of the diffusion: taking off everything above 10–12,000 Hz before starting, and bringing it back slowly throughout the fading in. Do the opposite at the end: slowly bring the 10–12,000 Hz down at the beginning of the fade-out, then fade out to silence.

Never, ever, big contrast !!!

Flyer for "Kyema" with Éliane Radigue at GERM, Paris, May 9, 1989. Courtesy Fonds Éliane Radigue.

BEING AND NONBEING: AN ANALYSIS OF *KYEMA*
Daniel Silliman

Adapted from the third chapter of Silliman's 2023 dissertation "Transcendent Machine: An Analysis of Éliane Radigue's ARP 2500 Synthesizer Music," this text offers an unprecedented technical analysis of Radigue's *Kyema* (1988), later designated as the first movement of the *Trilogie de la Mort* (1988–93). Silliman's reverent explication of Radigue's complex relationship with her instrument is complemented by measured speculation regarding the composer's broader thematic concerns.

In the opening ninety seconds of Éliane Radigue's 1988 composition *Kyema*, we hear two ARP 2500 oscillators, close in frequency to each other, create an undulating effect called beating. Beating is caused by a cyclical pattern of constructive and destructive interference between closely tuned sounds, and the rate of beating is determined by their difference in frequency.[1] Considering the well-documented fact that Radigue did not directly alter the frequencies of her ARP's oscillators once work on a new composition had begun, one would expect that the rate of beating would remain constant, but it doesn't. Instead, it gradually speeds up and slows down.[2]

While this question of variable beat frequencies may seem like a small thing to concern oneself with, beating is a defining characteristic of Radigue's synthesizer works, achieving some of her practice's most important ends. Beating animates what might otherwise be a static, opaque musical texture—thus lending the synthesized sounds a lively and rhythmic character. At the same time, by sounding out a difference between two or more tones, beating brings an actively engaged listener into close apprehension of the physical fact of sound's propagation in space.

This question began a years-long investigation into the arcana of analog modular synthesizers and magnetic tape recording. I needed to understand those gently undulating tones, so I pored obsessively over technical documentation of the ARP 2500, listened repeatedly to recordings of *Kyema* and Radigue's other synthesizer compositions, and ruled out the explanations that were incompatible with the evidence. It took some time for me to realize that I had been attributing an autonomy to these sounds that may not have been there in the first place. I had assumed that these subtle variations in beating were due to some innate quality of the sounds themselves, or an automatic process of electronic synthesis, which Radigue was simply observing and capturing on tape. This was only partially correct, as I would eventually discover that the beating at the opening of *Kyema* was speeding up and slowing down *because of something Radigue was doing with her hands*. In fact, her hand is ever present, subtly directing the flow of events from one moment to the next with meticulous attention.

Modular synthesizers like the ARP 2500 can be patched in various ways with novel combinations of signal processing modules.

This open architecture can yield a sound that lasts indefinitely, unbound by the note-on/note-off binary of keyboard presses.[3] The ARP 2500 keyboard is detachable from the cabinet that houses the other modules, and after Radigue purchased her ARP in New York in 1971, she returned to Paris with the cabinet alone.[4] Thus began a nearly three-decade partnership with the instrument that would yield nineteen compositions, of which *Kyema* is among the most well known. When I finally saw Radigue's ARP myself, I became possessed of a newfound appreciation for the depth of feeling and concern that Radigue extended toward this instrument. As my hands traced the movements that Radigue herself made to produce this unusually still and slowly moving music, I recalled her remark that the ARP has a "voice" all his own.[5]

Once an ARP 2500 is powered on, signals flow through the circuits, ready to be patched together in virtually endless combinations. While the designers of these instruments typically dichotomized signals intended for sound and those intended for the manipulation of sounds, from her early experiments with the ARP Radigue freely mixed these two domains to create complex webs of interdependence in which the slightest adjustment of one parameter could have a disproportionately dramatic effect on the overall sound.[6] These chaotic, nonlinear patterns are a general feature of Radigue's patching technique, and part of her role in these highly interdependent networks was that of a gentle and subtle supervisor, gradually and indirectly adjusting the system's behavior through careful and precise manual interventions. In this way, the synthesizer patch becomes much more like an ecosystem—a closed, *living* system bound by rules of relation. This ecological sense of signal flow finds support in Radigue's conviction that sound is alive—"an autonomous life that needed to be respected."[7]

Radigue placed the utmost importance on the active listening of an engaged audience, evidenced by her commitment to perceptually ambiguous, spare, and underdetermined musical materials. Her nontraditional formats of recital and presentation readily facilitated, even necessitated, such deep listening: consider, for example, *Vice-Versa, etc...* (1970), which was distributed not in concert but as a limited-edition tape reel for private use, to be duplicated and played back in "any combination of two tracks, in one direction or another, on several tape recorders, *ad libitum*";[8] *Labyrinthe Sonore* (1970), a proposed sound installation involving an actual labyrinth through which the audience would navigate;[9] or *Transamorem-Transmortem* (1974), which stipulated that the tape be diffused through four speakers, one in every corner of a carpeted room, with each listener composing their own version of the work through subtle movements of their head.[10] In advance of a presentation of her longer synthesizer works, Radigue would often collaborate with a venue's sound technicians to arrange the loudspeakers in such a way as to nullify stereophonic effects and create essentially equivalent listening experiences from any location in the space.[11] Radigue's disembodied presentation of her synthesizer works reveals latent tensions at the core of her practice. The "inner life" of sounds, to borrow Radigue's phrase, is disclosed through the composer's foregrounding of combination tones, waveform beats, and a filtering technique that reveals a sound's constituent elements; at the same time, by obscuring her role in its disclosure, this inner life takes on an aura of autonomy—sounds seemingly unfold at their own pace and on their own terms.

Radigue offers a warning to those, like myself, who would attempt to scrutinize this music, which she claims stands "in opposition to the analytic nature of trying to cut things up into little morsels in order to examine them"; "on the contrary," she says, "it's about the life that engenders things."[12] So, what is the life, or lives, that engender *Kyema*? One of these is Radigue herself. The composer's presence (and her absence) imbues her work with an uncommonly powerful intimacy, fostering encounters with the listener that are essential to Radigue's music in general. However, acknowledging the limitations of analysis should only draw one deeper into the act of listening, and what follows is an attempt to relate this act, in more or less real time, to the reader—a kind of guided journey through the sixty-one minutes and seven seconds that comprise *Kyema*.[13]

In my attempts to understand the somewhat esoteric technology Radigue used to create this music, I have found that the composer, despite the lengths to which she went to conceal her bodily presence in its presentation, is *there* all along; and I see this articulation of *the body that was always there* as one task of electronic music historians in particular. This is not least because so much of the body's presence in electronic music is obscured by a lack of familiarity with the connections between haptic actions and sonic outcomes. "[Electronic] music," as Deniz Peters rather succinctly frames the problem, "becomes an *interrogation* of human presence or absence by the very difficulty that composing this presence in fact entails."[14] I intend to counteract Radigue's mediated disembodiment by painting a vivid picture of the composer at work in the studio.[15]

In Radigue's aesthetic ethos, sound is alive, and in *Kyema*, she uses sound to convey a cyclical process of death and rebirth. These are grand ideas, but in elucidating the arcana of her creative process, I find much in the way of intimacy, afforded by Radigue's unique approach to working with melody, timbre, and harmony, and embodied in the physical traces of her deliberate recording techniques. If, as I will argue here, *Kyema* embraces the intentional listener, that is because it was made by one. At every moment Radigue is there, listening intentionally and directing the flow of the music with precision and care. The author's continuous presence is a distinguishing feature of Radigue's synthesizer music in general and does much to explain its power. If the reader's enchantment with this deceptively minimal music is somewhat muddled by the torn curtain, perhaps the revelation of the mechanisms behind the illusion can endear us to the complex and imperfect realities of being here, now, today.

Kyema from Afar

Radigue completed *Kyema* in September of 1988, first presenting the work in San Francisco in December of that same year. *Kyema* would become the first part of the *Trilogie de la Mort* (1988–93), which also includes *Kailasha* (1991) and *Koumé* (1993). Radigue composed the latter two pieces during a period of significant personal loss: in 1989, Radigue's son Yves died tragically in a car crash in Spain. Radigue would posthumously dedicate *Kyema* to his memory, though her initial inspiration for the composition came from a deep engagement with a compilation of Buddhist funerary texts. In the years immediately following Yves' passing, Radigue composed *Kailasha*, which allegorizes the difficult pilgrimage to Mount Kailash, a sacred peak that pilgrims do not ascend but rather circumambulate. *Koumé*, the final work in the cycle, is a response to the passing and cremation rites of Radigue's Tibetan Buddhist mentor, Pawo Rincpoche.[16]

The entire cycle takes just under three hours to complete, and *Kyema* is its longest movement. It is one of the more structurally complex compositions in Radigue's entire ARP 2500 output, cycling through several distinct thematic ideas in a compelling evocation of the liminal spaces between being and nonbeing. These various states blend into one another over the course of extremely slow crossfades and hazy superimpositions, encouraging listeners to attend to the almost imperceptible changes that comprise this music.

Early in the composition process, Radigue sought inspiration from passages in *The Tibetan Book of the Dead*, a syncretic document based partially on a seventeenth-century compendium of Buddhist funerary texts assembled by Rigdzin Nyima Dragpa called the *Bardo Thödröl*. With *Kyema*, Radigue sought to evoke the six intermediary states between death and rebirth, as outlined in the six verses found in the version of the text[17] that Radigue was instructed to read by her mentor.[18] While the question of how specifically these Tibetan Buddhist verses inform *Kyema* is beyond the scope of my expertise, I will nonetheless draw from time to time upon these cyclical ideas of death and rebirth as a metaphorical framing in my account of the work. Such a framing is hardly arbitrary. As noted by François J. Bonnet, the steward of Radigue's archive at the Groupe de Recherches Musicales (GRM), "the first step of the composition is *always* a mental image or story in her head."[19] Any consideration of Radigue's synthesizer work therefore ought to take these precompositional notions into account, if any record of them can be found.

Radigue has been quite effusive on the matter of *Kyema*'s inspirations, describing its title as a Tibetan expression invoking "the sigh we make when faced with inescapable fatality" and as a neologistic vernacular Latin construction "[referring] to beings born from a mother: *ma* is the suffix that marks the feminine, the maternal, and *kye* refers to birth."[20] With her customary linguistic erudition and play, Radigue thereby inscribes in the work's title a dual concept of birth and death, in which *each is constitutive of the other*. Radigue's electronic compositions frequently explore this cyclical understanding of life. For example, her 1971 composition *7th Birth*, one of her first for the ARP 2500, engages with this theme of repeated births, and her 1973 *Biogenesis* superimposes the auscultated heartbeats of her daughter, then pregnant with Radigue's granddaughter, with electronic synth tones, directly inviting comparison between somatic rhythms and Radigue's approach to the synthesizer.[21] While Radigue's conception of sounds as lifeforms is, in a sense, the enveloping context for engaging with her music, a work like *Biogenesis* readily complicates this reading by introducing recordings of the *sounds of the living*. While this is an important distinction, the slippage between Radigue's varied engagements with notions of life underline the composer's broader assertion of the inextricability of sound and its mediation by the

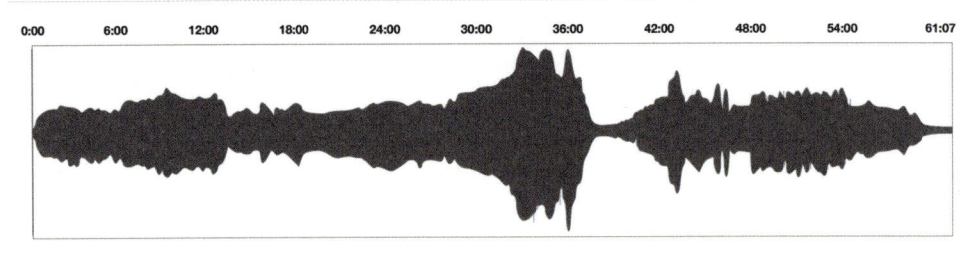

Figure 1 *Kyema*'s amplitude over time.

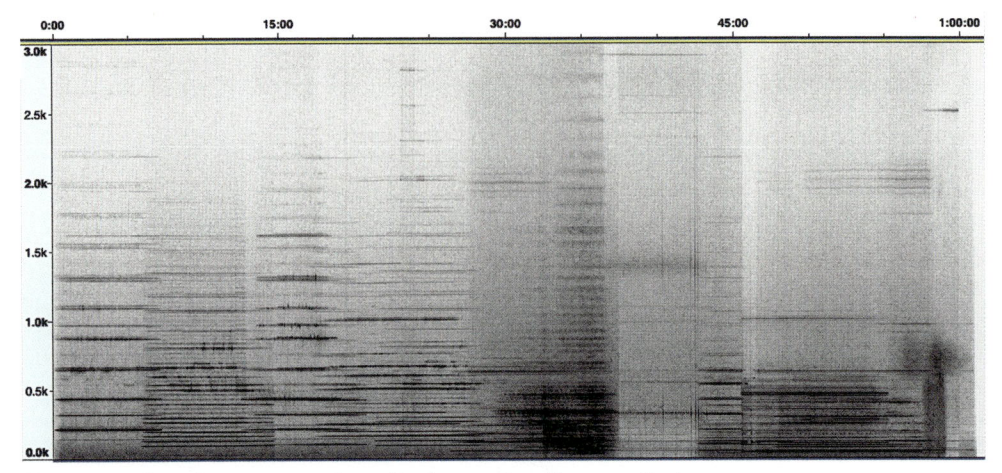

Figure 2 *Kyema*'s spectrum and amplitude over time (linear scaling).

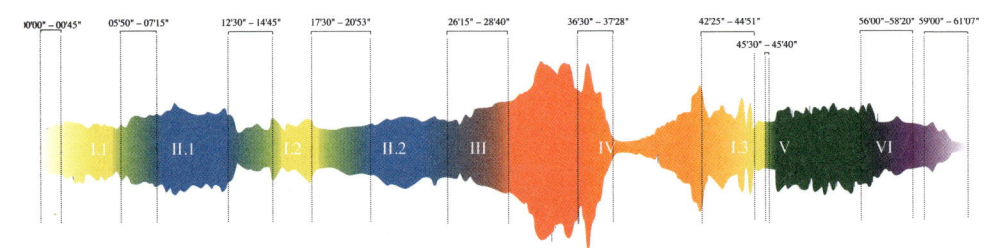

Figure 3 *Kyema*'s amplitude over time, color-coded to show cyclical structure. Bracketed regions denote crossfades between contiguous sections. All time markings are approximated within a few seconds.

corporeal mechanics of perception: "in this immense, vibrating symphony of the universe," asks Radigue in her 2009 aesthetic treatise "The Mysterious Power of the Infinitesimal," "[w]as there any sound if no ear was there to hear it?"[22]

Radigue organizes *Kyema* with one of the more dramatic, *telos*-driven structures of her synthesizer compositions. While her works are never, despite their slow progression of change, truly stationary, *Kyema*'s overall scale of contrast across many areas of analysis—register, dynamics, timbre, and rhythm—eclipses that of many of her other electronic works. *Kyema* also features relatively dramatic conceits: the use of repeated, cyclically developed, and contrasting sections, as well as a distinct climax around two-thirds of the way through the piece. The scope of this drama becomes visible only when one takes in a bird's-eye view of *Kyema* (Fig. 1)—a basic plot of *Kyema*'s amplitude over time. Around 36'00", just past the center mark, there's a clear highpoint, which is then followed by a massive drop in amplitude.

Accordingly, the spectrogram (Fig. 2) reveals a sudden drop in spectral saturation that corresponds with this highpoint in amplitude, while the distinctively blurry edges of each section beautifully demonstrate Radigue's adroit use of crossfades during the recording session for *Kyema*. Due to the spectrogram's linear scaling, bands spaced equidistantly in the frequency plot generally indicate a periodic signal, showing, for instance, a timbre with energy at integer multiples of a fundamental with frequency f (e.g., *2f, 3f, 4f,* etc.); while regions of unequally spaced bands of spectral energy generally indicate a noisier, or aperiodic, signal. Looking at the equally spaced bands on either side of the noisy climax, there is clearly a large-scale timbral contrast between periodicity and aperiodicity to be found in *Kyema*.

Building on the previous two figures, Figure 3 shows a plot of *Kyema*'s amplitude over time, color-coded and labeled using a hybrid Roman-Arabic numeral convention (according to which I.1, I.2, and I.3 are all thematically related). Figure 3's time markings show the temporal divisions of the work, denoting the approximate beginning of the fade-in and conclusion of the fadeout for each of its respective materials.[23]

As Radigue evidently sought to evoke the six *Bardos* in her composition, so, too, have I sought to identify six reasonably distinct kinds of music in *Kyema*. In her annotated works list, Radigue names these six intermediary states in Tibetan, French, and English:[24]

1. *Kyene—la naissance* [birth]
2. *Milam—la rêve* [dream]
3. *Samtem—la contemplation* [contemplation]
4. *Chikal—la mort* [death]
5. *Chönye—la claire lumière* [bright light]
6. *Sippaï—traversée et retour* [crossing and returning]

While Radigue remarks to Julia Eckhardt that, "[her] composition respects the text," the question of how *Kyema* evokes the six *Bardo* is not answered definitively. Radigue's own program notes for *Kyema*, while comparatively rich in detail, do not specify whether the six states are evoked musically through six temporally discrete movements, or as otherwise differentiated types of musical material. It's entirely possible that by "intermediary state," Radigue refers not to any discrete sections of music but rather to the six unique combinations of superimposed material found in the work (i.e., I+II, II+III, III+IV, IV+I, I+V, V+VI). The composer's lack of specification here is notable; in other multisection works, Radigue is typically quite specific about the correspondence between musical sections and their poetic intent. Take, for example, *Jetsun Mila* (1987), wherein the nine sections evoke nine phases of the life of the eponymous Tibetan spiritual leader; *Songs of Milarepa* (1983), which comprises distinct songs that are labeled and listed in chronological order; or *Adnos III* (1982), which is structured in four continuous movements, each of which is named by the composer in a program note.[25]

While I do not know how my six kinds of discrete musical material correspond, if at all, with the six intermediary states in the *Bardo Thödröl*, I offer this provisional outline of the work's possible thematic structure, with each of the six *Bardo* corresponding to each of the six sections, along with brief descriptions of each section and reduced transcriptions of their main harmonic ideas in European classical notation.[26]

I.1	II.1	I.2	II.2	III.	IV.	I.3	V.	VI.
(1st) Birth	(1st) Dream	(2nd) Birth	(2nd) Dream	Contemplation	Death	(3rd) Birth	Bright light	Crossing & returning

Birth, or I.1 (00'00"–07'15"), opens the piece. It is stated a total of three times throughout the work in varied forms: I.2 (12'30"–20'53") and I.3 (42'25–45'40). Harmonically, I.1, I.2, and I.3 consist of detuned approximations of integer multiples of an implied and occasionally audible ~110 Hz fundamental (~A2, m≈45.0) that beat at various rates.[27] This musical material generally entails the gradual revelation of beating harmonics through a technique called resonant bandpass filtering that iteratively and rhapsodically builds melodies out of the harmonics of this implied fundamental. For the synthesizer novitiate, the bandpass filter allows a band, or section, of the input spectrum, to pass through the filter at a greater amplitude than spectral components outside the band. Roughly speaking, the more resonant a bandpass filter is, the greater the difference in amplitude between the spectra within and outside the passband. Single partials can be selected by the ARP 2500's multimode filters using this technique.[28] Sections I.1 and I.2 possess a generally stable and periodic character, and to my ears function structurally as a kind of refrain; however, in I's final appearance (I.3) at 42'25", a low partial at around 60 Hz (~B-flat 1, m≈34.51) produces a subtle yet unyielding tension by suspending the harmony over a dissonant bass. This gradual transformation of returning and otherwise familiar material is one of *Kyema*'s defining characteristics.

The two statements of Dream, II.1 and II.2 (5'50"–14'45" and 17'30"–28'40") are mostly centered around an implied ~67-Hz fundamental (~C2, m≈36.41) (Fig. 5). This music is generally of a thicker, mellower, darker timbre than that of I. Over its two iterations, II further develops the technique of melodies constituted by resonantly filtered partials. I think of II.1 and II.2 as the *shadows* of I.1 and I.2, respectively, existing in a kind of axial opposition to that earlier music. I mean *axial* as precisely as spatial metaphors in musical analysis permit: II and I have many shared characteristics—such as a generally harmonic distribution of partials, and the use of resonant bandpass filtering to emphasize those partials—while also exhibiting a strikingly different affect. To my ears, II is more melancholic and reflective, and I attribute this difference in affective valence to II's thicker texture, generally lower pitch level, and more elaborate partial melody. The variations between each statement of II are subtle; when the material recurs a second time

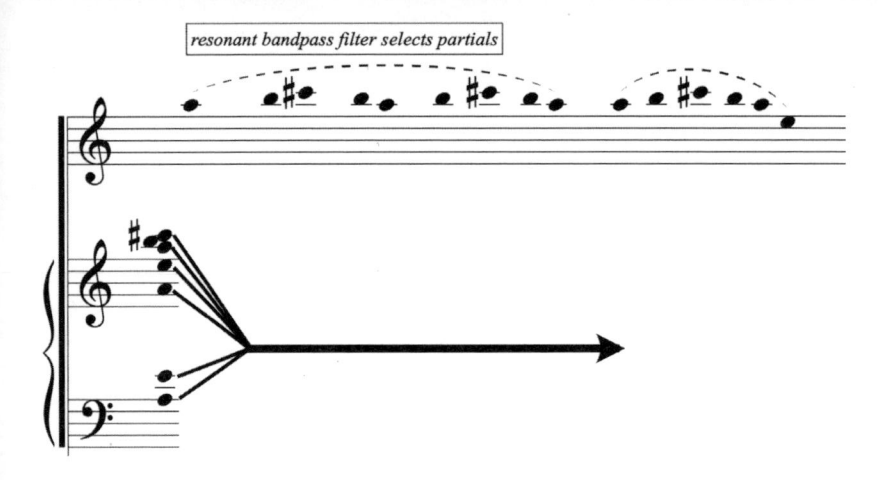

Figure 4   Reduction of I.1, including the main drone and the melody of partials 1'30"–2'30".

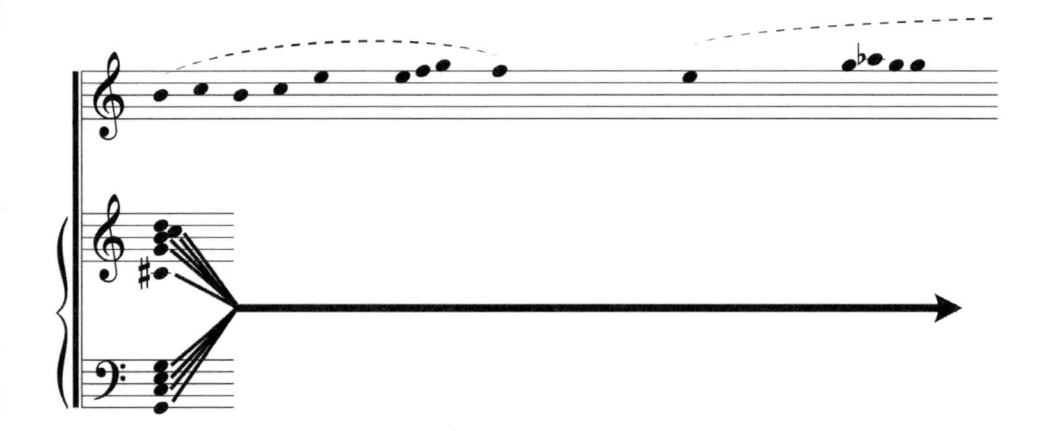

Figure 5   A transcription of a part of II.2, with approximations of the main partials of the drone at the partial melody heard between roughly 9'00" and 10'00".

(as II.2), the pitch is shifted up between 1 and 2 percent, prompting the rates of beating to adjust in response. This change in pitch may be the result of analog oscillator pitch drift caused by fluctuations in ambient temperature, or of slight variations in the playback or recording speed of the tapes used to capture these two sections.

Contemplation, or III (26'15"–37'28"), occurs only once, or possibly twice depending on how a later passage is interpreted. Constituting the most dramatic departure in *Kyema*, III contains a teleological swell toward the work's loudest and perhaps most dissonant moment, while superimposing a low, harmonic 61-Hz drone (~B1 fundamental, m≈34.79) with several partials that dissonate with the harmonic tone (Fig. 6). Bands of noise and electronically processed recordings of *gyaling* and *rag-dung*, two Tibetan wind instruments, contribute to the passage's overall increase in both thematic and timbral complexity. (There's an argument to be made for a brief recurrence of III starting around 57'00", as this music bears strong spectral affinity with the beginning of III heard around 26'30", but it's a fleeting appearance.)

In Death, or IV (36'30"–44'51"), we mostly hear a crackling band of noise that at first is indistinguishable from the noise floor of the tape itself. IV occurs at a structurally significant moment, immediately following the roiling climax of III; in this way, IV provides one of the starkest contrasts in *Kyema* between saturation and emptiness. A soft, striking tone accompanies the band of noise, sounding once every nine or ten seconds, corresponding roughly to either the same general frequency region of the bandpassed noise, or an octave below it, with approximate peaks at 330 Hz (~E4, m≈64.01) and 1,387 Hz (~F6, m≈88.88). The uneven spacing of this tone imbues the moments between its sounding with a sense of anticipation that implies an embodied presence; Radigue seems to *wait* before sounding it again (Fig. 7). As a constituent partial of the returning I.3 music around 42'25", this gently striking tone facilitates a smooth transition into the final restatement of the work's opening material.

Bright light, or V (45'30"–58'20"), constitutes the longest unbroken section of unique material in the work. Timbrally, it's so dense and underdetermined that it's easier to describe its constituent elements than to attempt a summary description of its total harmonic effect. This lack of equivalence between part and whole finds accord with Radigue's vitalistic conception of sounds, as well as the dynamic between those sounds and their listeners—each listener will draw out details that are personally significant to them, and no single perspective may be considered ideal or definitive;

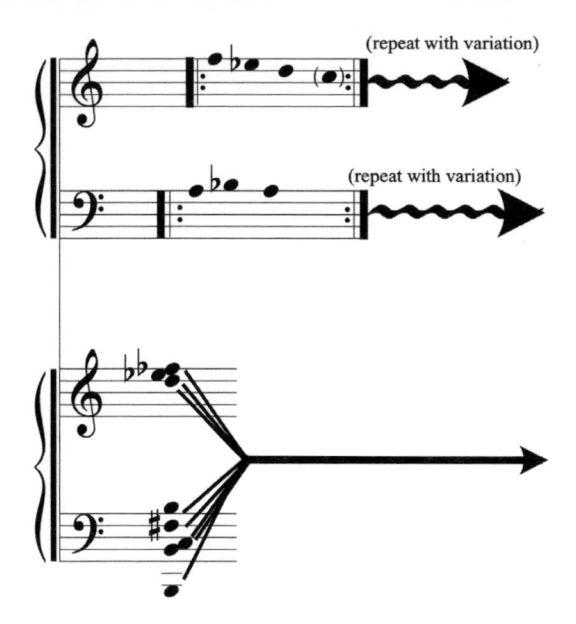

Figure 6   Reduction showing the main spectral peaks in the drone accompanied by approximations of the electronically processed *gyaling* and *rag-dung* loops. The pitches of the Tibetan wind instruments are quite difficult to pin down in the recordings, in part because they have very similar spectral profiles to the synth drones with which they are mixed.

Figure 7   Reduction of the beginning of section IV, from about 37'30" to 38'30". Note the unevenly spaced bell tones in the upper staff.

rather, through shifting attentional focus, each listener has a unique perception of the musical texture. Even if it cannot account for the variety or the significance of these individual responses, spectral analysis can offer some meaningful insights. Looking at its spectral peaks, V's texture appears to comprise two superimposed harmonic timbres with fundamentals approximately a major third apart, at 50 Hz (~G1, m≈31.34) and 62 Hz (~B1, m≈35.07). Further complicating any single reading of V's harmony are several other dissonant partials, accompanied by bands of filtered noise. Starting around 47'30", soft striking tones not unlike those heard in section IV ring out at approximately D-sharp 4 (m≈63) and G-sharp 4 (m≈68) (Fig. 8).

Crossing and returning, or VI (56'00"–61'07"), is the final material heard in the piece, comprising a band of dark, filtered noise that gradually gives way to a brighter and softer band of noise, through which cuts a faintly keening sinusoid around 2,515 Hz (~D-sharp 7, m≈99.18). VI offers a kind of elliptical, open ending that does not so much provide closure as it does point toward an ongoing process of spectral transformation. Musical notation is a poor medium for conveying such an abstract texture, and I think a spectrogram (Fig. 9) better conveys the austerity of *Kyema*'s final section.

A structure of such thematic complexity, unfolding over the course of an hour, clearly required significant preparation on Radigue's part. While the recording process Radigue used at the beginning of her career was nonstandard, themes of duplication, superimposition, and iterative rerecording can be identified throughout much of her oeuvre. For example, the final composition of *USRAL* (1969) was created through the successive rerecording of ultrasonic feedback tones at increasingly slower speeds, gradually bringing the music into the range of audibility.[29] *Chry-ptus* (1971), an early composition using the Buchla 100-series modular synthesizer, had unique performance instructions: a pair of desynchronized tape machines superimposed different recordings of the Buchla in real time, producing minute variations over the course of about twenty-four minutes.[30]

By the time of *Kyema*'s composition in 1988, Radigue had standardized a process of recording for these extremely long synthesizer compositions, which she would do in a single take in her Paris apartment. This unforgiving process involved the preparation of two reels with alternating sections of previously recorded material, between which she would crossfade in real time while recording

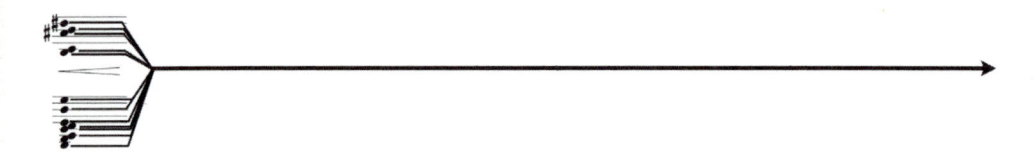

Figure 8   Reduction from 45'30" to about 48'00", showing the cloudy aggregate of tones, a low partial melody, and, toward the end of the passage, the soft striking tones.

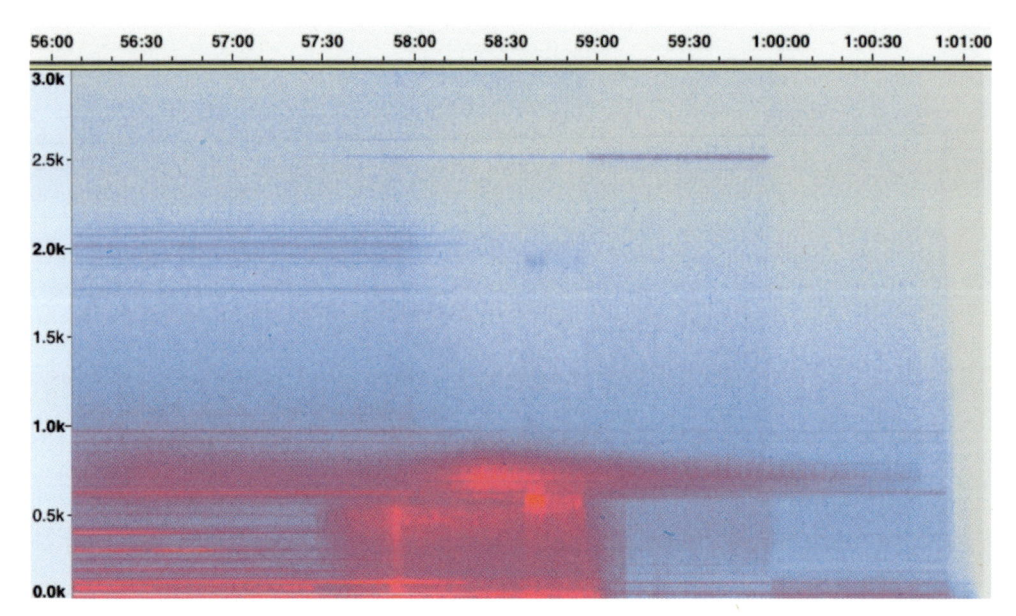

Figure 9   Spectrogram for the final section of *Kyema*, what I call VI (linear scaling). Note the band of noise with peak energy between 600 and 800 Hz and the lone sine tone at 2,515 Hz.

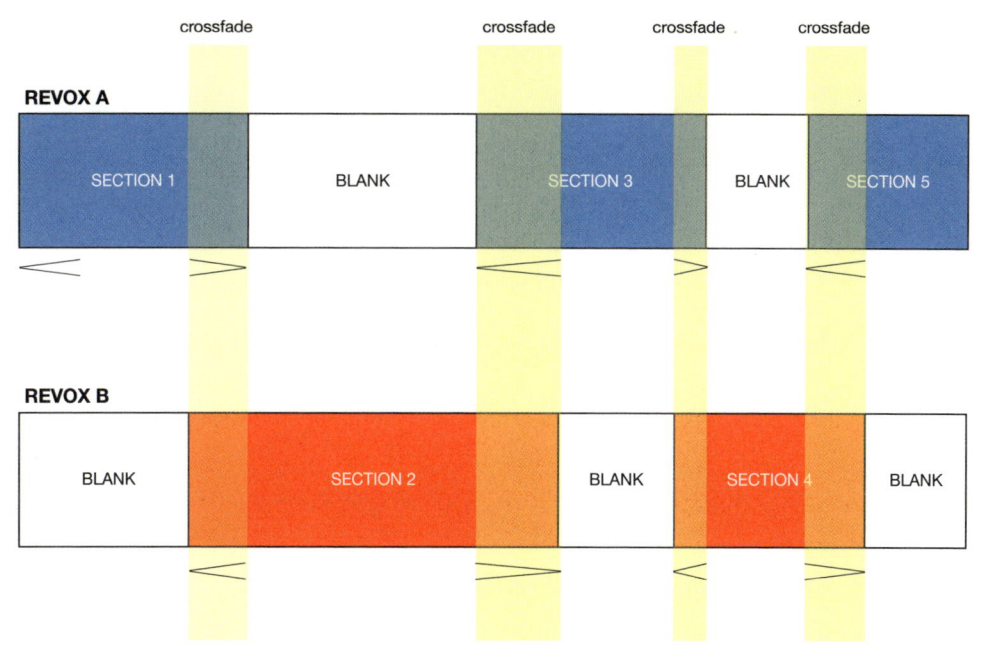

Figure 10   General concept showing how the two playback reels are prepared for the final recording session. Manually and in real time, Radigue would create the crossfade points using faders on the mixing console.

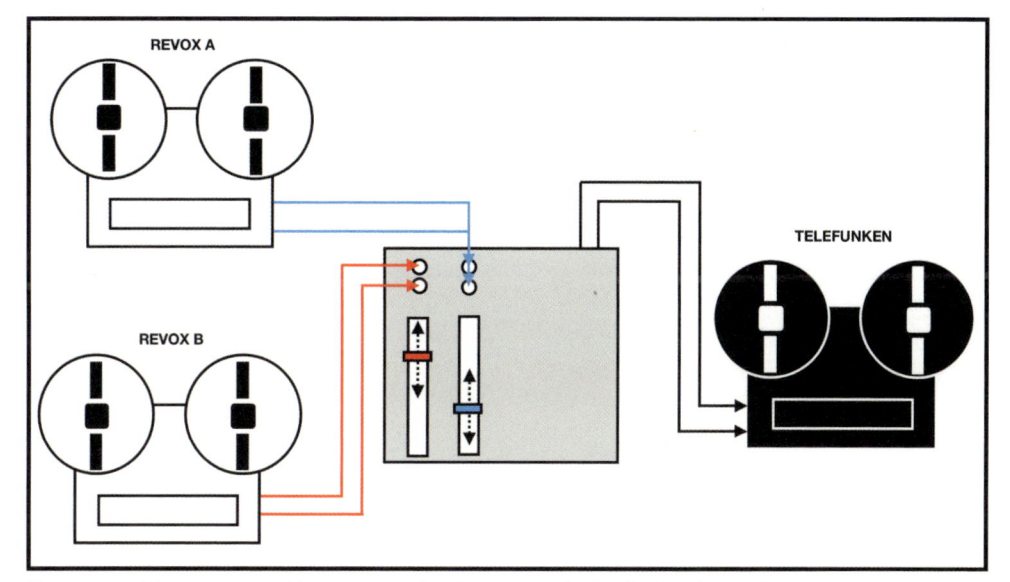

Figure 11   Three-tape machine setup with mixing console for the final recording session.

onto a third tape machine (Figs. 10 and 11). The compositing of prerecorded material is reminiscent of Radigue's compositional strategy for *USRAL*, and the two-tape machine setup is reminiscent of that of *Chry-ptus*, but the indeterminacies of fuzzy timing and ultrasonic points of origin have been removed. To ensure a successful recording session, all actions in this scheme would have to be precisely timed with a chronometer—everything from the length of blank segments of tape between sections on each reel to the length of each fade-in and fadeout executed on her mixing console.[31]

Considering the difficulty of this recording technique lends even greater credence to Bonnet's claim that the seeding metaphor of a synthesizer work is one of the most important parts of Radigue's compositional process. Radigue could orient the recording session, and evaluate its success, on its correspondence with her precompositional metaphor. Radigue explains that *Kyema* "is constructed with the six stanzas at the end of the [*Bardo Thödröl*]. These [stanzas] summarize the six intermediary stages that constitute a continuum of the evolution of consciousness through the transmigration and development of these 'Bardos,' meaning 'intermediary states'. . . My composition respects the text."[32] The *Bardo Thödröl*'s evocation of cyclical death and rebirth is mirrored in *Kyema*'s structure, which is built upon successively greater departures away from familiar material. The digressions from the introductory Birth material lengthen as the work unfolds, up until the point at which the once-familiar actually begins to contrast with the far more timbrally and thematically remote material of V (Bright Light) and VI (Crossing and Returning). As the familiar and unfamiliar trade roles, the exchange evinces a kind of fluidity between self or other, figure and field, evoking what Radigue may have referred to when she speaks of "the continuum of the evolution of consciousness through transmigrations . . . of these intermediary states."

In the Beginning

In the beginning, there was the air's powerful breath, violent intimidating tornados, deep dark waves emerging in long pulsations from cracks in the earth, joined with shooting fire in a flaming crackling. Surging water, waves streaming into shimmering droplets . . .

Was it already sound when no ear was tuned to this particular register of the wave spectrum in this immense vibrating symphony of the universe? Was there any sound if no ear was there to hear it? The wind then turns into a breeze, the base of the earth into resonance, the crackling fire into a peaceful source of heat, water, the surf against the bank, cooing like a stream.

—Éliane Radigue, "The Mysterious Power of the Infinitesimal"

As is typical of Radigue's synthesizer works, *Kyema* opens with a slow fade-in from nothing—or, *almost* nothing. Close listening reveals that the crackling noise on the tape is actually quite audible. All of Radigue's electronic works have some amount of constant noise, but *Kyema*'s signal-to-noise ratio is especially low. Whether this effect is intentional or accidental is amply obscured by Radigue's fondness for the irregularities of analog recording media; "the occasional accident, a disrupted relation between recorder—transmitter—recorder—playback," according to Radigue, is precisely where "our medium assumes some independence."[33] Her preference for electronic aberrations is evident in early feedback works like *USRAL*, which uses slowed-down recordings of chaotic, nonlinear analog feedback sounds to generate opaque yet mysteriously lively textures. After all, "life," Radigue says, "is made of little defects."[34]

On its own terms, *Kyema*'s persistent noise floor constitutes an important element of the work, framing through spectral contrast the generally periodic character of the other sounds, which seem to arise *from* the noise itself. From this crackling near-silence emerges a classic Radigue texture: the polyrhythmic jostling of various tones at various frequencies, all beating at rates independent of one another. A texture of this sort is likely what Radigue has in mind when she uses the phrase "*le jeu des harmoniques*" (meaning "the game," or "play," "of partials") in her writings and interviews.[35] This curious verbal construction certainly calls to mind what Tara Rodgers calls "audio-technical discourse," within which sounds have historically been described as differentiated, lively individuals.[36]

In a Radigue *jeu*, some elements are mixed somewhat louder than others, gently implying a hierarchy of attentional focus. In the first minute of this opening *jeu*, the element that is heard most dominantly is likely the beating sinusoid at around 220 Hz (A3, m≈57), which completes a cycle of beating between four and five times a second. Notably, there is a slight variation in this tone's rate of beating over time; around 1'55" the beating of the 220-Hz tone gradually speeds up and slows down. This subtle change has the compelling effect of preventing the resultant texture from ever sounding too periodic or predictable.

It's quite likely that Radigue achieved this effect by tuning two of her ARP 2500's five oscillators within a few Hertz of each other, with fundamentals in the neighborhood of 220 Hz (or perhaps an octave lower). Manually adjusting the base frequencies on one of these closely tuned oscillators would change the resultant beat frequencies, but Radigue is clear about leaving the base frequencies of her oscillators unchanged once composition for a given work began. While there is always some natural drift in analog oscillator frequencies caused by ambient temperature changes, this is unlikely to be the cause of shifting beat frequencies, as the ARP 2500 oscillators were generally very stable, with their pitch drifting only about 0.1 percent per hour across a wide range of temperature conditions.[37] Here, the change in beat frequencies is closer to 0.1 percent per *second*.

As I experimented with Radigue's ARP myself, I was able to recreate the effect heard in *Kyema* another way. I tuned two of its five oscillators close together and then engaged the pair in a basic, exponential frequency modulation (FM) scheme, according to which one oscillator serves as the carrier and the other serves as the modulator. The two oscillator outputs were then summed and routed to the output of the system, rendering the results audible. Finally, through careful and gradual adjustment to the amount of exponential FM exerted on the carrier, I was able to gain significant control over the rate of beating—all through *very* gradual knob movements (clockwise yielding more modulation; counterclockwise, less). If the lower of the two oscillators serves as the modulator, the resultant beat frequency continues to speed up as the index increases and their base frequencies are driven further apart. When the higher of the two oscillators is modulating the lower of two, the beat frequency slows down as their frequencies get closer together, then speeds up again as they pass. To understand why this happens, one must consider the fact that as the amount of audio-rate frequency modulation in an exponentially controlled oscillator increases, so too does the perceived pitch of the oscillator's fundamental. This change in pitch follows a curve according to which it is rather gradual at a lower amount of modulation before becoming quite rapid as the depth increases.[38] Since audio-rate frequency modulation spectra increase in timbral complexity as the amount of modulation increases, introducing more audible sidebands, to achieve such subtle variations in the rate of beating, along with minimal timbral change or perceptible pitch variations, one would need focus their attention on deliberate adjustments of the carrier's depth of modulation at low values. Thus, when one hears this variation in beat frequencies in *Kyema*, one is quite possibly hearing the results of Radigue very slowly and carefully rotating a knob within a span of just a few millimeters. This level of care and precision extends to nearly every aspect of *Kyema*'s composition and recording process.

Timbre as Melody

A longer passage from Julia Eckhardt's interview with Radigue beautifully introduces the question of the composer's approach to melody and timbre in her synthesizer compositions in general, and *Kyema* in particular:

> In my electronic music, I never bothered to define the intervals, since I was working on sustained sounds, for which the construction relied on an initial construction of various frequencies, which stayed the same throughout a given piece. It was the proportion of the constituents alone [depth of modulation, mixing levels, redistribution of spectral energy through filtering] that made the sound evolve 'from the inside' through different types of internal modulation . . . I'm not looking to construct a melody, but to frame the soft singing being shaped by itself through the interactions within the sound.[39]

On the one hand, there is the composer's intention expressed as a "framing"; on the other, there is sound's imagined autonomy, which "through the interactions *within* the sound" is "shaped by itself." While seemingly contradictory, the tension between external and internal modulation is an essential, and rather productive, tension in her practice. Instead of conceiving a melody in advance, Radigue would look to the constituent elements of a given sound—more specifically, its spectral components—as a constraining yet generative factor in the creation of melodic ideas. Around 1'30", one hears the first suggestions of how she would apply this aesthetic precept in *Kyema*. From the manifold, an A5 (~880 Hz, $m \approx 81$) subtly emerges. This A5 is then chained together with a B5 (~990 Hz, $m \approx 83.04$) and a C-sharp 6 (~1,100 Hz, $m \approx 84.86$) to create a sort of naturally tuned mi-re-do melody. However, while I call this passage a melody, it's quite important to distinguish Radigue's

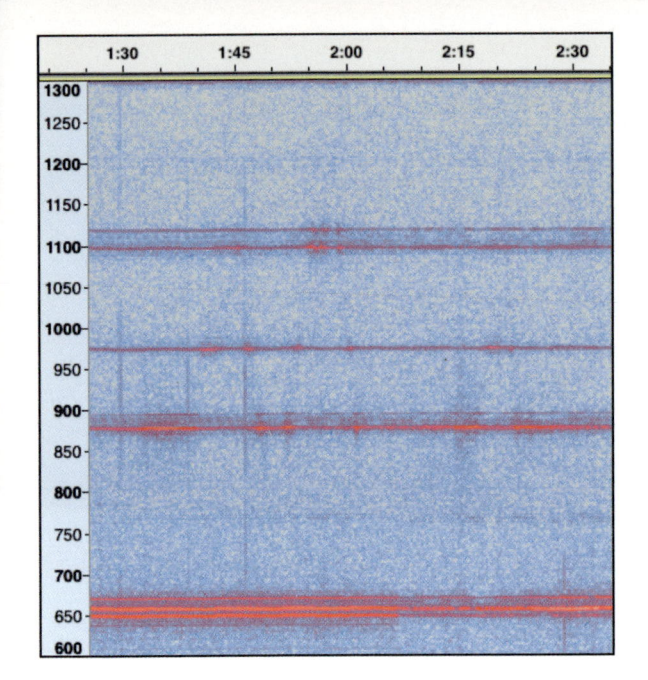

Figure 12   Resonant bandpass filtering periodically emphasizes the beating partials that are already present in the mix. Note the occasional bumps in each line of spectral energy: these are moments in time when the bandpass filter emphasizes a particular partial.

specific understanding of melody from that of melody as an analytically distinct category in European classical music. For Radigue, melody and timbre are inextricably linked, as opposed to separate categories.[40] Looking at a spectrogram for a segment of I.1 (Fig. 12), it becomes evident how Radigue uses resonant bandpass filtering to bring forth partials that are *already present in the sounding music*, and that by slowly and manually varying the cutoff frequency on one of the ARP 2500's 1,047 multimode filters, emphasize subsequent partials one by one. In these moments of periodic spectral emphasis, Radigue depicts within each partial a fleeting subjectivity, emerging from the manifold before disappearing again beneath the waves. By simultaneously bypassing the filter and filtering that very same signal, Radigue effectively blends together these otherwise distinct concepts of melody and timbre.

The resultant pitches of this partial melody correspond strongly to what would be the 8th, 9th, and 10th partials of a harmonic signal, perhaps a ~110 Hz sawtooth wave, which has energy at all integer multiples of the fundamental frequency; however, it is not possible to be absolutely certain of this without documentation of how Radigue patched the synth for *Kyema*, and the patch score for *Kyema* is considered lost as of this writing, if indeed it ever existed.[41] Further complicating matters is the fact that exponential frequency modulation (which was the only form of FM available on Radigue's synthesizer) can yield harmonic spectra by upshifting the carrier's frequency to an integer multiple of the modulator's frequency.[42] In these more complex cases, the resultant collection of partials doesn't really square with the notion of harmonics and their cardinality—that is to say, while this partial melody might *sound* like the 8th, 9th, and 10th harmonics, this doesn't necessarily mean a sawtooth wave serves as the input signal of the filter here. In contrast to the classical sawtooth wave, the partials of which lose amplitude at a rate inversely proportional to their frequency (e.g., the 10th harmonic is one-tenth the amplitude), the upshifted, harmonic timbres created by exponential FM contain a less systematic distribution of spectral energy, meaning some of the higher sidebands can be appreciably louder than lower ones.[43] Given that these partial melodies seem to be using harmonics above what would be the 7th or 8th overtone, the upper region of a canonical sawtooth spectrum may have insufficient power to produce clearly audible partial melodies with a desirable ratio of signal to noise, Radigue's predilection for the latter notwithstanding.

Radigue's general patching technique creates even more uncertainty given that a single sound source could be routed to many

Figure 13   The upper two staves show the tunings for partials with evenly spaced frequencies, yielding approximations of harmonic series for 71 Hz (~C-sharp 2, m≈37.42) and 67 Hz (~C2, m≈36.41). Because this figure concerns the harmonic series, I also use Marc Sabat's extension of the Helmholtz-Ellis notation for just intonation, a tuning system based on the harmonic series.

The lowest staff shows an approximate reduction of the collection of partials used for the partial melody in section II.1, with enharmonic respellings of certain partials used in order to convey modal or scale affiliation.

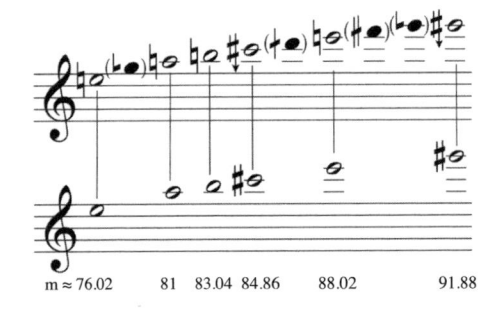

Figure 14   Upper staff shows theoretical gamut of available partials based on equally spaced frequencies, approximating the harmonic series of an A2 (110 Hz).

The lower staff shows the curated set of partials as heard in section I.2 (14'45" to about 20'00"). The 7th, 11th, 13th, and 14th harmonics are removed from the set.

destinations, simultaneously producing many altered versions of a signal acting in both the domains of audio and control. In any case, the rhythmic contour of this partial melody from around 1'30" to roughly 4'30" is certainly wandering, unfolding in a rhapsodic way, with each successive phrase increasing in length. In terms of loudness, Radigue has mixed this partial melody quite evenly with the rest of the music, making it difficult to discern; as *Kyema* progresses, this technique of building melodies out of partials becomes an important signifying and organizational element in the composition. Although the method of synthesis (i.e., using a bandpass filter to select partials from a timbrally rich input signal) is generally the same throughout the work, there are meaningful differences in Radigue's various applications of this technique, and in tracing its development and variation over the course of *Kyema*, a certain resonance emerges with respect to Radigue's notion of sound as a constrained form of life.

Around 9'00", II.1 further develops this technique of building melodies out of beating, resonantly filtered partials, but here the partial melody is less clearly derived from a single harmonic series. My guess is that Radigue superimposed two closely tuned harmonic spectra to generate a larger collection of partials from which she could build melodic fragments. An unequally spaced scale could then be derived using the resonant bandpass filter, yielding something more like ti-do-re-mi-fa-sol-*le*. By deliberately rotating the bandpass filter's cutoff frequency potentiometer, various partials in this somewhat chromatic collection would be selected one by one; however, not every partial in this aggregate is audible—some appear to have been skipped over (Fig. 13).

This curated presentation of a sound's constituent elements clearly demonstrates what Radigue describes as the "framing" of a sound's "soft singing"; however, this connection to the composer's philosophy does not explain how she might have achieved the effect. A compelling possible explanation emerges a bit later, when section I.2 begins to fade in around 14'40". Over the next several minutes, yet another development of *Kyema*'s partial melody technique becomes audible, giving the impression of a melody built out of a selection from something quite like the major scale (Fig. 14, lower staff); however, if Radigue was simply rotating a cutoff frequency potentiometer throughout this section, she would run into other partials at equally spaced points across the spectrum, which would then be audible on the recording (Fig. 14, upper staff).

Instead, it's much more likely that Radigue curated the set of available partials through a signal chain like the following: The

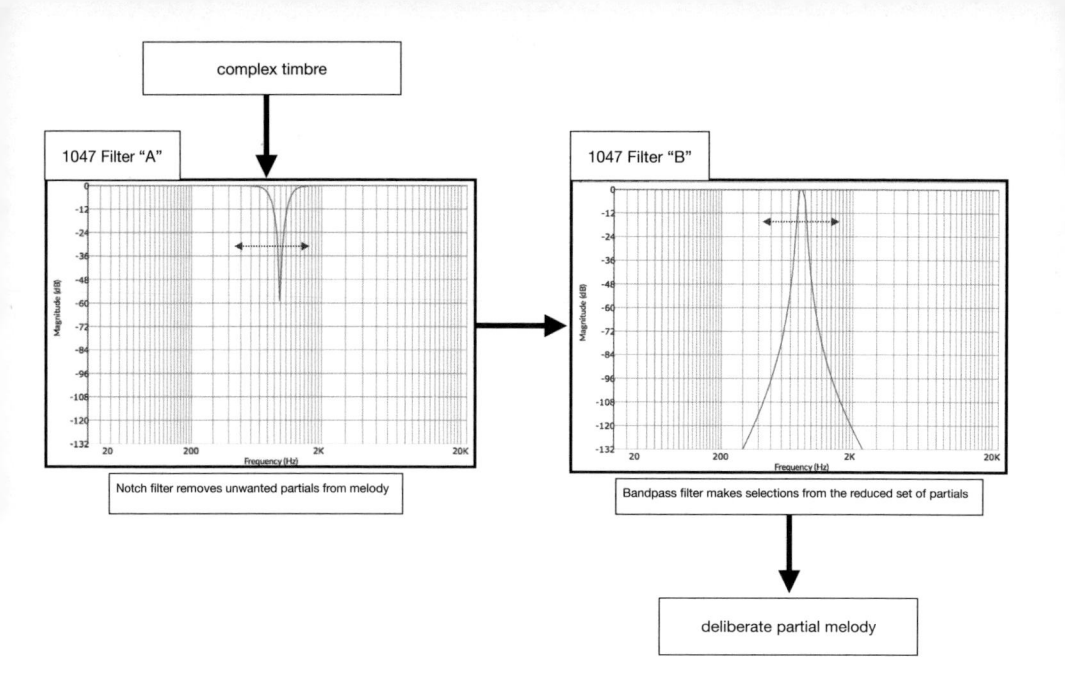

Figure 15   Dual filter signal path that may have been used to curate sets of partials from a complex timbre.

ARP's two multimode filters are routed in series, with the output of the first routed to the input of the second. The first filter's notch mode removes unwanted harmonics from the available set, with its resonance roughly determining the extent of rejection; the second filter's bandpass output, at a sufficiently high resonance, selects individual partials from the reduced set (Fig. 15). The output of this second filter is then passed on to the output for capture on a tape machine, recording the effect. This is some impressive prestidigitation, and while it may not be precisely the technique Radigue employed here, I welcome the synthesist-reader to try it out for themselves—with some practice, it works rather marvelously.

When the final restatement of the I material, what I call I.3, begins to fade in around 42'30", it's a mixture of old and new. This return to the opening material grounds the work in familiar territory before its murky conclusion, but once again there are meaningful differences in how the partial melodies are constructed. These melodies are now far more diffuse, taking the form of grand yet distant spectral swoops that reveal harmonics with each rise and fall of the filter's cutoff frequency (Fig. 16). These swoops are far more periodic and detached than prior emergences of partial melodies. At this point, the listener hears just one partial at a time; no more melodies per se, no more contrivances or signal processing sleight of hand. A reduction in the filter's resonance also smooths the transition between partials.

With the full progression of the partial melody technique in view, it becomes clear that I.3 constitutes a narratively meaningful departure from its earlier iterations. At this point, we're hearing the sound "as it is," without any elaboration or removal. For a more philosophical explanation of this turn, I look to Radigue's evocative comparison of filters and ears: "In the conch formed by the flow of sounds, the ear filters, selects, privileges, as would an eye fixed on shimmering water. Only listening is required, like a gaze that is absent and double, oriented toward an exterior image that lives as a reflection in the inner universe."[44] While she speaks here of the ear as a metonym of the listener's attentional focus over time, this linking of gaze and focus, of interiority and exteriority, is especially fruitful with respect to understanding Radigue's conception of sounds as forms of life, and the central role that filters play in framing that life. As the filter models a kind of attentional, directed subjectivity toward particular partials in a given sound, the slow rise and fall of the filter's frequency here finds rhythmic accord with the periodic, undulatory amplitudes of the beating partials themselves, coming and going in a continuous

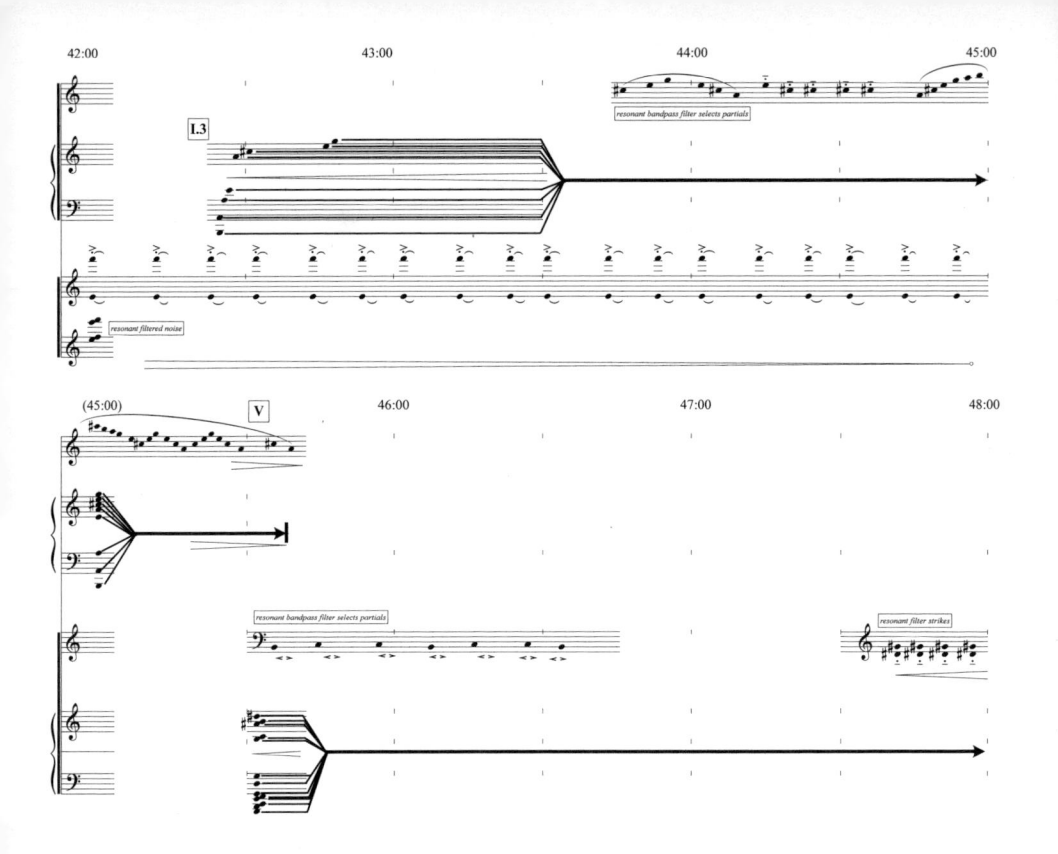

Figure 16   Reduction of the crossfade between IV and I.3, followed by the crossfade between I.3 and V. Note the smooth and gradual revelation of all harmonics in I.3, none of which are excised using notch filters or clever mixing techniques.

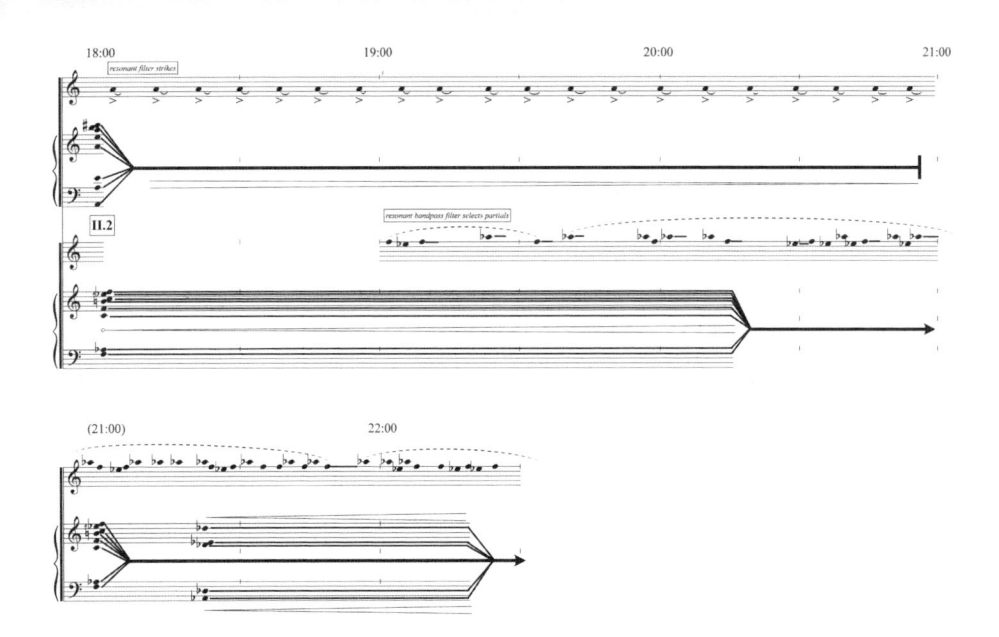

Figure 17   Reduction of the crossfade between I.2 and II.2.

Six prominent peaks from the FFT spectrum plot from 24′24″ to 24′26″ in 2021 INA/GRM recording

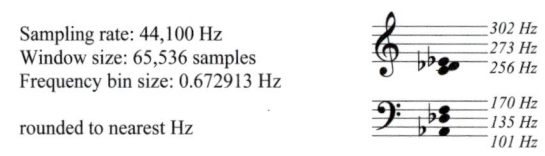

Sampling rate: 44,100 Hz
Window size: 65,536 samples
Frequency bin size: 0.672913 Hz

rounded to nearest Hz

— 302 Hz
— 273 Hz
— 256 Hz
— 170 Hz
— 135 Hz
— 101 Hz

Theoretical difference tones ($2f_2 - f_1$):

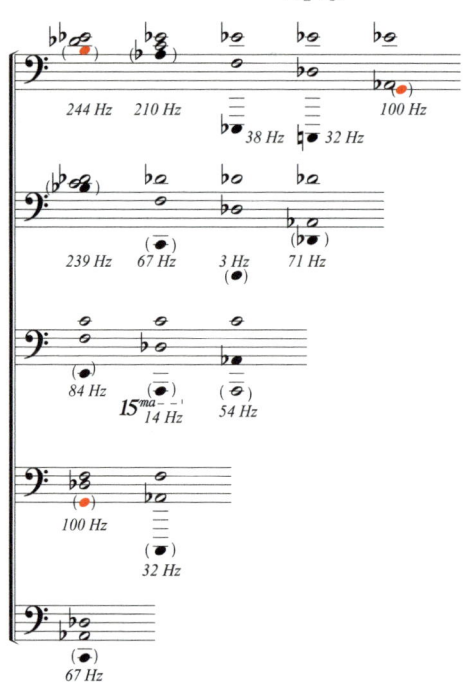

244 Hz   210 Hz   100 Hz
            38 Hz   32 Hz

239 Hz   67 Hz   3 Hz   71 Hz

84 Hz   14 Hz   54 Hz

100 Hz   32 Hz

67 Hz

Figure 18 $2f_2 - f_1$ combination tones for six prominent peaks in *Kyema* from 24′24″–24′26″.

exchange between figure and field. Listening to this passage, one finds an elegant articulation of the inherent tension in Radigue's understanding of her role as composer: accepting sounds "as they are," while simultaneously devising the context in which this acceptance of "sound as itself" can be allegorized.

Harmony as Experience

In a 1974 program note for *Transamorem–Transamortem*, Radigue engages in dialogue with an anonymous interlocutor, who states, "The consonant things are vibrating together." Radigue replies, asking, "Where is the changing point? Within the inner field of perception, or the external reality of something on the way to becoming." The interlocutor answers, "Time is no longer an obstacle, but the means by which the possible is achieved."[45] Close study of Radigue's approach to harmony in *Kyema* reveals a compelling interpretation of this text, offering further elaboration of the composer's complex conception of sound's inner life.

A long crossfade superimposing I.2 and II.2 begins around 18'00" (Fig. 17). This passage produces a remarkable ambiguity by superimposing harmonies that are mostly unrelated, creating an effect where the ground appears to shift depending on how one hears the tonality. This ambiguity is surely the sort that Radigue invokes in "The Mysterious Power of the Infinitesimal," wherein she affirms the virtue of "[the] freedom to be immersed in the ambivalence of continuous modulation with uncertainty of being and/or not being in this or that mode or tonality. The freedom to let yourself be overwhelmed, submerged in a continuous sound flow, where perceptual acuity is heightened through the discovery of a certain slight beating, there in the background, pulsations, breath."[46]

By 21'00", the I.2 material has faded out completely, but this does very little to alleviate the harmonic ambiguity. What remains is a kind of pseudochord that confounds the boundary between harmony and timbre. This suspended harmony turns out to be a kind of false return, as Radigue begins to gradually fade in the remaining partials of II.2 around 21'22", filling out the harmony with a clear fifth and root member. Around 22'30", the music finally sounds as though it has definitively *arrived* at a new point of stability; however, this stability is deceptive, and upon closer examination, yields to an additional layer of ambiguity.

Throughout her synthesizer works, Radigue demonstrates a propensity for superimposing multiple closely tuned harmonic spectra in order to produce kaleidoscopic undulations of amplitude between ever-so-slightly dissonant partials, or what I earlier referred to as a *jeu*. Considering the implications of this approach to harmony from not only an acoustic but also an otoacoustic perspective, complex ambiguities arise that are not easily resolved even by highly precise FFT analyses or other quantitative measures. The presence of multiple closely tuned harmonic spectra makes it very difficult in practice for a listener to differentiate between the beating caused by closely tuned partials and the dissonating combination tones that may be produced by those very same partials. Radigue's occasional use of ring modulation further confounds this distinction: in producing the sum and difference frequencies of all the partials for its two inputs, a ring modulator makes audible new sounds that share a strong spectral affinity with combination-tone otoacoustic emissions. Those emissions, even if strongly perceived in the inner ear, would not show up in a spectral analysis of *Kyema*; however, any sum and difference tones produced by ring modulation, for example, *would* be present in the analysis, as this device produces audible signals that can be captured on tape.

Further complicating the issue is the fact that Radigue often places into the mix additional tones that are close approximations of possible combination tones, yielding dissonances of a recursive complexity. An example drawn from the FFT of *Kyema* at 24'24" demonstrates this principle in action (Fig. 18). This chord is a somewhat idealized example, comprising six of the most prominent peaks over a two-second window, with each pitch representing a sinusoid at a particular frequency. Below the chord, I give the frequencies for a particularly common otoacoustic emission known as the *cubic difference tone*, which is given by $2f_1-f_2$; in red, I've noted combination tones that, if audible, would dissonate with frequencies that are already substantially present in the FFT (within -20 dB of the loudest peak).[47] This transcription makes apparent that Radigue's approach to harmony and dissonance resists the scrutiny of conventional forms of musical analysis by superimposing otoacoustic and acoustic phenomena.

While it's true that all music that uses irrationally tuned harmonies confounds acoustic and otoacoustic perception, this confounding merits particular emphasis in Radigue's case because of the decidedly glacial pace at which the music unfolds, affording a heightened degree of attentiveness to these phenomena, and to the complexities of hearing itself. In Radigue's work these phenomena can be understood as constitutive of, rather than merely incidental to, the music. "Time," after all, is not "an obstacle, but the means by which the possible is achieved."

There's another fascinating example of this approach to harmony and dissonance found later in the work. At 46'30" and throughout section V, the bass comprises two resonant sinusoidal peaks around 50 Hz (~G1, m≈31.34) and 62 Hz (~B1, m≈35.07). On a purely theoretical level, this dyad would be reasonably consonant given that it rather closely approximates the 5/4 syntonic major third. At the same time, the difference of their frequencies is 12 Hz, which means that a rapid beating at this difference is produced, complicating our ability to resolve these two tones into distinct pitches and obscuring the sense of a strong fundamental or root through the rapid undulation in amplitude. The effect is quite unsettling.

Returning to the question Radigue poses in *Transamorem-Transmortem*'s program note, "Where is the changing point?" we may find that it is not just "within the inner field of perception *or* the external reality of something on the way to becoming," but in *both* these places. What emerges in these passages of *Kyema* is a remarkable simultaneous articulation of multiple modes of listening: the acoustic and the otoacoustic, represented by waveform beats and combination tones, respectively. When one also considers resonant bandpass filtering as representative of a shifting attentional focus, it becomes possible to add to the mix Radigue's concern for the psychoacoustic: resonant filtering articulates certain individual spectral components, modeling a listener's cognitive process of differentiating between figure (partial) and field (timbre). With respect to harmony, the apprehension of consonance or dissonance in a Radigue composition is, therefore, an endeavor for one's whole being—mind and body—one in which the full and active participation of the listener is necessary.

Into the Breaks

For *Kyema*'s full duration of sixty-one minutes and seven seconds, there are no complete silences until the work's final fadeout. This continuous presence of sound is an important part of Radigue's aesthetic in general, and was made possible by her extremely deliberate recording process. The illusory continuity that results from this extremely gradual montage and superimposition obscures the composer's direct interventions by avoiding any moment-to-moment connections between haptic interventions (e.g., tape splices) and sonic outcomes (e.g., sudden changes in timbral or thematic content). Through the technique of slow, interlocking crossfades, listeners are instead given the impression that the music is *emanating from within itself*, unfolding at its own pace and on its own terms, an impression that is strengthened by the composer's practice of concealing herself during live presentations of these works.[48] Although in retrospect she considered this endeavor only partially successful,[49] the consequent impression of infinitesimal development through a particular method of recording and presentation nonetheless constituted Radigue's best attempt to create "an unreal, impalpable music, appearing and fading away like clouds in a blue summer sky."[50]

Pastoral metaphors like the above may seem to situate the composer outside the flow of the music, creating the impression that she is not in control but merely and only accepting things as they are. And, as listeners to this music, we may feel similarly passive in our reception of it, simply allowing it to wash over us. But Radigue's characterization of being "immersed in the ambivalence of continuous modulation" is hardly passive; rather, this immersion explicitly involves a "heightening of perceptual acuity"—even if such a heightening is accompanied by an "uncertainty of being and/or not being." In her tremendously deliberate approach to *Kyema*, Radigue creates conditions in which the listener must perpetually recalibrate their interpretation of the piece in key ways: employing long durations and minimal materials, foregrounding sound's physical fact (e.g., through beating and the emphasis of partials as constituents of sound), and aestheticizing oto- and psychoacoustic experience through combination tones and resonant filtering.

Even as Radigue's work is defined mostly by its continuous nature, *Kyema* is possessed of ruptures large and small. These moments of discontinuity merit attention, as in each of them are revealed further complications and elaborations of the themes of intersubjectivity and self-abnegation that characterize the composer's aesthetic. Consider what by now is a rather familiar section in *Kyema*: the long crossfade beginning around 18'00". Based on my general description of Radigue's recording process—not to mention all the smooth crossfades previously heard in the work—one could reasonably expect that I.2 will fade out imperceptibly to nothing; however, close listening reveals that I.2 suddenly drops off at 20'53", leaving II.2 hanging in the ether.

Earlier I showed how Radigue spaced segments in a given composition with blank sections during the final recording session (Figs. 10 and 11). She did this so that while fading in the next segment of music, it would begin playback at the proper time within her meticulously planned scheme. The sudden arrival of one such blank segment might be all that is happening at 20'53"; however, it is well established that Radigue's synthesizer recording process was rather unforgiving of error, in that any slip-ups would necessitate a complete restart. "If something went wrong at eighty minutes," she recounts to Julia Eckhardt, "I had to start all over again." Importantly, however, this does not mean that these works contain no errors; rather, as Radigue elaborates, "That's why, in all my [synthesizer] pieces, there's *always* a place where something goes wrong . . . there's a point where you need to know to stop yourself, too."[51]

Considering that this sudden removal of material does not take place at any other crossfade point in *Kyema*, it is of course possible—if not likely—that the sudden dropout of I.2 at 20'53" is merely an unintended consequence of Radigue's recording technique. However, the fact that this rupture occurred without Radigue's planning does not discount the fact that she *allowed* it to remain. The effect of this allowance is profound. For the first time in more than twenty minutes of music, we hear the subtle yet sudden removal of prior material. While the continuity of the already faded-in II.2 material smooths this transition, this moment challenges what may have been, up to this point, some fundamental assumptions about the work. Furthermore, what remains after this sudden break is tremendously ambiguous from a harmonic and timbral perspective, gaining clarity only when the lower tones are fully faded in around 22'15", in what turns out to be an iteration of the II material (II.2). The sudden break at 20'53", and the ambiguity in which it suspends the listener, makes manifest the participatory bridge between the inner world of the listener and the sounding reality of the music—in so many words, this moment of disjuncture invites reflection, anticipation, and an increased awareness of the passage of time.[52]

Taking a step back to consider *Kyema* as a whole, the structural significance of this disjunctive moment becomes clear. Figure 19 shows how this break anticipates the disruption of what up to this point has been a rather straightforward, repeated binary structure with variation (*aba'b'*). This return to II.2 is also the beginning of a departure into the quite timbrally and materially distinct music of III (Contemplation).

Timbrally, III features a less harmonically organized collection of partials, a higher prevalence of noise (which is audibly

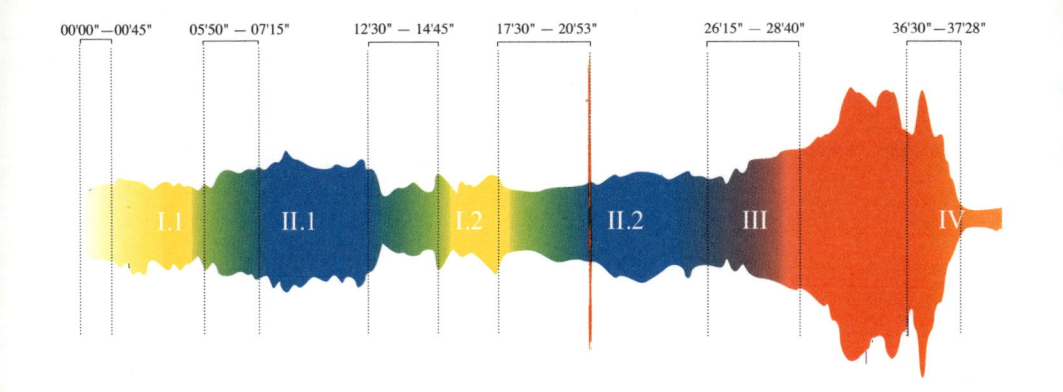

Figure 19 An excerpt of *Kyema*'s thematic structure. The rupture at 20'53" precedes a dramatic departure into thematically distinct material.

distinguishable from *Kyema*'s constant noise floor), and the electronically processed loops of two Tibetan wind instruments, rag-dung and gyaling. The former is a large horn and the latter is a reed instrument (the timbre of which Radigue compares to the oboe).[53] This inclusion of other instruments is not only a source of relatively substantial contrast in *Kyema*, it is also comparatively unique in Radigue's output. Of the nineteen works she composed with the ARP 2500 after 1971, only six use additional musical instruments.[54]

As the listener will note, starting around 29'20", she positively buries the rag-dung and gyaling beneath a cloud of electronic noise. In addition to the substantial spectral masking caused by Radigue's mixing technique, there is also some intentional degradation of the original recordings of the wind instruments. It's possible Radigue engaged the instrumental samples in a process of iterative degradation through rerecording akin to the techniques used in *Opus 17* (1970), what she called "*érosion électronisante*."[55] Radigue doesn't specify what exactly she means when she says she "electronicized" these instruments with her ARP, and given the instrument's wealth of available signal processing operations—filtering, amplitude modulation, and ring modulation—there are many possible ways this electronicization could have been achieved.[56] Whatever the means, this neologism-by-way-of-translation gets this idea across rather well: the inherent nonlinearities and distortions of analog electronic equipment impart unique colorations onto the recorded sounds that pass through them. Across iterations, electronicization erodes away a sound's initial purity to create something far more complex, unstable, and, to Radigue's ears, *alive*.

As Tibetan instruments, their connection to Radigue's spiritual practice is rather clear. As aerophones, the rag-dung and gyaling are representative of a kind of confounding of wind and breath and of a more conventional relationship between bodily intervention and sonic outcome. But Radigue obscures this relationship when she mixes these recordings at no greater loudness than the synthesizer and masks them with tones possessed of similar spectral profiles. This fleeting, heavily distorted appearance of the aerophones lends additional significance to the discontinuity that follows it. Around 36'30", the absolute peak of Kyema's amplitude, III begins to fade out as IV fades in, and at 37'27", what remains of III—gyaling, rag-dung, and all—is cut off quite abruptly: Contemplation (III) gives way to Death (IV). The instantaneous deletion of material is tremendously effective in part because of how rarely such a moment occurs in *Kyema* (I have noted only one such prior instance in my

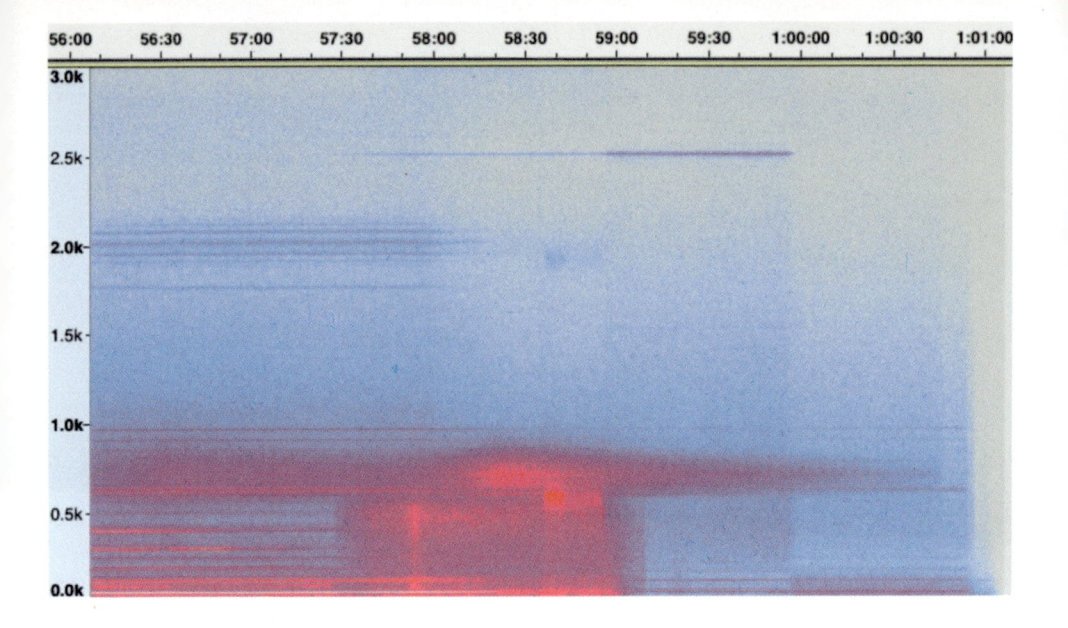

Figure 20   Spectrogram of *Kyema*'s final minutes. A lone sine wave at around 2,515 Hz soars over a cloud of noise.

account, occurring at 20'53"). By disrupting the music's flow, this exceptional discontinuity at 37'27" refocuses the listener's attention onto the bleeding edge of the present—the infinitesimal movement of one moment giving way to the next.

If, as I speculated with the earlier discontinuity at 20'53", this moment is the accidental consequence of using blank leaders in the recording process, then Radigue's disinclination to rerecord the piece to remove this break elegantly allegorizes her notion of composition as a kind of dialectical exchange between acceptance and control, as well as her longstanding deference to a sound's inner life. Furthermore, considering Radigue's statement that "life is made of little defects" and her refusal to censor a sound's inelegant, unexpected ending, this instantaneous silencing of the rag-dung, gyaling, and their accompanying spectral mask perhaps offers a simple yet profound comment on the mutually constitutive nature of birth and death.

These subtle breaks in continuity may ultimately register as nothing more than blips. Even so, listeners stand to gain by allowing these interstitial moments to speak their full weight: as markers of time's passing and as invitations to reflect and to anticipate.

In the wake of this rupture at 37'27", we hear a band of mid-to-high noise around 330 Hz (~E4, m≈64.02), likely accomplished by passing noise through a resonant bandpass filter with its cutoff set around 330 Hz. Emerging from this fluctuating band is a soft striking tone at roughly the same frequency, growing in loudness to the point of surpassing it, marking time with an almost abject, yet inconstant simplicity. In *Kyema* and other works, Radigue often uses these transient events to mark important structural moments. It's a terribly effective technique, and to find it used so sparingly—and in music that is almost entirely defined by continuity—points to Radigue's full appreciation of the potentialities of her chosen musical materials. It may also be evocative of an earlier chapter in Radigue's musical life. At the conclusion of her high school studies, Radigue was sent away from her hometown of Paris to stay with family friends in Nice; while there, she took up studies at the Conservatoire, including a harmony class and a harp class. "I took a lot of pleasure from learning the harp," she recounts to Eckhardt. "I liked the physical contact with the instrument, but with great regret I have never been a good instrumentalist."[57] While I cannot be sure if these resonating filter strikes are conscious references on Radigue's part to her background as a harpist, I would very much like to challenge her appraisal of her musicianship. In the resonant "striking" of the synthesizer's filters, I hear something very much like the transient onset of a harp, played with all the skill of a talented instrumentalist, and at just the right moments, ushering us into *Kyema*'s murky, mysterious conclusion.

Crossing and Returning

Starting around 56'00", a dark and swirling cloud of noise gradually saturates the music before giving way between 59'00" and 59'15" to a thinner, brighter band of noise accompanied by a lone sine wave at about 2,515 Hz (D-sharp 7, $m \approx 99.18$) (Fig. 20). For a full minute, that high keening drone sounds, bright and aloof, before fading away and leaving nothing but a distant noise that gradually dissipates into the crackling background of the tape. I have long been mystified by this ending. By superimposing a single sine wave with a band of noise in mutually exclusive frequency spaces, Radigue achieves a kind of spectral differentiation: the lone sine wave soars above the noise, representing in timbral terms its opposite; the former is clear and precise, the latter disorderly and dense. In its own way, the conclusion of *Kyema* expresses a continuous process of transformation by superimposing these stark opposites and inviting their comparison without resolution or synthesis. I would suggest, provisionally, that the sine wave at *Kyema*'s close represents some idealized, willing, and nearly bodiless subjectivity emerging, if only momentarily, from a manifold of disorder. Eventually, that subjectivity fades away, folded back into the crackling noise of the tape that delimits, however unsteadily, *Kyema*'s boundaries.

1. Erik Heller, *Why You Hear What You Hear: An Experiential Approach to Sound, Music, and Psychoacoustics* (Princeton, NJ: Princeton University Press, 2013), 487.

2. Tara Rodgers, "Interview with Éliane Radigue," in *Pink Noises* (Durham, NC: Duke University Press, 2010), 57.

3. Some modular synths from the late sixties and early seventies did actually include a keyboard module, but unlike a dedicated keyboard instrument such as the Minimoog or the Fender Rhodes, modular synths generally do not require a keyboard to initiate sound.

4. Emmanuel Holterbach, "Peindre du temps et de l'espace avec des sons, la musique d'Éliane Radigue," in *Éliane Radigue: Portraits Polychromes* (Paris: Groupe de Recherches Musicales de L'Institut national de l'audiovisuel, 2013), 30.

5. Julia Eckhardt and Éliane Radigue, *Intermediary Spaces/Espaces intermédiaires* (Brussels: Q02/Umland Editions, 2019), 114.

6. Peter Blasser, "Stores at the Mall" (master's thesis, Wesleyan University, 2015), 27–28.

7. Eckhardt and Radigue, *Intermediary Spaces*, 32.

8. Emmanuel Holterbach, liner notes for Éliane Radigue, *Feedback Works 1969–1970*, L'Institut national de l'audiovisuel/Groupe de Recherches Musicales, July 2, 2021, https://elianeradigue.bandcamp.com/album/feedback-works-1969-1970.

9. Eckhardt and Radigue, *Intermediary Spaces*, 97.

10. Éliane Radigue, liner notes for Éliane Radigue, *Transamorem–Transmortem*, Important Records, IMPREC 337, 2011, compact disc.

11. Eckhardt and Radigue, *Intermediary Spaces*, 120–23.

12. Eckhardt and Radigue, *Intermediary Spaces*, 54.

13. The particular recording I have chosen is INA/GRM's 2021 release, which is part of a larger effort by INA/GRM to preserve and distribute works from Radigue's archive. While it was the 1994 XI Records release that I first fell in love with, the INA/GRM recording generally has a higher signal-to-noise ratio. The relatively clearer signal also makes spectral analysis less prone to error. This fact makes it easier to appreciate the moments where distortion and discontinuity persist, bringing us closer not to an authoritative interpretation of this music but rather to a more accurate account of how it was made.

14. Deniz Peters, "Touch: Real, Apparent, Absent," in *Bodily Expression in Electronic Music*, ed. Deniz Peters, Gerhard Eckel, and Andreas Dorschel (Abingdon, UK: Routledge, 2012), 19.

15. I elaborate on this aspect of mediated self-abnegation in "Presence and Absence: Notes on Éliane Radigue's ARP 2500 Synthesiser Technique," in "Éliane Radigue," special issue, *Contemporary Music Review* (2024): www.doi.org/10.1080/07494467.2024.2348272.

16. Eckhardt and Radigue, *Intermediary Spaces*, 140–42.

17. "The *Tibetan Book of the Dead* is essentially a Western invention based on selections from the *Bardo Thödol*. No text actually titled *Tibetan Book of the Dead* ever existed in Tibet . . . A plurality of Tibetan funerary texts could have been given the same title, but it is these passages of the *Bardo Thödol* that have come to represent how the West understands Tibetan notions of dying, death, and the process of taking rebirth." See Alexandra Kemp, "Tibetan Book of the Dead (*Bardo Thödol*)" (Oxford, UK: Oxford Research Encyclopedia of Religion, 2016), www.doi.org/10.1093/acrefore/9780199340378.013.200.

18. Eckhardt and Radigue, *Intermediary Spaces*, 184.

19. François J. Bonnet, email correspondence with the author, January 8, 2021. Emphasis mine.

20. Eckhardt and Radigue, *Intermediary Spaces*, 140.

21. Eckhardt and Radigue, *Intermediary Spaces*, 180.

22. Éliane Radigue, "The Mysterious Power of the Infinitesimal," trans. Anne Fernandez and Jacqueline Rose, *Leonardo Music Journal* 19 (2009): 47–49.

23. Again, based on the 2021 INA/GRM recording.

24. Eckhardt and Radigue, *Intermediary Spaces*, 184.

25. Eckhardt and Radigue, *Intermediary Spaces*, 182–84.

26. While archival evidence and interviews with the composer clearly support the fact that Radigue organized her synthesizer compositions by ear, using frequencies rather than discrete musical pitches, pitch is nonetheless an important factor in my analysis of *Kyema*, particularly when interpreting a passage in relation to the composition's larger-scale structures. In this text, I'll invoke the notions of pitches and chords, with the understanding that this analytical approach does not imply authorial intent.

27. The "m≈" convention approximates raw frequencies as pitches using floating point MIDI numbers (60 = C4 or middle C). The numbers after the decimal point indicate hundredths of an equally tempered semitone (i.e., cents).

28. Dennis P. Colin, "Electrical Design and Musical Applications of an Unconditionally Stable Combination Voltage Controlled Filter/Resonator," *Journal of the Audio Engineering Society* 19, no. 11 (1971): 926.

29. Eckhardt and Radigue, *Intermediary Spaces*, 130.

30. Eckhardt and Radigue, *Intermediary Spaces*, 178.

31. Daniel Silliman, *Transcendent Machine: An Analysis of Éliane Radigue's ARP 2500 Synthesizer Compositions* (PhD diss., Princeton University, 2023), 60–65.

32. Eckhardt and Radigue, *Intermediary Spaces*, 140.

33. Radigue, "The Mysterious Power of the Infinitesimal," 48.

34. Ian Nagoski, "Interview with Éliane Radigue," in *Éliane Radigue: Alien Roots* (New York: Blank Forms Editions, 2025), 223.

35. This phrase appears several times throughout her interviews and writings, including "The Mysterious Power of the Infinitesimal," and the interviews with Rodgers and Eckhardt. See Tara Rodgers, "Interview with Éliane Radigue," 54–60; and Radigue, "The Mysterious Power of the Infinitesimal," 47–49.

36. Tara Rodgers, "'What, for me, constitutes life in a sound?': Electronic Sounds as Lively and Differentiated Individuals," *American Quarterly* 63, no. 3 (2011): 509–30.

37. *ARP 2500 Owner's Manual* (Newton, MA: ARP Instruments, Inc., 1970).

38. Bernard A. Hutchins, "Frequency Modulation Spectrum of an Exponential Voltage-Controlled Oscillator," *Journal of the Audio Engineering Society* 23, no. 3 (1975): 202.

39. Eckhardt and Radigue, *Intermediary Spaces*, 164–67. Interpolations mine.

40. While often considered distinct in the analysis of European classical music, melody is considered an emergent property of timbre by some investigators. See William A. Sethares, *Tuning, Timbre, Spectrum, Scale* (London: Springer, 1998).

41. At a certain point, Radigue stopped using pencil-and-paper drawings to plan out and recall the state of her ARP 2500 between sessions. This fact is pointed out in Holterbach, "Peindre du temps et de l'espace avec des sons, la musique d'Éliane Radigue," 30. Even if a patch score for *Kyema* was ever made, many of these drawings were unfortunately destroyed in a flood several years ago, as François J. Bonnet relayed to me in an email on January 8, 2021.

42. Bonnet, email correspondence with the author, January 8, 2021.

43. Hutchins, "Frequency Modulation Spectrum of an Exponential Voltage-Controlled Oscillator," 203–4.

44. Éliane Radigue, liner notes for Éliane Radigue, *Adnos I–III*, recorded 1975, 1981, and 1983, Table of The Elements, The Sandwalking Company, SWC551, 2002.

45. Radigue, liner notes for *Transamorem-Transmortem*, 2011.

46. Radigue, "The Mysterious Power of the Infinitesimal," 49.

47. G. Frank and M. Koessl, "The acoustic two-tone distortions $2f_1-f_2$ and f_2-f_1 and their possible relation to changes in the operating point of the cochlear amplifier," *Hearing Research* 98 (1996): 105–6.

48. Eckhardt and Radigue, *Intermediary Spaces*, 120–23.

49 Radigue writes: "I have known the enchantment of discovery by forgetting all I had learned, I have of course also encountered doubt, denial, and the feeling of absurdity during long years, alone with my ARP (Fig. 2) and all of the difficulties 'we' had to go through, before perhaps understanding each other . . . a little." Radigue, "The Mysterious Power of the Infinitesimal," 49.

50 Radigue, "The Mysterious Power of the Infinitesimal," 49.

51 Eckhardt and Radigue, *Intermediary Spaces*, 119. Emphasis mine.

52 Elizabeth H. Margulis, "Moved by Nothing: Listening to Musical Silence," *Journal of Music Theory* 51, no. 2 (2007): 245–76.

53 Eckhardt and Radigue, *Intermediary Spaces*, 140.

54 In addition to *Kyema*, there's the prepared piano in *Geelriandre* (1972); piano, flute, and voice in *Fc 2000/125* (1972); ondes martenot in *Schlinen* (1974); voices in *Songs of Milarepa* (1983); and finally the Serge modular in *L'Île re-sonante* (2000).

55 The 2021 digital release of *Opus 17* includes Emmanuel Holterbach's 2013 liner notes, where he translates this phrase as "electronicized erosion."

56 Eckhardt and Radigue, *Intermediary Spaces*, 140.

57 Eckhardt and Radigue, *Intermediary Spaces*, 61–62.

Mural of Guru Rinpoche (Padmasambhava), who is credited with bringing Buddhism to Tibet, with a small shrine near Thimphu, Bhutan. Courtesy Dagmar Schwerk.

SOUND, OFFERING, AND LIBERATION: LOCATING ÉLIANE RADIGUE'S *TRILOGIE DE LA MORT* (1988-93) IN TIBETAN BUDDHIST THOUGHT AND HISTORY
Dagmar Schwerk

Commissioned for this anthology, Tibetologist and Religious Studies scholar Dagmar Schwerk's "Sound, Offering, and Liberation" contextualizes Radigue's *Trilogie de la Mort* within Tibetan Buddhist thought and history. After giving an account of the content, Tibetan text genesis, and Western reception of *The Tibetan Book of the Dead*, she focuses on the *Root Stanzas of the Six Bardos* as the central tenet of *Kyema*. Schwerk traces the relationship between Tibetan Buddhist thought and practices and Radigue's musical output and life as a practitioner of Tibetan Buddhism, focusing on the composer's understanding of orality and transmission, her use of compositions as a Buddhist offering, and her integration of the Tibetan language and letters in the titles of her works.

The Sounds of the Bardos*

> One of the most significant and profound of all bardos lies between the beginning of the period during which we are completely unaware of the existence of our inherent buddha nature and the moment we awaken to it, which Buddhists describe as "enlightenment." In other words, everything that happens in between "not recognizing" and "recognizing" buddha nature is called a "bardo."
>
> —Dzongsar Jamyang Khyentse Rinpoche, *Living is Dying*[1]

Dzongsar Jamyang Khyentse Rinpoche (b. 1961), eminent Bhutanese Buddhist master, incarnated in the Tibetan Buddhist Khyentse lineage, and globally renowned filmmaker and author, summarizes here the very essence of how the Bardos, the six intermediate states, should be understood by a Buddhist practitioner: as the precious possibility inherent in each moment of one's experience to obtain liberation from Saṃsāra, the cycle of existence.[2] In that sense, the English translation of the Tibetan word *bardo* as "intermediate state" reminds one that, in fact, the intermediate state itself can be characterized by both recognition and nonrecognition of what really matters on the Buddhist path through life and death. The Bardos thus instill the possibility of reaching liberation—that is, enlightenment—in each moment of one's experience.[3]

However, as Dzongsar Jamyang Khyentse Rinpoche further elucidates, the six Bardos should not be understood as ultimately real or solid but as located between what he calls "illusory boundaries"—for example, between yesterday and tomorrow, this moment and the next, or birth and death—and as such are to a certain extent "imaginary," hence transitional or intermediate in nature.[4]

---

* Technical note: As this writing is intended for an interdisciplinary audience, Tibetan and Bhutanese proper names, places, and terms are spelled phonetically according to the THL Simplified Phonetic Transcription of Standard Tibetan by David Germano and Nicolas Tournadre. In addition, some Tibetan terms are provided in their proper Tibetan spelling. In that case, the transliteration of Tibetan characters follows the system of Turrell V. Wylie, and I set them apart in italics and occasionally also in parentheses, i.e., (Tib. *kye ma*). Sanskrit characters are transliterated according to the International Alphabet of Sanskrit Transliteration (IAST) with some terminologies provided in parentheses/italics, i.e., (Skt. *pramāṇa*). Birth and death dates of Tibetan and Bhutanese persons follow the standard reference work, the Buddhist Digital Archives (BUDA).

It is exactly these Bardos, which are the topic of a specific prayer, the *Root Stanzas of the Six Bardos* from *The Tibetan Book of the Dead*, that Éliane Radigue's Tibetan Buddhist teacher, the Tenth Pawo Rinpoche (1912–91),[5] personally instructed her to practice, and that would ultimately become the starting point for her 1988 composition *Kyema*.[6] The six Bardo states referred to in these root stanzas are the Bardo of Living (Tib. *rang bzhin bar do*), the Bardo of Dreams (Tib. *rmi lam bar do*), the Bardo of Meditative Concentration (Tib. *bsam gtan bar do*), the Bardo of Death (Tib. *'chi kha'i bar do*), the Bardo of Reality (Tib. *chos nyid bar do*), and the Bardo of Rebirth (Tib. *srid pai'i bar do*).[7]

In Tibetan Buddhism, there are different translations of the six Bardo states, as well as varying pronunciations of each of the terms, depending on the dialect of the Tibetan speaker. Radigue uses, for example, in her annotated works list, the following Tibetan, French, and English terms: *Kyene*/*la naissance*/birth, *Milam*/*la rêve*/dream, *Samtem*/*la contemplation*/contemplation, *Chikal*/*la mort*/death, *Chönye*/*la claire lumière*/bright light, and *Sippaï*/*traversée et retour*/crossing and returning.[8]

Unlike some of Radigue's other longform compositions, *Kyema* is not explicitly divided into submovements; she does not denote six sections that would correspond to the six Bardo states. However, the composer's ambiguity here provides a great opportunity for the listener: with the *Root Stanzas of the Six Bardos* as the starting point of my analysis, I will set the Tibetan Buddhist teachings (Skt. *dharma*) of the *Root Stanzas of the Six Bardos* in dialogue with the flow of sounds as they unfold in *Kyema*.

In general, I use the term *Dharma* to refer to the Buddhist teachings that comprise the entire doctrinal and philosophical content transmitted from the historical Buddha Shakyamuni Siddhartha Gautama (ca. sixth century BCE) in the form of texts but also oral transmissions. Over time in Asia (and later globally), many distinct Buddhist schools of interpretation developed. The complex historical development of Buddhism is generally described in terms of a doxographical distinction between "three vehicles" (Tib. *theg pa*; Skt. *yāna*): Śrāvakayāna/ Nikāya Buddhism, Mahāyāna, and Tantric Buddhism/Vajrayāna/Mantrayāna. Each of these "vehicles" has the capacity to lead all sentient beings from the cycle of endless rebirths (Skt. *saṃsāra*) to liberation (Skt. *nirvāṇa*), but differ in their respective approaches, philosophical views, texts, and practices. In Buddhist scriptures, this process is often described using the analogy of a ship crossing a river or ocean and leaving the ship of Buddhist teachings and methods behind at the other shore.

Most authoritative Buddhist texts have been preserved in the different Buddhist canons in Pāli, Sanskrit, Tibetan, Chinese, or Japanese, and each of these canons also contains a very extensive exegetical and commentarial literary corpus spanning about 2,500 years of authorial activity. In this essay, I focus on the Tibetan Buddhist tradition, which combines aspects of Mahāyāna and Tantric Buddhism. The *Root Stanzas of the Six Bardos* from *The Tibetan Book of the Dead* originally belong to this Tantric tradition.[9]

My particular approach to listening, experiencing, and interpreting *Kyema* can be understood as *taking sound as Dharma*. In Tibetan Tantric Buddhist meditation instructions and other canonical Buddhist scriptures, the perception of all sensory and mental phenomena as pure, and as such, as Dharma, is a recurring theme in descriptions of Yogic practices. This intertwining logic of sound and meaning is not always straightforward and requires a certain level of in-depth spiritual training to comprehend. Consequently, the experience of listening to *Kyema* is unique for each Buddhist practitioner, depending on the extent of their individual progression along the spiritual path and, in this context, their understanding of the specific doctrinal content of the *Root Stanzas of the Six Bardos*. In sum, in Tibetan Tantric Buddhism, different levels of perception are possible, gradually ascending from the ordinary to the pure, in which, according to certain practices, sound can be interpreted as Dharma.[10]

An additional aspect of taking sound as Dharma, exemplified in the particular case of *Kyema*, is that these possible linkages between sound and meaning can be revealed only through practices of both immersive, repeated listening and mindful reflection on the meaning of the *Root Stanzas of the Six Bardos*. I will use the term *sound metaphors* to describe some of these nearly imperceptible connections. Metaphors and other related forms of figurative language are able to establish communication and transport meaning between two otherwise semantically unrelated spheres (referential/attributive) of our thinking and feeling by transferring aspects or qualities from a source domain (music) to a target domain (Dharma/religion), thereby creating a likeness or analogy between two otherwise semantically unrelated areas.

In the Tibetan Buddhist context, metaphors and other figurative language feature very prominently as a means to create associations that lie beyond rational thinking in the realm of spiritual practice and experience. One of the most used metaphors in Buddhism, for example, is "the medicine of Dharma," which refers to the Buddhist teachings' capacity to alleviate our suffering at its roots. I use *sound metaphor* to denote this complex movement between multiple meanings of Tibetan Buddhist thought and philosophy and the sounds in Radigue's work.[11]

It follows that, for a Buddhist practitioner, the overlap or (re)appearance of different sound patterns and figures throughout *Kyema* provides an additional level of experience and thematic interpretation of this composition, thereby bringing the disciplinary perspectives of musicology and religious studies into a lively conversation, especially with respect to the auditory sensory experience.[12] One possible approach to this interdisciplinary project of taking sound as Dharma is an *autoethnography of the senses*, which would expand upon conventional musicological analysis by including a systematic consideration, analysis, and documentation of the listener's (in this case, my own) direct sensory and perceptual experiences, as well as their accompanying reflexive processes, from a Tibetological and religious studies perspective.[13] Such an approach, according to which one deliberately considers personal experiences influencing the research process, holds the possibility of a more holistic analysis of Radigue's work.[14]

Typically, in a Western academic context, depending on the questions driving one's research, the musical aspects of Tibetan Buddhism would be approached according to the discrete disciplinary methodologies of musicology, anthropology, ethnomusicology, or religious studies. Within the field of religious studies, my research on *Kyema* would most likely be categorized as belonging to the subfield of the "aesthetics of religion," which accounts for music, sounds, and soundscapes (*Klangwelten*).[15] By including the methods of autoethnography, I hope to establish a shared basis for engaging in a transdisciplinary and transcultural conversation about Radigue's work beyond the field of religious studies.[16] I will attempt to demonstrate my approach using Radigue's *Kyema* as an example.

In *Kyema*, from 13'10" onward,[17] what sounds like the characteristic striking of a Tibetan gong in a monastery, a common sound in Buddhist communities, is described by Daniel Silliman as "a soft, striking tone [accompanying] the band of noise"[18] and by Charles Curtis as "bell-like sounds."[19] These sounds also reappear along with the band of noise following 37'27", after what is surely the main caesura of the whole piece.

Kyema's caesura is very striking for a Buddhist practitioner acquainted with Tibetan philosophy, as it can be heard as marking the moment of a person's death and therefore as denoting a major transition in the cycle of existence. If one accepts this sound metaphor, then the preceding musical section (from 28'40" onward) can be understood in terms of what in *The Tibetan Book of the Dead* is described as the transition from the Bardo of Living to the Bardo of Death, the turbulent process of dying for which the entire spiritual practice of a Buddhist practitioner is supposed to prepare. This critical phase leading up to a person's physical death is described in the fourth of the *Root Stanzas of the Six Bardos* as follows:

> Alas, now as the intermediate state of the time of death arises before me,
> Renouncing (all) attachment, yearning and subjective apprehension in every respect,
> I must undistractedly enter the path, on which the oral teachings are clearly understood,
> And eject my own awareness into the uncreated expanse of space.
> Immediately upon separation from this compounded body of flesh and blood,
> I must know (this body) to be like a transient illusion.[20]

After the massive drop in amplitude that follows the caesura at 37'27", sounds subside into near-total silence. Understood as Dharma, this subsiding corresponds to the Buddhist concept of the subsiding of experiences and mental images into ground consciousness. In Tibetan epistemology, the categorization of different kinds of consciousness is very complex and varies according to different schools of thought. Generally speaking, however, ground consciousness (Tib. *kun gzhi rnam par shes pa*) can be understood as the underlying foundation for all other forms of consciousness and as the place where the imprints of past experiences and lives are stored.[21]

The section of *Kyema* after the massive drop in amplitude can thus be interpreted as the first phase of the Bardo of Reality following physical death, in which more concrete sense perceptions slowly reappear in what is called a *mental body*, where thoughts and appearances linger between lives. The listener dwells in this experience of the Bardo of Reality until 42'43", when the emergence of a sinister, deep, and wavering sound indicates (for the Buddhist practitioner) the appearance of the assembly of the Maṇḍala of the Hundred Peaceful and Wrathful Deities.[22] These forty-two peaceful and fifty-eight wrathful deities symbolize the enlightened nature of all sentient beings, and their appearance can help a practitioner in the Bardo to recognize the nature of their mind and lead to their liberation.[23] From 45'40" onward, the Bardo of Reality finally gives way to the Bardo of Rebirth, which consists of different phases depending on whether a more or less favorable rebirth is attained.

Radigue's decision to not explicitly name or identify submovements within the composition leaves the division of *Kyema* up to the listener. As demonstrated above, any provisional identification of submovements from the perspective of a Buddhist practitioner is particularly interesting considering the fact that, according to Tibetan Buddhist teachings, some of the Bardo states are not experienced subsequently but simultaneously, and some characteristics persist throughout all of them, such as the aforementioned ground consciousness.

It can be said, for example, that anyone reading this text at this moment is experiencing, in a Buddhist sense, the Bardo of Life, and will also, at some point today, probably experience the Bardo of Dreams (and perhaps even the Bardo of Meditative Concentration as well, if the reader is pursuing a spiritual practice). Consider the first of the *Root Stanzas of the Six Bardos* that Radigue took as her inspiration for *Kyema*:

> Alas, now as the intermediate state of living arises before me,
> Renouncing laziness, for which there is no time in this life,
> I must enter the undistracted path of study, reflection, and *meditation.*
> Taking perceptual experience and (the nature of) mind as the path
> I must cultivate actualisation of the three buddha-bodies.[24]
> Now, having obtained a precious human body, this one time,
> I do not have the luxury of remaining on a distracted path.[25]

Here, meditation is explicitly designated as part of the Bardo of Living. However, the three Bardo states that lie between rebirths—namely the Bardo of Death, the Bardo of Reality, and the Bardo of Rebirth—are usually taught as a sequential experience that can last up to forty-nine days in total. As taught in *The Tibetan Book of the Dead*, the particular sequence of these three Bardos depends on the spiritual capability of the Buddhist practitioner at that particular moment to either realize and achieve liberation (enlightenment) or not. Not all three Bardos of Death, Reality, and Rebirth necessarily have to be experienced; in fact, this is only the case if liberation (enlightenment) during one of these Bardo states is not achieved, and one is reborn in one of the six classes of beings conceptualized in Buddhism: gods, semigods, humans, animals, hungry ghosts, and hell beings.[26]

In other words, the Bardo states between two rebirths can be visualized as a kind of spiritual highway along which different exits to liberation are accessible but are also easily missed, in which case one would continue on to the next Bardo state and eventually rebirth, thus remaining in the cycle of Saṃsāra. In this sense, the teachings of *The Tibetan Book of the Dead* are extremely important for Buddhist practitioners because they offer very detailed advice and guidance on how to escape this cycle of Saṃsāra and reach liberation.

From the perspective of a Buddhist practitioner well versed in Tibetan Buddhist epistemology and philosophy, the simultaneous nature of one's experience of the Bardos and that of the blurred boundaries between these intermediate states finds articulation in Radigue's refined technique of seamless crossfading between musical sections. Moreover, Radigue's use of long sustaining sounds, slow crossfades, and timbral changes at the lower limit of perceptibility in *Kyema* can be further interpreted as audible representations of ground consciousness, which is experienced throughout all the six Bardo states and therefore persists throughout every moment of a person's experience. Understanding this connection between sound and meaning enables a Buddhist practitioner in their listening experience to align the progression of *Kyema* with the constant flow of their own consciousness and their personal knowledge and practice of the teachings of the *Root Stanzas of the Six Bardos*.

When contextualizing the Bardo states in Buddhist thought, it is important to note that several earlier Indian Buddhist texts—written before Buddhism came to Tibet in the seventh century—dealing with the authoritative means of gaining knowledge (Skt. *pramāṇa*) concentrate only on the three Bardo states between rebirths. According to the previously mentioned enumeration of six Bardo states in Tibetan Buddhism, this would refer to the three Bardo states of Death, Reality, and Rebirth; surely, this crucial transition between two rebirths is the focus of many Buddhist teachings. Tenzin Gyatso, the Fourteenth Dalai Lama (b. 1935), comments on this important transition as follows: "When we look at life and death from a broader perspective, then dying is just like changing our clothes! When this body becomes old and useless, we die and take on a new body, which is fresh, healthy and full of energy! This need not be so bad!"[27]

The importance of the transition between rebirths—this life and the next—is the core message that Tibetan Buddhists have traditionally drawn from *The Tibetan Book of the Dead*. Western cultures, often spurred by a general fascination with uncovering new ways of coping with mortality, have similarly interpreted this transition as the central concern of *The Tibetan Book of the Dead* since it was first translated into English in 1927.[28]

The Many *Tibetan Books of the Dead*

To understand the role of the *Root Stanzas of the Six Bardos*—the core theme of *Kyema*—within Tibetan Buddhist thought and history, *The Tibetan Book of the Dead* must be contextualized historically and doctrinally. Such a contextualization will also provide the background for understanding the global popularity of this particular text among Buddhists and non-Buddhists alike, as well as the text's subsequent reinterpretation, recontextualization, and secularization through Western media and culture.

What today is commonly known as *The Tibetan Book of the Dead* was first translated and published under this title in 1927 by the Sikkimese scholar and translator Lama Kazi Dawa Samdup (1868–1922) and the American orientalist Walter Yeeling Evans-Wentz (1878–1965), with a foreword by the eminent Swiss psychoanalyst Carl Jung (1875–1961). Their translation, though, included only three out of twelve chapters of a Tibetan work called the *Bardo Thödröl* (*Great Liberation Upon Hearing in the Intermediate States*).[29] Chapter Eleven, which today is generally understood as synonymous with *The Tibetan Book of the Dead*, is essentially a guide to be read aloud to the dying and dead.[30] Henceforth, I will use *Bardo Thödröl* to refer to the original, complete Tibetan work with its origins in the fourteenth century, and *The Tibetan Book of the Dead* to refer to the global perception and imagination of the work more generally focusing on Chapter Eleven.

For many centuries, the *Bardo Thödröl*'s teachings on how to prepare for and deal with death and dying have been central to the practices of Tibetan Buddhists of all four traditions of Tibetan Buddhism.[31] Today, in a global context, these teachings have found relevance with a much more diverse audience, including convert-Buddhists and non-Buddhists, who have interpreted aspects of them in new and unexpected ways. The answer of students in my classes, when asked about their first point of contact with Tibetan culture, speaks for itself, as it is almost always the same: either the Fourteenth Dalai Lama Tenzin Gyatso or *The Tibetan Book of the Dead*. Today, examples of Buddhist and non-Buddhist interpretations of *The Tibetan Book of the Dead* across different media and art forms are too numerous to name.

One of the most popular and widely consumed versions of *The Tibetan Book of the Dead* is the translation and commentary by Chögyam Trungpa Rinpoche (1937-89) and Francesca Freemantle, read (in audiobook form) by the prominent actor and longtime Buddhist practitioner and activist for the Tibetan cause, Richard Gere.[32] Chögyam Trungpa Rinpoche was an eminent and very controversial Tibetan Buddhist teacher who was pivotal in the transmission of Tibetan Buddhism to North America from the seventies onward and in the enculturation of Tibetan Buddhist arts into American counterculture. Moreover, Robert A. F. Thurman, renowned Tibetologist, Buddhist practitioner, and father of Uma Thurman, has concentrated in his Buddhist teaching activities quite prominently on *The Tibetan Book of the Dead*.[33]

One example of a non-Buddhist adaptation occurs in a section of Art Spiegelman's graphic novel *Maus*, which addresses the horror of the Holocaust and documents, based on the firsthand account of his father, his parents' persecution as Polish Jews by the Nazis and their survival of Auschwitz. Spiegelman includes parts of an earlier comic strip called *Prisoner on the Hell Planet* about his feelings and experiences following the suicide of his mother, in which passages from *The Tibetan Book of the Dead* are read at her Jewish funeral (Spiegelman leaves it open to the reader to determine whether this was fictitious or real).[34]

Of course, the popularity of *The Tibetan Book of the Dead* must be understood in the broader cultural and political context of the tragic fate and exile of the Tibetans from Tibet since the sixties, which precipitated the availability of Tibetan Buddhist teachings on a much larger, global scale. This globalization of Tibetan Buddhism met the generally heightened fascination with "Eastern" philosophies and worldviews in Western counterculture from the fifties and sixties onward, as exemplified by Timothy Leary (1920-96).[35]

Today, there are many examples of popular music (mostly in meditative, electronic dance, and ambient styles) that make excessive use of allusions to Buddhist and Eastern philosophies and Tibetan Buddhist ritual sounds—such as Tibetan throat-chanting[36] or Sanskrit Buddhist Mantras—often completely removed from their original meanings and cultural contexts.[37] For example, Mantras and prayers have been used quite prominently in electronic dance music since the nineties.[38]

Such superficial practices must be differentiated from the reception and adaptations by those of convert-Buddhists who have addressed Tibetan Buddhist topoi in their artistic practices, as Radigue has done in her musical idiom as a long-term Buddhist practitioner. In fact, the composer makes a point to emphasize her sincerity and great respect for the Buddhist teachings alluded to in her work when she says of *Kyema*, "my composition respects the text." Radigue elaborates further, stating, "there are also other parts where I use recordings I'd made of a gyaling, a double-reed instrument similar to an oboe, as well as a ragdung, the big horns, which I nevertheless 'electronicised' with my ARP."[39] Tibetan wind instruments, like the medium-sized brass trumpet (Tib. *rag dung*) and "Chinese flute" (Tib. *rgya gling*), have traditionally been used exclusively in Tibetan Buddhist ritual contexts (as opposed to string instruments). Learning to play these instruments and memorizing the repertoire of rituals that must accompany them is an integral part of the Tibetan Buddhist monastic curriculum; in that sense, they are solely religious instruments. Such contextual specificity offers a possible explanation for Radigue's decision to incorporate these sounds only after they had been sufficiently mediated by her various electronic processes.

Listening to *Kyema* (and to the rest of the *Trilogie de la Mort* [1988–93]), the presence of these "electronicized" Tibetan religious instruments became perceivable to me because of my familiarity with the daily ritual routines and corresponding soundscapes of the Tibetan monastery that I lived in for several months in 2010 while conducting my field research. With repeated, immersive listening of the *Trilogie de la Mort*, I was able to hear, recollect, and identify those sounds, as well as their possible metaphoric content, more clearly. Radigue's subtle use of these religious instruments gestures toward a whole semantic field of ritual, doctrinal content and practiced Buddhism.

Within its more recent, nearly century-long, global history of diverse interpretations both religious and secular, *The Tibetan Book of the Dead* has supported both convert-Buddhists and non-Buddhists alike in the often-challenging process of dying and/or accompanying others through the process, which is also known as "liberation by hearing." The *Bardo Thödröl* (*Great Liberation Upon Hearing in the Intermediate States*) belongs to a specific set of Buddhist teachings within Tibetan Tantric Buddhism that elucidate in detail how to utilize one's senses (in this case, hearing) as a deliberate—and often more effective, compared to other methods in Tibetan Buddhism—means to reach liberation. In other words, the *Bardo Thödröl* proposes that liberation can be achieved *through the senses* instead of by *overcoming the senses*.[40]

Interestingly, when the instructions for the dying and/or dead from *The Tibetan Book of the Dead* are read aloud, sound itself takes on an important, salvific role. As the eminent Bhutanese scholar Dasho Sangay Dorji (1946–2020) writes in an introduction to Chapter Eleven, "the voice of the Lama [teacher], who calls out the dying person should be very melodious, so that merely upon hearing the sound of the instructions the person feels soothed, elevated and attracted."[41]

The *Root Stanzas of the Six Bardos*, Orality, and Transmission

> In music, for example, the composer is not the only person, but the performers also, from the leading instrument to the most subordinate accompanyist. Then there must be the maker of the musical instruments, and the audience too, if they are connoisseurs, do not merely receive, but each one in his own way also has his work.
>
> —Friedrich Schleiermacher, *On Religion: Speeches to its Cultured Despisers*[42]

The complete *Bardo Thödröl* includes much more than the important and popular teachings in Chapter Eleven. In fact, the original, multilayered Tibetan work contains extensive and detailed teachings about Tibetan Tantric Buddhist meditative practices, such as how to recognize death approaching and avoid premature death; detailed information about the dying process, such as the dissolution of the elements of the psychophysical complex of the aggregate of form (Tib. *gzugs kyi phung po*), which according to Buddhist philosophy makes up the physical entity of a person; and aspirational prayers for the time of death. Following the famous Chapter Eleven is an allegorical drama (intended for staging in the Tibetan masked-theater tradition) about the workings of cause and effect (Karma)—which to this day is a very popular production in Bhutan and Tibet[43]—as well as instructions on how to wear a Mantra amulet that promises "liberation by wearing."[44] In other words, the "complete" *Bardo Thödröl* deals not only with the three Bardos of Death, Reality, and Rebirth between births, but addresses all six of the Bardo states experienced throughout the full cycle of existence in Saṃsāra.[45]

The *Root Stanzas of the Six Bardos*, which Radigue acknowledges as the inspiration for *Kyema* and for her practice as a Buddhist more generally, make up the very short third chapter of the *Bardo Thödröl*. They also appear in the tenth chapter and throughout the eleventh chapter (as Radigue explains in her interview with Julia Eckhardt).[46] From a Western perspective, the verse in which the *Root Stanzas of the Six Bardos* were composed would be associated with poetry; however, in the context of the Tibetan language, form does not necessarily determine or limit the content of a text.[47] In Tibetan literature, rather, one finds philosophical, doctrinal, literary, and even medical treatises written in verse. In religious literature, the very deliberate rhythm of the words functions didactically as a mnemonic means for the Buddhist disciple to memorize, recite, and understand the particular Buddhist teaching at hand.

Root stanzas (Tib. *rtsa ba*) play a crucial role in Tibetan Buddhist literature, often carrying the core message of the entire work. The *Root Stanzas of the Six Bardos*, for example, encompass all there is to know for a Buddhist about Saṃsāra and Nirvāṇa, and hence how to reach liberation. In other words, the content of the *Root Stanzas of the Six Bardos*, in essence, encompasses the entire *Bardo Thödröl* (*Great Liberation Upon Hearing in the Intermediate States*). Moreover, Tibetan root stanzas are often very dense, elliptical, and cryptic.[48] They can be understood fully only when they are studied along with additional textual commentaries and the oral guidance of a teacher. A Buddhist practitioner may deepen their understanding of the *Root Stanzas of the Six Bardos* by reciting and reflecting upon them on a regular (optimally, daily) basis throughout their life. This practice serves as crucial preparation for one's own death.[49]

Despite the popularity and availability of the *Bardo Thödröl* today, it is important to point out that in their original context, its teachings were what one might call esoteric in nature and could be transmitted only according to a strict set of rules, as is common for the Tantric aspects of the Tibetan Buddhist tradition. Traditionally, such teachings required a direct and close relationship between a teacher—in Sanskrit, *Guru*, and in Tibetan, *Lama*—and a suitable disciple. Such a disciple would need to possess certain qualities and be quite advanced along the spiritual path—only then could the teachings be transmitted authentically and the transmission lineage of the teachings be properly continued. As evidence of their validity, many Tibetan Buddhist texts list at the beginning all the persons in the transmission lineage of the particular teaching. However, in contemporary Buddhist practice, the *Bardo Thödröl* is more like Radigue describes it when she says, "[the] *Bardo Thödöl* is not a secret tradition, but one of the foundations of Buddhism, with multiple planes of comprehension, a bit like a Russian doll."[50] Here, Radigue refers not only to the fact that *The Tibetan Book of the Dead* (understood generally as the eleventh chapter of the *Bardo Thödröl*) is taught more publicly today, but also that the different layers of understanding and meaning can be apprehended only through an authentic Buddhist practice and transmission (as described above).

In the large corpus of Tibetan Buddhist literature, the *Bardo Thödröl* belongs to the category of *treasure literature* within the Nyingma tradition of Tibetan Buddhism, but is now practiced in all four traditions of Tibetan Buddhism. Such treasures (Tib. *gter ma*)—which are mostly texts, but can also be ritual objects or relics—are said to have been hidden by the eighth-century Buddhist master Guru Rinpoche (also known as Padmasaṃbhava), who is credited with bringing Buddhism to Tibet. Guru Rinpoche and his consort Yeshe Tsogyal, an eminent Buddhist master in her own right, are said to have hidden these treasures all over the Tibetan cultural area, both in physical places and in the minds of "treasure finders" (Tib. *gter ston*).[51] Many of these treasures were prophesied by Guru Rinpoche, along with the treasure finders, who, according to his prophecy, would become qualified to reveal these treasures through their spiritual realization when the conditions are considered right. To this day, treasures continue to be revealed by treasure finders in the Tibetan cultural area, with many still hidden and yet to be discovered.

One such eminent treasure finder was Karma Lingpa (ca. fourteenth century), who is credited with unearthing the *Bardo Thödröl* cycle. After their discovery, those teachings were then only very gradually and secretively taught over the proceeding generations. Gyarawa Namkha Chöki Gyatso (b. 1430) was the first to publicly teach them, and Rikdzin Nyima Drakpa (1647–1710) was an important editor who, at a late stage in his life, compiled and standardized the *Bardo Thödröl*.[52]

Furthermore, any authentic transmission of Tibetan Tantric Buddhist teachings requires a "reading transmission" (Tib. *lung*) to the ear of the Buddhist practitioner or disciple. If one reads the text of a teaching alone, no sufficient transmission of its content can take place; rather, a Buddhist teacher—who is themselves capable and has been authorized to transmit the specific teaching at hand—must read the text aloud to the disciple for the transmission to be valid. Reading transmissions often happen very quickly, and it is not important that the disciple understands the text conceptually at this point; rather, here, the sonic dissemination of the text (its recitation) is the most important factor in an authentic transmission of Buddhist teachings. The teachings are then further studied and practiced with additional instructions (Tib. *khrid/bshad*) from a qualified teacher.[53]

Textuality and orality are closely intertwined in the *Bardo Thödröl* (*Great Liberation Upon Hearing in the Intermediate States*), but more generally, it is the fact that the lineage of transmission in Tibetan Tantric Buddhism is always constituted by a direct Guru-disciple relationship that is the most essential feature of a valid or authentic transmission of its teachings.

In sum: while in general, orality and hearing are necessary aspects of the transmission of all the teachings in the Tantric forms of Tibetan Buddhism, in the case of the *Bardo Thödröl*, orality and the use of one's hearing sense itself is stressed as an enormously important *means for liberation* and as a Buddhist practice in and of itself. With this in mind, one can better sense what Radigue might possibly be alluding to when she states, "oral transmission is the most widespread method in all the world's music and actually not only for music but also for speech—the vehicle of thought."[54]

Radigue's own variations on orality are abundant in both her solo compositions and her collaborative engagements with her audience, performers, and performance itself. Such variations are exemplified in her electronic music by her practice of recording in a single take with no formal musical notation and by her *propositions sonores*' invitation to listeners to create their own unique versions of her compositions. In Radigue's later acoustical work, concepts of orality and transmission take on even greater significance: in the complex collaborative process of cocomposing with a performer; in the transmission of the work to the performer through this process; in that the work is stored singularly in the mind of the performer, with the possibility of being transmitted subsequently to another performer (if desired); and, generally speaking, in that each performance is unique and impossible to reproduce in identical form.[55]

Similarly, according to the Buddhist ideal of the authentic transmission of Buddhist teachings in an unbroken lineage since the historical Buddha or the treasure teachings revealed in the minds of treasure finders, there are no clear boundaries between author, text, teacher/lineage holder, and recipient/Buddhist disciple. Such conceptual boundaries are likewise blurred in Radigue's music. As listeners, we become an indispensable part of a complex and dynamic cocreation process. Thus, Radigue's fluid conception of the roles of composer, composition, performer, and listener can more generally be related back to Dzongsar Jamyang Khyentse Rinpoche's conception of the "illusory boundaries" that separate each moment of the six intermediate states of experience.[56]

Radigue's Music as a Buddhist Offering

> Apart from the sound and music that are used in religious practices and religious references in secular music cultures, many more forms of relationships exist between sound, music and religion that have gone virtually unnoticed to date.
>
> —Isabel Laack, "Sound, Music and Religion"[57]

While Radigue's compositions are not specifically intended for a Buddhist audience and have a very diverse, global listenership, as a long-term practitioner of Tibetan Buddhism she has persistently included Tibetan Buddhist topoi and literature in her work, interpreting their spiritual content in her musical idiom and using sound to give it shape. It is important to note that Radigue does not conceive of her music as formally religious, or, as she states, not as "religious music *sensu stricto*."[58] Radigue explains, "I do not presume to provide meditative music. People called it that even before I encountered Buddhism, which is a strange coincidence. My music is profane, but undoubtedly inspired by the sacred."[59] Here, I must emphasize that in my approach as a scholar of Tibetology and Religious Studies, I trace associations and connections between Radigue's sounds and Tibetan Buddhist thought and history and then combine those insights with those gained from immersive listening as a musician and my reflections on that listening through an autoethnography of the senses. In this section, I would like to point to some examples of sound metaphors in Radigue's work that I personally find intriguing; however, I do not intend to speculate about Radigue's intentions or feelings.

Radigue belongs to the first generation of Western European convert-Buddhists who were able to study very closely with the Tibetan Buddhist masters who so tragically fled from Tibet to India, Nepal, Bhutan, Europe, and the Americas after the occupation of Tibet by the Chinese People's Liberation Army in the fifties. As refugees, many of these eminent Tibetan Buddhist masters were invited to places in Asia, Europe, and North America, and Tibetan Buddhism began to flourish and spread as many new monasteries and retreat centers of all four Tibetan Buddhist traditions were founded across the globe.

The region of the Dordogne (*le Perigord*) in the South of France is one of these places, and was chosen as such deliberately. While visiting the Côte du Jor and taking in the stunning view of the Vézère Valley it offers, the eminent Tibetan Buddhist master Düdjom Jigdral Yeshe Dorje Rinpoche (1904–87) had a vision of this region being associated with the Maṇḍala of an important Tibetan Buddhist deity (Vajrakīlāya). It was therefore deemed fit as a place to build up the future of Tibetan Buddhism in the wake of the Buddhists' tragic exile from Tibet. Many Tibetan Buddhist teachers in exile were dependent on wealthy donors and patrons who sponsored Buddhist activities and provided land for monasteries and retreat centers; in the Dordogne, the first of these patrons was an English businessman and devoted Buddhist named Bernard Benson.[60] To this day, one still finds in the Dordogne a high concentration of Tibetan Buddhist centers of different lineages, with both lay and monastic Buddhist communities and retreat centers. Radigue's Tibetan Buddhist teacher, Pawo Rinpoche, came to the Dordogne in 1975 and founded his retreat center, Nehnang Samten Chöling (casually referred to as *Les Tranchats*).[61]

Raised Catholic, with an interest in spirituality from an early age, Radigue was first brought in direct contact with Tibetan Buddhism during her travels to North America; after presenting *Adnos I* in San Francisco in 1975, three French Buddhists in the audience approached her and gave her the address of a Buddhist center in Paris. This eventually led Radigue to Pawo Rinpoche, who would be her teacher in France for thirteen years. In the same year that Radigue was introduced to Tibetan Buddhism, she also discovered that she had suffered irreversible damage to her inner ear, and, as she puts it, "the two events together made me decide to mark a break in my path as a composer."[62]

Most of the first-generation convert-Buddhists such as Radigue had direct and very intimate relationships with their teachers, very much resembling the model of the traditional Indian and Tibetan Guru-disciple relationship (which is less often the case today). "At that time," Radigue recalls, "we were very lucky because in France, we had wonderful visitors, great Tibetan masters who've now disappeared. It was like fireworks. . . . And then, I came to meet Pawo Rinpoche, who was a great Tibetan lama. He had a more personal approach. He had a very small monastery on an old farm in the south of France in Dordogne, and at that time, I decided that this was the place I wanted to live, and that I would stay there for the rest of my life!"[63]

After returning to France and visiting the center in Paris, Radigue began to study and practice Buddhism intensively, and stopped making music for two to three years. During this period, she spent substantial time in Pawo Rinpoche's retreat center in the Dordogne before he returned to Kathmandu in 1988. It was Pawo Rinpoche himself who put an end to Radigue's hiatus as a composer, convincing her to resume composing and advising her to always conceive of her "music as an offering." Radigue has heeded this advice ever since.[64]

Radigue's first composition as a Buddhist offering was *Les Chants de Milarepa* (1983),[65] based on the *Hundred Thousand Songs of Milarepa*, which in their original cultural context are an intriguing example of both Tibetan Buddhist poetry and music.[66] They belong to the literary and musical genre of "songs of realization" or "songs of experience" (Tib. *mgur*; Skt. *dohā*), which dates back to earlier eminent Indian Buddhists, in whose lineage Milarepa (1052–1135), the great Tibetan Yogīn and cultural hero, also stands. These songs were a crucial part of Milarepa's teachings, and many of them were thus quite didactic, serving as a dialogic means—similar to the Socratic method—of transmitting Tibetan Buddhist doctrines and practices from a Guru (such as Milarepa) to a disciple, thereby preserving the teachings. Here, orality is once again foregrounded as one of the most important features of maintaining an authentic Tibetan Buddhist transmission lineage.[67]

In Radigue's version, the songs of realization are recited and sung in both Tibetan (by Lama Kunga) and English (by Robert Ashley). Without knowing Radigue's exact reasons for presenting a bilingual recitation, it strikes me personally as a very meaningful aesthetic gesture. Here, Radigue preserves the unique Tibetan tradition of singing spiritual songs, and she offers the listener the possibility of witnessing this tradition firsthand. With the English recitation, Radigue provides access to this doctrinal content to listeners unfamiliar with Tibetan. To those listeners on the spiritual path, however, Radigue offers the soteriological possibility—liberation through hearing. One peculiar characteristic of the Tibetan tradition of singing spiritual songs is that the story or narrative of a song is recited at the same time, both parts of the original Tibetan text are transmitted during the performance, so that the performer must alternate between the story and the song, which differ from each other in speed, rhythm, and melody.[68]

Other tape works directly connected to Tibetan Buddhist thought and conceptualized as Buddhist offerings are *Adnos II* (1980), *Adnos III* (1982), *Jetsun Mila* (1986), *Kyema* (1988), *Kailasha* (1991), *Koumé* (1993), and "Danse des Dakinis" (1998).[69]

Within Tibetan Buddhism and its ritual contexts, pleasing or beautiful music can be conceived as an offering to the senses (Tib. *mchod pa*; Skt. *pūjā*). From the common daily water offerings to very complex and intricate arrangements of Tantric Buddhist offerings, many different kinds of offerings exist in the Tibetan Buddhist world. One common practice is to present a set of seven or eight different kinds of offerings (Tib. *mchod pa bdun/mchod pa brgyad*).[70] In his praise of a Buddhist deity, Tibetan author Lopön Kongwa Jin gives an example of one of these arrangements: "having taken up in awareness (*blo*) flowers, incense, butter lamps and perfumed water, food, music and whatever more there is, offer with a respectful mind (*yid*)."[71]

In a Buddhist context, offerings are the lived expression of the virtue of generosity. Generosity is one of the Six Pāramitās that a Buddhist practitioner trains themselves in as they progress along the Buddhist path. The Six Pāramitās are generosity, morality, patience, perseverance, meditative concentration, and wisdom. The constant cultivation of generosity, and thereby the daily practice of offerings, plays an enormous soteriological role in reaching enlightenment for the Buddhist practitioner. Beyond all the technicalities of what, how, and whom to offer to, many Buddhist texts emphasize that the most important aspect of a Buddhist offering is the intention and motivation it is carried out with. Offerings must be free from the "three spheres" (Tib. *'khor gsum rnam dag*), that is, the person offering must refrain from conceptualizing or clinging to the subject themselves (the person making the offering), the object that is offered, and the act of offering itself. Only with such a pure intention does the very act of offering create wholesome merit for the Buddhist practitioner (and, by extension, for the recipient).

A more nuanced understanding of the Buddhist offering casts Radigue's compositions in a new light. Listeners, conceived as the recipients of the composer's offerings, are inextricable from the compositions themselves, as they are conceptually and practically part of the three spheres. For me, the importance of purity of intention in Buddhist offerings speaks to many aspects of Radigue's practice as a composer, from her solitary work over years without institutional support or material rewards to the technical process of drawing sound from within the complexity of electrical current *itself*—as in the feedback works—or from the instrument *itself*—as in the wolf sonority of *Naldjorlak*—independent of concerns about the sounding result of these processes. From a Buddhist perspective, the dynamic and fluid relationship between composition, performance/performer, and listener becomes not only an artistic activity but first and foremost a meritorious, indeed, liberating activity.

Radigue and the Sound of the Tibetan Language

> The golden letters arrayed
> Are like the stars and planets arranged in a line.
> —Chögyel Phagpa Lodrö Gyeltsen[72]

One particularly remarkable aspect of several of Radigue's works associated with Tibetan Buddhist topoi is her choice of Tibetan titles, which often involve creative yet very thoughtful play with the sounds, meanings, and spellings of Tibetan words. This is very well exemplified by the titles of the three "movements" of the *Trilogie de la Mort*, in each of which Radigue plays with the homophonic nature of different Tibetan words and syllables. Tibetan homophones can differ in spelling with the addition to a root letter of certain pre-, super-, sub-, or postscripts that change the meaning of the word but not the pronunciation. It is important to note here that the Tibetan language and alphabet are highly regarded in Tibetan culture, and in Tibetan Buddhism in particular, as the introduction of Tibetan script in the seventh century is directly linked to the introduction of Buddhism to Tibet via Guru Rinpoche from India.

All three parts of the *Trilogie de la Mort*—*Kyema*, *Kailasha*, and *Koumé*—bear titles beginning with the first letter in the Tibetan alphabet, "ka" (ཀ).[73] This Tibetan letter is also beautifully rendered by Arman (1928–2005), Radigue's former husband, in his artwork for the album cover for the 1998 release of the *Trilogie de la Mort*.[74]

Regarding *Kyema*, Radigue has explained that the title comes from the expression used at the beginning of each of the *Root Stanzas of the Six Bardos*. An evocative phrase, *kye ma* connotes grief or suffering; in Radigue's own words, it "evoke[s] the sigh we make faced with inescapable fatality."[75] The term is perhaps best translated into English as "alas!"[76] However, Radigue interprets the Tibetan term *kye ma* very differently, as meaning "beings born from a mother," with *kye* referring to "being born" (Tib. *skyes*) and *ma* (Tib. *ma*) as a "marker for the feminine."[77] With that, she created a new Tibetan homophone and thereby a neologism. For me, her interpretation places stronger emphasis on the divine feminine aspects of Tibetan Tantric Buddhism, and carries a much lighter and more positive note compared to the original meaning.

Kailasha also begins with the first consonant letter of the Tibetan alphabet, but this word remains unchanged in Radigue's use of it. In the cosmologies of the Buddhist, Jain, Hindu, and Bön religions, the Kailash Mountain is considered the center of this world, the sacred mountain Meru. The mountain is integral to Tibet's sacred landscape, with crucial pilgrimage routes encircling it. For Radigue, the composition of *Kailasha* took place during the very difficult mourning period after the unexpected death of her son Yves, and she describes the work as an "imaginary pilgrimage," inspired by photographs from a friend who had undertaken the journey in person and Radigue's own readings about it.[78] In Tibetan Buddhism, a pilgrimage consists of many different stages and serves to purify the Karma of pilgrims and people associated with them. Often, one sets out on a pilgrimage because oneself or a relative is seriously ill, or a loved one has died.

Regarding *Koumé*, Radigue explains that the title comes from her own "pidgin Tibetan" (as this word does not exist in Tibetan) combining *kou*, meaning "the sacred body," and *me*, meaning "fire," thus disclosing as the work's inspiration the composer's experience at the cremation ritual for her teacher, Pawo Rinpoche, in Kathmandu.[79] I assume that Radigue adds "sacred" because *kou* (Tib. *sku*) is an honorific Tibetan term for "body" that would be used when referring to the body of a venerated person, such as a Buddhist teacher. For oneself, one would always use the humbler term *lü* (Tib. *lus*).

When I first listened to the composition, before knowing Radigue's rationale behind the title *Koumé* as "sacred body [and] fire" (Tib. *sku me*), I thought of another possible Tibetan homophone: *sku med*, meaning "without [our] physical bodies," nearly in the sense of "*beyond* our physical bodies."

Another poignant example of Radigue's playful engagement with the Tibetan language is *Naldjorlak I–III* (2005–2009). Here, Radigue adds as suffix the honorific marker *lak* (Tib. *lags*) onto the substantive *Naldjor* (Tib. *rnyal 'byor*), which means "yoga." However, grammatically speaking, the honorific marker can only be added to a person, not to a concept or thing.

Radigue titles her works very deliberately to denote the ideas and interpretations that inspired them, including these very intricate references to Tibetan Buddhist thought and meaning embodied in the Tibetan language. Moreover, it is important to point out that the interplay between sound and meaning in her titles adds an additional dimension and function to Radigue's compositions. For the listener, this interplay creates an intermediate space that allows for the coexistence of multiple meanings evoked by sounds and the constant flux between meanings and their phonetic presence in different Tibetan words. In this lively and mutual interdependence, multiple meanings are not in contradiction with one another but unfold in the very personal experience of the listener—simultaneously and anew in each moment. Listeners are in a constant flux between not recognizing and recognizing certain meanings while immersed in the experience of listening (Tib. *nyams*) to Radigue's sounds.[80]

Experiencing Sound as Dharma in the *Trilogie de la Mort*

> These approaches raise the question of what is to be gained through description; the pieces exist for themselves, and it is hard to imagine how the immersive listening experience they call forth would benefit from informational pointers of this kind. The attempt to identify or label or graph its features may distract from a music that is fundamentally conceived as moment-to-moment entrainment in the lived time of its being listened to—a music, for lack of a better term, of personal experience.
>
> —Charles Curtis, "Éliane Radigue and an 'Unreal, Impalpable Music'"[81]

Listening to the *Trilogie de la Mort* as a scholar and practitioner of Tibetan Buddhism, I find that Radigue's sounds are deeply evocative of the content of the Buddhist teachings (Skt. *dharma*). More specifically, as shown in this essay, the different sound patterns and figures that populate this music offer an additional level of experience and spiritual engagement for the Buddhist practitioner, who may thematically connect Radigue's music with Tibetan Buddhist thought and history, become part of the music itself within the framework of the Buddhist offering, or reflect on the sounds of Tibetan words and letters in the titles of the works. Perceiving and reflecting on the sounds that Radigue produces in her compositions as Dharma is therefore one possible way of approaching the immense complexity and "impalpability" of her oeuvre, while simultaneously acknowledging the limitations of trying to analyze and describe this music rationally and conceptually. An autoethnography of the senses that is built upon listening to and experiencing the sounds and music of the *Trilogie de la Mort* can therefore provide a framework to analyze and describe a distinctly religious practice for a Buddhist,[82] or, more broadly speaking, also a spiritual practice.[83]

To conclude, I would like to extend this autoethnography of the sensory experience of *Kyema* to the two other movements of the *Trilogie de la Mort* in the hopes of further articulating the contours and potential significance of such an approach. *Koumé*, the last part of the *Trilogie de la Mort*, was composed by Radigue after participating in the elaborate cremation funeral rites for her Buddhist teacher, Pawo Rinpoche. While I have not been able to locate any documentation of Pawo Rinpoche's cremation, it is nevertheless safe to assume that for such an eminent Buddhist master, the event would have been massive and quite lengthy. Such an event is traditionally considered to hold immense blessings, and Buddhist masters and clergy from different Tibetan Buddhist traditions would have been present, along with many of Pawo Rinpoche's own Buddhist followers.[84]

As I listen to *Koumé*, before my inner eye, I can see and hear the elaborate fire rituals, the diverse forms of Buddhist liturgical texts and prayers being chanted, and their accompaniment by complex ritual music, including many different Tibetan ritual instruments and drums—all this taking place over many hours in an open space in the Kathmandu Valley with a very specific "architecture of sacral sound."[85] After the cremation rites, Pawo Rinpoche's ashes were installed in a new reliquary *Stūpa* in the main temple of his retreat center in the Dordogne, which today Buddhist practitioners can still visit to receive blessings from his ashes.[86] Such a practice exemplifies the religious and soteriological importance that the cremation of a Buddhist master holds for their Buddhist disciples.

According to Radigue, these experiences evoked for her "the transcendental side of death, which exists in all traditions." And, in an eclectic fashion, Radigue's program notes combine allusions to the Tibetan Buddhist cremation rituals with those to classical Christian liturgy and music by including four quotations: one referring to Mozart's Requiem Mass in D Minor, another to Bach's St. Matthew Passion, and two biblical references associated with death.[87]

In an interview with Ludger Brümmer on the occasion of her acceptance of the 2019 Giga-Hertz Award for her life's work, Radigue describes her experiences concerning *Koumé* in the following terms:

"We are made of spirituality, we are made of intuition also, even though in our civilization we give a big privilege to ratio[nalism], to intellect and all that. But, anyway, spirituality [is] there, intuition is there. And even though it was saddening somehow because this master was very important for me in my life, there were also this feeling of a kind of *transcendency of death*, which is universal."[88]

The *Trilogie de la Mort* is an ideal point of departure for a systematic analysis of Radigue's work and its relation to Tibetan Buddhism. This is primarily because of its in-depth consideration of death and mortality as one of *the* most crucial topics in Tibetan Buddhist thought, Radigue's deep, personal relationship with Tibetan Buddhism, and the direct connection between *Kailasha* and *Koumé* and the losses of her son and Tibetan Buddhist teacher. "Everything I've been doing has always its story," Radigue states, and "this one [the *Trilogie de la Mort*] is probably the one which is the most involved also with the physical, mental experiences."[89]

In *Koumé*, what Radigue calls the "transcendency of death" can be perceived by a Buddhist practitioner very clearly, as cremation rites denote one's transition into the different Bardo states after death and thereby represent the unique possibility for the deceased Buddhist practitioner to transcend death and reach liberation during the Bardo of Reality (as previously pointed out in my analysis of *Kyema*). The cremation of a Buddhist master demonstrates their own mastery over death to the disciples. Such mastery is said to be evidenced by the appearance of wondrous signs, such as unusual weather, double rainbows, gatherings of wild animals, mild earthquakes, or the appearance of relics or other materials from the ashes.

The transcendency of death is palpable in the dronelike sounds that, beginning around 20'59", evoke the very typical overtone throat-chanting of Tibetan monks, and then the gradual overtaking of these sounds, from around 27'21" onward, by a noise that resembles the crackling of fire as it consumes the body of the Buddhist master along with the wooden structure and firewood of the cremation Stūpa.[90] Beginning around 28'53", one hears the traces of chanting and ritual music as sounds resembling traditional Tibetan instruments, such as the Chinese flute (Tib. *rgya gling*), begin to fade in softly. These sounds continue to build up into ever more polyphonic and intense overlapping structures with the addition of what resembles yet more Tibetan instruments, such as the Tibetan big horn (Tib. *dung chen*) and drums. These electronicized sounds are interwoven into a tapestry that echoes the dense soundscape of the ritual that would indeed have accompanied the cremation of a Buddhist master like Pawo Rinpoche—which then slowly subsides from 38'50" onward into the final, much calmer phase of transcendency.

In *Kailasha*, the soundscape of the storied pilgrimage around the eponymous mountain is perceivable for a Buddhist practitioner from the very first moment of the piece, as sounds that evoke the whipping of winds as they blow over the vast Tibetan plateau envelop the listener in one of the most typical of all Tibetan geophones. And then there are sounds that resemble the distant chiming of bells at the temples and monasteries along the pilgrimage route—stretched by Radigue and varied in pitch and timbre throughout the piece, fading in more audibly from 15'15" onward. With *Kailasha*, Radigue enables a Buddhist practitioner to embark on a very individual pursuit—independent from her own painful inner journey during its composition—of spiritual purification and pilgrimage across a complex and sacred inner and outer landscape with each listening.

In sum, the methodological and theoretical framework of an autoethnography of the senses enables the listener (as well as the reader) to understand and trace more concretely the intricate interplay between sounds and meaning—*sound as Dharma*—in Radigue's *Trilogie de la Mort*, thus revealing yet another transitional state between the realm of the impalpable and the palpable.

1. Dzongsar Jamyang Khyentse, *Living is Dying: How to Prepare for Dying, Death and Beyond* (Siddhartha's Intent: 2022), 30, accessed May 15, 2024, https://siddharthasintent.s3.ap-southeast-2.amazonaws.com/Resources/Publications/LiDbookv13.pdf. Quotation marks have been standardized according to American English.

2. As common in the Tibetan tradition, I use the title *Rinpoche* to refer to a Tibetan Buddhist teacher who is also an incarnation.

3. In this essay, I use "intermediate state" as the English translation for *bardo*. Theoretically "intermediary state" is also a possible translation, but is less common in English.

4. Khyentse, *Living is Dying*, 30.

5. Tibetan Buddhist masters often have different names, for example, denoting family origin, ordination, or incarnation lineage. Pawo Rinpoche was also known as Nenang Pawo Rinpoche, Tsuklak Mawä Wangchuk, and Tsuklak Nangwa Wangchuk.

6. See, for example, Julia Eckhardt and Éliane Radigue, *Intermediary Spaces/Espaces Intermédiaires* (Brussels: Q02/Umland Editions, 2019), 140. See also Bernard Girard, "Conversations with Éliane Radigue," in *Alien Roots: Éliane Radigue* (New York: Blank Forms Editions, 2025), 279.

7. My translation of the *Root Stanzas of the Six Bardos* follows Gyurme Dorje's translation; see Graham Coleman and Thupten Jinpa, eds., *The Tibetan Book of the Dead: First Complete Translation*, trans. Gyurme Dorje (London: Penguin, 2006), 32–34.

8. Eckhardt and Radigue, *Intermediary Spaces*, 184. The differences in the phonetic transcription in Latin script result from the differences in the actual pronunciation of Latin consonants and vowels in the respective native language of the non-Tibetan speaker. For example, a French person would use "ou" instead of "u" in German, as also seen in the example of "Koumé," which a native German speaker would transcribe as "Kume."

9. For a detailed introduction to the complexities of the Tibetan Buddhist canon, see Phillip Stanley, "The Tibetan Buddhist Canon," in *The Wiley Blackwell Companion to East and Inner Asian Buddhism*, ed. Mario Poceski (Hoboken, NJ: John Wiley & Sons, Ltd., 2014), 383–99.

10. See, for example, Dagmar Schwerk, *A Timely Message from the Cave: The Mahāmudrā and Intellectual Agenda of dGe-bshes Brag-phug-pa dGe-'dun-rin-chen (1926–1997), the Sixty-Ninth rJe-mkhan-po of Bhutan* (Hamburg: Universität Hamburg, Department of Indian and Tibetan Studies, 2020), 111 ff; 141 ff.

11. For a detailed introduction to metaphor analysis, see Katrin Kohl, *Metapher* (Stuttgart: J.B. Metzler, 2007).

12. See, for example, Daniel Silliman, "Being and Nonbeing: An Analysis of *Kyema* (1988)" in *Alien Roots: Éliane Radigue*, 287 ff.

13. In my case, an autoethnography addresses the fact that I am a researcher in Tibetology and Religious Studies, a practitioner of Tibetan Buddhism, and a musician. Here, I offer a sketch of some of my initial findings with this approach without the accompanying research notes; however, I plan to elaborate on this more systematically in a future article. For an introduction to autoethnography as a qualitative research method, see Tony E. Adams, Stacy H. Jones, and Carolyn Ellis, *Autoethnography* (New York: Oxford University Press, 2015).

14. I would especially like to thank Charles Curtis, Lawrence Kumpf, Anna Morcom, Regine Hahn, and Clara Ragnitz for their insights and feedback, which have contributed significantly to this essay. My essay also interacts with Daniel Silliman's systematic musicological analysis. Moreover, I am very grateful to Lily Bartle for her thorough editing.

15. For more information on this subfield, see Hubert Cancik and Hubert Mohr, "Religionsästhetik," in *Handbuch Religionswissenschaftlicher Grundbegriffe, Band I*, ed. Hubert Cancik, et al. (Stuttgart: Kohlhammer 1988), 121–56.

16. For a comprehensive introduction to the current status of research, challenges, and possible ways of studying music within the field of religious studies, see Guy L. Beck, introduction to *Musicology of Religion: Theories, Methods, and Directions* (Albany: SUNY Press, 2023), 1–40.

17 Time indications throughout this essay are based on Éliane Radigue, *Oeuvres Électroniques*, INA 6060/74, 2021, compact disc.

18 Silliman, "Being and Nonbeing," 299.

19 Charles Curtis, "Éliane Radigue and an 'Unreal, Impalpable Music,'" in *The Oxford Handbook of Spectral Music*, ed. Amy Bauer, Liam Cagney, and William Mason (online edition, Oxford Academic, 2022), www.doi.org/10.1093/oxfordhb/9780190633547.013.24.

20 Translation according to Coleman and Jinpa, eds., *The Tibetan Book of the Dead*, 33. Parentheses are the translator's. To complicate matters, the Western concept of physical death is in some respects not completely transferrable to the Tibetan medical system. The Tibetan Buddhist tradition has reported and also visually documented cases of Buddhist masters who, after physical death, have remained for days in a *postmortem* meditative absorption (Tib. *thugs dam*); see also Schwerk, *A Timely Message from the Cave*, 58, 84. For a detailed documentation from the field of visual and medical anthropology, see Donagh Coleman, dir., *Tukdam: Between Worlds* (Ireland/Finland/Estonia: Martha O'Neill, Kaarle Aho, Pille Rünk, 2022), HD, 91 mins.

21 See Coleman and Jinpa, eds., *The Tibetan Book of the Dead*, 444.

22 For the technical musicological analysis of this part (in Silliman's numbering I.3), see Silliman, "Being and Nonbeing," 313–17.

23 For a description of the iconography of these different Buddhist deities and their Maṇḍalas, see "Bardo (Peaceful & Wrathful)," Himalayan Art Resources, last modified January 1, 2022, www.himalayanart.org/search/set.cfm?setid=227. For a detailed explanation of their symbolism, see also Coleman and Jinpa, eds., *The Tibetan Book of the Dead*, 387–402.

24 The spiritual path culminates in what is usually known as *enlightenment* and is expressed in Tibetan Buddhist doctrinal and exegetical works through the theory of the three (or more) Buddha Bodies. In brief, the Buddha Bodies represent different aspects of enlightenment caused by different accomplishments on the spiritual path, for example, by the accumulation of wisdom or merit; see Schwerk, *A Timely Message from the Cave*, 244n540.

25 Translation according to Coleman and Jinpa, eds., *The Tibetan Book of the Dead*, 32. Emphasis is my own. Parentheses are the translator's.

26 For further explanation, see Coleman and Jinpa, eds., *The Tibetan Book of the Dead*, 509.

27 Tenzin Gyatso quoted in Graham Coleman, "Editor's Introduction," in *The Tibetan Book of the Dead*, xxxvii.

28 See Coleman and Jinpa, eds., *The Tibetan Book of the Dead*, xxxvii, 479.

29 The first complete translation of the *Bardo Thödröl* was Coleman and Jinpa, eds., *The Tibetan Book of the Dead* (2005). My account of the history of *The Tibetan Book of the Dead* follows Gyurme Dorje's comprehensive but concise "A Brief Literary History of the *Tibetan Book of the Dead*," in Coleman and Jinpa, eds., *The Tibetan Book of the Dead*, xxxviii–li. I also follow their numbering of the chapters. Two more chapters were added by the translators and editors to the twelve chapters of the *Bardo Thödröl* on the advice of the eminent Tibetan Buddhist master, scholar, teacher, and artist Dilgo Khyentse Rinpoche (1910–91).

30 Ideally, a serious Buddhist practitioner would get acquainted with the different phases between rebirths during their life to prepare for the dying process.

31 Most of the Tibetan doxographical texts count four major traditions within Tibetan Buddhism: Nyingma, Sakya, Kagyü, and Geluk; but the reality is much more complex. Radigue's teacher Pawo Rinpoche belonged to the Kagyü tradition.

32 Their translation and commentary focus again only on parts of the *Bardo Thödröl*; see Trungpa, Chogyam, and Francesca Freemantle, trans./eds., *The Tibetan Book of the Dead: The Great Liberation Through Hearing in The Bardo* (Boulder, CO: Shambhala Publications, 2000).

33 See, for example, Robert A. F. Thurman, "Meeting the Miss-Titled Tibetan Book of The Dead: Robert A.F. Thurman on Death & Dying," Tibet House US Menla,

September 17, 2018, YouTube video, accessed June 13, 2024, www.youtube.com/watch?v=W2xJNrbZlHM.

34 Art Spiegelman, *Maus: Die Geschichten eines Überlebenden*, trans. Christine Brinck and Josef Joffe (Frankfurt am Main: Fischer Verlag, 2022), 102.

35 For a detailed analysis of the reception history of *The Tibetan Book of the Dead*, see Donald S. Jr. Lopez, *The Tibetan Book of the Dead: A Biography* (Princeton, NJ: Princeton University Press, 2011). See also Timothy Leary, Ralph Metzner, and Richard Alpert (Ram Dass), *The Psychedelic Experience: A Manual Based on The Tibetan Book of the Dead* (New York: University Books, 1964), with parts of it adapted by The Beatles in "Tomorrow Never Knows" (1966), which interestingly also incorporates Indian music–style "drone" elements.

36 While Tibetan monastic and ritual music moves the basic pitch up rather than maintaining a constant drone (as Anna Morcom has pointed out to me), the specialized Tibetan multiphonic throat-chanting (low-tone/high-tone), known as overtone singing, where the singer, usually a monk, individually creates a complete chord by learning to control the muscles of the vocal cavity while singing, sounds almost like a form of natural drone music, using the body as an instrument. While beyond the scope of this essay, a consideration of overtone singing from the perspective of spectral music would be interesting.

37 For a detailed introduction to and a categorization of Tibetan music, including ritual music, see Isabelle Henrion-Dourcy, "Studying the Tibetan Performing Arts: A Bibliographic Introduction (1986–2017)," *Revue d'Etudes Tibétaines*, no. 40 (July 2017): 5–54.

38 See, for example, Deniz Bul, "The Arrival," November 5, 2021, YouTube video, accessed June 18, 2024, www.youtube.com/watch?v=AfgG8ERdOM8, in which Bul uses parts of the Vajrasattva Mantra as a mere stylistic element. This crucial mantra belongs to the preliminary practices of Tibetan Tantric Buddhism. The description of the video exemplifies the crass but stereotypical detachment from the original religious and cultural content, reading: "With his new single 'The Arrival' Deniz pays homage to the fabulous classic 303 sound. The old-school rave sound paired with *some deep vocals* during the breaks is bringing back the 90's [*sic*] vibe." Emphasis is my own.

39 Eckhardt and Radigue, *Intermediary Spaces*, 140.

40 For a detailed analysis of the use of the "eleven sense encounters" (seeing, hearing, tasting, touching, recollecting, cultivating, drinking, wearing, training, smelling, and making offerings) as an effective tool for liberation on the Tibetan Tantric Buddhist path, see James D. Gentry, "Liberation through sensory encounters in Tibetan Buddhist practice," *Revue d'Etudes Tibétaines*, no. 50 (June 2019): 73–131. See also Donald S. Lopez and Robert DeCaroli, eds., *Buddhism and the Senses* (Somerville, MA: Wisdom Publications, 2024).

41 Coleman and Jinpa, eds., *The Tibetan Book of the Dead*, 221.

42 Friedrich Schleiermacher, *On Religion: Speeches to its Cultured Despisers*, ed. and trans. John Oman (1899; New York: Harper & Row, 1958), 158n43.

43 This masked drama is shown in detail in Khyentse Norbu, dir., *Hema Hema: Sing me a song while I wait* (Bhutan: Pawo Choyning Dorji, and Sarah Chen, 2016), streaming video, 96 mins.; see also Sonthar Gyal, dir., *Lhamo and Skalbe* (China: Sonthar Gyal, Jiamei Feng, 2019), DVD, 110 mins. For context, Norbu Khyentse is the artistic name of the previously mentioned Dzongsar Jamyang Khyentse Rinpoche.

44 Coleman, "Editor's Introduction," in Coleman and Jinpa, eds., *The Tibetan Book of the Dead*, xxxi–xxxii.

45 The three Bardos of Death, Reality, and Rebirth are addressed in detail in two movies by Bhutanese filmmakers: Khyentse Norbu, dir., *Pig at the Crossing* (Bhutan: Norling Studies, 2024), streaming video, 119 mins; and Namgay Retty, dir., *49th Day* (Bhutan: Namgay Tshering & NT Sound and Vision, 2006), DVD, 135 mins.

46 See Coleman and Jinpa, eds., *The Tibetan Book of the Dead*, 31–34, 235, 288, 407; see also Eckhardt and Radigue, *Intermediary Spaces*, 140.

47 The traditional standard forms in Western literature have been usually defined as prose, verse, and drama (excluding postmodern developments).

48 This is intensified by the fact that the Tibetan language generally allows sentences to be elliptical by leaving away constituents of the sentence, especially if they have already been mentioned before (such as the subject or object), without being considered grammatically incorrect (which is different from most Indo-Germanic languages). Extensive use of this grammatical rule is made in verse literature.

49 See Coleman and Jinpa, eds., *The Tibetan Book of the Dead*, 31. For an open-access English translation of the *Root Stanzas of the Six Bardos*, see, for example, Adam Pearcey, "Root Verses on the Six Bardos," Lotsawa House, 2016, accessed July 8, 2024, www.lotsawahouse.org/tibetan-masters/karma-lingpa/root-verses-six-bardos.

50 Eckhardt and Radigue, *Intermediary Spaces*, 140.

51 The Tibetan cultural area is here understood not only as the Tibetan Autonomous Region within today's People's Republic of China but includes in this broader definition Bhutan, as well as parts of Western China, the Indian Himalayas, Nepal, Mongolia, and the former Soviet Union, depending on the point in Tibetan history one is studying.

52 See Coleman and Jinpa, eds., *The Tibetan Book of the Dead*, xlv–xlviii. For a detailed study of the complex transmission and compilation history of the *Bardo Thödröl*, see Bryan J. Cuevas, *The Hidden History of The Tibetan Book of the Dead* (New York: Oxford University Press, 2003).

53 On the importance of the sonic dimension in religions, see Guy L. Beck, introduction to *Musicology of Religion*, 34 ff.

54 Quoted in "The Universe of Éliane Radigue: Stages of a Music Pioneer – A Tribute on the Occasion of her 90th birthday," *Maerz Musik*, 2022, accessed June 30, 2024, www.berlinerfestspiele.de/en/maerzmusik/stories/2022/story-eliane-radigue.

55 See also Curtis, "Éliane Radigue and an 'Unreal, Impalpable Music,'" 14–15. For an in-depth analysis of those fascinating aspects, see Anthony Vine, Charles Curtis, and Madison Greenstone "An Anti-Ideal: Radigue and the Paradoxes of Recording," in *Alien Roots: Éliane Radigue*, 389–407.

56 Dzongsar Jamyang Khyentse, *Living is Dying*, 30.

57 Isabel Laack, "Sound, Music and Religion: A Preliminary Cartography of a Transdisciplinary Research Field," *Method and Theory in the Study of Religion* 27, no. 3 (2015): 235.

58 Eckhardt and Radigue, *Intermediary Spaces*, 136.

59 Eckhardt and Radigue, *Intermediary Spaces*, 140.

60 See, for example, Dechen Dolma, "Tibetan Buddhism in the Dordogne, a Brief History," Dechen Journal, August 24, 2018, www.dechenjournal.com/2018/08/tibetan-buddhism-in-dordogne_24.html; see also Joseph McClellan, "Dudjom Rinpoche Jigdrel Yeshe Dorje," Treasury of Lives, February 2024, accessed July 12, 2024, www.treasuryoflives.org/biographies/view/Dudjom-Rinpoche/10019. To my knowledge, the information about Düdjom Jigdral Yeshe Dorje Rinpoche's vision has been transmitted orally within the Tibetan Buddhist tradition, and I am not aware of a specific written source for this information. I thank Regine Hahn for this information.

61 For more information, see the webpage of Nehnang Samten Chöling, accessed July 12, 2024, www.nehnangsamtencholing.wixsite.com/nehnang-france. While the globalization of Tibetan Buddhism since the sixties is the broader context for Radigue's conversion, it must, of course, be noted that Buddhism already had an important presence in France before that time, in, for example, esoteric, scholarly, artistic, but primarily theosophical and occultist circles from the 1890s onward. An important figure in this history was Alexandra David-Néel (1868–1969). For information on a new research project addressing the history of Tibetan Buddhism and Yoga

in France and Europe from the 1890s to the 1960s, see Lukas K. Pokorny, "Yogic Icons in the Making," Religion and Transformation in Contemporary Society, University of Vienna, www.religionandtransformation.at/forschung/yogic-icons-in-the-making/.

62 Eckhardt and Radigue, *Intermediary Spaces*, 132–33.

63 See Ian Nagoski, "Interview with Éliane Radigue," in *Alien Roots: Éliane Radigue*, 236.

64 Eckhardt and Radigue, *Intermediary Spaces*, 132–33. See also Nagoski, "Interview with Éliane Radigue," 236–37.

65 See Bernard Girard, "Conversations with Éliane Radigue," 278.

66 For a new and complete English translation of Milarepa's songs of realization, see Christopher Stagg, *The Hundred Thousand Songs of Milarepa: A New Translation. Tsangnyön Heruka* (Boulder, CO: Shambhala Publications, 2016).

67 For an interesting discussion of the oral aspects of songs of realization, see Matthew T. Kapstein, "Dohās and Gray Texts: Reflections on a Song Attributed to Kāṇha," in *From Bhakti to Bon: Festschrift for Per Kvaerne*, ed. Hanna Havnevik and Charles Ramble (Oslo: Novus Forlag, 2015), 291–303.

68 See Girard, "Conversations with Éliane Radigue," 278.

69 Eckhardt and Radigue, *Intermediary Spaces*, 137 ff, 182 ff; see also Nagoski, "Interview with Éliane Radigue," 236.

70 See Michael Monhart, "Listening with the Gods: Offering, Beauty and Being in Tibetan Ritual Music," *Revue d'Etudes Tibétaines*, no. 40 (July 2017): 92 ff. See also Karma Phuntsho, "Yönchap: Water Offering," Bhutan Cultural Library, Mandala Collections, University of Virginia, accessed July 11, 2024, www.texts.mandala.library.virginia.edu/text/y%C3%B6nchap-water-offering.

71 Translated and quoted in Michael Monhart, "Listening with the Gods," 93. This passage is from Lopön Kongwa Jin's *Praise of Wisdom Illuminating White Varahi* from the Tibetan Tenjur (Commentaries on the Buddha's Words). Butter lamps traditionally work by burning yak butter, but one could also use butter from a different animal, such as a cow, or vegetable oil.

72 This poetic ode to scriptural works by the eminent Tibetan scholar and ruler Chögyel Phagpa Lodrö Gyeltsen (1235–80) has been translated and quoted in Kurtis R. Schaeffer, *The Culture of the Book in Tibet* (New York: Columbia University Press, 2009), 132. I thank Patrick Dowd for pointing me to this quote.

73 The Tibetan alphabet begins with three different *k*'s: (1) "ka" (unaspirated/of high sound/the one on the album cover); (2) "kha" (aspirated/of high sound); and (3) "ga" (unaspirated and softer/of low sound/similar to a German "g").

74 See page 219 in this volume.

75 Eckhardt and Radigue, *Intermediary Spaces*, 140.

76 Heinrich A. Jäschke, *A Tibetan-English Dictionary* (1881; New York: Dover Publications, 2003), 8, provides this lemma for *kye ma*: "Oh! Alas! Mostly expressive of sorrow, often combined with *kyi-hud*; also a sign of the vocative case, seldom it expresses joy."

77 See, for example, Eckhardt and Radigue, *Intermediary Spaces*, 140.

78 See Girard, "Conversations with Éliane Radigue," 279; see also Eckhardt and Radigue, *Intermediary Spaces*, 141.

79 Eckhardt and Radigue, *Intermediary Spaces*, 141. At the time of *Koumé*'s composition, however, the pieces were independent from one another. They would not be assembled into the *Trilogie de la Mort* until 1993.

80 This paragraph was influenced by a very fruitful conversation with Charles Curtis about sound and meaning, which enabled me to understand my analysis of Radigue's Tibetan-language titles in a much broader context.

81 Curtis, "Éliane Radigue and an 'Unreal, Impalpable Music,'" 33.

82 For a detailed analysis of these aspects, see Michael Monhart, "Listening with the Gods," 92–102.

83 Here I use the terms *spiritual*, *sacred*, and *religious* more casually, but I have paid close attention to Radigue's own use of these words, and any future, more thorough analysis would have to address the exact definitions, boundaries, and use of such terms more systematically. Consequently, acknowledging the subjectivity of the listener provides concrete information about their individual positionality as the starting point of their experience.

84 For comparison, the footage from the cremation rites of the famous Tibetan Buddhist master, scholar, teacher, and artist Dilgo Khyentse Rinpoche provides good insight into the typical soundscape, anthrophones, and community sounds of Tibetan Buddhist cremations and rituals for an extraordinary Buddhist master; see Neten Chokling and Shechen Rabjam, dir., *Brilliant Moon: Glimpses of Dilgo Khyentse Rinpoche* (UK: Axiom Films International Ltd., 2010), DVD, 58 mins.

85 In religious studies, the "architecture of sacral sound" would describe the space in which sacred music is performed and the acoustic features that bring forth a certain sounding result and listening experience for the religious practitioner. For example, if one listens to Bach's St. Matthew Passion in the St. Thomas Church of Leipzig, it will have a different effect than it would if listened to in a concert hall.

86 Stūpas exist in all Buddhist traditions in many different architectural styles, materials, and sizes. Typically, they are somewhat dome-shaped structures that serve as Buddhist shrines.

87 Among the first generation of Western convert-Buddhists, who often came from a Christian background, there is an observable interest in bringing Buddhist and Christian elements together. Tina Turner, for example, combined her Baptist upbringing with Buddhism after she converted to a form of Nichiren Buddhism (Sōka Gakkai) in 1973; see, for example, her 2009 album *Beyond: Buddhist and Christian Prayers*, in which Christian liturgical traditions are combined with the chanting of the Buddhist *Lotus Sūtra*.

88 Éliane Radigue, "Interview with Ludger Brümmer: Im Rahmen des Giga-Herz-Preis 2019," November 11, 2019, video, ZKM/Videostudio, 46'46"–47'24", accessed June 25, 2024, www.youtube.com/watch?v=YH4DwKaJktA&list=WL&index=16&t=2884s. Transcription of and emphasis in the interview are my own, as are any possible mistakes. See also Eckhardt and Radigue, *Intermediary Spaces*, 141.

89 Radigue, "Interview with Ludger Brümmer," 42'07"–49'32".

90 In our example, a more systematic musicological analysis of *Koumé* could also include *key tones* (typical background sounds in a specific environment) or *anthrophones* (sounds made by humans); see Udo Tworuschka, "Vom 'Visible' zum 'Auditive Turn,'" in *Praktische Religionswissenschaft: Ein Handbuch für Studium und Beruf*, ed. Michael Klöcker and Udo Tworuschka (Köln/Weimar/Wien: Böhlau Verlag, 2008), 80; see also Wolfgang Welsch, "On the Way to an Auditive Culture?" in *Undoing Aesthetics* (London: Sage, 1997), 150–65.

Éliane Radigue, *Vice–Versa, etc…* box, ca. 1970. Private collection.

CONTOURS OF THE SENSES
Madison Greenstone

Commissioned for this anthology, "Contours of the Senses" situates Radigue's feedback works (1969–70) in relation to contemporaneous artistic currents such as *nouveau réalisme* and *musique concrète*. Drawing on their experience working with feedback in acoustic instrumental performance, Greenstone examines Radigue's output in light of the basic phenomenological premise that the senses and the world's phenomena mutually shape each other, making additional connections between Radigue's technical innovations and perceptual estrangements to those of artists like Jimi Hendrix, Gordon Mumma, and Yves Klein.

> Art does not reproduce visible things, but renders things visible.
>
> —Paul Klee, *Creative Confessions*[1]

1.

In an interview with Georges Haessig, Éliane Radigue describes her work with feedback as "an education of perception and sensations."[2] These works, produced between 1969 and 1970, mark Radigue's first engagements with the qualities that have since become emblematic of her music: an experience of sound that is specific to the listener, thus engendering an ensemble of perspectives rather than a single ideal one; an apparent autonomy of sound, its development seemingly propelled from within and revealing some sort of inner life; confounding durational mirages, in which the mind's perceptive faculties are challenged by the inability to ground the sound's duration in linear time; and an empirically vivid experience of sound, highlighting the contours of perception created by a heightened awareness of one's own hearing.

More than a passive form of observation, Radigue's own listening is a fundamental part of the compositional act and her sounds' coming into being. Her process of composing entails a kind of simultaneous listening and responding to the sound as it emanates and fills a space. Radigue's listening is also key to the manual finesse and precision with which she approaches composition. When dealing with the inherent unwieldiness of feedback, such a high level of attentiveness is critical to set and keep this volatile process in motion. The complex entanglement between Radigue's agency and responsiveness, the varied perceptions of listeners, and the way listening itself materializes within the sound amounts to a feedback paradigm wherein the senses reflect back on themselves.

2.

Generally, Radigue worked with two types of feedback: larsen, the feedback created between a microphone and speaker, and reinjection, Radigue's own term denoting a somewhat ambiguous feedback technique created by linking two tape machines together to record and play off the same loop.[3] These two sound production techniques are the building blocks of Radigue's feedback music, and in both of them Radigue herself plays an important role within the feedback loop, performing the delicate balancing act necessary to sustain such unruly processes. In the case of reinjection feedback, the composer carefully managed gain and amplitude levels at the mixing board; in the case of larsen, she adjusted the location of the microphone in relation to the speakers to maintain the sound.

Radigue's listening is guided by the quality of the sound, reflecting in its changes subtle fluctuations of attention and the composer's exceptional manual finesse. In the performance of feedback, Radigue listens for points where the tones stabilize, pulsate, beat, fluctuate, sustain, or blip, indexing the minutiae of movement between the mic and the speaker or the electrical fluctuations in a particular gainstage in the circuitry, sustaining feedback through a narrow frame of precision. The composer's attention is embodied in the minute physical adjustments necessary to sustain the feedback; the emergent sound ultimately reflects the intensity of her listening—an outward expression of an inner nature, a "mirror of the mind" as it listens.[4]

Radigue seemingly aspires to bring the acts of listening and of responding to the sound closer together to narrow, or even collapse, the window of time it takes to reflect on the present, to close the intractable syntonic comma of difference between the mind's percepts. Though Radigue first began to experiment with this autopoietic mode of listening in the feedback works she composed between 1969 and 1970, she would continue to develop this technique over the course of her career, perhaps reaching its most salient expression in her later work with acoustic instruments, especially in *Naldjorlak* for solo cello (2005), the first of her works made exclusively for an acoustic instrument and live performer.

3.

Radigue presented her feedback works using a repertoire of combinatorial processes, like desynchronized tape loops of different lengths and vinyl discs or tapes that could be played in any combination, speed, or direction, leaving the moment-to-moment realization of the work up to the aleatoric encounters that she created the conditions for, but, importantly, did not have direct control over. These works are thus wholly contingent upon their perception by the audience-listener, nongeneralizable, specific, and dependent on the qualities that a particular listener brings to the moment of encounter. Radigue designed the conditions for the presentation of her music so that no singular experience of the work would be definitive. Instead of a stable, repeatable aesthetic product, these early compositions are but an ensemble of specific and varied perceptions; in this sense, there are as many feedback works as there are listeners.

In *USRAL* (1969) and *OMNHT* (1970), Radigue used three desynchronized tape loops of different lengths to create what she termed a *musique sans fin* ("music without end") or a *musique combinatoire* ("combinatory music"). Radigue refers to recorded excerpts that comprise these works as "musical citations" or "aleatoric moments," insisting that no particular arrangement of these temporally bounded excerpts should be understood as the definitive version of the composition.[5] Instead, over the course of their respective installations in galleries, the tape loops of feedback recordings desynchronize, creating sonic environments that transform over long (potentially infinite) periods of time, and yet are made up of elements with fixed durations. *USRAL* and *OMNHT* are thus inseparable from their installation-based presentations, existing somewhere between nonrepetitive structural properties and personal empirical experience.

In the *propositions sonores*, like $\Sigma = a = b = a + b$ (1969) and *Vice-Versa, etc...* (1970), Radigue provided the listener with vinyl records and tapes of her feedback recordings, along with open-ended instructions for their playback in infinite combinations and arrangements, inviting the listener to participate directly in the composition of the works themselves and prioritizing the process of realization over an ideal sounding result.[6] $\Sigma = a = b = a + b$ comprises two identical seven-inch vinyl discs engraved with feedback recordings, and premiered at Como Festival in 1970, performed live by Giuseppe Englert, who, according to Radigue's instructions, freely mixed between the different sides at different playback speeds. This work was later presented alongside *OMNHT* at Galerie Yvon Lambert in 1972 with turntables available to the public, who were encouraged to experiment with the playback speed and layering of the records.[7] In his review of the Yvon Lambert diffusion, Jack Gousseland keenly notes that gallery visitors left to their own devices attempted to make "musical events" with the feedback recordings, thus reimbuing them with a sense of narrative and drawing the listener out of the timelessness and nonreferentiality that *OMNHT* evoked.[8]

With *Vice-Versa, etc...*, Radigue similarly relinquished her control over the realization of the composition to the listener.

In a small edition of ten copies, Radigue dubbed feedback onto two-track stereo tapes, with each track corresponding to either the left or right channel. The tape came with instructions for the listener to play the tracks separately or simultaneously, "in one direction or another, on several tape players, *ad libitum*."[9] The *propositions sonores* invite listeners to take on the role of the performer and composer, assembling Radigue's sonic provocations at their own will and to their own liking, while developing their own practices of mixing and listening. These works thus transform the technologies and spaces of at-home musical reproduction and consumption into instruments, challenging notions of musical reproduction that hinge only on replication and passive listening.

Radigue ingeniously activates the aleatoric potentials of materials with passive connotations, necessitating the listener's attention and participation in the experience of the composition for the work to coalesce. Such a practice raises fascinating and inherently unresolvable ontological questions about where and what "the composition" actually is, while challenging the dominant, idealized notion of works as complete and discrete entities. These works ask whether a definitive composition is even possible amidst such a rich overflow of specificity, determined by the proclivities, circumstances, and sensibilities of the listener-performer.

The complexities of the ontological inseparability between experience and piece come to a head with the shapeshifting nature of *Labyrinthe Sonore*, an installation unrealized in its initially intended form, which would have premiered at the World Exposition in Osaka in 1970, comprising seven different desynchronized tape loops disseminated through wall-mounted speakers pointing in different directions, creating a sonic environment of varied depth through which the listener would walk at their own pace. In this complex spatial configuration, the movement of the listeners, alongside their varied listening habits and attentional focus, constitute a kind of live mixing between Radigue's sound sources. The dynamic nature of the listener's experience of the work would have allowed for a spatial-relational experience of sonic transformation, the pace of movement determining and influencing the objective unfolding of the music.

4.

Of all the feedback works produced, *Opus 17* stands out as a formal oddity, and as such signals the conclusion of this body of work. Made in 1970 for the Satie-esque *fête en blanc* ("party in white") at the Centre Artistique de Verdonne,[10] it is the first composition since the start of her work with feedback to employ a fixed overall duration.[11] *Opus 17* is also the only work from this period where the generation of feedback is not governed by a moment-to-moment listening necessary to the sound's coming into being. Rather, the process through which feedback gradually accrues plays out almost passively, removed from Radigue's active participation as performer.

Though it is not definitively certain how Radigue created *Opus 17*, she presumably set up a microphone and speaker in her closet, leaving her clothes inside to dampen any resonance in the space. For the starting loop, Radigue used a 1933 recording of Alfred Cortot performing Chopin's Prélude no. 17 in A-flat Major, Op 28. She sent the signal of the Prélude from her record player into the closet, which the microphone picked up and recorded onto a separate tape reel. That recording was then played back into the closet through the speaker and recorded again onto a second tape deck. This process continued successively until the original allegretto character of the Prélude gave way to what Radigue termed "electronified erosion."[12]

The subsequent movements begin where "Étude" leaves off, with Radigue mixing and composing freely with the feedback produced in the process of "erosion." "Maquette" is drawn from Wagner's *Parsifal*—specifically, as Radigue reveals, from the transformation scene.[13] The source recordings for "Épure" and "Safari" are unknown, and the feedback for "No. 17" is drawn from the preceding movements.

The "Étude" of *Opus 17* is one of the rare instances in Radigue's oeuvre where a recording is presented to the listener unaltered, recognizable as a referent to the world outside of the electrical current and pulsations of her synthesizer or home studio. Soon after this initial presentation, however, "Étude" lays bare its own process of sonic transformation.[14] The static in the original recording of Cortot's performance is gradually amplified as Radigue rerecords the initial loop, in which the hissing and crackling of the record player's needle against the grain of the record's surface, as well as the record player's slight wobble in speed, are already audible.[15] The listener hears the incremental change from the recognizable opening minutes of Chopin's Prélude to a sonic blur, wherein harmonic palette, rhythm, and melodic contours gradually metamorphose into blooms of feedback resonance, completely transforming anything that would have been recognizable as the piano.

The articulation of the piano is the first aspect to distort. By the second time the loop is played, the definition of the lower register of the instrument is muddied. By the third, the higher frequencies are muffled, and the bass and midrange tones of Cortot's left hand are elongated like pedal tones. The timbre of the piano sounds more akin to that of a steel drum, with a low thrumming for what would have been the tones played by the left hand. At this point, the higher registers of Cortot's right hand are no longer sustained, sounding increasingly distanced and otherworldly. As the process continues, how and to what extent the different registers are distended and elongated becomes varied—the feedback sustains the middle voices of Chopin's counterpoint for different lengths of time than the bass voice in the left hand. One still hears the articulation of the downbeats in the left hand on one of the repeated loops—more intoning and sustained. Part way through the process of erosion, higher tones not indicated in Chopin's notation emerge, suddenly very present. The notes played by Cortot's right hand intone in their own rhythm and sustain at a more or less stable frequency. As these elongated ephemeral moments overlay, creating dissonances, one is given the impression of a distended present in which adjacent notes bleed into one another. These dissonances could be the result of the slowing of Radigue's record player in the initial instantiation, which would cause a pileup of slight frequency variations that only in later repetitions would be audible as overlaid harmonic dissonance. Between the two registers—high and low—an arrhythmic, asynchronous pulsating separates them from their original interdependence, each register evolving in its own timeframe, made possible by the frequency response of the microphone and the premixing of the speaker's output.

The act of overlaying and rerecording the peripheral feedback creates unexpected amplifications and distortions of the original signal. As "Étude" progresses, one loses the ability to discern when the Prélude begins, let alone at what point in the excerpt the listener is located at any given moment. What was vivid in the sonic variation between registers is honed by the composer into a sonic constancy—a continual oscillation between two registral extremes. Once established, these extremes persist through the entirety of the

Prélude according to different prosodic rhythms. And, by the end, no trace of Chopin's original harmonic variance remains.

5.

Much can be learned from pieces that displace, defer, or completely resist their own realization. Radigue's sketches for the unrealized work *Œuf Primordial* ("Primordial Egg") from 1970 place it squarely within her feedback period. The sketches suggest an unspecified number of tape loops of unspecified sound content, phasing in such a way that it would take centuries for them to realign at their point of origin. These tapes would have been diffused through speakers at the top and the base of a giant sphere, in which listeners could sit, ensconced in the externalization of what Radigue calls an "interior universe."[16] In her sketch for *Œuf Primordial*, Radigue invokes the imagery of a flowing river—perhaps prefiguring the water imagery that defines the *Occam* series—describing a gaze "fixed on the eternal movement of the iridescence of the river, always similar in essence . . . "[17]

In its use of desynchronized tape that would require centuries to realign, *Œuf Primordial* conjures an ever-emerging and ever-renewing present, as opposed to a more conventional chronological time that extends linearly. Immersed in a sound logic that evades prediction, the listener's sense of consequence and relation is unmoored; they are asked to bring a different kind of presence to the moment, one that isn't concerned with gauging duration but with experiencing the narrow window of the present. *OMNHT* and *USRAL* also create this quality of an ever-unfolding present that refuses to yield to a past or future. All three works—*OMNHT*, *USRAL*, and *Œuf Primordial*—propose an experience of temporality that emphasizes the constantly evolving *moment* of hearing, extending the instant of perception into infinity.

Radigue's *Tour Sonore* ("Sonic Tower") is another speculative sound sculpture drafted in 1970, wherein a listener would enter a cylindrical tower and stand atop a floor vibrating with frequencies below the human threshold for audibility, while overhead, ultrasonic frequencies above 18,000 Hertz are transmitted.[18] This piece was partially realized in 1973 at The Kitchen, but only the overhead aspect of the cylinder was presented, transmitting ultrasonic frequencies comprising a perfect fifth. Radigue understood that while ultrasonic frequencies cannot necessarily be heard, they can be felt by the body, and she makes reference to this sensitivity in conversations about her feedback work.[19]

Radigue addresses this dynamic poignantly in *USRAL*, where ultrasonic frequencies are radically slowed down into the range of human hearing, creating a texture of eerie pulsations, glassy harmonics, Morse code–like transmissions, abrupt swoops in frequency, and voicelike sustained humming.[20] The process of slowing down itself causes these ultrasonic frequencies to take on certain sound qualities; *USRAL* is particularly revelatory in its coupling of peripheral ultrasonic feedback and these sonic qualities produced by transformation processes. The playback speeds possible on Radigue's tape machines, the extent to which and how these frequencies are slowed down, and the electrical-acoustic transformations bring into the realm of audibility a host of sounds that were otherwise imperceptible.

Radigue drew inspiration for *Tour Sonore* from a diagram of different wavelengths—from subatomic particles, visible color, and sound scaling up to wavelengths with a single periodic cycle that would encompass the distance between the earth and sun.[21] The installation's spatial registration of frequencies, with high frequencies "above," low frequencies "below," and humans situated in between, creates a kind of sonic bracketing of the human body—evoking an awareness of the waves of vibratory energy that constitute the universe and the sensory experience of that universe at all levels, and thus placing the body of the listener in the midst of this expansive vibratory field.

6.

Radigue's work can be contextualized in terms of the broader aesthetic output of and discourse surrounding two musical and artistic movements of the fifties and sixties: *musique concrète* and *nouveau réalisme*. In both movements, perceptual apparatuses and the senses were central concerns for the creation and experience of the artwork produced. That which was peripheral or merely taken as a given subliminal process, like the gestalt function of sight and hearing to apprehend identifiable and stable forms, was reframed as artistically meaningful.

As an assistant to Pierre Henry and Pierre Schaeffer in the fifties, Radigue learned the compositional and technical methods of *musique concrète*, assisting in the realization of large-scale works and even traveling to lecture on their techniques. During the peak of Radigue's involvement with *musique concrète*, she was married to the visual artist Arman; together, they participated as lively interlocutors in a circle of friends that included Yves Klein, Daniel Spoerri, and others who comprised the Nice School. Later, this group named themselves the *nouveaux réalistes*,[22] uniting under Pierre Restany's 1960 manifesto with artists like Jean Tinguely, Christo, and affiliates of the *ultra-lettrists* literary movement.[23] While there are not many similarities between the outward expressions of Radigue's music and the work of the *nouveaux réalistes*, there are some compelling connections on underlying structural levels.

Restany's assertion that *"Nouveau Réalisme = new ways of perceiving reality"* acknowledges that the expressions and conceptions of what makes up reality are as varied as the temperaments of the members of the group.[24] There was, however, a throughline that connected their work: the use of everyday objects and detritus.[25] In Arman's *Accumulations*, for example, mundane objects (and even trash) are elevated to the status of art through their contextual framing.[26] Recontextualizing mass-produced commodities associated with the commercial sphere was a means of demystifying the auratic value that enshrouds art objects. Leaving aside its implicit critique of capitalism, waste, and mass production, the reframing of these otherwise worthless objects as art prompts the viewer to perceive them in a context that emphasizes their material qualities over their use or exchange value, calling into question the defining criteria of artwork itself. In a direct response to Yves Klein's *Le Vide* (1958), which consisted of an empty gallery with empty display casings, Arman's *Le Plein* (1960) piled trash into a gallery space, physically impeding viewers from entering. By foregrounding the objects that would normally blur into the background of a person's everyday life, the viewer is confronted with their innocuousness transformed into an overflow of presence.

Yves Klein's monochrome paintings invite the viewer to experience the *act of seeing* as central to that which is seen, instilling in the viewer a heightened awareness of the fluctuating nature of sight in apprehending and constructing a visual field. One sees blue that does not claim to be anything else, but one also sees how this blue interacts with the transformations in light and differences in one's position within the exhibition space. Sight is no longer an invisible means of rendering the object beheld; rather, sight itself *becomes* the object beheld. Klein's paintings thus present a fascinating paradox: the seeming constancy of the visual field sharpens the viewer's awareness of differentiation and change—their body's position in relation to the painting, changes in light and environmental conditions, their shifting attention over time. The materiality of the paint and canvas magnify those perceptual and circumstantial attributes that are normally sublimated in the apprehension of a representation or an object, revealing how the modulating nature of perception (in this case, vision) is integral to the identity of the object being perceived.

Capturing the act of seeing in all its dynamism has played a significant role in the development of French painting since the period just before the turn of the century—with the work of Paul Cézanne in particular. The perforated and bent qualities of Cézanne's horizon lines, of the planes of a table, of wood paneling in a room, or of a windmill, can be interpreted as physical traces of the empirical experience of seeing.[27] Through a kind of depiction of the act of seeing, the inextricability of the body's percepts and presences brought upon a point of address are magnified. In beholding Cézanne's depiction of *seeing*, sight is thus made to reflect back upon its own mechanisms, revealing the unstable nature of perceptual states, or as the *nouveaux réalistes* put it, *new ways of perceiving reality*.

Through the extreme empirical listening conditions of her feedback works, Radigue engages just as intently with emanations and emergences of the *real* of *reality* as the *nouveaux réalistes*. They all seemed concerned to some extent with the reality, rather than the representation, of details and elements at play.

7.

The founders of *musique concrète* were similarly concerned with new perceptions of reality, challenging their listeners to perceive noises—sounds of the everyday, of nature, sounds that were not made with a musical intention in mind—to be heard as musically capacious. Italian futurist Luigi Russolo's *Intonarumori* (made between 1910 and 1930) had already begun to set the stage for this experience of noise, as had the sounds of industrialization, world wars, and other rapidly emerging technologies. In conjunction with this evolving openness to noise and other nonmusical sounds was the growing access that musicians had to portable recording technology. It was the wire recorder that enabled Egyptian composer Halim El-Dabh to create one of the first pieces of *musique concrète*, *The Expression of Zaar*, in Cairo in 1944, years before Pierre Schaeffer founded Studio d'Essai. El-Dabh had access to a radio broadcasting station where he manipulated his recordings to elicit what he termed their "inner sound," an objective shared by Radigue.[28] Emblematic of *musique concrète* was the manipulation of recorded sound through highly inventive studio techniques, ranging from the interventionist montages of cut-up and spliced magnetic tape to rerecording sounds in spaces with different acoustical and reverberant qualities to bring out different harmonic elements of the sound.[29]

8.

Radigue's work with feedback, and with feedback-like paradigms, can be situated within a continuum of investigations by composers and musicians into the volatile and self-generative nature of electronic, computer, and amplified instrument systems. Her use of feedback can also be understood in terms of a general enthusiasm for the artistic potential of cybernetics, alongside the emerging discipline of computer sciences and (as mentioned above) the increasing availability of experimental technologies.[30] A number of the key actors in this sphere of technological exploration were Radigue's friends and colleagues, including James Tenney, Alvin Lucier, David Tudor, and John Cage. It's beyond the scope of this essay to give a complete account of the influence of cybernetics on experimental music, or even to give an overview of feedback in experimental music; however, regarding Radigue's conception of the "life" within sound, a fruitful comparison can be made with experimental composer Gordon Mumma's 1970 *Notes on Cybersonics*, in which he attributes an "artificial intelligence" to his instruments, which, accordingly, must be viewed as "collaborative equal[s] in a democratic society."[31] Mumma's comments have potent resonances with Radigue's conception of feedback phenomena as deserving of respect and as capable of engaging in "dialogue."[32] As Radigue herself puts it, "I put the tapes among themselves to 'discuss' while saying: 'There you are, you have said many things to me . . . Now I would like to hear what you say to each other, without my intervening.' There is no doubt that my vocabulary is based on that, to observe and enter into dialogue with the fundamental behavior of these electronic sounds."[33] These sounds, as Radigue conceives them, take on a subjective or autonomous quality that finds expression in the volatility of recording and amplification processes.

Looking beyond the horizon of experimental music, Jimi Hendrix's astonishing and unprecedented use of feedback in his live performances expanded not only the possibilities of instrumental virtuosity but of the very instrumentality of electricity itself. Considering that Hendrix and Radigue were direct contemporaries, it's possible to discern how Hendrix's truly experimental approach to live guitar performance and studio recording parallels the sound manipulation techniques of *musique concrète*—though, admittedly, his experimental techniques probably have less to do with Hendrix's proximity to the lineages of French experimental music than they do with his and Radigue's generation's tireless search for what lay beyond the expressive limits of the technologies that were available to them at the time. Hendrix astonished recording engineers when he "knew how the solos he took against music played on a tape machine running backward would sound when run normally."[34] The deliberate use of phase discrepancies in the initial mixes of *Electric Ladyland* (1968) achieved unique spatial emergences—sounds hovering in front of the speakers or buzzing around the listener's head. However, audio engineers who weren't up to pace with Hendrix's skill and imagination only heard the recording as out of phase and "corrected" these three-dimensional phasing phenomena.[35]

In his performances with feedback, one can hear Hendrix's consciousness of pitch and harmony, as well as his awareness of the Promethean power of the amplifier to evoke the falling of bombs, the orbits of the planets, and otherworldly expanses of space and time. In his solos, one hears Hendrix cultivating feedback as an instrument in its own right through an uncanny ongoing awareness of his guitar's proximity to the amp. Hendrix achieved a state of such synchrony with his equipment that those who knew him often remarked on his ability to reach a type of oneness with his guitar and pedals, as if he were "inside" them.[36]

9.

Like Hendrix's, Radigue's use of feedback blurs the boundaries between recording equipment and sound-producing instruments. Radigue understood feedback as a kind of natural phenomenon, intrinsic to recording and playback systems, and that these systems have a tendency to feed back at certain resonant frequencies.[37] Feedback draws from sound a richly self-generative sonic agency; sounds, seemingly with a life of their own, are propelled from within. In Radigue's work, feedback is drawn out as a type of *musique concrète* from her studio equipment-as-instrument—rather than reappropriating the noises of the everyday world as her primary compositional material, she identified and deployed the noise latent within the recording and playback equipment itself. This noise, or feedback, which in turn indexes the resonant qualities, gain staging, and any variance in the distance between the microphone and speaker, takes on an instrumental quality through Radigue's carefully managed collapse of input and output.

Generally considered as an aberration or undesirable effect of electrified sound-production systems, feedback can cause real physical damage to equipment, as well as to one's ears. Radigue herself warns that the feedback loop between the two tape recorders must be scrupulously monitored at the mixing board, as explosive and out-of-control sounds can erupt from the equipment, and the equipment itself may physically burst apart.[38] Radigue's use of feedback—reconceived from technical byproduct to an object of aesthetic consideration in its own right—is based in the intersection of technological experimentation and modern recording equipment, the uncontrollability and unpredictability of feedback phenomena, and the empirically rooted modes of listening and experimentation that are characteristic of *musique concrète*.

That the act of perception itself inevitably inflects the thing being perceived comes to a head in Radigue's formulation of music as a "mirror of the mind." By embodying and necessitating an intensive form of listening, Radigue's music invokes a state of mind attuned to continually renewed presence. The composer's feedback works lack the markers of discernible and referential sonic events—pulse, gesture, harmonic ground—that would enable the listener to locate themselves within the framework of chronological, linear time. Untethered by repetition, one's experience of these works occurs in a continuously unfolding present in which the listener's fluctuations of attention confounds their perception of the passage of time.

In Radigue's feedback works, the contours of the works themselves are thus absolutely contingent on the listener's encounter with them—the movement, through perception, of sound from a state of latency and unknown potential to a state of groundedness in the empirical experience of the individual listener. As Cézanne's and Klein's paintings depict the modulating nature of vision, in Radigue's work the dynamic nature of embodied listening plays a constitutive role in forming the sound phenomena apprehended by that listening. This inseparability between the *object* and *the ways in which it is perceived* is one of the core pillars of the phenomenological understanding of the world's formation mediated through the body's percepts.

At its most mundane, the listener's physical presence changes the acoustics of a space of listening, inflecting the sound that is actually heard. Alvin Lucier's *Music on a Long Thin Wire* (1977) addressed the acoustic reflections and absorptions of a space. The installation created a sonic register of changes to the space, such as the opening or closing of a door or the entrance or exit of a visitor, and was anecdotally known to inexplicably go silent for periods of time. The relationship of sound indexing listening can also encompass the ear's synthesis of difference tones or the production of otoacoustic emissions—both of which occur in direct response to what is sounding outside the body, and subsequently affect that which is heard. Further, difference tones often serve as transitory guides for tuning pure intervals.[39]

As Maurice Merleau-Ponty formulates, the contours of the senses are determined by the things that they bring into being, and the contours of that which is brought into being are determined by the senses:

> There is vision, touch, when a certain visible, a certain tangible, turns back upon the whole of the visible, the whole of the tangible, of which it is a part, or when suddenly it finds itself surrounded by them, or when between it and them, and through their commerce, is formed a Visibility, a Tangible in itself, which belong properly neither to the body qua fact nor to the world qua fact—as upon two mirrors facing one another where two indefinite series of images set in one another arise which belong really to neither of the two surfaces . . .[40]

This mutually constitutive nature of the material world and its apprehension through sense perception, first explored by Radigue in her work with feedback, finds its ultimate articulation in Radigue's later work with acoustic instruments, particularly in *Naldjorlak*.

10.

Naldjorlak I (2005), the solo cello piece for Charles Curtis, explores the mechanical feedback system created when the cello is tuned to the so-called wolf tone, an acoustical anomaly deriving from the cello's natural mode of resonance. While it was composed decades after her work with electronic feedback, the continuity between Radigue's early works and *Naldjorlak* is particularly salient in the latter composition's contingent formation through the listening of the performer, the fact that its duration is determined in response to the endemic resonating potentials of the instrument, and in that it reveals the irreducible nature of the aberration of the wolf tone as a marker of identity.

In *Naldjorlak*, every tunable component of the cello is adjusted to approach the wolf resonance of the instrument. The wolf tone is less a singular tone and more a dynamic relation between sets of mechanical actions, like anomalous string vibration patterns or irregular impedance changes in the bridge, due to overresonance within the cello. Like the feedback generated by electronic systems, the wolf tone is typically considered a malfunctioning of the instrument when, in fact, it is indicative of the resonant properties inherent to the instrument. Radigue herself articulates the correlation between the wolf and feedback:

> [The wolf] recalls a similar phenomenon. My first electronic pieces were made on the basis of feedback, which is considered a recording mishap. The wolf tone is also somehow a mishap. It's notorious with classical musicians; it's considered an anomaly, a somewhat unpleasant and unstable sound . . . It made me think of feedback, for which to keep subtle control and maintain the fragile stability, you need to give a lot of attention to the distance between the mic and the speaker.[41]

In the discipline of instrument acoustics, the term *wolfing action* denotes a contingency that occurs when an instrumentalist bows one of the two lower strings at the fundamental resonant frequency of the cello's backplate.[42] This causes the backplate to resonate sympathetically with the frequency of the bowed string, setting into motion a whole host of nonlinear resonance patterns, altered impedances,[43] interferences,[44] and unstable transductions[45] that affect the directionality of mechanical vibrations within the body of the instrument and the vibration of the bowed string.[46] It is perhaps interesting to note here that in the sixties and seventies, it was a common methodology in instrumental acoustics to model the mechanical interferences built up in a bowed string instrument using analogous electrical circuit diagrams.[47] Empirically, the wolf is characterized by the beating, warbling, or any of the other unruly vibrations that might occur within the body of the instrument, as well as a change in the instrument's playability.

When one attempts to tune a cello to this fundamental resonating frequency, the varied tension of each string affects the tension of the body of the instrument, which in turn causes the fundamental resonant frequency to change. The shifting nature of the fundamental resonant frequency requires the instrumentalist to continuously search for a tuning state that is always slipping out of reach, as every adjustment to the whole of the cello's tuning will affect the frequency and the character of its wolfing action. Tuning thus becomes a never-ending attempt to bring all resonating components into alignment, and in so doing, to coax out the elusive wolf.

The phrase *just wolfing* refers to the occurrence of wolfing when bowing an open string—the open string will vibrate at a frequency that causes sympathetic resonance with the backplate of the cello.[48] If the tuning of *Naldjorlak* is an attempt to bring the tunable components into alignment to create just wolfing action, the entire body of the cello can be seen as a highly sensitive feedback system through which a performer navigates, quite literally feeling their way through an unstable environment. This tuning creates resonating conditions that are unruly and unpredictable, verging on the chaotic. In a performance I saw of *Naldjorlak* in February 2020, the cello began to shake violently as resonance built up within the instrument, making latent vibrations visible and audible.

What is centered in *Naldjorlak* is a responsive mode of listening and performing: listening to oneself listen, sensing vibration through the bow, and finding the aural manifestation of these dynamic relationships. Rather than attempting to master certain sounds or emotional affects, the performer responds to the resonant state of the instrument, hearing out in real time the unforeseeable variance within it. *Naldjorlak* thus reorients highly ingrained notions of instrumental mastery, unlocking yet another central tension in Radigue's work: that the high level of skill, attentiveness, and refinement necessary to navigate the unstable terrain of the wolfing cello influences, instead of controls, the ways sound is stewarded into being and tended to through listening. There is thus a certain level of adaptability or plasticity required to achieve a state of seeming constancy. In the midst of this dynamism, within any given performance and across a performance practice, such a technique gives rise to an aesthetic state that is continuously evolving, rather than seeking to repeat stable states.

11.

Radigue's feedback works invite, and invoke, irreversible change as a constitutive part of their identities. The transformation of listening mediates the works' transformation, where, in perfect complement, the edges of the work's ontological shape meet the contours of listening through which the work is formed, expressing in sound the transformation of the listener's own *inner life*.

1   Kerstin Stremmel, *Realism* (Cologne: Taschen, 2004), 8.

2   Georges Haessig and Éliane Radigue, "*Dans la réalité cinglante,*" *Musique en jeu*, no. 8 (1972): 69–70.

3   Julia Eckhardt and Éliane Radigue, *Intermediary Spaces/Espaces Intermédiaires* (Brussels: Q02/Umland Editions, 2019), 8.

4   Eckhardt and Radigue, *Intermediary Spaces*, 37.

5   These terms are used in what appears to be a draft communication with a gallery about presenting *OMNHT*. In addition to the instructions she provides regarding the diffusion of the sound, its mixing, and the type of cassette players to be used, Radigue emphasizes that the excerpt recording she is sending for demonstration purposes should not be confused with the actual piece.

6   Haessig and Radigue, "*Dans la réalité cinglante,*" 69–70.

7   Eckhardt and Radigue, *Intermediary Spaces*, 174.

8   "For one of the pieces using vinyl instead of tape loops, the listener had to intervene by means of potentiometers to select such or such a source. Guided by ear, it necessarily recreated sonic 'events,' a spontaneous structure: music regained its anecdote." Jack Gousseland, "Music to Exhibit by Éliane Radigue," in *Alien Roots: Éliane Radigue* (New York: Blank Forms Editions, 2025), 92.

9   Eckhardt and Radigue, *Intermediary Spaces*, 106, 178.

10 The central theme of the event was the color white: swans and doves were released, white food was served, the attendees stayed awake all night to participate in a *nuit blanche* or "white night," and a pageant of sorts was held. There is a possible connection between the work of Erik Satie and Radigue's endless loops—especially in "Étude," where a piano loop is consumed by feedback over successive playbacks. Satie's *Vexations* for solo piano consists of a short and highly dissonant phrase, with the instruction to repeat that phrase 840 times, possibly with the intent of facilitating a sort of meditative spiritual trance for the performer.

11 Eckhardt and Radigue, *Intermediary Spaces*, 176.

12 The process used by Radigue is similar to that used by Alvin Lucier in the production of his works *I Am Sitting in a Room* (1969) and *Exploration of the House* (2005).

13 Emmanuel Holterbach, liner notes for Éliane Radigue, *Feedback Works 1969–1970*, L'Institut national de l'audiovisuel/Groupe de Recherches Musicales, July 2, 2021, https://elianeradigue.bandcamp.com/album/feedback-works-1969-1970.

14 A kindred analogy would be a pianist playing the tone row before performing a piece by Schoenberg, Berg, or Dallapicolla, or playing the King's Theme before the subsequent transformations it undergoes in Bach's Musical Offering. The performer's intent is for the listener to attend to the mechanistic transformations the original theme undergoes.

15 In a comparative listening of the 1933 recording to the incipient excerpt of *Opus 17*, the slight drift in speed is only present in the latter, along with a slight halo of feedback.

16 See Éliane Radigue's sketch, *Œuf Primordial*, 1970, reprinted in this volume, 75.

17 Éliane Radigue, *Œuf Primordial*, 1970, reprinted in this volume, 75.

18 The lower threshold of human hearing is around 20 Hz, and any frequency below this threshold is termed *infrasonic*.

19 Holterbach, liner notes for Éliane Radigue, *Feedback Works 1969–1970*.

20 Holterbach, liner notes for Éliane Radigue, *Feedback Works 1969–1970*.

21 The diagram of the different wavelengths, from subatomic to cosmic proportions can be found in Eckhardt and Radigue, *Intermediary Spaces*, 26–27.

22 Stremmel, *Realism*, 13.

23 The *nouveaux réalistes* and the *ultra-lettrists* intersected through François Dufrêne, Raymond Hains, and Jacques Villeglé. The latter movement was concerned with extreme forms of concrete and sound poetry, creating a strong affiliation with *musique concrète*. In fact, listening to Dufrêne's *ultra-lettrist*

poetry readings, one gets the impression that they are listening to a fully fledged piece of *musique concrète*, replete with distortion techniques, field recordings, and other inscrutable processes of transformation applied to the words and phonemes of speech. One of Raymond Hains's *ultra-lettrist* décollage films was even scored by Pierre Schaeffer.

24 Stremmel, *Realism*, 11.

25 Stremmel, *Realism*, 13.

26 A decades-long series of pieces that was first shown in a 1959 exhibition called "Accumulations in Plexiglass."

27 For an excellent discussion of Cézanne's empiricism and sight, see Rackstraw Downes, *Nature and Art are Physical: Writings on Art, 1967-2008* (New York: Edgewise Press, 2014).

28 Thom Holmes, *Early Synthesizers and Experimenters*, 3rd ed. (Oxford, UK: Taylor & Francis, 2008), 156.

29 Experimental reamping is related to the process of successive rerecording used in Alvin Lucier's *I Am Sitting in a Room*.

30 Further sources on this subject can be found in Hannah B. Higgins and Douglas Kahn, eds., *Mainframe Experimentalism: Early Computing and the Foundations of the Digital Arts* (Berkeley: University of California Press, 2012).

31 Gordon Mumma, *Cybersonic Arts: Adventures in American New Music* (Urbana, Chicago, and Springfield: University of Illinois Press, 2015), 90.

32 Holterbach, liner notes for Éliane Radigue, *Feedback Works 1969-1970*.

33 Holterbach, liner notes for Éliane Radigue, *Feedback Works 1969-1970*.

34 Greg Tate, *Midnight Lightning: Jimi Hendrix and the Black Experience* (Chicago: Chicago Review Press, 2003), 36.

35 Tate, *Midnight Lightning*, 126-27.

36 Tate, *Midnight Lightning*, 184.

37 In her interview with Georges Haessig, Radigue says, "I believe that these new sound materials must also have their internal logic; like with traditional music, and the natural resonance of a sounding body, the relations between fourths, fifths, why, in electroacoustic music, this tendency to always return to the frequency of a larsen, or to certain frequencies that come spontaneously, naturally?" Haessig and Radigue, "*Dans la réalité cinglante*," 69-70.

38 Eckhardt and Radigue, *Intermediary Spaces*, 88-89.

39 An even more extreme example of the mechanics of hearing being registered by sound would be the role of hearing damage and tinnitus in filtering and producing sound in response to that which is heard.

40 Maurice Merleau-Ponty, *The Intertwining—The Chiasm*, trans. Alphonso Lingis (Chicago: Northwestern University Press, 1968), 139.

41 Eckhardt and Radigue, *Intermediary Spaces*, 153.

42 "The wolfing-action occurs when the bowed frequency of one of the strings (most often the C and G strings of the cello) is within a very close range of the fundamental resonant frequency of the body of the cello. Between the string and the body, these frequencies phase and modulate amplitude in a way similar to coupled oscillators, causing a kind of mechanical feedback." I. M. Firth, "The Wolf Tone in the Cello: Acoustic and Holographic Studies," *STL-QPSR* 15, no. 4 (1974): 42-56.

43 Firth, "The Wolf Tone in the Cello," 52.

44 Firth, "The Wolf Tone in the Cello," 43, 46.

45 Ailin Zhang and Jim Woodhouse, "Playability of the wolf note of bowed string instruments," *Journal of the Acoustical Society of America* 144, no. 5 (November 2018): 2852-54.

46 Vasilij Centrih, "Violin and the Wolf: The Wolf Tone on Violin Family Instruments" (seminar paper, University of Ljubljana, Physics Department, Ljubljana, Slovenia, February 2011).

47 A 1974 acoustics paper by J.C. Schelleng discusses the nature of the wolf tone, analogizing it to what Ailin Zhang and Jim Woodhouse call "equivalent coupled electrical resonant circuits." In Schelleng's use of electrical circuit vocabulary to describe the wolf, a compelling resonance with Radigue's early work with feedback emerges. Feedback constitutes a throughline from her

early work with those wild tones, through the circuit feedback paths she created in her ARP patches, to wolfing action. This throughline reveals Radigue's marked commitment to the autopoietic potentials of sound (electrical or acoustic) as an undergirding ethic and organizing principle of her oeuvre. Taking a speculative step beyond Schelleng's conception of the wolf tone as an electrical circuit, one might imagine the wolf-tone tuning of *Naldjorlak* itself modeled in circuitry, which then raises the possibility of a playable synthesizer-instrument employing a circuit design modeled on the mechanical feedback of acoustic wolfing. John C. Schelleng, "The Physics of the Bowed String," *Scientific American* 230, no. 1, (January 1974), 87–95.

48 Firth, "The Wolf Tone in the Cello," 53–54.

Éliane Radigue's studio at 22 rue Liancourt, Paris, ca. 1980s. Courtesy Fonds Éliane Radigue.

AN ANTI-IDEAL: RADIGUE AND THE PARADOXES OF RECORDING
Anthony Vine, Charles Curtis, and Madison Greenstone

This roundtable discussion, conducted over email in 2023, was originally published (in slightly different form) in *Contemporary Music Review* 42, no. 5–6 (2023), a double issue celebrating Éliane Radigue's ninetieth birthday, which was accompanied by a two-day conference in Paris at which Curtis spoke and performed.

CHARLES CURTIS

From my standpoint, the music presents an unusual set of interlocking paradoxes. To start with, I'm convinced that Éliane has always favored hands-on sound making over typical composerly concerns like pitch relationships, formal patterns, score making, representational or symbolic structures. From the feedback pieces to the acoustic music, she has worked directly with sound as physical presence, with all its unpredictabilities and roughnesses, embracing the impossibility of ever exerting full control. In fact, seeking a kind of rapport with the uncontrollable, skirting the edge of the rational and the known, working in a region that just exceeds her considerable knowledge and manual finesse. But, up until the end of the nineties, her work is captured on tape, and then experienced by listeners from tape, a circumstance that by definition eliminates most of the unpredictability of the process through which it was made. So here is the first paradox: even in a recording, one hears the difficulty and the struggle with sound as a physical force, but only after the fact, as a second-order representation of the event.

But then we have the many examples of recordings that are designed by Éliane to recover some of that first-order unpredictability in the listening situation: multiple playback sources, tapes or discs played at different speeds and nonsynchronously, backward as well as forward, and so on. She insisted on presenting her tape music in concert, under her own direction, and she was notoriously idiosyncratic about her speaker setups: doubling stereo signals at odd angles in the room, pointing speakers at the wall or into corners, doing everything "wrong" from a conventional stereophile standpoint. So this brings up the second paradox: that the flattened, predictable medium of recorded sound is upended, even subverted, to unleash again a new set of complications and uncertainties with respect to the behavior of sound in space.

Then we come to the moment in the mid-to-late nineties when the music is widely discovered by a younger generation of fans, largely coming from alternative music scenes, interested in "drone" and "ambient" and "sound art." A virtual explosion of CD releases ensues over the next decades; with an entirely new listenership and a mode of reception dictated by music consumption, the music takes on a more standardized identity within this new landscape of indiscriminate listening. I know this sounds a bit cranky, but along with the unarguable benefits of the music's wider dissemination, it's clear that for many listeners the music slips into the casual listening category—as background music, soundtrack, soundscape, atmosphere music—which is a huge loss for the music. And here's

391

the next paradox: it is at exactly this moment that the work with acoustic instruments and live performers begins. I'm interested in the relationship between these developments, how these new listening habits may inform aspects of the acoustic works.

ANTHONY VINE
For me, this "rapport with the uncontrollable" is the defining feature of Radigue's work. She seems to be drawn to acoustical energies that are recalcitrant, those that act on their own volition, like the mercurial emanations of microphone feedback or the unruly wolf tone of the cello. These sound sources and playback methods—desynchronized tape loops, off-kilter speakers, and structure-borne filtering—are often self-producing and in some cases self-structuring. Radigue mobilizes autopoiesis and similar devices across nearly all her work, relinquishing a certain degree of authorial control to the immanent expressivities of her instruments—synthesizers and acoustic instruments, even speakers and magnetic tape—as well as to the spatiotemporal circumstances of their sounding. The work was designed to be in constant flux, manifesting differently with each realization. This evanescence, or what you call "first-order unpredictability," is at odds with the inherent fixity, repeatability, and boundedness of recordings, which dilute a crucial and defining feature of her work: its continual movement, its restlessness.

CC One aspect of this fixity is that the recording appears to capture not just a particular sounding result but a specific aesthetic state. In effect the commercial recordings promote an illusion that there is not just a repeatable sound image but a repeatable affect, a repeatable experience—that the recording has captured an aesthetic, or a feeling, as if it were an idealized thing, and reproduces it on command.

AV What you are describing brings to mind the [2012] *Feedback Works 1969–1970* release, a collection of audio excerpts from Radigue's early protoinstallations. These recordings belie the works' limitlessness and interactivity with their surroundings, ossifying them into generalizable, consistent, and replicable things. With that said, I would be remiss to not acknowledge the value of the glimpse this archival release provides into a crucially formative period of Radigue's work, which is rarely, if ever, staged as it was intended.

Part of the slipperiness of capturing a work like *OMNHT* [1970] on a recording is its duration. A back-of-the-napkin calculation reveals that it would take just over 334 days for all three different tape loops to totally realign. Without even accounting for the ontological complexities of reassembling a piece like this, its sheer length makes it impossible to apprehend in its full continuity. This brings me to something I want to explore further: the idea of recordings as *re*-productions. I actually want to problematize this word a little, or possibly recuperate it. In recuperating reproduction, I want to emphasize its deeply active aspect—to produce again, or to produce anew. I think this relates strongly to the ideas of contingency, performance specificity, and autopoiesis of form that you've both addressed. What I think these commercial recordings do is create replications (or with *Chry-ptus* [1971], curated remixes) of her work, which strip them of their contingency, of the momentary character of their being attuned to a space (*OMNHT*, *Labyrinthe Sonore* [1977], *Transamorem–Transamortem* [1973]).

I also want to point out here that I notice a preponderance of *re-* in this conversation, and would possibly like to relate this to the multitude of *re-*'s that are involved in constructing an understanding of listening/sounding paradigms—resonance, resounding, reflection, reverberation, reiteration, returning—and how those terms are somewhat aligned with paradigms of feedback, a signal *re*-introduced into a system, amplifying its own *re*-sonant characteristics. In *Listening* [2007], Jean-Luc Nancy writes that the doubling of hearing back upon itself—the reverberation of hearing—creates a type of subjecthood, an apperceptive awareness of one's own perception. In the actual doubling back of the sound, sound confronts itself: in phase cancelation, in standing waves, in beating. And an audience member will perceive these consequences empirically, in material ways: if they shift their location slightly, their heads will be in minima or maxima of phase cancellation or amplitude modulation. I think this folding back is part of the autopoietic return of Radigue's music, and gives rise to this central knot of self-generativity, material volatility, and the creation of the performances' own time of becoming.

AV Another relevant duality is contained within the prefix *re-* itself, meaning either "again," "anew," "once more," or "back, backward, undoing." The latter sense, the notion of going or looking back, of recapitulating, is on one hand completely alien to Radigue's work, particularly its formal unfolding. Sounding surfaces continuously transform, moving outward, always away from where they started, where they are and were. Frustrating this sense of movement is the imperceptibility of change, the dearth of distinct events or rhetorical indicators. But the notion of "back, backward, undoing" also reveals itself to be an essential force, paradoxically, for stimulating the music's renewal, transformation, and forward momentum. There's feedback, as Madison mentioned, a signal from a system sent back into itself, the output of which is indeterminable and irreplicable, always emerging anew. The entanglement of both senses of *re-* also surfaces in the endless tapes from Radigue's early feedback music, which loop again and again, but out of phase with one another, yielding an ever-changing output. The instrumental work contains this dynamic as well. The wolf tone in *Naldjorlak* [2005], for instance, is revisited and reactivated across different sites of the cello throughout the performance, but always manifests differently; and this formulation extends to the performance history of *Naldjorlak* too. In a later composition, *Occam XIII* [2015], Dafne Vicente-Sandoval activates a single bassoon multiphonic again and again, revealing a new part of its spectrum with each pass. Here and elsewhere in Radigue's work these two senses of *re-* merge, operating not just simultaneously but symbiotically.

MG Anthony, your series of connections and insights regarding just how far this paradigm of *re-* permeates Radigue's work unleashes a slew of questions concerning the entangled relationship between ontology and listening and its ramifications. How does one understand the identity of something that is different every time, something that needs to be *re-*created and *re-*produced each time? How does one understand identity over long periods of change—within a singular performance, and over the course of years of *re-*performance? A line from Rilke's "Ninth Duino Elegy" [1923] seems to resonate here: "What, if not transformation, is your deepest purpose?" Perhaps this purpose of transformation, as something active and productive, speaks to a particular ontology underlying Radigue's oeuvre. This leads me to wonder in what ways, if at all, does the abundance of commercial recordings inflect how one hears Radigue's music? In what ways, if at all, has the preponderance of replications of her music changed how listeners understand the active processes of *re*-production that undergird her music's coming into being? Have replications of her music occasioned a schism between a more readily apprehensible sonic surface and a substrative task of productive transformation?

CC I think this brings us close to the heart of the matter. What Anthony observes about the reactivations of the wolf sonority and the timbrally varied bassoon multiphonics, set against the idea of a purposive state of ongoing transformation, suggests that the supposedly *single* multiphonic actually exists in an infinite number of variations, each revealing different spectra. And likewise, that there are an infinite number of gradations of the wolf, of potential reiterations of the Chopin Prélude in *Opus 17* [1970], of possible speaker setups for the tape pieces, and so on. In this way the pieces, incomplete in themselves because they reveal only a selection of the possible, become pointers toward an incomprehensible totality. And this brings up yet another paradox—in my opinion, the most interesting one—that I'd like to try to lay out. On one hand, the incompleteability that is expressed in performance, whether in the skewed playback of the tape pieces or the instability and conditionality of *Naldjorlak*, expresses at the same time a different totality, perhaps even a completeness, but one that exceeds our frame of recognition. We don't have access to it; it's bigger than what we can think and feel and comprehend. But it is indicated by the incompleteness, by the nearness of failure and breakdown, the searching and seeking in performance. By fraying the demarcations of duration, form, and even sonorous content, by pointing beyond those local limits, the performance points outward and brings us an intimation, a glimmer, of this other totality. On the other hand, some of the *Occam* performances, in expressing their own completeness—as rounded, finished, reliably beautiful pieces, largely repeatable and impervious to changing conditions—express the larger incompleteness of chronological time, its inevitable breakdown into excerpts, fragments, and pieces, each finished and preserved as a past, to be recalled on command.

AV   Radigue's engagements with space also point toward the infinite. Feedback, for instance, is determined by a seemingly limitless array of spatial conditions, from the resonant frequencies of the room to the circuit paths of the equipment, which in no uncertain terms are also spaces, corridors of resistance and conductivity. Radigue then diffuses these feedback signals in ways that interact with the spaces in which they sound. Take, for example, *Labyrinthe Sonore*, which sounded from a spiraling pathway of outdoor speakers, or *OMNHT*, which was diffused through transducers in the walls of one of Tania Mouraud's meditation rooms. Adding to these interconnected spheres of spatial conditions is the vantage point of the listener, which as Madison pointed out, is a crucial determinant of the work too. In Radigue's modular synthesis work, we find this in the peculiar speaker positions that not only engender certain acoustic phenomena, like standing waves, but also give the music a sourceless presence, the illusion of it being a natural product of whatever space it inhabits. Notably, Radigue nods to the materiality of architectural space in the commercial release of *Ψ 847*, which includes both the original recording, transferred directly from Radigue's reels of magnetic tape, and the same piece played in a live concert setting. In the "Étude" from *Opus 17*, the notion of incompleteability surfaces once again in a litany of recordings of recordings and spaces within spaces that could precipitate ad infinitum. *Occam XIII* and *Naldjorlak* also explore the infinitude of spatial resonance, but in those works the focus is turned toward instrumental volumes, their vibratory energies and dimensions.

CC   You mentioned the multisensory environments that the early pieces formed a part of; that's one example of how the work tends to engage a field, to connect with what's around it, rather than to dominate it. The simultaneous playback strategies do this, too, by decentering the singular work into a plurality of elements. Along with the multiplication and desynchronization of sources, differences in playback speed and tape direction, there is a multiplication of points of address and perspectives. One of the results of this multiplication is that, through the elimination of a unified perspective, any hierarchy of listening is broken down; the authority implied in "this is what you should hear" goes away. And the listener is then faced with a task, that of assimilating, managing, *re*-assembling aurally and mentally *a* piece. It's not an easy task, and there is no ready aesthetic model or category to guide one through it. I would go so far as to say that the listener must construct the piece in the very moment of listening, with not just the sounds as composed or recorded but also out of the occurrence of those sounds in time, and the vantage point of the listener in space, in this expanded field. As you have both pointed out, in diffusion these sounds present differently at different points in the room, and Radigue has made it clear that there is no ideal or privileged listening location. These factors are largely absent from the experience of listening to a CD at home. Putting this all together, I see in the multisource and simultaneous playback pieces a kind of tacit acknowledgment that the piece itself does not preexist the act of listening. And that's a very interesting gambit for a composer.

MG Charles, the diffusion instructions Éliane gave to you relate to the task of the listener that you just began to elucidate: "Ideally," Radigue writes, "we should forget about the speakers and get the feeling of sounds coming from everywhere, like being immersed in a shell or in the body of an instrument." I find this idea that the sound, as well as the space of its diffusion, can act as an instrument in itself to be particularly profound, as it imbues the spatioactive qualities of the sound with as much agency as the composer. Her early feedback pieces (such as $\Sigma = a = b = a + b$ [1969]), performed live for no other listener than Radigue herself, inhabit a kind of protozoan core within layered frames of activity—the vinyl discs or tapes become the tools of diffusion and the instruments with which the listener manually *re*-constructs and *re*-constitutes the piece for their own hearing. The feedback is the starting point for something malleable, creating itself in real time, as Anthony elucidated. That baseline of Radigue's performance responds flexibly within the space; the performance of the feedback is inextricably bound up with the performance of her own listening, mediated through her manual technique. One hears her live hand, ephemeral moments of touch, something coming into being and continuously renewing itself. But in the *propositions sonores* like $\Sigma = a = b = a + b$ and *Vice–Versa, etc...* [1970], Radigue's is only the initial realm of performance, before the responsibility of physically reconstituting an iteration of the piece is passed on to the listener. Going further, beyond the technical materials at play, I'm interested in exploring what happens with the sound in and as air as it's disseminated—the clashing of frequencies and spectra inflected by space—how the piece exists only as it is experienced in the real-time act of its creation. Perhaps the live sound is a type of phantasm mediating between sense and making sense, and the tapes create the conditions for its emergence.

CC   It is a phantasm, and true to its nature it changes with the changing conditions of performance. Even in the long single-tape pieces made with the ARP, which are not about layering or desynchronized sources, a whole series of time- and space-dependent factors act upon the piece in critical ways. The totality of the piece can be conceived as a kind of sequence of morphisms, whereby each stage adds or alters the previous one in unforeseeable ways. One might begin with the oscillators of the ARP and the waveforms shaped by Radigue through mixing and filtering; then these provisional results are captured and altered by the electromagnetic response of the tape machine, its preamps and circuits, and the tape itself. But this nominal "composition" then moves into the performance realm, where it is again subjected to all the factors we've discussed, including speaker placement and room responses. And finally, the ongoing variation in frequencies that is the formal shape of the piece in time comes to harbor in the space of the listener, their particular location in the room, the presentational powers and proclivities of their mind. If we follow this sequence of changes, we ultimately find ourselves far removed from what would nominally be thought of as "the composition" or "the work," or indeed from any kind of a preformed aesthetic object. And while one could say that all of this is always at play in any work in sound, here these morphisms—and the phantasmal image they bring about—are desired and made central to the identity of the music; they are not just unavoidable and regrettable collateral effects. In no sense are we dealing with a definitive object, "Radigue's creation," that can be relied on to produce intact a particular aesthetic physiognomy. Rather, we're dealing with a continuously varying structure, and to be true to its nature we, whether as listeners or as performers, must seek out its potential for difference and nonidentity.

AV Seen this way, the construction of her electronic music can be viewed as a continuous, interminable process, never complete, existing beyond the moment when sounds are etched onto magnetic tape and spilling into the realm of *performance*, a term that I find better suited to Radigue's music than *playback* or *diffusion*. Playback implies passivity and uniformity, the rehearing a self-contained, immutable work, like listening to a CD, LP, or tape. Diffusion does not seem right either; it brings to mind the act of shaping the directionality and color of the sound at the mixing board, foregrounding certain instances based on momentary and subjective predilections. A reversal of this dynamic seems to be at play in Radigue's work. The space and speakers perform, inflecting and variegating the surface of the music, effectuating its presence and directionality within the room. In fact, Radigue's performance and setup instructions explicitly advise technicians to make only "very few light corrections" at the mixer. And nested inside this performance is another type of performance, which both of you outlined earlier: listening as a dynamic act of creation.

CC Madison, your calculation of the total duration of *OMNHT* raises another interesting angle and might clarify the idea of incompleteness just mentioned by Anthony. The piece, at a duration of 334 days, will never be completed. No one will hear it or comprehend it in its totality. Each loop, though, has a closed duration—the time it takes to loop—and once it's fixed on a CD, this closed duration gives the impression of being something like a composed duration. But the purpose of the three loops is to generate an incomprehensible totality that no one will ever hear. The "Étude" from *Opus 17* could go on indefinitely, while its constituent source recordings are comfortably finite at a length of about two minutes each. Here, the fixed durations are in support of a kind of open and inherently incomplete extension in time, not a composed duration. I think one could argue that the long pieces made on the ARP continue this project using different methods, inscribing this programmatic incompleteness into the composition itself. The incompleteness is at the heart of the creative act. The constant varying of filters and modulators at the threshold of audible change, the long manual crossfades, the searching out of complex beating patterns and partial relationships are all ways of constructing sonority in real time, testing and searching through a listening process that is fused with the production of sound itself. And this is very much a process of tuning; this is how one tunes if one takes it seriously. I think this analogy is helpful. La Monte Young's statement "tuning is a function of time" means that sound is shaped continuously in time, that there is no completed state. For Young, as Spencer Gerhardt puts it, intervals are not "completed points in 'musical space,' but rather subject-dependent constructions." And this is equally true of Radigue's way of shaping sonority. One could commute La Monte's statement to the formulation that musical time is a function of tuning, or that time, as experienced in this music, is under the sway of the act of bringing it into audibility, not the other way around. If you are coming to the music from the experience of commercial releases with fixed durations, you are experiencing it as a music that claims to be complete. And I think that some of the pieces in the *Occam* series function in this way and therefore relate back to the multisource pieces that make an incomprehensible totality out of excerpts. They announce their boundaries and their boundedness—they are in fact excerpts, which the title of the overall piece, *Occam Ocean*, actually makes clear. And, I should add, they function beautifully in this way. But they are fundamentally different from the work that embraces tuning, in this extended sense, as constitutive of musical time, expressing a state of incompleteness as its deepest purpose.

MG   Charles, I want to expand on your consideration of the interrelations (or dissonances) between Radigue's work for acoustic instruments in the *Occam* series and the constitution of musical time through tuning. I think there is a definite correlation between this notion of tuning as a continual process and that of generative listening. The notion of hearing/listening as *creating* an experience of temporality is closely tied to the autopoietic nature of Radigue's music. This is especially salient in *Naldjorlak*, in which a scaffolded multiplicity of tunings is brought into play. Listening, in conjunction with a live negotiation with the instrument, draws a vibratory latency out from within the instrument. But that which is latent, immanently present yet hidden, is also late in arriving. And in this way the emanation of sound is always after the fact of its manual instigation (literally impeded by the mechanical vibrations of the cello), yet the hearing of that sound in return (as it's reverberated by the space) is always after the performer has moved on to the next instigation. The hearing of the returning sound, which is decisive in how the performer proceeds, is simultaneously active and reactive. What occurs is a navigation of the flickering between past and future, mediated through sound and matter. In the performance of live sound, there is an attention to its spectral-harmonic content, which acts as a directive for physical adjustments in relation to the material qualities of the instrument. The sound and the haptic feel of performing take on the role of a score (in an extended sense), though one that both leads and is continuously being led by the way that sound, the instrument, and one's own listening are experienced momentarily before. The boundaries between acting and reacting within the sound's mechanical capaciousness are decisively blurred (or flickering between one and the other). The performer listens to the instrument itself to discern how to proceed, affording it with just as much agency as the performer. The cello, much like the feedback setups and even the speaker setups for her tape pieces, becomes an active field of possibility.

CC   What you call a latency in performance, the time lag between action and reaction and action again, is really a key to understanding how the performance emerges in time. This flickering between past and future opens a gap that moves forward in the time of performance, and it is in this gap that the performance lives. In a good performance, one never leaves that tiny space of intensive listening and responding, and the performance is entirely directed and monitored through this solitary act. A few very specific corollaries to this arise: the pacing of the piece, its time, its temporal shape and duration, the durations of its individual sections, all this must be decided then and there, or must emerge from the performance. The inaccessibility of the sonorities in a piece like *Naldjorlak* means that a preformed duration is not possible, and that the proportionate durations of its sections cannot be determined in advance either, not even approximately. How long it takes to get from here to there, and then to the next, and so on, can be determined only within the act itself.

The other corollary has to do with the presence of the sounds in space, their being brought into presence, and the variability of the sounds' amplitude across a space. You've both described this eloquently. This is a kind of mix, but a mix in three dimensions. One has to acknowledge that the mix is beyond the control of the performer, and that control over it is not desired. I guess this is part of what you both see as autopoiesis, the apparent agential energies in the sounds themselves and in the ways they propagate in space. Whether as standing waves, as shifting nodes of constructive interference, or in the inevitable phase incoherencies due to Radigue's insistence on doubling speakers at cross-angles—and equally in the complex sounds coming from the acoustic pieces—we are dealing with a sound image that is not stable and neither uniform nor balanced across a room. What a performer hears is different from what a listener hears, and what one listener hears is different from what another listener hears. This is built into the music. Thus, to my mind, the idea that an idealized sonorous or aesthetic result can be achieved, or even sought, is at odds with the meaning of the music.

I attended a performance in Geneva last spring of *Occam Ocean* with the ONCEIM orchestra, and this was a listening experience of great sensuous beauty. I puzzled over the function of the conductor, and over what it means for a music that is so profoundly and radically shaped around the individual act of constructing sound in time to be overseen or supervised by a surrogate listener, a conductor. I asked Frédéric Blondy what he viewed as his role in conducting, and he responded with two points: gauging the pacing of the performance and managing the balance, or mix, of the instrumental groups. As he is not actually making sound himself but listening from outside the task of actual making, he must be deciding these parameters based on an idealized aesthetic result, ultimately determined by taste and subjective discrimination. The performance was arresting, beautiful—even ravishing—and very gratifying to listen to, but I had none of the thrill of witnessing an impossible task being undertaken, of an antiaesthetic yielding an unknown expressivity, of being in the presence of the unforeseeable—the incommensurable—worked out in sound, of the palpable possibility of failure.

AV   This question of the conductor brings to mind Madison's idea of following a particular kind of score that emerges from physical contact with the instrument and the sound itself. The score, like the conductor, is a rather unexpected concept to bring into a discussion of Radigue's work. The *Naldjorlak* and *Occam* pieces are often distinguished, in contrast to most other concert music, by the complete lack of a notational object and in its stead a focus on the oral transmission of musical ideas—intimate, dialogic explorations of the particularities of the individual, instrument, and relationship therein. It makes me wonder whether the memory space that each performer possesses—the meetings with Radigue, the performance history of a given piece, etc.—is a sort of score? And if so, how does it interface with this intangible, ever-morphing score that Madison invokes?

CC   For me, the past performances or recordings of a piece, the origins of its planning and making, recede into the unconscious. I have no interest in consulting notes or timings or memory aids, and I have rarely listened to recordings of previous performances. So, the piece moves forward through time, anchored only unconsciously to its point of origin. My sense is that the piece is actually constructed each time in performance. And it might be worth trying to tease out what that means: not just realized or performed but actually *brought into being*. I think that's exactly what was going on when Éliane was making the tape pieces alone in her studio. And this is closely tied to the elusiveness and unreliability of the sounding states that are so characteristic of her music: you must find them, and then once you have found them you still must coax them out of their somnolent state and sort of build them up, or build up the conditions within which they can be heard, felt, foregrounded. In *Naldjorlak*, no matter that I have tuned the cello for days and carefully practiced the desired techniques; when the moment to play the wolf arrives, I still need to look for it, I still need to circle around it and find not just the particular frequency area but the bow speed and pressure, the contact point of the bow, the differences between upbow and downbow, and how the wolf responds to each of these factors. All this has to be worked out in real time with the audience right there. And once I have found it—if indeed I have, because not even this is guaranteed—then I need to continue to build it up and explore how strong it is, how responsive, how rhythmic, how fast in pulsation it happens to be at that very moment. And then I continue to try to take it to its furthest-most point, at which I sense that I have exhausted its possibilities and can then go on to the next transition into the next section, and so on. And this is true of every section, every technique and sonority in that piece; I mention the wolf because it is the most conspicuous case.

My point in describing this is threefold: first, that the sonorities favored in this music are elusive and unstable, in ways that necessitate a process of searching and constructing; second, that this process must be undertaken in real time—it's a task-oriented music, and the task plays out differently each time; and third, that a particular expressive state arises from this engagement, that of a human involved in an act of construction, listening and searching and thinking, and materially building a set of possible sounds. This expressivity is categorically different in kind from that of a performance providing a desired aesthetic result. If you are genuinely involved in this task, you are not even thinking about an aesthetic result, you are not even thinking about how it sounds. You are in the middle of a struggle so concentrated that there is no room to consider the effect it is having upon listeners on the outside. That kind of expressivity, if we can call it that, I find incredibly valuable and inspiring as a practice of resistance against fixed and scripted aesthetic states.

MG   This practice or ethos of resistance allows the perceiver—be it the performer caught in the task of extremely focused listening or an audience member witnessing this negotiation between performer and instrument—to encounter what might actually be real and uniquely specific *to that moment in time.*

The creation of a scripted aesthetic state does not allow for an encounter with what is actually being brought into being. Rather, it forces specificity into a prefabricated framework of perception and expectation, one that asks what an entity *should* be, and how to sculpt it into conformity with the idealization. This process requires a kind of standardization of perception, according to which emergent details are glossed over and smudged out. The anti-ideal holds the possibility for recognition, experience, and knowledge of phenomena on their own terms, beyond the bounds of prescribed taste, to allow the particular qualities of time and space to flourish and inflect what emerges. According to this ethos, a work doesn't benefit from comparison with its past iterations; rather, it calls into question how one forms knowledge of that which emerges anew, instead of knowledge of the memory of past emergences, or of the afterimages they leave behind. This opens up into broader questions about how one perceives and experiences time flowing through life, how one might navigate through it with an attunement to, and celebration of, change—a celebration of the difference inherent in all things, of the flux of their nonidentity, and that which resists fixed definition.

Éliane Radigue, ca. 1970s. Courtesy Fonds Éliane Radigue.

EDITORS

LAWRENCE KUMPF is the founder and Artistic Director of Blank Forms. He has curated exhibitions such as "Open Plan: Cecil Taylor" with Jay Sanders at the Whitney Museum of American Art, New York (2016); "Catherine Christer Hennix: Traversée du Fantasme" at Stedelijk Museum, Amsterdam (2018); and "Organic Music Societies: Don and Moki Cherry" at Blank Forms, New York (2021). Kumpf is the editor of the anthologies *Catherine Christer Hennix: Poësy Matters and Other Matters* (Blank Forms Editions, 2019) and *The Shadow Ring: 1992–2002* (Blank Forms Editions, 2024).

CHARLES CURTIS is a cellist. He has performed and recorded widely in the worlds of experimental and classical music; his close working relationship with Éliane Radigue dates to 2004. He is Distinguished Professor of Music at the University of California, San Diego.

CONTRIBUTORS

ÉLIANE RADIGUE is a pioneering French composer of undulating continuous music marked by patient, virtually imperceptible transformations that unfold to reveal the intangible, radiant contents of minimal sound. Radigue began working with synthesis in 1970, painstakingly assembling series of subtle, pulsating ARP recordings to be later mixed into hourlong suites of precise, perpetual mutation before permanently abandoning electronics for acoustic composition in 2004. Radigue has maintained an obstinate focus throughout the flow of her career, her dedication to the materiality of sound earning her numerous accolades and ensuring her place as one of the most important composers of our time.

MADISON GREENSTONE is a clarinetist, writer, and member of TAK Ensemble. Their solo practice, *exstatic resonances*, explores phenomenological, material, and spatial expressivities of sound through richly noisy timbral actions. Madison performs across the US and internationally as a soloist and chamber musician.

DAGMAR SCHWERK is a Professor of Tibetology at the Institute for South and Central Asian Studies at Leipzig University, Germany, with a main research focus on Tibetan and Bhutanese Buddhism, the history of the Tibetan cultural area, and environmentally engaged Buddhism. She has researched and worked in Germany, Bhutan, India, Canada, and the UK, and received the 2012 Khyentse Foundation Award for Excellence in Buddhist Studies. As a musician and violinist, she has experimented across genres—classical, folk, experimental rock, and manouche jazz.

DANIEL SILLIMAN is an American musician. He's presented work at Carnegie Hall, Palacio de Bellas Artes, CCRMA, and The Kitchen. He holds a PhD in music from Princeton.

ANTHONY VINE is a composer based in New York City. He creates music about spirituality, beauty, and sound itself.

"Dreaming Machines" by Helene Cingria (page 50), "Music to Exhibit by Éliane Radigue" by Jack Gousseland (page 91), "Les musiques sans fin" by Éliane Radigue (page 55), "... In Reality" by Georges Haessig (page 101), "Interview with Éliane Radigue" by Patrick de Haas (page 143); letters from December 9th, 1969 (page 64), January 14, 1970 (page 66), from Pierre Restany (page 76), from Georges Haessig (page 98), from Patrick de Haas (page 140), from Lama Kunga Rinpoche (page 182), from Christian Marclay (page 206); notes for "Labyrinthe Sonore" (page 69), "Tour Sonore" (page 72), "Les bulles d'ecoute" (page 74), "Auditorium permanent" (page 75); press release for "Exposition Sonore" (page 94), "Espace et Lumière" (page 49), notes for *Adnos* (page 154) translated to English by Madison Greenstone.

"Combinatory Music" (page 53), "$\Sigma = a = b = a + b$" (page 59), "Mode diffusion electronique" (page 285) by Éliane Radigue and "Conversations with Éliane Radigue" (page 243) by Bernard Girard translated to English by Adrian Rew.

Edited by Lawrence Kumpf and
　Charles Curtis
Copyeditor: Lily Bartle
Proofreading: Heather Holmes
Design: Alec Mapes-Frances

BOARD OF DIRECTORS
Arani Bose, Walker Carpenter, Moriah Evans, Angela Goding, David Grubbs, Hannah Hoffman, Lawrence Kumpf, Robbie Lee, Josiah McElheny, Louise Neri, David Nuss, Christian Nyampeta, Marina Rosenfeld, Kim Schnaubert, Jacques Louis Vidal, and Andros Zins-Browne.

CURATORIAL ADVISORY BOARD
Charles Curtis, Neneh Cherry, Thulani Davis, Kim Gordon, Shelley Hirsch, Sanya Kantarovsky, Arto Lindsay, Branden W. Joseph, Tommy McCutchon, Ikue Mori, Joe McPhee, Aki Onda, Tony Oursler, Benjamin Piekut, and Mónica de la Torre.

Blank Forms Editions is supported by the Mellon Foundation, Robert Rauschenberg Foundation, The Andy Warhol Foundation for the Visual Arts, and the 2024 Blank Forms Publisher's Circle, including Gisela Gamper, Linden Renz, and Charline von Heyl and Christopher Wool.

Blank Forms is a nonprofit organization supporting emerging and historically significant artists who produce work across disciplines, often rooted in traditions of experimental and creative music. We aim to establish new frameworks to preserve, nurture, and present these artists' work and to build platforms for practices underrepresented in art's commercial, institutional, and historical fields. Blank Forms collaborates with artists on commissions, exhibitions, publications, as well as archival and estate projects within contemporary cultural ecosystems and in perpetuity. In presenting and documenting this work, Blank Forms seeks to foster an artistic community founded upon engaged and equitable conversations across continents, media, and generations.

ISBN 978-1-953691-22-4

Printed by Ofset Yapımevi in Turkey
©2025 Blank Forms Editions

Blank Forms
468 Grand Avenue
#1D/#3D
Brooklyn, NY 11238
blankforms.org

ALSO FROM BLANK FORMS EDITIONS

Loren Connors, *Autumn's Sun*
Catherine Christer Hennix, *Poësy Matters and Other Matters*
Joseph Jarman, *Black Case Volume I & II: Return From Exile*
Maryanne Amacher, *Selected Writings and Interviews*
Thulani Davis, *Nothing But the Music*
Alan Licht, *Common Tones: Selected Interviews with Artists and Musicians 1995–2020*
Stephen Housewright, *Partners*
Kazuki Tomokawa, *Try Saying You're Alive!: Kazuki Tomokawa in His Own Words*
The Cricket: Black Music in Evolution, 1968–69
Tori Kudo, *Ceramics*
Wesley Brown, *Blue in Green*
Curtis Cuffie
Ahmed Abdullah, *A Strange Celestial Road: My Time in the Sun Ra Arkestra*
Steve Cannon, *Groove, Bang and Jive Around*
Spencer Gerhardt, *Ticking Stripe*

Blank Forms 01: Magazine
Blank Forms 02: Music from the World Tomorrow
Blank Forms 03: Freedom is Around the Corner
Blank Forms 04: Intelligent Life
Blank Forms 05: Aspirations of Madness
Blank Forms 06: Organic Music Societies
Blank Forms 07: The Cowboy's Dreams of Home
Blank Forms 08: Transmissions from the Pleroma
Blank Forms 09: Sound Signatures